Rick Bushnell

Sun Certified
Network Administrator
for Solaris™ 8

Operating Environment
Study Guide

ISBN 0-13-064669-5

90000

9 780130 646699

Sun Microsystems Press
A Prentice Hall Title

Prentice Hall books are widely used by corporations and government agencies for training, marketing, and resale. For information regarding corporate and government bulk discounts please contact Corporate and Government Sales (800) 382-3419 or corpsales@pearsontechgroup.com.

Editorial/production supervision: *Carol Wheelan*
Cover design director: *Jerry Votta*
Cover designer: *Anthony Gemmellaro*
Cover illustration: *Karen Strelecki*
Manufacturing manager: *Alexis R. Heydt-Long*
Marketing manager: *Debby vanDijk*
Executive editor: *Gregory G. Doench*
Associate editor: *Eileen Clark*
Editorial assistant: *Brandt Kenna*
Sun Microsystems Press Publisher: *Michael Llwyd Alread*

10 9 8 7 6 5 4 3 2 1

ISBN 0-13-064669-5

Sun Microsystems Press
A Prentice Hall Title

This book is dedicated to my parents, Dorothy and Harry Bushnell. Your children—Dawn, Tracy, Mark, and I—have always been inspired and motivated by your love, passion, and energy for life and for teaching us the importance of family values and fairness in all we do. Your children thank you for being what all children deserve to have, which is loving and caring parents. Although father passed away on July 5, 2001, he will not be forgotten. Thank you, Mum and Dad. This book is dedicated to you.
—Rick P. Bushnell
April 2002

C O N T E N T S

Preface   *xix*

Acknowledgments   *xxvii*

C H A P T E R   1

Network Models and Protocols   *1*

Layered Network Models   2
    The OSI/ISO 7-Layer Reference Model   *3*
    The TCP/IP 5-Layer Model   *4*
    Benefits of Using Network Models: A Summary   *5*

The Layers of the TCP/IP 5-Layer Model   6
    Application Layer (5)   *6*
    Transport Layer (4)   *8*
    Internet Layer (3)   *9*
    Network Interface Layer (2)   *10*
    Physical Layer (1)   *11*

Network Protocols   *11*
    Transport Layer Protocols: TCP and UDP   *12*
        Transmission Control Protocol (TCP)   *12*
        User Datagram Protocol (UDP)   *13*
    Internet Protocol (IPv4)   *14*
    Internet Control Message Protocol (ICMP)   *15*

Peer-to-Peer Communication   *16*

TCP/IP Protocols by Name and Function   *17*

CHAPTER 2
Introduction to Local Area Networks   *23*

LAN Basics, Advantages, and Disadvantages   *24*

LAN Topologies   *26*
  Bus LANs   *27*
  Star LANs   *27*
  Ring LANs   *29*

LAN Components   *30*
  Backbone   *30*
  Segment   *31*
  Repeater   *31*
  Hub (Multiport Repeater)   *31*
  Bridge   *32*
  Switch (Multiport Bridge)   *33*
  Router   *34*
  Gateway   *34*
  Concentrator   *34*

Non-TCP/IP LAN-Based Technologies and Protocols   *35*

CHAPTER 3
The Ethernet LAN   *41*

The Ethernet Specification   *42*
IEEE Ethernet Identifiers   *42*
The Ethernet Address   *45*
  The Scope of Ethernet Addresses   *46*
    Sending Data to a Single Ethernet Host (Unicast)   *46*
    Sending Data to a Group of Ethernet Hosts (Multicast)   *46*
    Sending Data to All Ethernet Hosts on Subnet (Broadcast)   *47*
  Global versus Local Port Ethernet Addresses   *47*

The Ethernet Frame V2   *50*
  Frame Overhead Fields   *52*
    Minimum Frame Length   *52*
    Maximum Frame Length   *52*
  Ethernet V2 Frame Fields   *53*
    Destination Ethernet Address   *53*
    Source Ethernet Address   *53*

Type Field   53
Data Field   54
Cyclic Redundancy Check (CRC)   54

The Ethernet Access Method   55

Using ndd to Set and Get Protocol and Interface Driver Parameters   58
Protocol Variables   *59*
Getting Parameter Settings   *63*
Setting Parameter Settings   *64*

Sun Ethernet Controllers   65
Fast Ethernet Cards   *65*
Slow Ethernet Cards   *66*

```
C  H  A  P  T  E  R       4
```

The ARP and RARP Protocols   *71*

Address Mapping with ARP and RARP   72

The ARP/RARP Protocol Format   73

ARP and RARP Operations   74
ARP   *75*
ARP Request, Operation 1 (Opcode 1)   75
ARP Reply, Operation 2 (Opcode 2)   79
RARP   *82*
RARP Request, Operation 3 (Opcode 3)   83
RARP Reply, Operation 4 (Opcode 4)   85
Configuring the RARP Server   *87*

The ARP Cache and arp Command   89
The ARP Cache   *89*
The Arp Command   *90*
Checking a Single Cache Entry   90
Viewing the Entire ARP cache with **arp –a**   *91*
Deleting an ARP Cache Entry with **arp –d**   *92*
Adding a Static ARP Cache Entry with **arp –s** *and* **-f**   *93*

```
C  H  A  P  T  E  R       5
```

The Internet Layer and IPv4   *101*

IPv4 Address Classes, Netmasks, and the Broadcast Address   *102*
IPv4 Address Classes A, B, C, and D   *102*
Class A Networks and Addresses   105

Class B Networks and Addresses   106
Class C Networks and Addresses   107
Class D Multicast Identifiers and Multicast Groups   109
Netmask (Subnet Mask)   *111*
Truth Tables, Binary Logic, and the Netmask Value   112
Computing the Network Number Using the Netmask Rule   113
The Broadcast Address   *114*
Special-Case IP Addresses   *116*
Special Broadcast Address Types   117

Subnetting   *119*
Why Subnet?   *119*
Creating Multiple Logical Networks from a Single Network Address   119
Traffic and Protocol Isolation   119
Increased Security   120
Delegated Subnet Administration   120
How Subnetting Works   *120*
Subnetting on a Non-Byte Boundary   *123*

The IPv4 Datagram Header and Datagram Fragmentation   127
The IPv4 Header   *127*
IPv4 Header Fields   127
Datagram Fragmentation   *131*

Classless Inter Domain Routing (CIDR)   *134*

The Netmasks File   *136*

Variable Length Subnet Masks (VLSM)   *137*

Configuring a Network Interface   *139*
Types of Solaris 8 Interfaces   *140*
Configuring the Three Types of Solaris Interfaces   *141*
Example 1   142
Example 2   142
Example 3   143
Example 4   143
Example 5   144
Example 6   144
Plumbing in a Temporary Virtual Interface   *149*
Creating a Permanent Virtual Interface   *150*

CHAPTER 6
Routing over TCP/IP with Solaris 8   *155*

IP Routing—An Introduction   *156*
    Non-router Host Behavior   *156*
    Router Host Behavior   *157*
    A Routing Example   *158*

Solaris 8 Routing Protocols and Daemons   *160*
    The Routing Information Protocol (RIP)   *162*
        RIP Features   163
        The RIP Routing Process   163
        Stability Properties of RIP   165
    The Router Discovery Protocol (RDP)   *167*
        Building the MAC Address for a Multicast Group   169

Solaris 8 Router Configuration Files and Their Functions   *171*
    Adding Default Routes through the /etc/defaultrouter File   *173*
    Direct and Indirect Routing   *175*
    Working with the /etc/gateways File   *176*
        Example 1: Adding a Network Route to the Routing Table
           on Host voyager   176
        Example 2: Adding a Default Route to the Routing Table Using the
           /etc/gateways File   177
        Example 3: Preventing RIP from Entering or Leaving an Interface   177

Configuring a Solaris 8 System as a Router   *178*

Administering the Solaris 8 Routing Table Using the route
        and netstat Commands   *182*
    Adding and Deleting Routes Using the **route** Command   *182*
        Example 1: Adding a Network-Specific Route on mars   182
        Example 2: Adding a Network-Specific Route on pluto   183
        Example 3: Adding a Default Route on voyager   183
        Example 4: Deleting the Network-Specific Route Added in Example 1   184
        Example 5: Deleting the Network-Specific Route Added in Example 2   184
        Example 6: Deleting the Default Route on voyager Added in Example 3   185
    Continuously Monitoring Routing Information Using
        the **route** Command   *185*
    Getting Routing Information and Displaying on Standard Output   *186*
    Viewing the Routing Table with **netstat**   *187*
        Line 1   187

Line 2   188

Line 3   188

Line 4   188

Line 5   189

Using **netstat –rn** *189*

Additional **in.routed** Options *190*

Capturing Routing Information in a Log File   190

Capturing Routing Information and Displaying on Standard Output   191

C H A P T E R   7

The Transport Layer Protocols *195*

TCP Encapsulation, Header, and Features   *196*

TCP Encapsulation *196*

The TCP Header *197*

Source and Destination Port Numbers   197

32-Bit Sequence Number   199

32-Bit Acknowledgment Number   200

4-Bit Header Length   201

Control Bits   201

Window Size   202

Checksum   202

Urgent Pointer   204

Options   204

Padding   204

TCP Data   204

TCP Features *205*

Connection Establishment and Release   205

Positive Acknowledgment with Retransmission   213

Sliding Window Protocol   215

UDP Encapsulation, Header, and Features   *216*

UDP Encapsulation *216*

The UDP Header *217*

Source and Destination Port Fields   218

The UDP Length Field   218

The UDP Checksum Field   218

UDP Features *219*

Line 1   222

Line 2   222

Comparison of TCP and UDP   *223*
The IP Interface to the Transport Layer   *223*

C H A P T E R   8

The Client-Server Model   *229*

Servers, Clients, and Services   *230*
Client/Server Applications: An Overview   *230*
ONC+ Applications   *231*
eXternal Data Representation (XDR)   *232*
Transport Layer Interface (TLI)   *233*
Sockets   *233*
Network File System (NFS)   *233*
Network Information Service (NIS/NIS+)   *233*

Configuring Solaris 8 Servers   *234*
Starting Servers   *235*
Starting Standalone Servers   *235*
Starting Services through inetd   *237*
Allocating Port Numbers to Traditional and TI-RPC Servers   *243*
Port Allocation to Traditional Servers via /etc/inet/services   *243*
Port Allocation to TI-RPC Servers via **rpcbind**   *245*
TI-RPC Server Program Numbers   *246*

Monitoring Services and Servers   *247*
Server Monitoring with the **netstat** Command   *248*
Server Monitoring with the **rpcinfo** Command   *252*
rpcbind *Fields*   *253*
mountd *Fields*   *255*
The /etc/rpc File   *255*
Official Server Name   *256*
Program Number   *256*
Aliases   *256*
Comparing **inetd** and **rpcbind**   *257*

C H A P T E R   9

Dynamic Address Allocation with DHCP   *261*

Overview of DHCP   *262*

DHCP Terminology   *262*
  DHCP Client   262
  DHCP Server   263
  BOOTP Relay   263
  DHCP Binding   264
  Lease   264
Advantages of Using DHCP   *264*
Disadvantages of Using DHCP   *265*
DHCP IP Address Allocation Modes   *266*
  Automatic Allocation of Permanent IP Addresses   267
  Dynamic Allocation of IP Addresses   267
  Manual Allocation of IP Addresses   267
  Allocating a Specific Address to a DHCP Client   268

DHCP Configuration Files   *269*
The /etc/dhcp/inittab File   *270*
  Option Type STANDARD   *271*
  Option Type SITE   *273*
  Option Type VENDOR   *273*
  Option Type FIELD   *274*
  Option Type INTERNAL   *274*
The /var/dhcp/*dhcp_network* File   *275*
The /var/dhcp/dhcptab File   *277*
  Name   278
  Type   278
  Value   278
  Lease Negotiation   280
The /etc/dhcp.interface File   *283*
The /etc/default/dhcp File   *283*
The /etc/default/dhcpagent File   *284*
  Example 1   284
  Example 2   285

Administering DHCP Clients and Servers   *286*
DHCP Server Installation Using **dhcpconfig**   *286*
Managing the/var/dhcp/dhcp_network File with
  the **pntadm** Command   *288*
  The **–c** *Option   289*
  The **–a** *Option   289*
  The **–m** *Option   289*
  The **–d** *Option   290*
  The **–p** *Option   290*

The **–r** *Option*   *290*
The **–l** *Option*   *290*
Managing the /var/dhcp/dhcptab File with the dhtadm Command   *291*
The **–C** *Option*   *291*
The **–A** *Option*   *291*
The **–M** *Option*   *292*
The **–D** *Option*   *292*
The **–R** *Option*   *292*

The DHCP Server Daemon in.dhcpd   *293*

CHAPTER   10

Network Management Using SNMP   *299*

Network Management: An Overview   *300*
Network Management as Defined by ISO   *300*
Network Management Tools   *301*

Introduction to the Simple Network Management Protocol (SNMP)   *302*
SNMP Functions: **get**, **set**, and **trap**   *303*
Structure of Management Information and the OID Tree   *304*
Management Information Bases (MIB) and ASN   *305*
Sun's SNMP-Based Management Tools   *306*

CHAPTER   11

Domain Name Service (DNS)   *311*

DNS: The Glue of the Internet   *312*

DNS and Berkeley Internet Domain Name (BIND) Software   *313*
Solaris 8 Version of DNS and BIND   *313*
Solaris Name Services: A Comparison   *314*

The DNS Namespace   *316*
Domain Name Basics   *316*
*Fully Qualified Domain Names (FQDN) versus Relative Domain Names
(RDN)*   *317*
Top Level Domains (TLDs)   *317*
Zones of Authority and Delegation   *321*

Types of DNS Servers   *323*
Root-Level DNS Servers   *324*
Nonroot Master DNS Servers and the named.root File   *324*

DNS Master Servers   *327*
DNS Slave Servers   *327*
DNS Caching-Only Servers   *328*
DNS Forwarding Servers   *329*
Querying Servers: Recursion versus Iteration   *329*

The Main Configuration File /etc/named.conf   *333*
Named.conf Entries   *334*
The /etc/named.conf Main Configuration File   *335*
The Directives in /etc/named.conf   *335*
Options   *335*
Server   *337*
Zone   *338*
The **acl** *Directive*   *341*
The **include** *Directive*   *342*

The Zone Database Files and the Resource Record (RR) Format   *343*
Syntax of the Resource Record (RR)   *344*
[NAME] *Field*   *345*
[TTL] *Field*   *345*
[CLASS] *Field*   *345*
[RECORD-TYPE] *and* **[RECORD-DATA]** *Fields*   *345*
The Zone Database Files   *346*
A Forward Zone File Example   *346*
The Reverse Zone File   *351*
The Root Zone File   *353*

Creating a DNS Server and Client Step by Step   *354*
Creating a DNS Server   *354*
Creating The Main /etc/named.conf File on Server rigel   *355*
Creating a /var/named Directory and Desired Subdirectories   *355*
Creating Zone Files for Each Zone Supported   *356*
Modifying the /etc/nsswitch.conf File   *359*
Starting **in.named**   *358*
Creating a DNS Client   *359*

DNS Debugging and Dumping the DNS Cache   *361*
Sending Signals to in.named   *361*
The INT Signal—Dumping the DNS Server's Cache   *361*
The HUP Signal—Reloading the Server's Configuration Files   *362*
The USR1 Signal—Activating Real-Time Debugging   *362*

The TERM and KILL Signals—Killing **in.named**   *363*
Additional Tools   *363*

C H A P T E R   1 2

The Network Time Protocol (NTP)   *367*

Solaris 8 NTP Features and Terminology   *368*
NTP Basic Terminology   *368*
A Brief Description of Solaris 8 NTP   *369*
Solaris 8 NTP Configuration Files   *371*
The Primary NTP Configuration Files   *371*
/etc/inet/ntp.conf   *371*
/var/ntp/ntp.drift   *372*
/etc/init.d/xntpd   *372*
/var/adm/messages   *372*
Verifying That Solaris 8 NTP Packages Are Installed   *372*
Configuring a Solaris 8 NTP Client and Server   *373*
Configuring a Solaris 8 NTP Server   *374*
Creating the NTP Server Main Configuration File   *374*
Configuring the NTP Server   *374*
Configuring a Solaris 8 NTP Client   *379*
Configuring the Client's ntp.conf File   *379*
Running the **xntpd** *Daemon*   *380*
Client Synchronization and the Log File Entries   *380*
Some Useful NTP Commands: **ntpq** and **ntptrace**   *382*

C H A P T E R   1 3

The New Internet Protocol: IPv6   *387*

IPv6, the New Internet Protocol   *388*
The IPv6 Datagram Header   *389*
Fields of the IPv6 Header   *389*
Version   *389*
Traffic Class   *389*
Flow Label   *390*
Payload Length   *390*
Next Header   *390*

Hop Limit   391
Source IP Address   391
Destination IP Address   391
Comparing the IPv6 and IPv4 Headers   *392*
IPv4 Options Field   392
Checksum Field   392
Router Fragmentation Field   392

The IPv6 Address Format   393
Text Representation of IPv6 Addresses   *394*
Colon Notation Example Using an IPv4 Address   394
Colon Notation Example Using IPv6 Addresses   396
IPv6 Subnet Prefixes   *400*

The Three Types of IPv6 Addresses   401
The Three Types of IPv6 Unicast Addresses   *402*
Aggregatable Global Unicast Addresses   402
Site-Local Unicast Addresses   404
Link-Local Unicast Addresses   405
IPv6 Special Unicast Addresses   406
IPv6 Multicast Addresses   *409*
The IPv6 Multicast Address Format   409
Multicast Addresses Used by the Network Time Protocol (NTP)   411
Node-Local, Link-Local, and Site-Local Multicast Addresses   412
IPv6 Anycast Addresses   *413*

Configuring an IPv6 Network Interface   414
Autoconfiguring IPv6 Link-Local Addresses   *415*
Obtaining the Host's Ethernet Address   416
Converting to Binary   417
Inverting Bit 7 (High-Order Byte)   417
Inserting 0xFF and 0xFE between the CID and VID   417
Adding the Prefix   418
Configuring an IPv6 Permanent Address Manually   *418*
Plumbing in Interface hme0:10   419
Bringing Up and Assigning an IPv6 Address   419
Testing with the **ping** *Command   420*

APPENDIX A

Multiple-Choice Answers   *425*

APPENDIX B

Free Response Answers   *435*

APPENDIX C

Examination Objectives   *449*

Index   *453*

PREFACE

Why Certification?

What is all the commotion about technical certifications? Is it just hype—or is there really something to it? What is the true value of a certification? In the quest for competitive advantage among IT professionals, certification is rapidly becoming a key distinguishing characteristic for those able to attain it. Here is what industry analysts are saying:

- *Certification in leading technologies (such as Solaris) is a key to higher pay.* This reflects a trend where companies are paying more for knowledge, rather than just experience.

- *Certification is becoming the new standard for professionalism in business.* Although the college degree is still very important, the technical certification is evidence of proficiency with a particular technology or product. Certification is an independent, objective verification of knowledge.

- *Having a certification may make the difference between getting invited to the interview—or not.* Technologists need differentiators—not just accomplishments, but objective measures of technical proficiency—in order to stay competitive and stand out from the crowd of "wanna-bes."

- *Managers value certification because it increases quality and productivity of work.*

- *Solaris is the market leader in the UNIX space.* UNIX is the leader in the server OS space. Solaris does the heavy lifting on Wall Street, in compute-intensive engineering and biotechnology, and in E-commerce.

You need a certification if you want to stay ahead of the competition. This book will guide you to Solaris certification.

Intended Audience

Solaris 8 Certification is intended for experienced UNIX network administrators who wish to prepare for the *Sun Certified Network Administrator for the Solaris 8 Operating Environment* exam.

If you wish to take the exam but feel that you need to learn more, contact Sun Education at *http://suned.sun.com/*. There you can find out about training materials and classes in your area. You can also contact Sun Education at:

Sun Education
UBRM12-175
500 Eldorado Blvd.
Broomfield, CO 80021

Phone: (800) 422-8020, or (303) 464-4097
Fax: (303) 464-4490

Registering for the Exam

Follow these steps to register for the exam:

1. Purchase a Certification Voucher by calling Sun Education at 1-800-422-8020. Outside the U.S., contact your local Sun Education office. If you do not know the location of your local Sun Education office, you can find it here:
   a. http://suned.sun.com/USA/certification/global_contacts/index.html
   b. The exam costs US $150.00.
   c. You will be given a voucher number, which will be the letters "SE" followed by eight digits, for example, SE01470053. Save this number—you will need it to schedule the examination.
2. Schedule your examination by visiting the Prometric Services Web site at http://2test.com/.
   a. Select *Information Technology Certifications*. You'll then be taken to a login page; you must log in to continue (you will have an opportunity create a login if this is your first visit to the site).
   b. After logging in, you will see the Certification Program page; select *Sun Education* from the pull-down menu.
   c. Select the country where you will take your exam.
   d. Select *310-043 SUN CERTIFIED NETWORK ADMINIS-TRATOR FOR SOLARIS 8 OPERATING ENVIRONMENT* from the pull-down menu. Select the state or province if this option appears on your screen.

   e. The exam is available only in English.

   f. Select the exam location and schedule most suitable for you.

   g. You'll be given a confirmation, which includes more numbers that you will need in order to take the exam. For U.S. locations, you can also print a map showing the exam location.

Be sure to understand the policy for changing your exam date and time in case you need to reschedule your exam. Also be sure you understand any time limitations regarding the starting time for your exam. If you are late, you might not be able to take your exam. Restrictions and penalties for cancellations and/or late arrivals may apply. Carefully read all of the terms and conditions printed on your exam confirmation.

Taking the Exam

Allow plenty of time to travel to the exam site, including time for finding a parking space and the location of the exam building and room. It is advisable to call in advance if you are not familiar with the exam site.

No food or beverages are allowed in the exam room. You must check in any computer, laptop, PDA, calculator, recorder, or cell phone you bring in with you. The exam center will supply pencils and one sheet of paper for you to make calculations, draw diagrams, etc., and you will have to surrender that piece of paper at the end of the exam. You are not allowed to take any written notes with you out of the exam.

You will have 120 minutes to take the exam. That's about 2 minutes per question, as there are 58 questions in the exam. The amount of time remaining is always visible on the screen. You may take a restroom break if you wish (according to rules at the testing center), but the time clock will continue counting.

Exam Questions

The exam contains 58 questions, which are a combination of multiple choice and free response. There is more than one version of this exam. Each version has questions that were carefully selected from a much larger pool of questions, so that each version of the exam covers the same subject area and has an equivalent degree of difficulty.

The process for developing the exam questions is not trivial. Exam questions are carefully written according to a strict set of guidelines and then tested. There is a whole field of study called *psychometrics* that is used to measure and evaluate each question. Only after passing careful scrutiny will an exam question ultimately find its way onto the exam.

Questions will appear one at a time on the screen. You will be able to see each question and, in the case of multiple-choice questions, you will be able to see all of the possible answers. In some longer questions, you can scroll down to see these.

If you are not sure of the answer, you may skip the question and return to it later. You can also "mark" any exam question that you wish to review later.

Multiple-Choice Questions

The exam contains two types of multiple-choice questions: some with one correct answer, and some with two or more correct answers. Multiple-choice questions with one correct answer will present radio buttons for selecting your answer, allowing you to select only one answer. If two answers appear to be similar, be very careful because only one answer is correct.

Multiple-choice questions with more than one correct answer will specify the number of correct answers. You must select *all* of the correct answers in order to get credit for the question. These questions will present checkboxes, allowing you to select more than one answer.

Here are two sample multiple-choice questions—one with one correct answer, and one with multiple answers.

1. *What is the default main DNS server configuration file called?*

    A. /etc/resolv.conf

    B. /etc/named.root

    C. /etc/named.cache

    D. /etc/named.conf

    E. /etc/nsswitch.conf

2. *Which of the following DNS clients/servers usually ask recursive questions? Choose two.*

    A. root level servers

    B. master servers

    C. slave servers

    D. forwarding servers

    E. clients

Free-Response Questions

Free-response questions require that you type the correct answer into a blank text field. You must be very careful that you get the answer exactly right. But what about the order of options in a command? The exam is smart enough to figure this out—the exam knows about all possible variations. For instance, *netstat –rn*, *netstat –r –n*, and *netstat –n –r* are all correct answers and will be accepted.

Here is an example of a free-response question:

> *If a DNS slave server fails to synchronize with the DNS master, what is the most likely reason?*

Reviewing Test Answers

After you have answered all of the questions, you will be able to see a list of all the exam questions and the answers you selected (or filled in). Each question will have a special marking if you marked it for later review.

You may start at the beginning and review each question, you may review questions you marked earlier, or you may just skip around and check questions in any order you wish. You may unmark questions you marked, and you may mark other questions. You are free to review questions, change answers, and mark and unmark questions until time runs out or you finish the exam early.

Scoring the Exam

Once you have finished the exam, it will be scored immediately. You must answer at least 67 percent of the questions correctly to pass the exam

You will receive a temporary certificate that will show whether you passed or failed the exam. The certificate will include your name and the number of questions you answered correctly. A chart on the lower half of the certificate will indicate how you scored on each subject area. You will not know how you did on any individual question.

Retaking the Exam

If you failed the exam, you may take it again as soon as two weeks later, but you cannot take the exam more than three times in a calendar year. You will have to register and pay for another examination. You can be assured that the version of the exam will not be the same one you took previously.

Conduct

You may not discuss the details of the exam with any other individual. You may not offer or accept help of any kind.

How This Book Is Organized

Each chapter begins with a list of exam objectives. These objectives were developed by Sun Microsystems; they define the subject matter covered by the certification exam and this book. Here is an example exam objective:

- Describe IP address, broadcast address, netmask, datagram, and IP fragment.

All of the certification objectives appear in Appendix C, along with the chapter number associated with each objective. This will allow you to quickly find the technical information behind each objective.

Examples from real sessions appear in `courier` font, as in the examples below.

```
# pkill -TERM named
```

To restart the DNS server, just type

```
# in.named
```

 Note   Notes and warnings are enclosed in boxes so that they will stand out.

Throughout the book, at the end of every section are Key Learning Points, which I strongly recommend you read and learn. They list the most important points made in the section and should be understood.

Each chapter ends with a Summary and a Test Yourself section where there are ten multiple-choice and two free-answer questions. Because the exam contains few drag-and-drop questions, no sample drag-and-drop questions appear in this book.

The answers for test questions from all of the book's chapters are found in Appendixes A and B.

Feedback

Despite the presence of reviews and controls at every level, from executive direction to copy editing, some mistakes are bound to slip through. That or an unannounced change in behavior or functionality in Solaris itself, is bound to create a discrepancy between this book, the exam, and reality.

If a mistake is found in this book, all is not lost. Changes in the way books are published these days lead to the fact that this book will undergo several printing runs, each of which represents an opportunity to fix a mistake here and there.

Please send us feedback about any mistakes you find in this book, or about any ideas or comments you may have for future editions of this book.

Prentice Hall PTR
Attn: Rick Bushnell
One Lake Street
Upper Saddle River, NJ 07458
E-mail: ptr_feedback@phptr.com

We also publish an errata list online. Please visit us at http://www.phptr.com/bushnell.

ACKNOWLEDGMENTS

The author's name is on the cover of this book, but the contributions of others are watermarked indelibly throughout the pages of this text. Although I am the author, others have helped along the way, and I would like to thank them now.

I would like to thank my family—wife Sunita and my three very special children (Rebecca, age 10, Lisa, age 8, and Arron, age 6)—for suffering my absences during the writing of this book. You are a devoted and wonderful mother to our children, Sunita, as their happy, contented, lovely faces reveal.

I would like to thank my administrator, Caroline Newton, who helped with the appearance and layout of the chapters prior to copyediting. I would also like to extend my appreciation to Geoff Carrier and Diane Hudlin of Sun Microsystems for asking me to guide and lead the technical team who wrote the Sun Solaris 8 Network Administration exam in October 2000. Geoff, you inspired the team with your endless energy and passion for perfection. This year we will write an even better Solaris 9 exam. I want to thank you as a colleague and friend for your unique, individual contribution.

Thanks also to the team at Prentice Hall—Greg Doench, Eileen Clark, Brandt Kenna, Carol Wheelan, Debby vanDijk, and Mark Taub—whose editorial, marketing, and production skills this book has already, and will in the future, greatly benefit from. I would like to thank Paul Smart, Phil Potter, Peter Parsons, and Keith Lawrence for their assistance in technically reviewing the draft chapters of the book as it neared completion in the winter of 2002, and my old friend Gary Meehan for his assistance with the graphics. Thanks also to my work colleague and friend John Wilkie, for listening to *book* talk, as we enjoyed the very *occasional* beer down at our local pub.

Thanks also go to Rachel Borden and Michael Alread of Sun Press for asking me to write this book, which has been a labor of love. I would very much like to thank Sybil Ihrig of Helios Productions in San Diego, California, for coordinating the page composition, indexing, and proofreading stages of production, for editing this book with brilliant and painstaking accuracy, and for wonderful rewrites of some of my less-than-elegant prose. Sybil, I know your hair is now quite gray with grief, but I think we worked well together and I, for one, would like to repeat the performance upon a different stage in some future act. I thank you for your kind patience and for enabling me to produce a far better first book, which, at last, is finished.

Rick P. Bushnell
BA (Hons), P.G.C.E., M.B.C.S, SCNA
April 2002

Network Models and Protocols

EXAM OBJECTIVES

1.1 Layered Network Models

1.2 The Layers of the TCP/IP 5-Layer Model

1.3 Network Protocols

1.4 Peer-to-Peer Communication

1.5 TCP/IP Protocols by Name and Function

A fter completing this chapter, you will be able to meet the following Network Administration Exam objectives:

- Identify the purpose of each layer in the TCP/IP 5-layer model.
- Describe the functionality of each of the following Network Protocols: TCP, UDP, IP, and ICMP.
- Describe the relationship between the following Network Protocols: TCP, UDP, IP, and ICMP.
- Describe peer-to-peer communication.

To help you meet these objectives, this chapter covers the following topics:

- layered network models
- the layers of the TCP/IP 5-layer model
- network protocols
- peer-to-peer communications
- TCP/IP protocols by name and function

1.1   Layered Network Models

This chapter first introduces layered network models and then describes the services provided by each layer of the model. We then briefly describe, in the context of a *protocol stack*, the *network protocols* that provide the services to upper layer protocols or applications at each layer. You will learn about the features of the most important network protocols, TCP/UDP/IP and ICMP, and this information will serve as the foundation for later chapters that cover these protocols in greater detail. This gradual or phased introduction of the important network protocols will allow you to understand the basics of each protocol before we explore their more complex aspects.

Network protocols are modular by design and function at specific layers of a hierarchical protocol stack. Each layer in the hierarchy provides services to the layer above it and uses the services of the layer beneath it. There are instances in which nonadjacent layers communicate directly, but these are exceptions to the rule.

Through this hierarchy, each layer provides an *abstraction* to the layer just above it. This abstraction is desirable, as upper layers need not know how their data is routed across the Internet, or over which network their data will travel.

To understand how applications such as **sendmail**, **telnet**, and **ftp** interface with the Transmission Control Protocol/Internet Protocol (TCP/IP) suite of protocols, we must examine how the protocols communicate with each other and how they offer a service to applications. Each protocol was designed to offer a service to another protocol or application and will be explored in that context.

We can best view the protocols as an ordered stack of modules based on a set of hierarchical relationships. The hierarchy is of fundamental importance because it explains and exposes not only the relationships among the interacting protocols but also the properties of each protocol, revealing why a particular protocol is able meet the requirements of a particular application.

There are many protocol families and models. This book explores two models, which are covered by Sun course SA-389, Solaris Operating Environment TCP/IP Network Administration:

- the OSI/ISO 7-layer reference model
- the TCP/IP Sun/DoD 5-layer model

The two models are different in several respects, although both perform the same function, which essentially is to reveal the hierarchical, modular nature of network protocol design and operation. The network models also provide guidance for network protocol designers. Throughout this book, we will refer to the Open Systems Interconnection OSI/ISO 7-layer reference model simply as the OSI model and to the DoD TCP/IP Sun/DoD 5-layer model as the TCP/IP model.

The OSI/ISO 7-Layer Reference Model

The OSI/ISO 7-layer reference model was created in the early 1980s. Table 1.1 shows the seven layers of the model.

Table 1.1 *Layers of the OSI Model*

LAYER (NUMBER)	DESCRIBES/DEFINES
Application (7)	Applications and network services
Presentation (6)	The way data is presented
Session (5)	Manages connection terms of a session
Transport (4)	End-to-end messaging between applications
Network (3)	Data addressing and delivery between networks
Datalink (2)	Error detection and packet framing across a physical network
Physical (1)	Network hardware, electrical voltage and current

Note that:

- The OSI model was developed by the International Standards Organization (ISO).
- The layers of the OSI model are numbered from the base upward.
- The Physical layer (1) is at the base and the Application layer (7) is at the top.
- The OSI model is a generic networking model.
- The OSI model was designed in the early 1980s and intended for multiple manufacturers and standards.
- The OSI model was originally focused on open systems and interfacing multiple stacks.

- Chronologically, the OSI model was created long after the TCP/IP family of protocols.

The model is to some degree an ideal, as it does not pertain to any specific protocol family, but rather provides a framework within which network protocol designers and hardware manufacturers may work as they strive to produce modular products.

We next outline the TCP/IP model and compare and contrast it with the OSI model.

The TCP/IP 5-Layer Model

The Department of Defense (DoD) TCP/IP 5-layer model was created in 1969. Table 1.2 shows the layers of this model and the service provided by each layer.

Table 1.2 *Layers of the TCP/IP Model and Purpose of Each Layer*

LAYER (NUMBER)	PURPOSE
Application (5)	Reserved for applications and protocols
Transport (4)	Provides end-to-end delivery service for layer 5 applications and protocols
Internet (3)	Provides a network routing service to upper layers
Network (2)	Provides a framing service to the Internet layer
Physical (1)	Provides an electrical signal bit transmission service to the network

With this model, aimed specifically at TCP/IP conventions, we can identify the protocols at each layer, as shown in Table 1.3.

The most important points to note about the TCP/IP model are:

- The TCP/IP protocols were developed and funded by the USA DoD for purposes of research and experimentation.
- The TCP/IP model was conceived in 1969.
- The TCP/IP model accommodates only the TCP/IP protocols.
- The TCP/IP model has only five layers.

Table 1.3 *Layers of the TCP/IP Model and Entities That Function at Each Layer*

LAYER (NUMBER)	NETWORK COMPONENT THAT OPERATES AT THIS LAYER
Application (5)	HTTP, FTP, telnet, SMTP, NTP, POP, IMAP, and others
Transport (4)	TCP/UDP
Internet (3)	IP, ICMP, ARP, RARP
Network (2)	Data Link: Ethernet, Token Ring, FDDI, ATM, and others
Physical (1)	Coaxial, fiberoptic, twisted pair

Benefits of Using Network Models: A Summary

It is beneficial to consider the organization of any network model because the network model

- reveals the hierarchical, modular nature of network protocol design and implementation.
- enables us to think in terms of each protocol performing a given function or service at a specific layer.
- visually reveals a host's protocol stack as implemented in the kernel.
- reveals the order of the protocol stack.

The striking differences between the models are shown in Table 1.4.

Table 1.4 *Differences Between the OSI 7-Layer and TCP/IP 5-Layer Models*

OSI MODEL	TCP/IP MODEL
Devised 1983	Devised 1969
Created by ISO	Created by USA DoD
Multiple vendors/multiple protocols/ ISO protocols	TCP/IP protocol family
Seven layers	Five layers
Generic networking model	TCP/IP-specific model

KEY LEARNING POINTS

- The OSI model is used as a frame of reference when describing protocol architectures and functional characteristics.
- The TCP/IP model is specifically intended for the TCP/IP family of protocols.
- The TCP/IP model and protocols chronologically predate the OSI model and protocols.
- Traditional TCP/IP applications talk directly to the Transport layer and have no distinct session and presentation layer protocols.

Next, we examine the TCP/IP 5-layer model in more detail to illustrate which protocols operate at each of the layers. The TCP/IP model and the protocols that function within each of its layers constitute the basis for the rest of this book. A brief description of each protocol appears in this chapter; later chapters examine the individual protocols in greater detail.

1.2   The Layers of the TCP/IP 5-Layer Model

A closer examination of the layers of the TCP/IP 5-layer model follows. The layers of the protocol stack are numbered, as you saw in Table 1.3. This examination starts at the Application layer (layer 5) of the protocol stack and works downward to the level of the Physical layer (layer 1) at the bottom of the stack.

Application Layer (5)

There are literally hundreds of applications that function at the Application layer, and more are being developed as the Internet evolves. Well-known TCP/IP applications include:

- Web browsers/servers using the HyperText Transfer Protocol (HTTP)
- mail applications and related protocols
  - Post Office Protocol (POP)

- Internet Message Access Protocol (IMAP)
- Simple Mail Transport Protocol (SMTP)
- File Transfer Protocol (FTP)
- **telnet** and **rlogin**
- Domain Name Service (DNS)
- Network File System (NFS)
- Network Information Service (NIS) and Network Information Service Plus (NIS+)

Application layer protocols and applications are unable to deliver their own data across a network or Internet unassisted and so need to be *encapsulated* in a Transport protocol such as TCP or User Datagram Protocol (UDP). The Transport layer provides this *transport service* (also known as a *delivery service)* to the Application layer. The Transport layer protocol in turn relies on the Internet Protocol (IP) to provide an end-to-end routing service.

You will visit these concepts again when IP (Chapter 5), routing (Chapter 6), TCP/UDP (Chapter 7), and the Client-Server model (Chapter 8) are investigated in greater detail.

Focus on the following important points that summarize features of the Application layer. Chapter 8 examines how these applications interact with Transport layer protocols.

EXAM NOTES

KEY LEARNING POINTS

- Many protocols function at the Application layer.
- HTTP, SMTP, POP, FTP, and DNS are the most heavily used Application layer protocols on the Internet.
- Web browsers, mail clients, news readers, **ftp, telnet, sendmail** are just a few of the thousands of layer 5 applications.
- The Application layer uses the Transport layer for delivery.
- Users often interact directly with Application layer programs.
- The Application layer (5) is at the top of the stack.

Transport Layer (4)

TCP and UDP are the only two protocols that function at the Transport layer (4). They encapsulate or carry the layer 5 protocols and offer an end-to-end transport service. They accept data from a client network application on a client host and deliver it to the server application on the server host that is providing the client with the service. The client and the servers are usually on different systems and therefore need a network to connect them. Data travels between the client and server across one or more networks.

For example, a **telnet** client on the client host needs to reach the **in.telnetd** server daemon running on the server host. The **telnet** client process uses the TCP Transport layer protocol to connect to the **in.telnetd** server process (which usually exists on a different system). Other Application layer protocols use the UDP transport protocol, which offers a nonguaranteed transport service, trading guaranteed delivery for speed and minimized overhead. DNS queries, for example, use UDP, as speed is of the essence, and failure considerations are not so critical.

The choice of using either TCP or UDP at the Transport layer is made by the network programmer and is based on the type of service required. Some well-known network protocols that function at the Application layer use both TCP and UDP for different functions— DNS, for example, which is fully explored in Chapter 11. Some applications that were originally designed to use UDP, such as Sun's NFS that allows file sharing between systems, have switched to using TCP. Version 2 of NFS used UDP, but version 3 uses TCP.

Focus on the following important points before proceeding to the next section on the Internet layer.

EXAM NOTES

KEY LEARNING POINTS

- Most Solaris applications use TCP and UDP for end-to-end delivery.
- TCP and UDP are transport protocols.
- TCP and UDP are encapsulated in IP.
- TCP and UDP are not able to route their own data and so use IP to perform this task.

Chapter 7 explores the Transport layer protocols (TCP and UDP) in detail, examining why a given application may be better suited to using TCP than UDP, or the converse. In Chapter 8 we examine the client-server model and learn how the applications that use TCP/UDP are configured.

We next examine the Internet layer, on which the Transport layer relies for routing the data it is transporting. The Transport layer provides client and server applications with an end-to-end delivery service (which is not the same as routing), which you will see in Chapter 7, whereas IP (described in Chapter 6) provides an end-to-end IP datagram routing service.

Internet Layer (3)

At every other layer of the TCP/IP network model, multiple protocols exist to carry out similar tasks. The Internet layer is an exception, with only the IP protocol capable of performing the critical routing function. Although other protocols function at the Internet layer, only the IP protocol offers a datagram-based routing service to the upper layers of the stack. IP is the only protocol able to encapsulate and route packets to a destination IP address (identified in the IP datagram header), understand the IP address scheme, and route data for upper-layer protocols such as TCP, UDP, and ICMP. These, in turn, carry encapsulated application layer data.

The Internet layer protocol, IP, makes the *routing decision* and handles the routing of IP datagrams. IP is also responsible for the fragmentation of IP datagrams, which might be necessary if the underlying Network Interface layer (2) demands it. Chapter 5 covers IP fragmentation in detail.

IP does not build the routing tables; it merely uses the kernel routing table information in an attempt to route the IP datagram(s), as you will learn in Chapter 6.

IP was designed to run over any LAN or WAN technology. An IP's address is essentially a logical or software address that is *mapped* onto a Network layer (2) address so that IP datagrams can be packaged up *(framed)* and carried across a specific type of Network Interface layer technology, such as Token Ring or Ethernet. ARP manages the mapping between the Internet layer (3) where IP resides and the Network Interface layer where Ethernet resides. Chapter 4 examines ARP further. Chapter 5 covers IPv4 in detail and Chapter 13 explores IPv6.

EXAM NOTES

KEY LEARNING POINTS

- IP makes the routing decision and routes IP datagrams.
- IP routes datagram(s) to the destination IP address in the IP header.
- IP datagrams typically carry (encapsulate) TCP/UDP application data.
- IP functions at the Internet layer.
- IP's header is a minimum of 20 bytes and can be larger.
- IP's unit of data is an IP datagram.

Network Interface Layer (2)

Ethernet functions at this layer. There are alternatives to Ethernet at this layer, but Ethernet is dominant in terms of UNIX LANS and is the only LAN examined in detail in this book. Ethernet frames or encapsulates the data it is carrying, prior to transmitting its packet onto the Ethernet bus.

Network Interface layer technologies have Maximum Transmission Units (MTUs) of various sizes. (The MTU determines the maximum number of bytes that can be transmitted in a single frame, not including the headers.) As Table 1.5 shows, MTU size varies according to the Network Interface layer technology.

Table 1.5 *Network Layer MTUs*

NETWORK TYPE	MTU (BYTES)
Hyperchannel	65,535
16 MB/second Token Ring (IBM)	17,914
4 Mbits/second Token Ring (IEEE 802.5)	4,464
Fiber Distributed Data Interface (FDDI)	4,352
Ethernet	1,500
IEEE 802.3/802.2	1,492
Point to Point (low delay)	296

Ethernet's MTU is especially significant because it determines whether an IP datagram carried by Ethernet needs fragmenting. See Chapter 5 for further information.

KEY LEARNING POINTS

- **The Network Interface layer MTU determines the maximum number of bytes carried in a single frame.**
- **Ethernet is a Network Interface layer technology.**
- **Network Interface layer technologies have MTUs of various sizes.**

Physical Layer (1)

This layer at the base of the stack identifies the LAN transmission media, typically fiberoptic or wire-based media. This layer concerns the transmission of bits across a physical media with very little interpretation of the data.

Chapter 3 examines the copper wire and fiberoptic-based media used by Ethernet, FDDI, and ATM in greater detail.

So far, we have examined the network protocols in the context of a network model. The ensuing discussion of the most important network protocols reveals their features and provides a foundation for chapters that follow.

1.3   Network Protocols

This section is a brief introduction to TCP, UDP, IP, and ICMP. First, we briefly examine the two transport protocols, TCP and UDP, and then take a cursory look at IP and ICMP.

Transport Layer Protocols: TCP and UDP

We briefly mentioned the TCP and UDP protocols in the context of the TCP/IP model described earlier in this chapter. We now examine the Transport layer in greater detail.

The Transport layer offers either a high-overhead, guaranteed, connection-oriented transport service such as that offered by TCP, or a low-overhead, connectionless, nonguaranteed service such as the one offered by UDP. See Chapter 7 for more information about the Transport layer protocols and Chapters 5 and 13 for details about the IP protocols (IPv4, IPv6) that route the Transport protocols data.

Transmission Control Protocol (TCP)

TCP provides a connection-oriented, guaranteed, reliable transport service. TCP has significant overhead because every byte of transmitted data is both acknowledged and sequenced by both ends of the connection. The data itself is delivered in one or more *segments*, which are TCP's basic units of data. In addition, TCP establishes a connection at the Transport layer, which must be formed before transmission of client data may occur over the Transport layer.

Although TCP guarantees data delivery, it must be remembered that TCP is routed over IP and therefore uses the same underlying packet-based routing service as UDP—namely, IP, which is not guaranteed. Both TCP and UDP use IP to route their data, but they impose different levels of reliability and overhead as determined by their own specifications as Transport layer protocols. TCP extensively monitors the quality of data sent and received, whereas UDP has only a simple checksum error checking method, which is often turned off and therefore ignored.

The cost of TCP reliability, as just stated, is significant overhead. The TCP protocol sends a sequenced (numbered) *byte stream* of segmented data. The sequence numbering of bytes ensures that the destination TCP protocol at the receiving end orders the data stream correctly. Unfragmented IP datagrams that arrive in the wrong order (which have encapsulated TCP segments) are simply passed up the stack to TCP, which ensures that the data is delivered to the application in the correct order. Fragmented IP datagrams, on the other hand, are reassembled by IP itself before being passed to TCP based on fragment offset information stored in the IP header. Some example TCP client applications are

telnet, ftp, and **sendmail**, all of which require a guaranteed delivery service and therefore use TCP rather than UDP.

EXAM NOTES

KEY LEARNING POINTS

- TCP is a connection-oriented protocol.
- The segment is the TCP unit of data.
- TCP is a Transport layer protocol.
- TCP is encapsulated and routed by IP.
- TCP is said to offer a guaranteed, reliable, connection-oriented service that creates significant overhead.

Essentially, if data security must be guaranteed, TCP is a better choice than UDP, although more expensive in terms of both the amount of control data transmitted and the control overhead incurred. Chapter 7 examines the TCP protocol in greater detail.

User Datagram Protocol (UDP)

UDP is a connectionless transport protocol, which means that no connection is established at the Transport layer prior to data being sent between client and server applications.

Some applications—for example, a router propagating routing information every 30 seconds—can afford to lose an occasional data packet. Routing clients that miss the occasional routing table update do not usually suffer adverse effects. The Routing Information Protocol (RIP) uses UDP. DNS queries also use UDP, as speed is more important than reliability for this application. UDP applications tend to send small packets that can be transported in a single UDP datagram. UDP has an optional checksum error check, which introduces minimal overhead and is usually turned off.

To check the UDP checksum variable (**udp_do_checksum**) under Solaris 8 use **ndd**:

```
# ndd -get  /dev/udp udp_do_checksum
0
```

A value of 0 means false; that is, disable the UDP checksum feature. A value of 1, which means true, indicates that the UDP protocol checksum feature is enabled.

To enable the UDP checksum feature, issue the following command:

```
# ndd -set /dev/udp udp_do_checksum 1
```

To check the current value of **udp_do_checksum**:

```
# ndd -get  /dev/udp udp_do_checksum
1
```

EXAM NOTES

KEY LEARNING POINTS

- UDP is a connectionless protocol.
- UDP is a transport protocol.
- UDP is encapsulated and routed in IP.
- UDP is not guaranteed.
- UDP does minimal error checking.
- UDP has a simple checksum for error checking.
- UDP's header is only eight bytes.

Chapter 7 looks at the UDP protocol in greater detail.

Internet Protocol (IPv4)

IPv4 is a connectionless protocol like UDP. Unlike UDP, however, IP is not a transport protocol but instead offers a datagram routing service to the Transport layer (a datagram is the unit of data for the IP layer). The Transport layer protocols, TCP and UDP, use IP to route their client data between application client and server hosts. It is worth stressing, therefore, that IP routes data between hosts, and in effect, between the Transport layers on end-to-end hosts, but not between clients and server processes. The Transport layer protocols, TCP and UDP, transport the data between client and server processes, using IP to form a bridge between hosts. IP as a protocol is responsible for the following:

- fragmenting of IP datagrams if the Network Interface layer MTU demands it
- reassembly of IP fragments
- making the IP datagram routing decision

EXAM NOTES

KEY LEARNING POINTS

- **IP is a connectionless protocol.**
- **IP is an Internet layer protocol.**
- **IP is encapsulated in many different datalink technologies such as Ethernet, Token Ring, and Point-to-Point Protocol (PPP).**
- **IP is not guaranteed.**

Chapter 5 looks in detail at IPv4, and Chapter 13 explores IPv6. Next we look at ICMP, which also functions at the Internet layer (3).

Internet Control Message Protocol (ICMP)

ICMP is considered almost part of the IP protocol, even though it is a separate protocol in its own right. ICMP generates messages, which receive a response either from the IP layer itself or a higher layer protocol such as TCP or UDP. Although ICMP is at the same layer as IP, it is not an alternative to IP; rather, it assists IP with IP error detection and correction.

ICMP data is encapsulated in IP datagram(s), as is TCP and UDP data, but ICMP is not a Transport layer protocol. Error messages such as **network unreachable**, **host unreachable**, and **port unreachable** are examples of ICMP error messages.

See Chapter 5 for further details about ICMP.

1.4   Peer-to-Peer Communication

The term *peer-to-peer* identifies two communicating entities, functioning or operating at the same layer of the stack, as *peers*. The peers are usually on different systems that are connected by one or more networks, as shown in Figure 1-1.

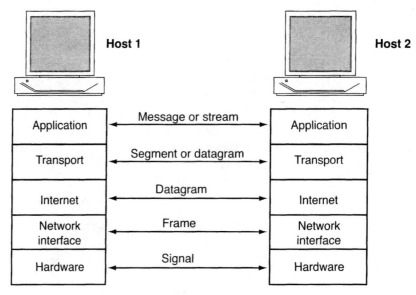

Figure 1–1   *Peer relationships*

KEY LEARNING POINTS

- The two ends of a communication are at the same layer of the stack.
- The peer entities may be application processes or protocols.

The following section identifies protocols by the Requests for Comments (RFCs) that formally describe them.

1.5   TCP/IP Protocols by Name and Function

In this chapter we already looked briefly at some TCP/IP protocols. It is, however, worth summarizing each protocol formally in terms of its name and the RFC that describes it. Some of these protocols will be explored in later chapters as indicated in Table 1.6.

The following list of RFCs and protocols is not definitive. Listed are the most useful RFCs, but not all RFCs that relate to the subject, as the list is extensive for the more complex protocols. The RFC column of the table lists the chapter of this book that covers the protocol where applicable. We work down the stack from the Application layer (5), again, taking the journey that application data takes.

The Application layer has literally hundreds of applications and many protocols that the applications at this layer use. They are listed in Table 1.6 by relevant RFC, protocol name, and a brief description.

Table 1.7 lists the important Transport layer protocols. Chapter 7 explores these in detail.

Table 1.8 describes the protocols of the Internet layer. Chapter 4 covers ARP/RARP, and Chapters 5 and 13 cover IPv4 and IPv6, respectively.

Table 1.9 shows the Network layer protocols, with many technologies to choose from. Ethernet is by far the most important LAN technology to understand. Alternatives such as Token Ring and Token Bus exist, but they are far less important than Ethernet.

Table 1.6 *Application Layer Protocol Descriptions*

RFC	PROTOCOL	DESCRIPTION
1034,1035 *Chapter 11*	DNS	Domain Name Service is a text-based, distributed host-to-IP address (and IP address-to-host) mapping solution based on Berkeley Internet Name Domain (BIND) library routines. It also provides, through mail exchanger (MX) information, the IP addresses and names of servers that accept inbound e-mail for given domain names.
959	**ftp**	File Transfer Protocol transfers a file by copying a complete file from one system to another system.
854,855	**telnet**	This service provides a remote connection and login facility, which runs over any TCP/IP network.
1258,1280	**rlogin**	This service, offered by UNIX systems, enables users of one machine to connect to other UNIX systems across the Internet and to interact as though their terminals were connected directly to the machines.
2131 *Chapter 9*	DHCP	Dynamic Host Configuration Protocol automates the assignment of IP addresses in an organization's network.
821	SMTP	Simple Mail Transfer Protocol transfers electronic mail messages from one machine to another.
1157	SNMP	Simple Network Management Protocol is the language that allows for the monitoring and control of network entities.
1939	POP3	Post Office Protocol lets users collect e-mail from a POP server over any TCP/IP network. The user's host runs a POP client application, and the server runs the POP server software, which gives the user authenticated access to his or her mailbox.
2060	IMAP4	Internet Message Access Protocol, like POP, lets users collect e-mail from an IMAP server over a TCP/IP network. The user's host runs an IMAP client application, and the server runs the IMAP server software, which gives the user authenticated access to his or her mailbox. IMAP4 is more powerful and offers more features than POP3.
1945,2068	HTTP	HyperText Transfer Protocol is used by the World Wide Web to display text, pictures, sounds, and other multimedia information with a Web browser.

Table 1.7 *Transport Layer (4) Protocol Descriptions*

RFC	PROTOCOL	DESCRIPTION
793 *Chapter 7*	TCP	Transmission Control Protocol is a connection-oriented protocol that provides the full-duplex, stream service on which many application protocols depend. It is encapsulated in IP.
768 *Chapter 7*	UDP	User Datagram Protocol provides a datagram delivery to application and is encapsulated in IP.

Table 1.8 *Internet Layer (3) Protocol Descriptions*

RFC	PROTOCOL	DESCRIPTION
826 *Chapter 4*	ARP	Address Resolution Protocol defines the method used to map a 32-bit IP address to a 48-bit Ethernet address.
903 *Chapter 4*	RARP	Reverse Address Resolution Protocol is the reverse of ARP. It maps a 48-bit Ethernet address to a 32-bit IP address.
791,950 919,922 *Chapters 5 and 13*	IP	Internet Protocol determines the path a datagram must take, based on the destination host's IP address.
792 *Chapter 5*	ICMP	Internet Control Message Protocol communicates error messages and other controls within IP datagrams.

Table 1.9 *Network Layer (2) Protocol Descriptions*

RFC	PROTOCOL	DESCRIPTION
1055	SLIP	Serial Line IP encapsulates IP datagrams on serial lines.
1661	PPP	Point-to-Point Protocol transmits datagrams over serial point-to-point links.
826, 894 *Chapter 3*	Ethernet	Ethernet is a broadcast-based, contention-bus LAN technology.

KEY LEARNING POINTS

- The OSI/ISO 7-layer reference model is a generic network model.
- The DoD 5-layer model is specifically for the TCP/IP protocol family.
- TCP and UDP are transport protocols that provide a delivery service to the Application layer.
- IP is an Internet layer protocol that offers a datagram-based routing service to the Transport and Application layers.

SUMMARY

This chapter explored network models, specifically the OSI 7-layer model and the TCP/IP 5-layer model. Having contrasted the models, it should be apparent that OSI is a generic model in contrast to the TCP/IP model, which is specifically aimed at the TCP/IP family of protocols. An examination of the protocol stack revealed a hierarchical approach to network management and a modular approach to protocol implementation and design. The five layers of the TCP/IP model were examined and the main network protocols at each layer introduced. A discussion of peer-to-peer communications described how the communicating protocols or applications are considered peers when they are both functioning at the same layer in the stack.

Finally, we provided a tabular summary of relevant protocols and applications that function at various layers of the protocol stack, listed by RFC, protocol, description, and the chapter of this book that discusses them.

TEST YOURSELF

MULTIPLE CHOICE

1. *Which of the following are layers of the OSI/ISO 7-layer reference model? Choose three.*

    A. Session layer

    B. Application layer

    C. Semblance layer

    D. Service layer

    E. Presentation layer

2. *Which of the following are layers of the TCP/IP 5-layer model? Choose three.*

    A. Transmit layer

    B. Physical layer

    C. Transient layer

    D. Transport layer

    E. Internet layer

3. *At which layer of the TCP/IP 5-layer model does Ethernet function?*

    A. Application layer

    B. Transport layer

    C. Internet layer

    D. Network Interface layer

    E. Physical layer

4. *At which layer of the TCP/IP 5-layer model does the UDP protocol function?*

    A. Application layer

    B. Transport layer

    C. Internet layer

    D. Network layer

    E. Physical layer

5. *What does the acronym UDP mean?*

    A. User Distance Protocol

    B. Uniform Data Protocol

    C. United Datagram Protocol

    D. User Datagram Protocol

    E. Ultimate Datagram Protocol

6. *What does the acronym TCP mean?*

    A. Transport Control Protocol

    B. Transmission Counter Protocol

    C. Transmission Control Protocol

    D. Transport Concert Protocol

        E. Transmission Count Protocol

7. *Which word describes communicating layers across hosts that are at the same layer within the stack?*

    A. partners

    B. peerers

    C. primers

    D. peers

    E. players

8. *Which protocol is ICMP encapsulated in?*

    A. TCP

    B. IP

    C. UDP

    D. ARP

    E. RARP

9. *What is the size of the UDP header in bytes?*

    A. 10

    B. 20

    C. 12

    D. 4

    E. 8

10. *What is the minimum size of the IPv4 header in bytes?*

    A. 20

    B. 18

    C. 12

    D. 40

    E. 25

FREE RESPONSE

1. State in your own words three advantages of modularizing the design of network protocols.

2. List the similarities and differences between IP and UDP as protocols.

Introduction to Local Area Networks

EXAM OBJECTIVES

2.1 LAN Basics, Advantages, and Disadvantages

2.2 LAN Topologies

2.3 LAN Components

2.4 Non-TCP/IP LAN-Based Technologies and Protocols

After completing this chapter, you will be able to meet the following Network Administration Exam objectives:

- Identify the LAN components repeater, hub, bridge, switch, router, and gateway.
- Identify the network topologies.

To help you meet these objectives, this chapter covers the following topics:

- basics of Local Area Networks (LANs) and their relative advantages and disadvantages
- bus, star, and ring LAN configurations
- backbones, segments, repeaters, hubs, switches, and other LAN components
- non-TCP/IP LAN-based technologies and protocols such as OSI, IPX, NetBIOS, and NetBEUI

2.1   LAN Basics, Advantages, and Disadvantages

A Local Area Network (LAN) is a network connecting machines and devices that are in geographical proximity to one another. By definition, LANs typically cover a geographically small area in contrast to Wide Area Networks (WANs), which cover greater geographical distances. An understanding of LAN technologies, especially Ethernet solutions, is important if you are to understand the crucial role played by LANs in modern networks. LAN technologies offer a fundamental service to upper-layer protocols such as IP because LANs deliver packets (frames) across *local* links. To describe LANs fully, it is essential to discuss the characteristics of available LAN technologies and both the hardware and software needed for a particular LAN.

Most businesses with two or more computers would benefit from using a LAN to share expensive resources like network or shared printers, to communicate using basic tools such as e-mail and the Internet, and also to share company information and data using file servers.

In this chapter we explore LANs and the devices found on a typical LAN. We explore some of the terms used and the available LAN technologies. LANs offer both benefits and disadvantages, as you will see shortly.

LANs offer multiple advantages. By connecting devices to a LAN, companies and organizations can share vital hardware and software resources, communicate, and share joint project areas, thus increasing workgroup synergy and productivity. Systems administrators can manage and monitor local systems and access remote networks through a LAN.

The disadvantages of a LAN relate primarily to security: The LAN offers a means by which a user can potentially access all systems on the LAN. Extend this reasoning a bit further. If the LAN is connected to a WAN such as the Internet, external users potentially have access to the systems on the LAN simply because a connection exists. LAN systems need to be protected behind *firewalls*, which essentially block unwanted inbound network traffic (and also outbound traffic if desired). Firewalls filter or restrict which protocols and services are allowed into the LAN and in this way protect component systems from attack.

Another potential disadvantage (in terms of cost specifically) is that a LAN requires network administrators who have the specialized knowledge to manage the services and connectivity that a LAN offers. Finally, devices on which companies rely heavily, such as file and print servers, affect a broader number of users when they fail if they are connected to a LAN.

The advantages and disadvantages of using a LAN are summarized in Tables 2.1 and 2.2.

Table 2.1 *Advantages of Using a LAN*

ADVANTAGE	DESCRIPTION
Shared hardware devices	Expensive devices, such as printers and scanners, can be shared by multiple users, thus representing a cost savings to the enterprise. Multiple users can also share other hardware components such as modems and CD-ROM drives.
Shared software and files	Application software can be shared via the application server.
	Project data can be shared via Sun's NFS and be seen by anyone who can access the LAN.
	Users can work at several different systems within the LAN and still access their data and home directories.
Platform integration	Platforms are more easily integrated. For example, UNIX directories can be shared using SAMBA and are seen by LAN-connected PCs as logical drives, for example as drive **G:**. This is useful for making backups and for the use of shared data areas across platforms.
Shared network services	All LAN users can share e-mail because they have access to the LAN-based mail server through their client applications.
	Domain Server information can be shared via DNS.
	Client systems can access LAN Web servers and use the LAN as the gateway to Internet Web and DNS services.
	Via **ftp**, LAN clients can move files between systems and across the Internet.
Remote management and access	LAN client software can be configured to manage remote servers on other networks.
	LAN clients can use remote connection tools, such as **telnet** or **rlogin**, to connect to remote systems.
Remote backups and archiving	Users can back up to remote tapes and disk systems using **rcp, rdist, ftp,** and Solstice Backup.

The advantages of using LAN technology easily outweigh the disadvantages, which helps to explain why they are so popular.

Table 2.2 *Disadvantages of Using a LAN*

DISADVANTAGE	DESCRIPTION
Security concerns	LANs make it possible for remote systems to access yours by using tools such as **telnet**. Also, e-mail viruses propagate via LANs and WANs. One solution is to provide better security by installing firewall-based solutions.
Additional staffing and skills	Depending on the complexity of the LAN and the number of systems connected, additional staff skills are needed to manage the LAN and connected devices. Usually, the extra staff skills needed are acquired through training courses (such as those offered by Sun), books, Web sites, and on-the-job experience.
Network failures	The failure of the LAN will affect all connected systems globally.

EXAM NOTES

KEY LEARNING POINTS

- There are both advantages and disadvantages to using local area networks.
- Communication and sharing are the main advantages of networking.
- LANs make remote backup, monitoring, and management possible.
- Potential security problems constitute the most important disadvantage of using LANs.
- Additional staff training is essential to install, maintain, and manage a LAN.
- Reliance on networking can lead to major problems if the network fails.

2.2 LAN Topologies

A LAN's *topology* describes how machines are connected together and the path taken by data traveling between systems on the LAN. The most popular topologies are:

- bus LANs
- star LANs
- ring LANs

Bus LANs

A bus LAN allows all connected systems to see all data passing between hosts because the transmitted data propagates through the entire bus. The best-known example of a LAN bus is Ethernet, which, since its inception 25 years ago, has typified and dominated bus technology. Ethernet is a typical bus network in which stations contend for bandwidth. For this reason, a bus-type LAN is often referred to as a *contention bus*. The bus has no bus server to decide when stations are allowed to transmit. The systems listen to the bus and transmit when they are able to. This process is analogous to a highway intersection where the traffic light that normally regulates vehicle flow is temporarily out of service: The drivers of individual vehicles decide when to stop and when to proceed of their own volition. (For more information about how a contention bus works, see Chapter 3.)

In an earlier era of computing, systems connected to a bus by means of a *backbone*, which consisted of a cable up to hundreds of meters long. Modern buses tend to use much smaller devices such as hubs and switches that do not take up nearly as much physical space as traditional backbones; these are collectively referred to as *collapsed backbone* technologies. The advantage of collapsed buses such as hubs is that systems connect to them through a single segment of cabling. If a particular systems cable breaks, it does not affect other systems because they connect through their own point-to-point segment of cable. If the bus itself breaks, on the other hand, the bus malfunctions regardless of whether that bus is collapsed (switch or hub type) or simply a length of backbone cable to which stations connect. Loss of power to the switch or hub affects all stations connected to it. Figure 2-1 shows a traditional cable bus.

Star LANs

In a star LAN, each host connects to a central device, such as a hub or switch. The distance between any two stations is normally two cable segments. A break in one segment normally affects only the system on the end of the segment. Ethernet, which uses a central hub or switch, is a popular example of a LAN using a star topology. The switch connected to it determines the port to which messages are transferred when data is to be delivered to a system that is connected to a switch.

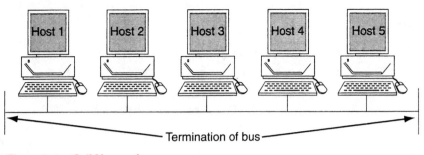

Termination of bus

Figure 2–1   *LAN bus topology*

Figure 2-2 shows three systems connected to a switch in a star topology. The switch usually has 4, 8, 16, or 32 ports. Special dedicated ports on the switch are often used for *uplinking*—connecting switches to enable a network to span a greater distance.

See section 2.3 discussing LAN components for more information about how switches work.

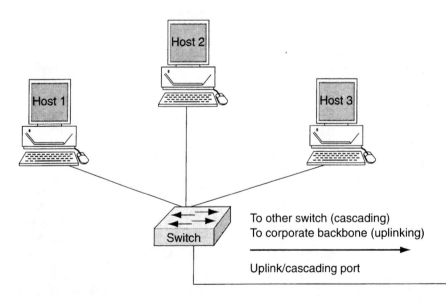

Figure 2–2   *An example of LAN star topology*

Ring LANs

A ring LAN consists of a logical single or dual ring. A well-known example is Token Ring, developed by IBM. With Token Ring, a token circulates around the ring and must be collected by any station wishing to transmit. The system that has successfully acquired the token may transmit. Following transmission, the system that removed the token from the ring must regenerate the token and transmit it back onto the ring so that other systems can acquire the token and transmit in turn.

Ring topology has traditionally had disadvantages similar to those of bus topology: A breakage in the ring or a failed host can lead to complete disruption of the entire ring. These days, however, intelligent central hubs implement dual rings to guard against a single breakage that could lead to a complete breakdown of the ring. In effect, the ring network is a logical ring with dual-ring capability.

Fiber Distributed Data Interface (FDDI), an IBM technology, is another example of how ring topology can be implemented. Each host in the LAN is connected to the ring in the series: The output of one node connects to the input of the next node. The hosts connect through a central device. Figure 2-3 shows a star-wired ring topology.

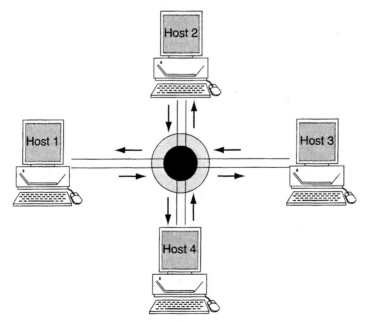

Figure 2–3   *Star-wired ring topology*

EXAM NOTES

KEY LEARNING POINTS

- Three basic topologies exist: bus, ring, and star.
- Machines connected to ring networks are connected in series.
- Ring topologies are typified by IBM's Token Ring.
- FDDI backbones use a ring topology and use Token Ring technology.
- Ethernet is a bus, but it may be implemented in a bus or star topology.

2.3   LAN Components

LAN components vary in function, purpose, and cost. Devices on a LAN are either equipment that users share (such as printers, scanners, and servers) or devices that enable other equipment to connect to the LAN or that connect one LAN to another. Devices such as hubs, switches, and routers fall into the latter category. In this section we will describe the various LAN devices and where they fit in the protocol stack that we discussed in Chapter 1.

Backbone

A *backbone* is the primary means by which devices connect to the network, be it a main cable, hub, or switch. On the embryonic Internet (originally called the Advanced Research Projects Agency Network or ARPANET), the main backbone connected the *core gateways* (important routers that connected distant networks) across the USA. When a hub or switch (which is much more compact than the older-style cables) is used as the backbone, the backbone is said to be *collapsed*—a common scenario among contemporary LANs.

A backbone can also be the main cable to which routers, switches, and bridges connect to link multiple LANs together, as in the example of an FDDI ring or an asynchronous transfer mode (ATM) backbone.

A backbone maps onto the physical layer of the protocol stack.

Segment

A *segment* is a length of unbroken cable (called *contiguous* cable) and is often referred to as a *link* because it links a device to the LAN. The segment is usually restricted in terms of length and is joined to other links or segments through repeaters if greater cable length is desired.

A segment could be

- a contiguous piece of cable connecting switches and/or hubs,
- a contiguous piece of cable linking a hub or switch to the main backbone, or
- a contiguous piece of cable linking a node or host to a hub or switch.

The length of a segment depends on the type of cable in use, and it tends to vary from one media type to another. A segment maps onto the physical layer of the protocol stack.

Repeater

A *repeater* is in essence an amplifier, ensuring that a signal's strength does not attenuate and degrade to the point of being corrupt. The repeater does not interpret the data; it simply amplifies the signal to allow the data to traverse greater distances. Repeaters allow multiple Ethernet segments to be joined, thereby achieving greater cable lengths. Repeaters are not the only type of device that can link segments together; other linking devices include bridges, switches, and routers. Repeaters are used when a segment has reached the maximum length allowed for that type of media.

A repeater maps onto the physical layer of the protocol stack. It amplifies a signal and prevents signal degradation, usually referred to as *attenuation*.

Hub (Multiport Repeater)

Multiport repeaters for 10-, 100-, or 1000-Mbps networks are usually called *hubs,* typically providing anywhere from 4 to 32 ports. A special port is usually available for *uplinking* or *cascading* multiple hubs, a process that connects LAN segments and allows networks to span greater distances.

A *collision domain* refers to a wiring range within which a collision may occur and includes the systems the collision will affect. Uplinking basic hubs simply extends the collision domain. That is, in an uplinked hub topology, a collision that occurs will affect all hubs, as they are all part of the same collision domain. The use of switches overcomes this problem, however, by separating collision domains and largely eliminating collisions. Refer to the "LAN Components" section of this chapter to learn more about switches.

The Ethernet standard defines a maximum, round-trip time in a collision domain of 576-bit periods or, to be exact, 5,120 nanoseconds. Each component in a network adds delay; the amount of delay is defined either as *latency port to port*, which is defined as the time it takes to process a single bit from input to output, or as a *round-trip delay*, which is the time it takes for a bit to be processed once in both directions. Delay equals 5.76 microseconds for a 100 Mbps Ethernet setup and 57.6 microseconds for a 10 Mbps network. The maximum allowed distance of the collision domain shrinks for fast Ethernet, from the 2500 m allowed for 10 Mbps Ethernet to a mere 205 m for 100 Mbps fast Ethernet. Exceeding the allowed maximum distances between devices and allowed cable lengths causes collision detection to fail, and chaos can ensue.

A hub can be the central device that connects hosts in a twisted-pair Ethernet installation, although in contemporary use, switches are replacing hubs at a rapid rate. In effect, the hub acts as a collapsed small bus, although the topology is starlike in shape. A hub is also commonly referred to as a multiport repeater as we just described, and it acts as a means of connecting segments.

A hub maps onto the physical layer of the protocol stack.

Bridge

A *bridge* connects network segments. A bridge forwards and filters network segments based on MAC addresses, but not between IP addressees. Bridges operate at the network interface layer of the stack. A bridge (unlike a hub) creates a separate collision domain on the segments it connects. A bridge learns or is programmed to know which systems exist on the segments it connects. It allows essential data to pass through the collision domain and prevents traffic from passing through it unnecessarily.

Two segments can be connected by a standard bridge, which are old technology by today's standards. If more connections are permitted, the device is usually referred to as an Ethernet *switch* (a multiport bridge), which is more popular than bridges today because a switch offers the same capability but with a richer feature set. We discuss switches in the next section.

All traffic within the bridge is forwarded through a single dedicated data path, which minimizes internal collisions. Switches and bridges store MAC addresses to enable them to decide which port data needs to pass through so that it can reach the appropriate system.

A bridge maps onto the Network Interface layer of the protocol stack.

Switch (Multiport Bridge)

Unlike a bridge, which typically connects just two segments, a *switch* provides multiple paths between multiple cable segments, thereby acting as a fast backbone with a fast internal bus. Collapsed backbone solutions cost much less than FDDI or ATM, but they limit the maximum geographical distances between nodes on a LAN.

Multiple connections or paths on a switch-based LAN may be used simultaneously. Consequently, switches tend to be more expensive than bridges or hubs. Switches translate the Ethernet bus technology into a star topology, allowing for simultaneous transfers between different segments.

Switches support several features worth mentioning briefly. For example, once they have received at least the destination address, switches are able to forward a frame before the complete frame has been received, which leads to greater throughput and a mere 40-ms delay in transmission time (also known as *latency*). On the downside, the entire frame is needed for an Ethernet Cyclic Redundancy Check (CRC), so with this method of transmission, the CRC might not be computed. Provided that the number of erroneous frames in the network is relatively small, however, this on-the-fly-switching or reduced delay time feature is desirable. Chapter 3 covers Ethernet and the CRC in greater detail.

Another feature is called *store-and-forward*. Fully supported by the Institute of Electrical and Electronics Engineers (IEEE) standard for multiport bridges, this feature enables the switch to wait until the entire Ethernet frame has been received correctly and in full, and only then forwards it. By this means, Ethernet switches provide dedicated pathways between devices, as the data is segmented and only sent to and heard by the appropriate destination. A switch maps onto the Network Interface layer of the protocol stack.

Be aware that the Internet layer (3) switches that route packets based on their IP addresses are available from some manufacturers. The Internet layer switch, behaving like a LAN-to-LAN router, reads all of the frames of the first IP packet, extracts the sender and destination address, and then forwards the IP packet. Subsequent packets can be switched or addressed based on the source and destination MAC address. LAN-to-LAN routers may be replaced by Internet layer switches, but this will depend on the network's topology. These Internet layer switches use both MAC addresses (Network Interface layer) and IP addresses (Internet layer).

Router

A *router* connects networks to one another and typically has multiple physical interfaces. A router (either a dedicated device such as a Cisco router, or a Sun system configured as a router) forwards IP packets between networks based on the packet's destination IP address. The source and destination IP address are found in the IP header. See Chapter 6 to learn more about routing over TCP/IP, Solaris 8 routing protocols, and using a Solaris 8 system as a router.

A router maps onto the Internet layer (3) of the protocol stack.

Gateway

Gateways are systems that are able to convert between protocols. For example, e-mail systems that use different protocols might have to convert headers from one e-mail standard to another. A system connecting an SNA and a TCP/IP network would have to convert protocols as packets passed between the two networks.

A gateway maps onto the Transport layer (4) and above of the protocol stack.

Concentrator

A *concentrator* is a device offering many of the functions described in previous sections, typically stacked in a single multilayered, modular unit. An excellent way of exploring the differences between devices is to study communications catalogs, such as those from Transtec (http://www.transtec.co.uk), and to examine both the technical features and specifications of concentrators (configurations of which vary widely) as well as the differences in pricing between a concentrator and a configuration involving a repeater, a hub, a switch, and a router. Prices tend to vary based on the complexity of the device, the number of interfaces and ports, and the vendor. Transtec provides an excellent information section in the back of its catalog, which you will find useful for its technical content and descriptions of network components.

Understanding how to use and deploy the devices just described is best learned in hands-on installation and configuration scenarios. Studying the technical specifications of the devices in the catalogs of manufactures is also extremely valuable.

EXAM NOTES

KEY LEARNING POINTS

- Networks use multiple devices from simple to complex.
- The devices function at different layers of the protocol stack and perform different functions.
- Hubs and switches are referred to as a collapsed bus.
- A collision domain can be made up of one or more devices.
- Switches and bridges use MAC addresses.
- Switches reduce the likelihood of collisions.
- Routers use IP addresses.
- Gateways convert between protocols and/or headers.

2.4 Non-TCP/IP LAN-Based Technologies and Protocols

This book focuses completely on the TCP/IP protocol family. There are other families of protocol to be aware of, too:

- *OSI*—The Open Systems Interconnection (OSI) family of protocols has not proved as popular as TCP/IP. Some OSI protocols such as X.400 mailing and X.500 directory services have become popular, however.

- *IPX/SPX*—Novell introduced Internetwork Packet Exchange in their network operating system known as Netware. The current version of Netware now uses IP as its default protocol.
- *NetBIOS*—IBM introduced NetBIOS as a nonroutable protocol for PC-to-PC, point-to-point communication. It is used by many LAN-based operating systems such as Windows 95/98/NT and others.
- *NetBEUI*—NetBIOS Enhanced User Interface is also used for inter-PC communication, especially across a LAN. Windows 98 and NT use NetBEUI, but TCP/IP is needed for Internet communication. DNS, for example, is not available through Net-BEUI and relies on TCP/IP as its underlying protocol family. As a result, both TCP/IP and NetBEUI are necessary for network-based PC applications.

EXAM NOTES

KEY LEARNING POINTS

- TCP/IP dominates the Internet but is not the only family of protocols.
- OSI X400 and X500 protocols are also very popular and are used on the Internet.
- NetBIOS and NetBEUI are popular LAN protocols.
- IPX and SPX are heavily used in PC server environments.

SUMMARY

In this chapter, we explored the benefits and disadvantages of using LANs and the various LAN topologies in use today. We then discussed the typical components likely to be found on most LANs, paying special attention to Ethernet, which is by far the most popular LAN in use today. We also explored LAN devices such as hubs, switches, and routers and described the role each device plays in the wiring tapestries found in most modern offices.

In the next chapter we explore Ethernet, the most popular LAN in the world, especially in the "bursty" Solaris UNIX environment where LAN bandwidth demands increase at a frenetic pace and the technology struggles to keep up.

TEST YOURSELF

MULTIPLE CHOICE

1. *Which of the following are LAN topologies? Choose three.*
   A. Star
   B. Pop
   C. Bus
   D. Ring
   E. Loop

2. *Which word specifically describes a length of continuous cable?*
   A. Backbone
   B. Segment
   C. Rail
   D. Repeater
   E. Hub

3. *What types of address does a bridge deal with? Choose two.*
   A. IP
   B. Software
   C. MAC
   D. Ethernet
   E. Signal

4. *What types of address does a router deal with? Choose two.*
   A. IP
   B. Software
   C. MAC
   D. Ethernet
   E. Signal

5. *Onto what layer of the TCP/IP 5-layer network model would a router map?*
   A. Application layer
   B. Transport layer
   C. Internet layer

D. Network Interface layer

E. Physical layer

6. *Onto what layer of the TCP/IP 5-layer network model would a bridge map?*

A. Application layer

B. Transport layer

C. Internet layer

D. Network Interface layer

E. Physical layer

7. *Onto what layer of the TCP/IP 5-layer network model would a repeater map?*

A. Application layer

B. Transport layer

C. Internet layer

D. Network Interface layer

E. Physical layer

8. *What is another description of a multiport repeater?*

A. Switch

B. Repeater

C. Hub

D. Router

E. Bridge

9. *Which of the following filters packets by Ethernet address? Choose two.*

A. Switch

B. Repeater

C. Hub

D. Router

E. Bridge

10.   *Which of the following devices uses IP addresses to route packets?*
      A. Switch
      B. Repeater
      C. Hub
      D. Router
      E. Bridge

FREE RESPONSE

1.   Describe briefly how a LAN specifically helps groups of users who are working on the same project and need to share files.

2.   What could you do to increase the responsiveness of a LAN?

The Ethernet LAN

EXAM OBJECTIVES

3.1 The Ethernet Specification

3.2 IEEE Ethernet Identifiers

3.3 The Ethernet Address

3.4 The Ethernet Frame V2

3.5 The Ethernet Access Method

3.6 Using **ndd** to Set Protocol Driver Parameters

3.7 Sun Ethernet Controllers

Afters completing this chapter, you will be able to meet the following Network Administration Exam objectives:

- State the purpose of the Ethernet address.
- Identify the commands for getting and setting driver configuration.

To help you meet these objectives, this chapter covers the following topics:

- the Ethernet specification and the types of cable used to build Ethernet LANs
- the cable types used in Ethernet LANs and the codes that identify them
- the 48-bit Ethernet address
- the fields of the Ethernet V2 frame and how to differentiate frame overhead from frame data
- the Ethernet access method and the process by which Ethernet systems contend for bus bandwidth
- the use of **ndd** to set protocol driver parameters
- Sun Ethernet controllers and the commands used to configure them

3.1 The Ethernet Specification

Local Area Networks (LANs) are networks that cover a small geographical area. Ethernet is the most popular LAN technology in use today. Ethernet is used extensively in UNIX environments and has been a great success, both commercially and technically. Ethernet Version 1 (V1) was developed initially by Xerox at the Palo Alto Research Center (PARC) in California and then developed further by a joint project cosponsored by Xerox, Digital Equipment Corporation, and Intel, which eventually led to the development of Ethernet Version 2 (V2).

Ethernet speeds are measured in megabits per second (Mbps). The several speeds of Ethernet in common use—10 Mbps, 100 Mbps, and 1,000 Mbps—coexist well. The high-speed 1,000 Mbps Gigabit Ethernet offers tremendous throughput and backbone performance that are much needed by today's demanding networks.

Ethernet uses two major types of cable:

- copper-based
- fiberoptic-based

The Electronics Industry Association (EIA) and the Telecommunications Industry Association (TIA) created a series of cablings standards with the following goals:

- support for multiple LAN technologies
- architecture that is easy to alter
- capacity for high data transmission rates and high bandwidth
- low cost
- ease of installation and upgrade
- vendor independence

Ethernet meets all of the above goals and uses both fiberoptic and copper-wire media to achieve transmission speeds of 10, 100, and 1000 Mbps.

3.2 IEEE Ethernet Identifiers

IEEE uses three-part identifiers when describing Ethernet media types. The *identifier* is made up of three components. Figure 3-1 shows the three parts of the example IEEE identifier 100BASET.

Table 3.1 shows the IEEE three-part components, a description, and the possible values.

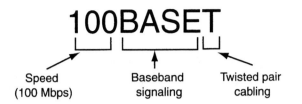

Figure 3–1   *Example identifier: 100BASET*

Table 3.1 *IEEE Ethernet Identifier Breakdown*

COMPONENT	DESCRIPTION	POSSIBLE VALUES
1	Speed (Mbps)	10,100,1000 Mbps
2	Signaling method	Baseband or broadband
3	Cable length or Cable type	2 (200m) or 5 (500m) T (twisted pair) or F (fiberoptic)

Table 3.2 shows the range of possible IEEE Ethernet identifiers and the identifier specifications in use today.

Table 3.2 *Ethernet Identifiers in Common Use*

IEEE THREE-PART IDENTIFIER	DESCRIPTION
10BASE5	Thick coaxial, baseband 500 m maximum segment length 10 Mbps only Original Ethernet, defined in 1980
10BASE2	Thin coaxial, baseband (cheaper or thinnet) 200m maximum segment length 10 Mbps only Defined in 1982
10BASET	Twisted pair CAT3 and CAT5 cabling Defined in 1990
10BASEF	Fiberoptic inter-repeater link (FOIRL) 200 m maximum segment length Based on original fiberoptic specification Slow Ethernet, developed in 1980

Table 3.2 *Ethernet Identifiers in Common Use (Continued)*

IEEE THREE-PART IDENTIFIER	DESCRIPTION
10BASE-FL (fiber link)	Replaced the original FOIRL and has both repeater-to-repeater and repeater-to-DTE capability 200 m maximum segment length Slow Ethernet, developed in 1980
10BASE-FB (fiber backbone)	The fiberoptic backbone standard. Not widely used today.
100BASE-TX (transmit)	100 Mbps twisted pair, two pairs of wires CAT5 cabling Defined in 1990
100BASE-T4	100 Mbps twisted pair, four pairs of wires 200 m maximum segment length CAT3, 4, or 5 cabling Fast Ethernet, defined in 1990
1000BASE-X: Three main types (SX/LX/CX)	Gigabit Ethernet Very fast, new technology Fiberoptic based IEEE 802.z, defined in 1995
1000BASE-SX	Fiberoptic using short-wave lasers 300 m maximum segment length over 62.5μ multimode fiberoptic (MMF) 500 m maximum segment length over 50μ MMF Defined in 1995
1000BASE-LX	Fiberoptic using long-wave lasers 550 m over 50 and 62.5μ MMF 300 m over 9-micron single-mode fiberoptic (SMF)
1000BASE-CX	Short-haul copper 25 m maximum segment length over twin axial cable Defined in 1995, IEEE-approved in 1999
1000BASE-T	IEEE 8.2.ab, Approved 1999 1000m maximum segment length over four pairs of CAT5 UTP Defined 1995

Table 3.2 demonstrates that Ethernet offers a variety of cabling types and speeds. Ethernet devices with different specifications can be mixed in a *multimode* Ethernet environment, thereby preserving businesses' past investments in equipment and easing transition to newer technology.

KEY LEARNING POINTS

- Ethernet has three bandwidth capacities: 10, 100, and 1000 Mbps.
- The IEEE defines types of Ethernet using a three-component identifier.
- BASE stands for baseband.
- T stands for twisted pair.
- F stands for fiberoptic.
- Ethernet cable types can be mixed in a multimode Ethernet environment.

3.3 The Ethernet Address

The Ethernet address is six bytes (48 bits) in length and is usually represented as six bytes in hexadecimal, separated by colons. The Ethernet address is also referred to by the following names:

- hardware
- physical
- media access control (MAC)

The IEEE manages the allocation of global Ethernet addresses by allocating to manufacturers a three-byte prefix that the manufacturers should use at the start of all the Ethernet addresses they allocate to the devices they produce. Some manufacturers, such as Sun, have more than one designator because of the large number of devices they have manufactured. A manufacturer uses the designated *prefix* as the first three bytes of all Ethernet devices it produces and adds a unique three-byte *suffix* to form a six-byte address. In effect, all Sun Ethernet devices begin with the same prefixes. Sun calls this IEEE-assigned prefix the Company Identifier (CID) and refers to the three-byte suffix added by the manufacturer as a Vendor Identifier (VID). Table 3.3 shows Sun's CIDs currently in use.

Ethernet addresses are displayed using colon notation. Figure 3-2 shows an example of a Sun Ethernet address.

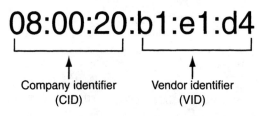

Figure 3–2 *Sample Sun Ethernet address*

Table 3.3 *Sun CIDs*

TYPE OF SYSTEM	GLOBAL CID
Sun E10K systems	00:00:be
Sunblade systems	00:03:be
Other Sun devices	08:00:20

The *scope* of an Ethernet address depends on whether it is associated with a single system, a group of systems, or all systems on a bus. We will explore that topic next.

The Scope of Ethernet Addresses

Sending Data to a Single Ethernet Host (Unicast)

An Ethernet address that belongs to a single host is a *unicast* address. A system needing to deliver data to a single destination host needs to acquire the destination system's Ethernet address using the ARP protocol discussed in Chapter 4. The system transmitting the data (the source) generates a frame with the destination host's Ethernet address in the *destination field* of the frame. The frame is then transmitted onto the Ethernet bus. Only the targeted host copies the frame off the bus and up the stack.

Sending Data to a Group of Ethernet Hosts (Multicast)

An Ethernet address to which multiple systems listen is known as a *multicast*. Multicast Ethernet addresses are associated with network protocols that need to communicate information to a group of systems. For example, the Router Discovery Protocol (RDP) uses a multicast Ethernet address to enable communication between RDP clients and servers. See Chapter 6 for more information about RDP.

Sending Data to All Ethernet Hosts on Subnet (Broadcast)

An Ethernet *broadcast* address is comprised of all ones, usually expressed in hexadecimal as ff:ff:ff:ff:ff:ff. Frames whose destination field is the broadcast address will be copied off the bus by all systems that are listening, because the broadcast address includes or targets all hosts. Remember that because Ethernet is a bus, all hosts hear all packets regardless of destination address; however, hosts pass up their protocol stack only those Ethernet frames that target them through their own unicast, through a shared multicast, or through the broadcast address that targets all hosts on the same physical subnet.

Global versus Local Port Ethernet Addresses

Sun has two approaches to managing Ethernet addresses on its Ethernet adapters:

- host-based, main-system programmable read-only memory (PROM), global
- port-based, network adapter PROM, local

With the host-based approach, the network interface drivers acquire the Ethernet address from the system main PROM and assign it to the Network Interface Card (NIC). Host-based Ethernet addresses are global (as described earlier in this section) and use an IEEE three-byte vendor prefix. With the port-based approach, the network interface software drivers acquire the Ethernet address from the network adapter's onboard PROM rather than from the main system board PROM. The port-based approach is especially useful when a system has multiple interfaces on the same subnet, and we need to assign a local Ethernet address to a specific port.

The value of the system's electrically erasable programmable read-only memory (EEPROM) parameter *local-mac-address?* determines whether the network interface drivers are permitted to use the local or port-based Ethernet address. The *local-mac-address?* EEPROM parameter may contain the values

- true
- false

The question mark (?) at the end of *local-mac-address?* **is a part of the parameter name; you must include it whenever you use the parameter.**

You may set the value of EEPROM parameter *local-mac-address?* at the Sun OpenBoot prompt as follows by entering

```
OK setenv local-mac-address? true
```

or issue the following UNIX command as the root user:

```
# eeprom 'local-mac-address?' -true
```

Both of these sample commands set the value of *local-mac-address?* to true.

Newer Sun network adapters use port-based Ethernet addresses that are encoded into their onboard PROM, not to be confused with the main system PROM recognized by IEEE.

The following Sun Ethernet cards have local Ethernet addresses:

- PCI FW-SCSI/FastEthernet combo
- QFE/Sbus (4 MAC addresses)
- QFE/PCI (4 MAC addresses)
- GEM/Sbus (Gigabit v2.0)
- GEM/PCI (Gigabit v1.0)
- VGE/Sbus (Gigabit v1.0)
- VGE/PCI (Gigabit v1.0)
- All new Sun network adapters

Having set the *local-mac-address?* parameter to *true*, you can create a local Ethernet address from a global Ethernet address. Given the following global Ethernet address

```
08:00:20:b1:e1:d4
```

you can calculate a local address by raising the seventh bit of the first byte as follows:

1. Express the first byte (08) in binary:

```
128   64   32   16  8   4  2  1
0     0    0    0   1   0  0  0
```

2. Raise the seventh bit by one to get

```
128    64   32   16 8 4 2 1
0       0    0    0 1 0 1 0
```

3. Convert to split binary notation, which we use to derive hexadecimal pairs:

```
8 4 2 1   8 4 2 1
0 0 0 0   1 0 1 0   =   0A
```

The A is derived by adding the 8 and 2, because the binary columns 8 and 2 both contain the value of 1. 8 plus 2 is 10 (decimal), which in hexadecimal is A. In this way the 08 is transformed to 0A, and the final address is

0a:00:20:b1:e1:d4

This valid address is now local, as the IEEE does not recognize the three-byte prefix **0a:00:20**.

There are several ways to display an Ethernet address on Solaris 8:

- Using the **ifconfig** command as **root**:

```
# ifconfig hme0
hme0:flags=1000843<UP,BROADCAST,RUNNING,MULTICAST,
IPv4>mtu 1500 index 2 inet 194.168.85.51 netmask
ffffff00
broadcast 194.168.85.255 ether 8:0:20:b1:ed:cf
```

- Using the **arp** command with the **–a** switch to print the Address Resolution Protocol (ARP) cache (the ARP protocol is examined in Chapter 4):

```
#arp -a
Net to Media Table: IPv4
Device IP Address        Mask            Flags Phys Addr
------ --------------    --------------- ----- --------------
hme0   hercules          255.255.255.255       08:00:20:b6:0c:08
hme0   alpha             255.255.255.255       00:60:b0:07:1a:3f
hme0   voyager           255.255.255.255 SP    08:00:20:b1:ed:cf
```

- Using the **netstat** command to display the ARP cache:

```
# netstat -p
Net to Media Table: IPv4
Device IP Address        Mask            Flags Phys Addr
------ --------------    --------------- ----- --------------
hme0   hercules          255.255.255.255       08:00:20:b6:0c:08
hme0   alpha             255.255.255.255       00:60:b0:07:1a:3f
hme0   voyager           255.255.255.255 SP    08:00:20:b1:ed:cf
```

Notice that the last field (Phys Addr) shows the Ethernet address.

KEY LEARNING POINTS

- Ethernet addresses are 48 bits in length.
- IEEE designates a three-byte prefix for Ethernet device manufacturers.
- The first three bytes of a global Ethernet address identify the vendor.
- Sun calls the first three bytes of the Ethernet address the CID.
- Sun calls the last three bytes of the Ethernet address the VID.
- A unicast Ethernet address belongs to a single Ethernet host.
- A multicast address is shared by a group of Ethernet hosts.
- A broadcast address is shared by all hosts on a given Ethernet bus.
- Global Ethernet addresses are managed by IEEE.
- Local port-based Ethernet addresses are not recognized globally.

Next, we examine the fields of the Ethernet V2 Frame, which encapsulates the data that the Ethernet frame is delivering across the Ethernet.

3.4   The Ethernet Frame V2

The Ethernet LAN operates at the Network Interface layer (2) of the protocol stack. Figure 3-3 shows where Ethernet operates in the Sun TCP/IP 5-layer model that we discussed in Chapter 1.

The Ethernet frame has a source and destination Ethernet address (MAC) field plus a data type, a checksum, and the data field itself. Figure 3-4 shows the fields of an Ethernet V2 frame.

Note The preamble is not part of the Ethernet frame proper; it synchronizes the transmitting and receiving devices prior to the transmission of the frame itself. It is not counted as overhead.

Table 3.4 describes the field names, field content, and field lengths (in bytes) of the V2 frame.

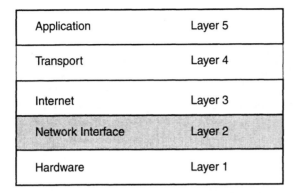

Application	Layer 5
Transport	Layer 4
Internet	Layer 3
Network Interface	Layer 2
Hardware	Layer 1

Figure 3–3   *Ethernet functioning at Layer 2 of the Sun TCP/IP 5-layer model*

| Preamble | Destination address | Source address | Type of data carried | Data field | CRC |

Ethernet frame

Figure 3–4   *Fields of the Ethernet V2 frame*

Table 3.4 *Field Values of Ethernet V2 Frame*

FIELD NAME	FIELD CONTENT	FIELD LENGTH (BYTES)
Destination Ethernet address	Ethernet address	6
Source Ethernet address	Ethernet address	6
Type	Code identifying the type of data in the frame	2
Data	46 to 1500 bytes of data	46 to 1500
Cyclic Redundancy Check (CRC)	A frame checksum	4

Frame Overhead Fields

Frame overhead describes all the fields of the Ethernet frame that are necessary for successful delivery of the frame to occur, but which are additional to the data field itself. The data field carries the data and headers of upper-layer protocols such as ARP, RARP, or IP and is therefore considered real data rather than overhead. There is both a minimum and a maximum length for the frame overhead.

Minimum Frame Length

The frame overhead consists of the destination and source addresses plus the type and CRC fields, which, when added up, amount to 18 bytes of overhead. The data carried must be at least 46 bytes and is padded to this size by zeros if necessary. When added to the 18 bytes minimum overhead, the minimum frame size is 64 bytes (18 bytes of overhead plus 46 bytes of data).

The minimum frame size of 64 bytes ensures that incomplete or damaged frames (which are truncated by the transmitting transceiver to less than 64 bytes) are detected. In addition, the minimum frame size of 64 bytes ensures that the smallest frame will reach the far end of the maximum allowed length of cable while the transmitting station is still transmitting. It is important that a frame propagates the entire bus while the sending station is still transmitting so that if a collision occurs, the sending station detects the collision and ceases the transmission. Collision detection must be guaranteed if the Ethernet Access Method is to work, but collision detection is less reliable if the bus length exceeds the maximum lengths specified by IEEE. Maximum bus lengths, in turn, are determined by the type of cable in use.

Maximum Frame Length

The maximum frame size is 1,518 bytes, comprised of the 18 bytes of overhead and a maximum of 1,500 bytes of encapsulated data. This total size of the frame is referred to as the maximum transmission units, or MTU. The MTU restriction ensures that all systems have a reasonable chance of transmitting on the bus.

Ethernet V2 Frame Fields

The fields of the Ethernet V2 frame include the destination Ethernet address, the source Ethernet address, the field type, the data field, and a field for the cyclic redundancy check (CRC). In this section we briefly describe the content of each field.

Destination Ethernet Address

The *destination field* of the Ethernet frame contains the 6-byte Ethernet address of the device to which the frame is targeted (the intended recipient of the frame). The address is one of the following:

- the unique Ethernet address of a particular system
- the broadcast Ethernet address that targets all systems on the Ethernet bus
- multicast Ethernet addresses

We explore these further in Chapter 5.

Source Ethernet Address

The *source Ethernet address* is the 6-byte address of the system transmitting the frame.

Type Field

This field identifies which upper-layer protocol is encapsulated in the Ethernet frame. Table 3.5 shows Ethernet type field codes.

Note

The values shown in Table 3.5 are not the only possible values found in Ethernet frames. They are the ones commonly found on the Sun Ethernet networks and the only codes relevant for the exam.

Table 3.5 *Ethernet Type Field Codes*

CODE IN HEXADECIMAL	IDENTIFIES PROTOCOL ENCAPSULATED IN FRAME
0800	Internet Protocol (IP)
0806	Address Resolution Protocol (ARP)
8035	Reverse Address Resolution Protocol (RARP)

Data Field

The minimum allowed data field size is 64 bytes, comprised of 18 bytes overhead and a minimum data field size of 46 bytes. The data field is padded with zeros if necessary to ensure this minimum size of 46 bytes is met. The maximum number of bytes allowed in the data field is 1,500 bytes, which, when added to the frame overhead fields (18 bytes), brings the total frame size to 1,518 bytes.

Cyclic Redundancy Check (CRC)

The CRC is calculated by the transmitting device and recalculated by the receiving device. If incorrect, the frame is deemed corrupt and is discarded. It is important to realize that the destination device does not send an acknowledgment to the sending device for the received data. We rely on the CRC and Collision Detection (CD) to make Ethernet reliable. Upper-layer protocols such as TCP introduce reliability when used over Ethernet, as they have their own means of error detection and correction. TCP is examined in Chapter 7.

The **snoop** command is an excellent tool for examining the fields of an Ethernet frame. An example of using **snoop** to capture an Ethernet frame follows. We use the **snoop** option **–c 1** to capture a single frame and then quit.

```
# snoop -vc 1 broadcast
ETHER:  ----- Ether Header -----
ETHER:
ETHER:  Packet 1 arrived at 12:23:39.75
ETHER:  Packet size = 60 bytes
ETHER:  Destination = ff:ff:ff:ff:ff:ff, (broadcast)
ETHER:  Source      = 0:1:42:a5:ea:56,
ETHER:  Ethertype = 0806 (ARP)
ETHER:
ARP:  ----- ARP/RARP Frame -----
ARP:
ARP:  Hardware type = 1
ARP:  Protocol type = 0800 (IP)
ARP:  Length of hardware address = 6 bytes
ARP:  Length of protocol address = 4 bytes
ARP:  Opcode 1 (ARP Request)
ARP:  Sender's hardware address = 0:1:42:a5:ea:56
ARP:  Sender's protocol address = 62.254.198.254,
nexus2.gvon.co.uk
ARP:  Target hardware address = ?
ARP:  Target protocol address = 62.254.198.222, 62.254.198.222
ARP:
```

```
1 packets captured
#
```

In this example, the Ethernet frame has ARP encapsulated (type 0806) and is addressed to the Ethernet broadcast address of ff:ff:ff:ff:ff:ff. The source address is 0:1:42:a5:ea:56.

EXAM NOTES

KEY LEARNING POINTS

- The minimum amount of data in an Ethernet frame is 46 bytes.
- The frame overhead is 18 bytes of header plus CRC information.
- The minimum size of the frame, including overhead, is 64 bytes.
- The MTU size of an Ethernet V2 frame is 1,518 bytes, including overhead.
- The type field defines which upper layer protocol is being delivered.
- The CRC field is used to detect corrupt frames.

3.5   The Ethernet Access Method

It is important to understand how Ethernet transmits data across the Ethernet bus. Ethernet's means of delivering Ethernet packets is based on broadcast bus technology. Fire alarms are broadcast in a similar way. Fire alarms communicate their message to the maximum audience almost simultaneously, rather than informing each individual of a fire. As you can imagine, the latter process would lead to more burn victims and a loss of faith in fire alarms.

Ethernet frames broadcast onto the Ethernet bus are heard by all systems. The Ethernet bus is shared equally by all stations connected to the bus, which are said to have *equal access*. Frames are transmitted onto the bus and heard by all listening stations.

Figure 3-5 shows the Ethernet Access Method, the technical name of which is Carrier Sense Multiple Access with Collision Detect (CSMA/CD). The figure shows how Ethernet devices contend for bandwidth, how they determine when to transmit, and how they determine whether their transmissions have been successful or not.

Figure 3-5 illustrates the following steps:

1. Ethernet stations listen continuously to the shared bus for inbound frames.
2. A station has a frame to transmit. (Not all stations have a frame to transmit at the same time.)
3. The station listens for a quiescent bus and then transmits.
4. If, during the transmission, a collision is detected, the station ceases transmitting, backs off exponentially, and then returns to step 3. If no collision is detected, the transmission is successful.
5. Having transmitted, the station must wait 9 microseconds before attempting to transmit any further frames. (This is known as the *interpacket gap*, or IPG.)
6. The station returns to step 1.

The CSMA/CD access method requires transmitting stations to leave a gap between transmitted frames. This gap is called an interpacket gap (IPG) and allows other stations to transmit. Ethernet has no server to arbitrate between stations waiting to transmit; each station is expected to behave correctly and to transmit only when the network is quiet or quiescent.

Collisions occur when multiple stations believe the network is quiescent and therefore transmit simultaneously. There is a *collision window* defined as the time it takes for a frame to propagate the bus, during which brief period a collision may occur. Ethernet hosts are always listening for frames addressed to their Ethernet address. You can see the number of collisions that have occurred by using the **netstat** command:

```
# netstat -in
Name  Mtu   Net/Dest      Address       Ipkts     Ierrs Opkts   Oerrs Collis Queue
lo0   8232  127.0.0.0     127.0.0.1     2647289   0     26729   0     0      0
hme0  1500  194.168.85.0  194.168.85.1  18792976  0     20759   0     55     0
```

The **collis** column shows a collision count of 55. The collision rate is defined as:

Output collisions / Total Output Packets * 100

Given the above command output, you can calculate as follows:

55 / 20759 * 100 = 0.265

A collision rate of **0.265** is acceptably low. Collision rates of 5 percent or higher are an indication of *network loading*—available network band-

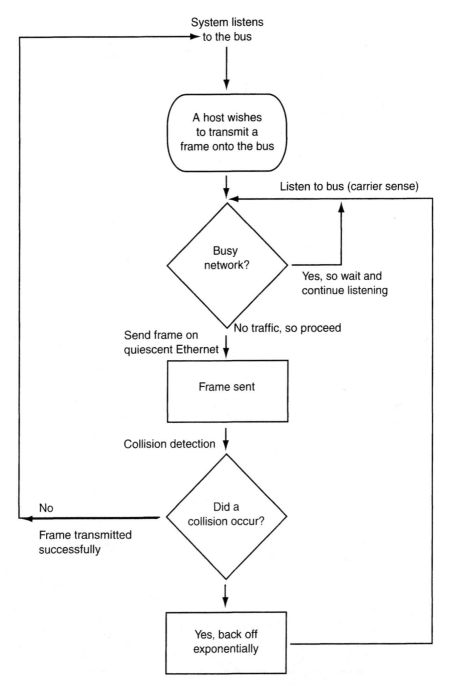

Figure 3–5   *The Ethernet Access Method*

width diminishes due to heavy use, with the result that network performance suffers.

Next, we examine **ndd**, used to modify the parameters for interface drivers.

KEY LEARNING POINTS

- Ethernet is a contention bus.
- Collisions occur when two or more systems transmit simultaneously.
- Systems back off and cease transmission when a collision occurs.
- The **netstat -i** command gives a collision count per interface.

3.6   Using **ndd** to Set and Get Protocol and Interface Driver Parameters

The **ndd** and **ifconfig** commands configure Solaris 8 interfaces. Like most UNIX commands, they have a range of options that you can set. You can use **get** and **set** parameters for the following five protocol modules by changing the driver value of the **ndd** command. In effect we access the parameter through a UNIX device file name such as /dev/ip, as shown in Table 3.6.

Table 3.6 *Configuring Interface Parameters Using*   **ndd**

PROTOCOL	PROTOCOL DEVICE NAME USED BY **NDD**
ARP	/dev/arp
IP	/dev/ip
UDP	/dev/udp
TCP	/dev/tcp
ICMP	/dev/icmp

Protocol Variables

Multiple variables are available for each protocol. Use **ndd** to display all the variables for a supported protocol by supplying the \? parameter.

Note

If a variable contains a time value, it is specified in milliseconds (ms) unless otherwise stated.

The following example shows how to display all the variables for the ARP protocol (variables for the RARP protocol are the same):

```
# ndd /dev/arp \?
arp_cache_report              (read only)
arp_debug                     (read and write)
arp_cleanup_interval          (read and write)
```

Notice that some parameters are read-only, while others are read-and-write. Read-and-write parameters have values that you can modify by using the **ndd** command. The **ndd** command allows you to modify and change protocol parameters without having to rebuild and recompile the *kernel*, the core of the UNIX operating system that loads into memory when the system boots.

Next are the variables for the IP protocol:

```
# ndd /dev/ip \?
?                                      (read only)
ip_respond_to_address_mask_broadcast(read and write)
ip_respond_to_echo_broadcast   (read and write)
ip_respond_to_timestamp        (read and write)
ip_respond_to_timestamp_broadcast(read and write)
ip_send_redirects              (read and write)
ip_forward_directed_broadcasts (read and write)
ip_debug                       (read and write)
ip_mrtdebug                    (read and write)
ip_ire_timer_interval          (read and write)
ip_ire_arp_interval            (read and write)
ip_ire_redirect_interval       (read and write)
ip_def_ttl                     (read and write)
ip_forward_src_routed          (read and write)
ip_wroff_extra                 (read and write)
ip_ire_pathmtu_interval        (read and write)
```

```
ip_icmp_return_data_bytes        (read and write)
ip_path_mtu_discovery            (read and write)
ip_ignore_delete_time            (read and write)
ip_ignore_redirect               (read and write)
ip_output_queue                  (read and write)
ip_broadcast_ttl                 (read and write)
ip_icmp_err_interval             (read and write)
ip_icmp_err_burst                (read and write)
ip_reass_queue_bytes             (read and write)
ip_strict_dst_multihoming        (read and write)
ip_addrs_per_if                  (read and write)
ipsec_override_persocket_policy(read and write)
icmp_accept_clear_messages       (read and write)
igmp_accept_clear_messages       (read and write)
ip_ndp_delay_first_probe_time    (read and write)
ip_ndp_max_unicast_solicit       (read and write)
ip6_def_hops                     (read and write)
ip6_icmp_return_data_bytes       (read and write)
ip6_forwarding                   (read and write)
ip6_forward_src_routed           (read and write)
ip6_respond_to_echo_multicast    (read and write)
ip6_send_redirects               (read and write)
ip6_ignore_redirect              (read and write)
ip6_strict_dst_multihoming       (read and write)
ip_ire_reclaim_fraction          (read and write)
ipsec_policy_log_interval        (read and write)
pim_accept_clear_messages        (read and write)
ip_forwarding                    (read and write)
ip_ill_status                    (read only)
ip_ipif_status                   (read only)
ipv4_ire_status                  (read only)
ipv6_ire_status                  (read only)
ip_ipc_status                    (read only)
ip_rput_pullups                  (read and write)
ip_enable_group_ifs              (read and write)
ifgrp_status                     (read only)
ip_ndp_cache_report              (read only)
ip_proxy_status                  (read only)
ip_srcid_status                  (read only)
lo0:ip_forwarding                (read and write)
hme0:ip_forwarding               (read and write)
```

The variables for the UDP protocol are:

```
# ndd /dev/udp \?
?                                (read only)
```

```
udp_wroff_extra                 (read and write)
udp_ipv4_ttl                    (read and write)
udp_ipv6_hoplimit               (read and write)
udp_smallest_nonpriv_port       (read and write)
udp_do_checksum                 (read and write)
udp_smallest_anon_port          (read and write)
udp_largest_anon_port           (read and write)
udp_xmit_hiwat                  (read and write)
udp_xmit_lowat                  (read and write)
udp_recv_hiwat                  (read and write)
udp_max_buf                     (read and write)
udp_extra_priv_ports            (read only)
udp_extra_priv_ports_add        (write only)
udp_extra_priv_ports_del        (write only)
udp_status                      (read only)
```

Here are the variables for the TCP protocol:

```
# ndd /dev/tcp \?
?                               (read only)
tcp_time_wait_interval          (read and write)
tcp_conn_req_max_q              (read and write)
tcp_conn_req_max_q0             (read and write)
tcp_conn_req_min                (read and write)
tcp_conn_grace_period           (read and write)
tcp_cwnd_max                    (read and write)
tcp_debug                       (read and write)
tcp_smallest_nonpriv_port       (read and write)
tcp_ip_abort_cinterval          (read and write)
tcp_ip_abort_linterval          (read and write)
tcp_ip_abort_interval           (read and write)
tcp_ip_notify_cinterval         (read and write)
tcp_ip_notify_interval          (read and write)
tcp_ipv4_ttl                    (read and write)
tcp_keepalive_interval          (read and write)
tcp_maxpsz_multiplier           (read and write)
tcp_mss_def_ipv4                (read and write)
tcp_mss_max_ipv4                (read and write)
tcp_mss_min                     (read and write)
tcp_naglim_def                  (read and write)
tcp_rexmit_interval_initial     (read and write)
tcp_rexmit_interval_max         (read and write)
tcp_rexmit_interval_min         (read and write)
tcp_deferred_ack_interval       (read and write)
tcp_snd_lowat_fraction          (read and write)
tcp_sth_rcv_hiwat               (read and write)
```

```
tcp_sth_rcv_lowat              (read and write)
tcp_dupack_fast_retransmit     (read and write)
tcp_ignore_path_mtu            (read and write)
tcp_rcv_push_wait              (read and write)
tcp_smallest_anon_port         (read and write)
tcp_largest_anon_port          (read and write)
tcp_xmit_hiwat                 (read and write)
tcp_xmit_lowat                 (read and write)
tcp_recv_hiwat                 (read and write)
tcp_recv_hiwat_minmss          (read and write)
tcp_fin_wait_2_flush_interval  (read and write)
tcp_co_min                     (read and write)
tcp_max_buf                    (read and write)
tcp_strong_iss                 (read and write)
tcp_rtt_updates                (read and write)
tcp_wscale_always              (read and write)
tcp_tstamp_always              (read and write)
tcp_tstamp_if_wscale           (read and write)
tcp_rexmit_interval_extra      (read and write)
tcp_deferred_acks_max          (read and write)
tcp_slow_start_after_idle      (read and write)
tcp_slow_start_initial         (read and write)
tcp_co_timer_interval          (read and write)
tcp_sack_permitted             (read and write)
tcp_trace                      (read and write)
tcp_compression_enabled        (read and write)
tcp_ipv6_hoplimit              (read and write)
tcp_mss_def_ipv6               (read and write)
tcp_mss_max_ipv6               (read and write)
tcp_rev_src_routes             (read and write)
tcp_wroff_xtra                 (read and write)
tcp_extra_priv_ports           (read only)
tcp_extra_priv_ports_add       (write only)
tcp_extra_priv_ports_del       (write only)
tcp_status                     (read only)
tcp_bind_hash                  (read only)
tcp_listen_hash                (read only)
tcp_conn_hash                  (read only)
tcp_acceptor_hash              (read only)
tcp_host_param                 (read and write)
tcp_time_wait_stats            (read only)
tcp_host_param_ipv6            (read and write)
tcp_1948_phrase                (write only)
tcp_close_wait_interval
   obsoleted- use tcp_time_wait_interval) (no read or write)
```

Finally, here are the variables for the ICMP protocol:

```
# ndd /dev/icmp \?
?                              (read only)
icmp_wroff_extra               (read and write)
icmp_ipv4_ttl                  (read and write)
icmp_ipv6_hoplimit             (read and write)
icmp_bsd_compat                (read and write)
icmp_xmit_hiwat                (read and write)
icmp_xmit_lowat                (read and write)
icmp_recv_hiwat                (read and write)
icmp_max_buf                   (read and write)
icmp_status                    (read only)
```

Getting Parameter Settings

In the following examples we examine how to get the current value of specific parameters. Observe the method of acquiring the parameter and the use of **ndd** rather than the example parameter itself.

In the first example, we **get** the value of IP variable *ip_forwarding*. This parameter determines whether the receiving station will forward IP datagrams it receives that are not addressed to one of its IP addresses:

```
# ndd -get /dev/ip ip_forwarding
0
```

A value of 0 means that the station will not forward IP datagrams, while a value of 1 means that it will forward them—this effectively constitutes routing.

In the next example, we **get** the value of TCP parameter *tcp_mss_def*, which defines the default Transmission Control Protocol (TCP) segment size for non-local destinations. TCP sends data over IP in data blocks called *segments*, which ideally will remain (for performance reasons) in a single datagram that is not further fragmented by IP.

During the three-way TCP handshake, the maximum segment size (MSS) may be announced by connecting systems; the maximum size must not exceed the MTU of the sending interface. Ethernet has an MTU of 1,500 bytes, but the segment must carry the 20-byte IP header and the 20-byte TCP header, which reduces the MSS to 1,460 bytes over Ethernet. If an MSS is not announced during the three-way TCP handshake, the default value specified in the *tcp_mss_def* variable is used. See chapter 7 for more information about the TCP three-way handshake.

```
# ndd -get /dev/tcp  tcp_mss_def
536
```

In the next example, we **get** the value of IP variable *ip_def_ttl*, which determines how many routers a datagram may pass through. This value limits the lifetime of a datagram and prevents the possibility of a datagram circulating the Internet forever in a routing loop. As a datagram passes through a router, the value is decremented. If the value reaches 0, the datagram is discarded,

```
# ndd -get /dev/ip ip_def_ttl
255
```

In the next example, we **get** the value of IP variable *ip_addrs_per_if*, which determines how many *virtual IP addresses* may be assigned to a single interface (a virtual address is one that shares an Ethernet interface with another IP address). The maximum value that can be set on Solaris 8 is 8192.

```
# ndd -get /dev/ip ip_addrs_per_if
256
```

Here, the interface is configured to allow for 256 virtual addresses on each interface. Refer to Chapter 5 for more information about virtual interfaces and how to configure them.

Setting Parameter Settings

You can also use the **ndd** command to **set** and **get** kernel network parameters. In the first example that follows, we set the value of the *ip_forwarding* parameter of the IP protocol module:

```
# ndd -set /dev/ip ip_forwarding 1
```

This example sets the *ip_forwarding* parameter to 1. The Solaris 8 kernel will now forward IP datagrams it receives that enter any of its interfaces and travel up the protocol stack, destined for another host. Data traveling in an upward direction through the stack is said to be *inbound*. Datagrams being forwarded to another host and traveling down the stack (leaving an interface) are said to be *outbound*.

In the next example, we set the value of the *ip_addrs_per_if* parameter of the IP protocol module:

```
# ndd -set /dev/ip ip_addrs_per_if 8192
```

This **ndd** command sets the number of IP addresses on a single interface to 8192, which is the maximum allowed.

EXAM NOTES

KEY LEARNING POINTS

- The **ndd** command can **set** and **get** protocol driver parameters.
- The IP, ICMP, ARP, TCP, and UDP protocols all have read and write parameters.
- The **ndd** command must be executed by the root user when a protocol parameter's value is being set. Non-root users may use **ndd** to read a parameter's value.
- Parameters set by **ndd** are lost across a reboot unless added to a startup file.
- **ndd** updates the protocol drivers in the memory-resident kernel.
- **ndd** does not write to the kernel in the file system.

3.7 Sun Ethernet Controllers

Sun produces the Ethernet controllers le, be, hme, qe, qfe, and ge. In a mixed Ethernet environment, several of the following Ethernet standards may be found.

Fast Ethernet Cards

Sun provides the following fast Ethernet controller interfaces (the interface name of each controller appears in parentheses):
- Sun Fast Ethernet 1.0 SBus controller (be0)
- Sun Quad FastEthernet 1.0 SBus controller (hme0-3)
- Sun Quad FastEthernet 2.0 SBus controller (qfe0-3)
- SunFastEthernet 2.0 SBus/PCI controller (hme 0)
- SunGigabitEthernet 2.0 Sbus controller (ge0)
- SunGigabitEthernet 2.0 PCI controller (ge0)

Slow Ethernet Cards

Sun provides the following slower Ethernet controller interfaces:

- Lance Ethernet SBUS controller (le0)
- Quad Lance Ethernet SBus controller (qe0-3)

So far, we have listed the Ethernet identifiers, Sun Ethernet controller names, and interface names. Focus on the following important key points.

EXAM NOTES

KEY LEARNING POINTS

- **Sun produces both slow (10 Mbps) and fast (100 Mbps) Ethernet controllers.**
- **Quad cards have four interfaces.**
- **Sun produces PCI and SBus Ethernet controllers.**
- **Sun produces Gigabit Ethernet cards for both PCI and Sbus.**

SUMMARY

This chapter explored the Ethernet LAN, with special focus on the Ethernet V2 specification. We also examined the contents of an Ethernet frame as well as the Ethernet access control method, called CSMA/CD. We discussed the 48-byte Ethernet address, which identifies either a specific Ethernet NIC (unicast), a group of systems (multicast), or all systems on the shared bus (broadcast).

Finally, we examined the **ifconfig, netstat, arp**, and **ndd** commands, which together configure and display Ethernet interfaces and their kernel module parameters. In the next chapter, we examine the ARP and RARP protocols that glue together the Network and Internet Layers that we discussed in the information on network models in Chapter 1.

TEST YOURSELF

MULTIPLE CHOICE

1. *What does the CD stand for in CSMA/CD?*
   - A. colliding detection
   - B. collision detect
   - C. collision data
   - D. colliding detection
   - E. collision databus

2. *Which word describes the result of two or more Ethernet hosts transmitting simultaneously, leading to a bandwidth contention situation?*
   - A. compression
   - B. contention
   - C. collision
   - D. crash
   - E. comparison

3. *IEEE standard 802.5 pertains to which type of LAN?*
   - A. Token Ring
   - B. CSMA/CD
   - C. Token Bus
   - D. Logical Link Control
   - E. Ethernet

4. *Which organization allocates CIDs to Ethernet card manufacturers in order to identify the specific manufacturer's Ethernet cards?*
   - A. CCITT
   - B. ITU
   - C. IEEE
   - D. IETF
   - E. OSI

5. *What is the size (in bytes) of the type field of a V2 Ethernet frame?*
   - A. 4 bytes
   - B. 2 bytes
   - C. 8 bytes

   D. 20 bytes

   E. 6 bytes

6. *What is the size (in bits) of an Ethernet source address?*

   A. 24 bits

   B. 48 bits

   C. 1,500 bits

   D. 12 bits

   E. 4 bits

7. *In a 64-byte V2 Ethernet frame, how much is overhead (frame header information) rather than the actual data being carried?*

   A. 24 bytes

   B. 18 bytes

   C. 28 bytes

   D. 12 bytes

   E. 16 bytes

8. *Which field of the Ethernet frame is used to detect damaged Ethernet frames?*

   A. CRC

   B. ACK

   C. NACK

   D. VID

   E. MTU

9. *Which of the following represents an Ethernet broadcast?*

   A. ff:ff:ff:ff:ff:ff

   B. 00:00:00:00:00:00

   C. 01:01:01:01:01:01

   D. ae:ae:ae:ae:ae:ae

   E. f0:f0:f0:f0:f0:f0

10. *Which of the following commands configures Solaris Interfaces?*

   A. ifconfig

   B. netstat

   C. arp

   D. prtconf

   E. drvconfig

FREE RESPONSE

1. *Which UNIX commands can you use to view a system's Ethernet address?*

2. *Describe Ethernet's strengths and weaknesses in brief.*

FURTHER READING

Tannenbaum, A. *Computer Networks*. ISBN 0-13-166836-6. Upper Saddle River, NJ: Prentice Hall, 1998.

"Sun Ethernet Interface." Sun Infodoc ID 12306, Sun Ethernet Interface Support Document/FAQ, 22 Feb 2000, available at http://docs.sun.com.

"Sun Fast Ethernet Interface." Sun Infodoc ID 17416, Sun Fast Ethernet Support Document/FAQ, 9 Mar 2000, available at http://docs.sun.com.

The ARP and RARP Protocols

EXAM OBJECTIVES

4.1 Address Mapping with ARP and RARP

4.2 The ARP/RARP Protocol Format

4.3 ARP and RARP Operations

4.4 The ARP Cache and **arp** Command

After completing this chapter, you will be able to meet the following Network Administration Exam objectives:

- Explain the process of address resolution using ARP and RARP.
- Identify the commands to manage the ARP cache.

To help you meet these objectives, this chapter covers the following topics:

- how ARP and RARP map IP addresses to physical addresses
- the message format for the ARP/RARP protocol
- observing ARP and RARP operations and configuring the RARP server
- working with the **arp** command and the ARP cache

4.1   Address Mapping with ARP and RARP

The Address Resolution Protocol (ARP) and Reverse ARP (RARP) build a mapping between a systems Internet Protocol (IP) address and its Ethernet address. There is no inherent or mathematical relationship between a machine's Ethernet address and its assigned IP address. When a network administrator chooses an IP address for a given host, the Ethernet address need not be referred to. If the Ethernet NIC or PROM containing the Ethernet address needs replacing, the IP address does not need to change.

The two addresses for a given host are mapped together by the ARP and RARP protocols. In this chapter, we refer to the Ethernet address variously as the MAC, the hardware address, or the physical address, and we describe it using the colon notation that we discussed in Chapter 3. The IP address, also known as the *logical* or software address, is usually shown using dotted decimal notation. For more information about IP addresses, you can refer to Chapter 5, which discusses IPv4, and to Chapter 13, which examines IPv6.

This chapter explores both ARP, which provides a mapping service between a 32-bit IPv4 address and the 48-bit Ethernet address, and RARP, which provides the same service in reverse. Figure 4-1 shows the direction of mapping for these two protocols.

The direction of the arrow indicates the direction in which the protocol functions. For example, ARP knows the 32-bit IP address of a host and uses that to acquire the 48-bit Ethernet address. RARP, however, begins by knowing the 48-bit Ethernet address of a host and needs to acquire the 32-bit IP address.

The process of sending IP packets between hosts across Ethernet requires the sending host (the source) to acquire the Ethernet address of the intended recipient of the Ethernet frame. If the intended recipient of IP traffic is not on the same network as the source host, the source host routes the packets to a local router on the same network as the source, which then forwards the packets to their ultimate destination on behalf of the source host. In such a case, the source host must acquire the *next-hop* local router's Ethernet address in order to forward the packets to it. (A next-hop router is so called because hosts use it to forward IP datagrams

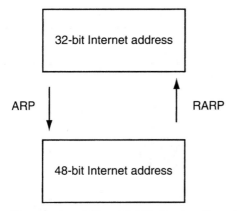

Figure 4–1   *ARP and RARP direction of mapping*

to other networks.) The basic principle is that in order to send IP datagrams to other networks, special systems called *routers* are used, which connect networks both physically and by virtue of their ability to calculate routing paths between networks. In Chapter 6 we examine the routing process in greater detail.

EXAM NOTES

KEY LEARNING POINTS

- ARP acquires an Ethernet address for a known IP address.
- RARP acquires an IP address for a known Ethernet address.

4.2   The ARP/RARP Protocol Format

Ethernet encapsulates the ARP/RARP message in the data field of the Ethernet frame (refer to Chapter 3 for more information about the structure of a frame). Figure 4-2 shows the format of the ARP/RARP protocol message and the number of bytes in each field of the frame.

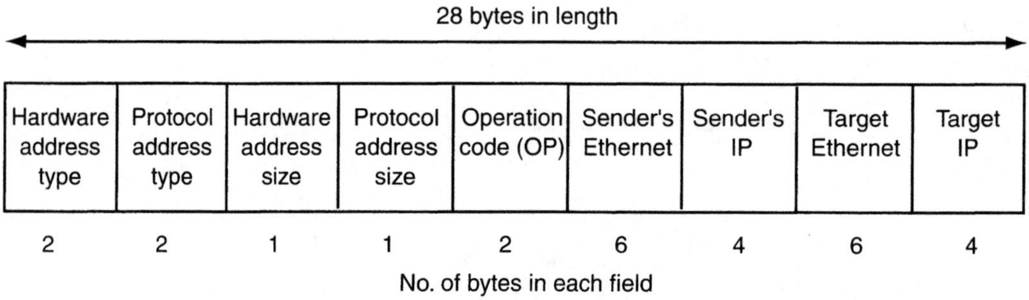

28 bytes in length

Hardware address type	Protocol address type	Hardware address size	Protocol address size	Operation code (OP)	Sender's Ethernet	Sender's IP	Target Ethernet	Target IP
2	2	1	1	2	6	4	6	4

No. of bytes in each field

Figure 4–2   *The ARP/RARP protocol frame format*

EXAM NOTES

KEY LEARNING POINTS

- The ARP/RARP frame is 28 bytes in length.
- ARP and RARP share the same frame format.
- The ARP/RARP frame identifies the operational code of a message.

4.3   ARP and RARP Operations

ARP and RARP make use of four *operational codes*, commonly referred to as *opcodes*, which identify the type of ARP or RARP packet. Here they are, with a brief description of each:

- *Opcode 1*   describes the ARP request and is used to acquire the MAC of a known IP.
- *Opcode 2*   describes the ARP reply and returns the MAC address as a response to Opcode 1.
- *Opcode 3*   constitutes the RARP request and is used to acquire the IP of a known MAC.
- *Opcode 4*   is the RARP reply and returns the IP address in response to Opcode 3.

Figure 4-3 depicts an example of a basic network that we will use to describe the opcodes. Over the next few sections, we describe sample transactions between two hosts, apollo and voyager, which are on the same segment of the Ethernet bus. We will refer to the examples in Figure 4-3 several times later in this book, specifically in Chapters 6, 7, 8, and 11.

Table 4.1 shows the IP and Ethernet addresses for the systems involved in the ARP and RARP messages that we examine in this chapter.

Table 4.1 *Addresses Used in Opcode Examples*

HOST	IP ADDRESS	ETHERNET ADDRESS
apollo	194.168.85.75	08:00:20:fc:8d:d6
voyager	194.168.85.51	08:00:20:b1:ed:cf
mars	10.1.1.1	08:00:20:0d:c7:7c
tannhauser	10.1.1.100	08:00:20:7b:33:a4

ARP

The ARP portion of an ARP/RARP message involves only opcodes 1 and 2. As we examine these opcodes, keep in mind that the two systems involved in the example shown in Figure 4-3 (apollo and voyager) are both source and destination in different ARP messages, depending on the direction of traffic. In opcode 1 (the ARP request), apollo is the source and voyager the destination, but in opcode 2, the reply to apollo from voyager, their roles are reversed: voyager becomes the source and apollo the destination.

ARP Request, Operation 1 (Opcode 1)

In opcode 1, apollo attempts to acquire the Ethernet address of voyager. When a station wishes to send an Ethernet frame to the unicast Ethernet address of a given host, it needs to acquire the Ethernet address of the destination host. Usually, the need to send an Ethernet frame is the direct result of attempting to send higher level packets, such as those of IP (layer 3), TCP (layer 4), or UDP (layer 4). The higher level protocols are carrying data on behalf of an Application layer process, such as **tel-net** or **ftp**, and the host needs to send the higher level data over Ethernet.

Apollo, the source host, needs to send an Ethernet frame to voyager but does not have voyager's Ethernet address. The sending station broadcasts an ARP request across the Ethernet in which it includes the

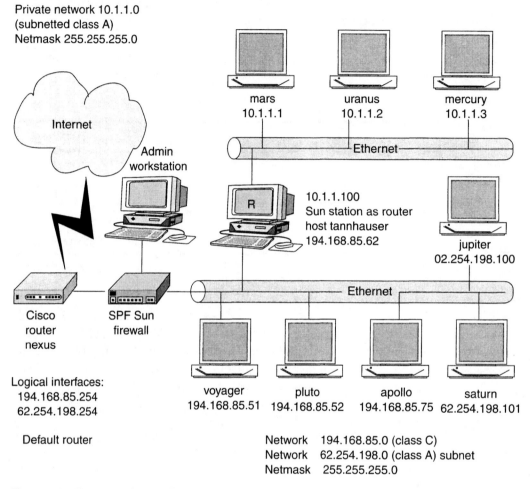

Private network 10.1.1.0
(subnetted class A)
Netmask 255.255.255.0

Internet

Admin workstation

mars
10.1.1.1

uranus
10.1.1.2

mercury
10.1.1.3

Ethernet

R

10.1.1.100
Sun station as router
host tannhauser
194.168.85.62

jupiter
02.254.198.100

Ethernet

Cisco
router
nexus

SPF Sun
firewall

Logical interfaces:
194.168.85.254
62.254.198.254

Default router

voyager
194.168.85.51

pluto
194.168.85.52

apollo
194.168.85.75

saturn
62.254.198.101

Network   194.168.85.0 (class C)
Network   62.254.198.0 (class A) subnet
Netmask   255.255.255.0

Figure 4–3   *Basic example network*

IP address of the target system voyager, whose Ethernet address it is attempting to acquire.

Opcode 1 always results in an Ethernet broadcast frame being transmitted because the unicast address of the destination system *voyager* is unknown. (If the Ethernet address of voyager were known, the ARP would not be needed!)

To illustrate ARP in action, let us examine the commands that were used to capture the ARP request message from apollo to voyager. First, here is the command that captures ARP packets into a file called `arpcapture`:

```
# snoop -o arpcapture arp
```

To view the **snoop** data, use:

```
# snoop -v -i arpcapture
```

The following **snoop** packets show the ARP opcode 1 from apollo to voyager. Notice that the numbers in the right margin are not part of the **snoop** output but are present to make it easier to refer to the code lines in the explanation that follows the code snippet.

```
ETHER:   ----- Ether Header -----
ETHER:
ETHER:   Packet 3 arrived at 15:19:25.19
ETHER:   Packet size = 42 bytes
ETHER:   Destination = ff:ff:ff:ff:ff:ff, (broadcast)        1
ETHER:   Source      = 8:0:20:fc:8d:d6, Sun                  2
ETHER:   Ethertype   = 0806 (ARP)                            3
ETHER:                                                       4
ARP:   ----- ARP/RARP Frame -----                            5
ARP:
ARP:   Hardware type = 1
ARP:   Protocol type = 0800 (IP)
ARP:   Length of hardware address = 6 bytes
ARP:   Length of protocol address = 4 bytes
ARP:   Opcode 1 (ARP Request)                                6
ARP:   Sender's hardware address = 8:0:20:fc:8d:d6           7
ARP:   Sender's protocol address = 194.168.85.75, apollo     8
ARP:   Target hardware address = ?                           9
ARP:   Target protocol address = 194.168.85.51, voyager      10
```

Now, let us analyze some of the lines of the **snoop** extract.

LINE 1

```
ETHER:   Destination = ff:ff:ff:ff:ff:ff, (broadcast)
```

The Ethernet destination address is a broadcast (`ff:ff:ff:ff:ff:ff`). because apollo needs to reach all machines on the LAN segment.

LINE 2

```
ETHER:   Source      = 8:0:20:fc:8d:d6, Sun
```

The source Ethernet address is that of apollo, the system that transmitted the ARP request on the bus. The system is a Sun system.

LINE 3

```
ETHER:  Ethertype = 0806 (ARP)
```

This line shows that the Ethernet frame is carrying ARP, identified by Ethertype code 0806.

LINE 4

```
ETHER:
```

Marks the end of the Ethernet header. The frame's CRC follows the ARP message, so we cannot say that line 4 marks the end of the Ethernet frame.

LINE 5

```
ARP:  ----- ARP/RARP Frame -----
```

This is the first line of the ARP message, which is encapsulated in the Ethernet frame's data field.

LINE 6

```
ARP:  Opcode 1 (ARP Request)
```

Line 6 indicates that the ARP packet is of type opcode 1, the ARP request.

LINE 7

```
ARP:  Sender's hardware address = 8:0:20:fc:8d:d6
```

This line contains the Ethernet address of the system that originated the ARP request (the sender), in this case, apollo.

LINE 8

```
ARP:  Sender's protocol address = 194.168.85.75, apollo
```

This line contains the IP address and name (apollo) of the system that originated the ARP request (the sender).

LINE 9

```
ARP:   Target hardware address = ?
```

Notice that in line 9, ARP refers to the address it is attempting to acquire as the *target*. This is important because the function of ARP is to target a specific Ethernet address and acquire it through the ARP request. This line reveals the need for the ARP request; the target hardware address is unknown, indicated by the ? character.

LINE 10

```
ARP:   Target protocol address = 194.168.85.51, voyager
```

This critical line shows the IP address of the system (voyager) whose Ethernet address the ARP request is attempting to discover. Voyager will hear the ARP request and reply with an ARP reply (opcode 2), which we examine next.

ARP Reply, Operation 2 (Opcode 2)

The reply from voyager to apollo is addressed to apollo's unicast address rather than being transmitted in a broadcast, as the ARP request was. Voyager does not need to broadcast its reply (opcode 2), because it learned apollo's IP address and Ethernet address from the ARP request (opcode 1) packet that it received from apollo. Keep in mind that in opcode 1, the target was voyager, but in the reply from voyager, the target is apollo.

Here is the **snoop** extract of relevance, showing the ARP reply from voyager to apollo. Once again, the important lines are numbered for easy reference.

```
ETHER:   ----- Ether Header -----
ETHER:
ETHER:   Packet 4 arrived at 15:19:25.19
ETHER:   Packet size = 60 bytes
ETHER:   Destination = 8:0:20:fc:8d:d6, Sun        1
ETHER:   Source      = 8:0:20:b1:ed:cf, Sun        2
ETHER:   Ethertype = 0806 (ARP)                    3
ETHER:
ARP:   ----- ARP/RARP Frame -----                  4
ARP:
ARP:   Hardware type = 1
ARP:   Protocol type = 0800 (IP)
```

```
ARP:    Length of hardware address = 6 bytes
ARP:    Length of protocol address = 4 bytes
ARP:    Opcode 2 (ARP Reply)                               5
ARP:    Sender's hardware address = 8:0:20:b1:ed:cf        6
ARP:    Sender's protocol address = 194.168.85.51, voyager 7
ARP:    Target hardware address = 8:0:20:fc:8d:d6          8
ARP:    Target protocol address = 194.168.85.75, apollo    9
```

Following is a line-by-line examination of the code snippet.

LINE 1

```
ETHER:   Destination = 8:0:20:fc:8d:d6, Sun
```

Line 1 specifies that the Ethernet destination address is apollo's. Apollo is a Sun system.

LINE 2

```
ETHER:   Source      = 8:0:20:b1:ed:cf, Sun
```

This line specifies that the Ethernet source is voyager, which is a Sun system.

LINE 3

```
ETHER:   Ethertype = 0806 (ARP)
```

Line 3 specifies that the frame type being carried is ARP (0806).

LINE 4

```
ARP:    ----- ARP/RARP Frame -----
```

Line 4 represents the start of the ARP message encapsulated in the Ethernet frame.

LINE 5

```
ARP:   Opcode 2 (ARP Reply)
```

This line specifies that the packet is an ARP reply (opcode 2).

LINE 6

```
ARP:   Sender's hardware address = 8:0:20:b1:ed:cf
```

This line specifies the Ethernet address of the sender of the ARP reply (voyager)

LINE 7

```
ARP:  Sender's protocol address = 194.168.85.51, voyager
```

Line 7 specifies the IP address of the sender of the ARP reply (voyager).

LINE 8

```
ARP:  Target hardware address = 8:0:20:fc:8d:d6
```

This line identifies the Ethernet address of the intended target of the ARP reply (apollo).

LINE 9

```
ARP:  Target protocol address = 194.168.85.75, apollo
```

Line 9 gives the IP address of the target of the ARP reply (apollo). The result of this ARP reply (opcode 2) is that apollo now has voyager's Ethernet address. Voyager, of course, now has apollo's Ethernet address too.

In summary, we have now examined both the ARP request (opcode 1) from apollo to voyager and the ARP reply (opcode 2) from voyager to apollo, in which it supplies its Ethernet address to apollo.

EXAM NOTES

KEY LEARNING POINTS:

- There is no inherent or mathematical relationship between a MAC address and an IP address.
- We acquire another system's Ethernet address using an ARP request.
- The targeted system replies using an ARP reply.
- Opcode 1 is the ARP request and uses a broadcast address.
- Opcode 2 is the ARP reply and uses a unicast address.
- ARP is identified by Ethernet as Ethertype 0x0806.

RARP

RARP is the inverse of ARP. It is used by a host that knows its own Ethernet address (because Ethernet is hardware-based) but needs to acquire its IP address from a RARP server running the **in.rarpd** daemon—a server process that listens on the network for hosts issuing RARP requests.

In this examination of RARP, we use two example systems, mars and tannhauser, to explore opcodes 3 and 4. In opcode 3, mars is the source and tannhauser the destination, but in the reply to mars from tannhauser, tannhauser becomes the source and mars the destination.

As we have seen, all systems use ARP to acquire the Ethernet address of all other systems. On the other hand, a system uses RARP specifically to learn its own IP address, so in this sense RARP has a narrower focus.

The RARP protocol allows a booting client to acquire the IP address of that booting client from a boot server running **in.rarpd**. Having acquired its IP address, the system may continue to boot. Some of the types of systems that typically do not know their own IP address at boot time are

- diskless clients
- X Terminal clients
- Jumpstart clients
- SunRay clients
- a network printer
- Java stations

In some of the foregoing cases a system is capable of storing an IP address, but the network administrator has chosen to allocate IP addresses using RARP.

Observe that the RARP server does not dynamically choose an IP address for a RARP client, but rather knows the IP address that is to be assigned to a given Ethernet address because it maintains a simple map called *ethers*, which we explore later in this chapter. You may also refer to Chapter 9, where we examine the Dynamic Host Configuration Protocol (DHCP), which, unlike RARP, may be configured to assign IP addresses dynamically.

To illustrate RARP in action, the following scenario uses mars as a boot client. Forcing mars to boot across the net (**boot net**) forces it to use RARP. At the Sun OpenBoot prompt, enter

```
ok boot net - install
```

RARP is broadcast based, so it is important that the client and server be on the same subnet. For the following explanation of RARP, mars is the RARP client and tannhauser the **in.rarpd** boot server.

RARP Request, Operation 3 (Opcode 3)

In the following examples, host mars is booting and broadcasting using RARP (Opcode 3) to learn its IP address. Host mars is booting as a Jumpstart client, but for this chapter, focus only on its use of RARP. (The details of Jumpstart are not covered by this book.)

The following **snoop** packet was captured as we described earlier in this chapter. The important lines are once again numbered for easy reference.

```
ETHER:  ----- Ether Header -----
ETHER:
ETHER:  Packet 1 arrived at 17:03:14.22
ETHER:  Packet size = 64 bytes
ETHER:  Destination = ff:ff:ff:ff:ff:ff, (broadcast)       1
ETHER:  Source      = 8:0:20:d:c7:7c, Sun                  2
ETHER:  Ethertype = 8035 (RARP)                            3
ETHER:
ARP:  ----- ARP/RARP Frame -----                           4
ARP:
ARP:  Hardware type = 1
ARP:  Protocol type = 0800 (IP)
ARP:  Length of hardware address = 6 bytes
ARP:  Length of protocol address = 4 bytes
ARP:  Opcode 3 (REVARP Request)                            5
ARP:  Sender's hardware address = 8:0:20:d:c7:7c           6
ARP:  Sender's protocol address = 0.0.0.0, OLD-BROADCAST   7
ARP:  Target hardware address = 8:0:20:d:c7:7c             8
ARP:  Target protocol address = ?                          9
```

Here's a line-by-line breakdown of the code snippet.

LINE 1

```
ETHER:  Destination = ff:ff:ff:ff:ff:ff, (broadcast)
```

The RARP request (opcode 3) uses a broadcast address, as it does not know the Ethernet address of the boot RARP server.

LINE 2

```
ETHER:   Source      = 8:0:20:d:c7:7c, Sun
```

The source address identifies mars, a Sun system.

LINE 3

```
ETHER: Ethertype = 8035 (RARP)
```

The Ethernet frame has RARP encapsulated, indicated by the hex code 0x8035.

LINE 4

```
ARP:   ----- ARP/RARP Frame -----
```

This line marks the beginning of the ARP packet, which is encapsulated in the Ethernet frame. Notice that even though the contents of the frame are RARP rather than ARP, **snoop** identifies both ARP and RARP as ARP.

LINE 5

```
ARP:   Opcode 3 (REVARP Request)
```

This line identifies the message as a RARP request (known as a REVARP request), which is an opcode 3.

LINE 6

```
ARP:   Sender's hardware address = 8:0:20:d:c7:7c
```

This line reveals the Ethernet address of the sender of the REVARP. It belongs to mars, as you can see by examining Figure 4-3.

LINE 7

```
ARP:   Sender's protocol address = 0.0.0.0, OLD-BROADCAST
```

Here the sender is using the OLD-BROADCAST address of 0.0.0.0. You can learn more about the full significance of OLD-BROADCAST (a reserved address) in Chapter 5, where we explore IPv4 in detail. For now, it is sufficient to understand that mars does not know its own IP address and therefore cannot use the specific broadcast address of the network to which it is connected. The network-specific broadcast is also called the *net-directed broadcast*, which we also discuss in Chapter 5.

LINE 8

```
ARP:  Target hardware address = 8:0:20:d:c7:7c
```

In line 8, notice that the target of the REVARP is the system that originated the frame (the RARP client), not the RARP server as you might expect.

This enables the **in.rarpd** server when it examines the RARP frame to identify the Ethernet address of the RARP client. The **in.rarpd** server returns the IP address that matches with this Ethernet client address in the server's *ethers table*. The server's ethers table is examined later in this chapter.

> **Be careful here. Notice that the target is mars—the client who is actually issuing the RARP request—not the target of the Ethernet frame, which is the RARP server. The Ethernet frame is broadcast and in this sense targets all hosts in the bus, but it is the RARP server that we hope will hear the frame and respond to the RARP client.**

LINE 9

```
ARP:  Target protocol address = ?
```

The whole purpose of opcode 3 (RARP request) is to enable the client host issuing the RARP request to learn its IP from a RARP server. In this request packet, therefore, the target IP address is unknown.

Next, we examine the opcode 4, the reply to the RARP request just examined.

RARP Reply, Operation 4 (Opcode 4)

In the RARP reply, tannhauser is replying to mars and informing mars of its IP address. This is the express purpose of RARP. Here are the RARP reply lines as revealed by **snoop**:

```
ETHER:  ----- Ether Header -----
ETHER:
```

```
ETHER:    Packet 2 arrived at 17:03:17.24
ETHER:    Packet size = 42 bytes
ETHER:    Destination = 8:0:20:d:c7:7c, Sun            1
ETHER:    Source      = 8:0:20:7b:33:a4, Sun           2
ETHER:    Ethertype = 8035 (RARP)                      3
ETHER:
ARP:    ----- ARP/RARP Frame -----                     4
ARP:
ARP:    Hardware type = 1
ARP:    Protocol type = 0800 (IP address)
ARP:    Length of hardware address = 6 bytes
ARP:    Length of protocol address = 4 bytes
ARP:    Opcode 4 (REVARP Reply)                        5
ARP:    Sender's hardware address = 8:0:20:7b:33:a4    6
ARP:    Sender's protocol address = 10.1.1.100, tannhauser  7
ARP:    Target hardware address = 8:0:20:d:c7:7c       8
ARP:    Target protocol address = 10.1.1.1, mars       9
```

Following is a line-by-line analysis of the code snippet.

LINE 1

```
ETHER:    Destination = 8:0:20:d:c7:7c, Sun
```

This line specifies the target address of the reply packet (mars).

LINE 2

```
ETHER:    Source      = 8:0:20:7b:33:a4, Sun
```

Tannhauser is the source of the reply packet. Tannhauser is the RARP server, so we expect the reply to originate from tannhauser.

LINE 3

```
ETHER:    Ethertype = 8035 (RARP)
```

This line specifies that the Ethernet frame has a RARP packet encapsulated. The code for RARP is hex 0x8035.

LINE 4

```
ARP:    ----- ARP/RARP Frame -----
```

Line 4 marks the beginning of the ARP packet that is encapsulated in the Ethernet frame. Notice that even though the contents of the frame are RARP rather than ARP, **snoop** identifies both ARP and RARP as ARP.

LINE 5

```
ARP:  Opcode 4 (REVARP Reply)
```

This line specifies that the RARP packet is a type RARP reply.

LINE 6

```
ARP:  Sender's hardware address = 8:0:20:7b:33:a4
```

Line 6 identifies the sending machine (source) of the RARP reply as tannhauser, the RARP server. We know it is tannhauser by its Ethernet address, as shown in Figure 4-2.

LINE 7

```
ARP:  Sender's protocol address = 10.1.1.100, tannhauser
```

The sending machine (source) of the RARP reply is once again tannhauser.

LINE 8

```
ARP:  Target hardware address = 8:0:20:d:c7:7c
```

Line 8 specifies mars as the target of the RARP reply. We can identify mars by its Ethernet address. See Figure 4-3.

LINE 9

```
ARP:  Target protocol address = 10.1.1.1, mars
```

Finally, line 9 gives the IP address of the target and the reason for the RARP request and reply. Mars issued its RARP request because it did not have this golden nugget of information.

In summary, mars has now been informed of its IP address by tannhauser the RARP server. The RARP server needs configuring as follows.

Configuring the RARP Server

The RARP server needs configuring because it relies on the content of files, which the administrator must populate. At minimum, the server needs to run the **in.rarpd** daemon and have a /etc/ethers file, which acts as a simple text database listing RARP clients, their Ethernet addresses, and their host names. NIS or NIS+ can be used instead of an ethers file. This chapter presumes you are using an ethers file, not NIS or NIS+, on the **in.rarpd** server.

To run the **in.rarpd** daemon, enter

```
#  in.rarpd -a
```

Create the /etc/ethers file, entering a line for each boot client your server supports, as in this example:

```
# cat /etc/ethers
8:0:20:d:c7:7c              mars
```

Note

Do not enter the IP address of mars in this file. Enter the Ethernet address and the hostname of the RARP client (mars in this example scenario). Ensure that mars and its IP address are in the /etc/inet/hosts file on the RARP server.

The IP address of mars is returned to mars by the RARP server, which it acquires from its own /etc/hosts file:

```
# grep  -i   mars /etc/inet/hosts
10.1.1.1                   mars
```

With this command, the configuration of the RARP server is complete.

EXAM NOTES

KEY LEARNING POINTS

- ARP's function as a protocol is to acquire an Ethernet address for a known IP address.
- RARP's function as a protocol is to acquire an IP address for a known Ethernet address.
- ARP's opcode 1 is the ARP request, which requires a MAC address.
- ARP's opcode 2 is the ARP reply to opcode 1, which returns the required MAC address.

- RARP's opcode 3 is the RARP request, which requires an IP address.
- RARP's opcode 4 is the RARP reply, which returns the IP address.
- The **in.rarpd** server daemon listens for RARP requests and answers RARP clients.
- The /etc/ethers file maps the client's Ethernet address to its host name.
- The /etc/inet/hosts file provides an IP address for the client host name in the /etc/ethers file.

4.4   The ARP Cache and arp Command

In this section we examine the ARP protocol cache and the **arp** command. The ARP cache stores learned IP-to-Ethernet address mappings, thus sparing hosts from the necessity of acquiring this information from across the network every time they need it. The **arp** command may be used to display, add, and delete ARP cache entries and make permanent (static) entries.

The ARP Cache

Hosts store the IP-to-Ethernet mappings they learn in a memory-resident *ARP cache*. The ARP cache is a per-system, memory-based table of IP-to-Ethernet address mappings, populated by information that is gleaned through the use of the ARP and RARP protocols. By building up a cache in memory of the addresses it learns dynamically through ARP, a system can avoid generating unnecessary broadcast traffic on the network. Essentially, then, entries in a host's ARP cache are either

- learned dynamically through the ARP/RARP protocol or
- added statically by a host at boot time or through **arp –s** or **–f**

The resulting advantages of using an ARP cache include

- fast retrieval of requested addresses
- reduction of load on hosts by reducing their need to use the network
- reduction of unnecessary traffic on a network

The information in an ARP cache is not stored indefinitely, because a system's MAC can change (although this is a rare occurrence). The cache retains learned addresses for about 20 minutes and then dumps them.

The Arp Command

The **arp** command displays and modifies the ARP cache. In this section we examine the **arp** command and methods for manually adding and deleting information from the ARP cache. Table 4.2 describes **arp** command options.

Table 4.2 *ARP Command Options*

OPTION	DESCRIPTION
Hostname	Shows the hostname's entry in the current host's cache.
-a	Views the ARP cache.
-d	Deletes an entry from the ARP cache.
-s	Adds a static entry to the ARP cache.
-f	Populates the ARP cache from a file.

Let us next examine each of the command options. We run the commands on the host called *apollo*, which we refer to in the examples as the current host.

Checking a Single Cache Entry

To view the name of the current host, use the **uname** command:

```
# uname -n
  apollo
```

You may also check the entries for voyager and apollo in apollo's ARP cache:

```
# arp voyager
voyager   (194.168.85.51) at 8:0:20:b1:ed:cf
# arp apollo
apollo (194.168.85.75) at 8:0:20:fc:8d:d6 permanent
published
```

Notice that the entry for voyager has been learned and is therefore a dynamic entry in the ARP cache rather than static. Static entries are like apollo's, with the word *permanent* displayed. *Permanent* indicates that apollo's entry has not been learned and will therefore not be deleted from the cache. This is because apollo has added this entry itself as the current host; it has not learned this address. Apollo is not a boot client (RARP client) and so had both its IP and Ethernet address at boot time.

Systems are usually able to respond to ARP requests for their Ethernet addresses; this is why *published* as well as *permanent* appears in the code. In short, apollo will publish (make available) its Ethernet address if it is asked to do so during an ARP request.

Note

The system apollo will never issue an RARP request, because it is not a boot client or Jumpstart client. It will never be asked for its IP address, because no other system will use it. Systems needing to contact apollo and acquire its IP address for this purpose will use either their own /etc/inet/hosts file or a naming service such as Domain Name Service (DNS).

Viewing the Entire ARP cache with arp –a

To view the contents of the current host's ARP cache, use the **–a** option. Here is an example of the command and its resulting output:

```
# arp  -a

Net to Media Table: IPv4
Device IP Address Mask                Flags  Phys Addr
------ --------------------- ----  -----------------
hme0   tannhauser 255.255.255.255          08:00:20:7b:33:a4
hme0   apollo     255.255.255.255 SP       08:00:20:fc:8d:d6
hme0   voyager    255.255.255.255          08:00:20:b1:ed:cf
hme0   nexus      255.255.255.255          00:01:42:a5:ea:56
```

Let us examine a particular entry more closely.

```
Device IP Address Mask                Flags  Phys Addr
------ --------------------- ----  -----------------
hme0   voyager    255.255.255.255          08:00:20:b1:ed:cf
```

Each column has a particular function:

- The *Device* column is the interface through which the MAC address was learned on the current host (the host whose cache we are examining). We are on apollo in this example.
- The *IP address* to MAC (physical address) mapping that we are examining belongs to voyager.

- The *Mask* broadcast address was used to learn the MAC address of voyager and is `255.255.255.255`. This value identifies a limited broadcast, which you can read more about in Chapter 5.
- The *Flags* field is empty, which usually means that this ARP cache entry was learned dynamically and not added statically.
- The *Phys Addr* (Ethernet address) of voyager is `08:00:20:b1:ed:cf`.

Table 4.3 lists the possible flags found in the *Flags* field of ARP cache entries. In our example, the current host is apollo. It is apollo's ARP cache table and entries that we are referencing in the table.

Table 4.3 *Possible ARP Cache Flags*

FLAG VALUE	MEANING	FUNCTION
P	Publish	Includes the IP address for the current host and the addresses that have explicitly been added by the **-s** option of the **arp** command. ARP will respond to ARP requests for this address.
S	Static	Not learned dynamically by the ARP protocol. The entry was either added statically to apollo's cache at boot time, added by **arp –s,** or added by **arp -f.**
U	Unresolved	Waiting for ARP response. Unresolved entries occur when a host fails to respond to the current host's ARP request. The host's IP address is entered in the cache by the current host, but its Ethernet address remains unknown and therefore unresolved.
M	Mapping	Used only for the multicast entry for 224.0.0.0. Multicast addresses are explored further in Chapter 5 on IPv4 and in Chapter 13, which covers IPv6.

Deleting an ARP Cache Entry with arp –d

In the following example, we delete host tannhauser from the current host's ARP cache.

1. First, ensure that host tannhauser is in the cache:
   ```
   # arp tannhauser
   tannhauser (194.168.85.62) at 8:0:20:7b:33:a4
   ```
2. Tannhauser is indeed in the cache. Now to delete it:
   ```
   # arp -d tannhauser
   tannhauser (194.168.85.62) deleted
   ```

3. Let us check to ensure that it has really been deleted:

```
# arp tannhauser
tannhauser (194.168.85.62) -- no entry
```

It is deleted.

When we access tannhauser, its Ethernet address is forced back into the current host's cache. In order to **ping** tannhauser, the current host must acquire tannhauser's Ethernet address through an ARP request like the following:

```
# ping tannhauser
tannhauser is alive
```

Let us check to ensure that it is back in the cache:

```
# arp tannhauser
tannhauser (194.168.85.62) at 8:0:20:7b:33:a4
#
```

The ARP request was successful, as tannhauser's Ethernet address is in fact back in the ARP cache.

Note

The ping command issues a small ICMP echo request packet, which is encapsulated in IP. Its purpose is to test whether another system is alive (booted or up). Because ping uses IP, which in turn is encapsulated in Ethernet, "pinging" a system forces the current host to acquire the "pinged" system's Ethernet address. If we ping a system on a network other than our own, we must use a local router to forward our IP packets. In this case, it is the Ethernet address of the local router that we need, because we encapsulate our IP packets in an Ethernet frame addressed to the local router, and that router forwards our IP packets to the system we are "pinging."

Adding a Static ARP Cache Entry with arp -s and -f

Next, let us examine how to force static entries into the ARP cache. Static entries are identified by the **S** flag. There are occasions when statically adding a mapping to the ARP cache is preferable to having the system learn an Ethernet address dynamically using the ARP protocol. Static address mapping is useful when

- we wish to add a static mapping to reduce network traffic so that a host need not acquire a given Ethernet address every time it is needed, or

- a host can be configured to answer on behalf of another host, which is referred to as proxy ARP.

Using the **arp** command with the -**s** option allows us to add a single static entry into the ARP cache. The -**f** option to the **arp** command allows the administrator to add multiple static entries that he or she has added to a text file. The syntax for the **arp** command's -**s** and -**f** options is the subject of the next two sections.

STATIC MAPPING USING -S

In the example that follows, we add a simple static mapping to the ARP cache. Keep in mind that on rebooting, any static mapping created in this way would be lost. To make a static mapping permanent, add the **arp** command to a startup script and use the -**s** or -**f** option.

The process of adding a static mapping involves removing a dynamic entry and replacing it with a static one. Follow these steps:

1. To begin the process of adding a static mapping, first delete a current voyager learned (dynamic) entry. Here is an example of the command and its resulting output:

```
# arp -d voyager
voyager (194.168.85.51) deleted
```

2. Next, add a static entry using the –**s** option:

```
# arp -s voyager 08:00:20:b1:ed:cf perm
# arp voyager
voyager (194.168.85.51) at 8:0:20:b1:ed:cf permanent
```

3. Finally, check voyager's entry in the cache and examine the flags field:

```
# arp -a | grep voyager
hme0 voyager  255.255.255.255   SP  08:00:20:b1:ed:cf
```

Notice the flags S and P. Also notice that the entry is permanent. This is because we added it with the -**s** option, so it will not be deleted from the cache. It is worth noting that when the system reboots, the entry will be deleted, and that adding to the cache with the -**s** option only adds it to the ARP cache in memory rather than writing it to a file.

We could put **arp -s** lines in a shell script and execute the shell script at boot time, but there is a better, recommended way of adding such entries. To make an entry permanent in the sense that it is added automatically at system boot, use the **arp -f** option, which we examine next.

STATIC MAPPING USING ARP -F

You can use the **arp -f** option to add static entries to the cache as in the following example:

```
# arp -f arplines
```

Here, the file called **arplines** contains

```
voyager  08:00:20:b1:ed:cf pub
```

Voyager is now added to the cache as a **permanent** (published) entry. The file syntax is

```
Hostname Ethernet-Address [temp] [pub]
```

A *shell script* is a program that is interpreted and executed by a UNIX shell as indicated by the first line of the script. Sun recommends that additional shell scripts be added to the /etc/init.d directory and then linked to the appropriate run-level directory, such as /etc/rc1.d. In the following steps, we will create a simple shell script that adds the host voyager to the current host's ARP cache at boot time. The script also creates a file called **arpadd** as it runs.

1. Create a shell script called /etc/init.d/arpadd that contains the following code. If you wish to add additional hosts at a later time, simply add lines beneath the *voyager* line in the script, but above the final bang (!):

```
#!/bin/sh
INITDIR=/etc/init.d
#create a file and add arp lines

cat <<!    >$INITDIR/arpadd
voyager  08:00:20:b1:ed:cf pub
!

#next, run arp -f on created file
arp -f  $INITDIR/arpadd

#End of Script
```

2. Next, hard link the script to the file /etc/rc1.d/S100arpadd. Here is an example using a hard link:

```
# ln  /etc/init.d/arpadd  /etc/rc1.d/S100arpadd
```

The shell script uses a feature of the shell called a *here document*. The `cat<<!>` `$INITDIR/arpadd` line starts the here document, and the exclamation mark (!) finishes it. Please ensure that the lines of the here document are not indented. They must be at the start of the line as in the foregoing example. Indenting the here document lines of the script result in breaking the script. Most other lines of shell scripts are *free-form*, meaning that the code can contain indentations and blank lines without the execution of the code being affected. So indentation is recommended if it makes the script more readable.

Scripts in the /etc/rc1.d directory beginning with a capital S are executed by the system process init automatically as the system transitions to run state 1.

EXAM NOTES

KEY LEARNING POINTS

- ARP maps a known 32-bit IP address to a dynamically learned 48-bit MAC address.
- RARP maps a known 48-bit MAC address to a dynamically learned 32-bit IP address.
- ARP and RARP requests (opcodes 1 and 3) use a broadcast address.
- ARP and RARP replies (opcodes 2 and 4) use unicast addresses.
- Use the **arp** command to add, delete, and view the cache.
- ARP cache entries are either permanent (static) or learned and therefore temporary (dynamic).

SUMMARY

In this chapter, you saw how ARP permits a known IP address to be mapped onto a learned MAC address through a broadcast using the ARP protocol. We examined RARP, which enables a boot client to learn its IP address from a RARP server running **in.rarpd**.

You also explored the ARP frame and the contents of the ARP header, as also shown and displayed using the Solaris packet sniffer **snoop**, an excellent tool for examining LAN traffic. (A packet *sniffer* allows us to examine network packets and their contents.) Having gleaned information from the network, hosts cache the mappings they have learned in an ARP cache for future use. Caching improves network performance and reduces unnecessary network traffic, which would result if ARP had to broadcast every time it needed a given destination's Ethernet address.

The next chapter examines IPv4, whose datagrams (ubiquitous byte barges) route most traffic across the Internet.

TEST YOURSELF

MULTIPLE CHOICE

1. *Which opcode identifies the ARP reply?*

    A. 1

    B. 4

    C. 5

    D. 3

    E. 2

2. *What type of data is Ethernet delivering when 0x0806 is in the Ethernet type field?*

    A. IP

    B. TCP

    C. ARP

    D. RARP

    E. ICMP

3. *When a host issues an ARP request (opcode 1), what is it attempting to learn?*

    A. An Ethernet address

    B. An IP address

    C. A hostname

    D. A broadcast address

    E. A unicast address

4.   *When a host issues a RARP request (opcode 3), what is it attempting to learn?*
    A. An Ethernet address
    B. An IP address
    C. A hostname
    D. A broadcast address
    E. A unicast IP address

5.   *A RARP server must run which of the following daemons?*
    A. **rarpd.in**
    B. **in.rarp**
    C. **in.arpd**
    D. **in.rarpd**
    E. **in.macd**

6.   *The **arp** command -**d** option does which of the following?*
    A. Display the ARP cache
    B. Delete the entire ARP cache
    C. Delete a selected entry from the arp cache
    D. Display a selected ARP cache entry
    E. Define an ARP cache entry

7.   *The U flag found in **arp -a** output indicates what?*
    A. A complete entry
    B. An unresolved entry
    C. A Sun Ethernet mapping
    D. A ubiquitous broadcast entry
    E. A broadcast message

8.   *For what length of time are ARP entries usually cached?*
    A. 1 minute
    B. 5 minutes
    C. 20 minutes
    D. 100 minutes
    E. 2 minutes

9.   *How many bytes does the ARP/RARP protocol frame contain?*
    A. 52
    B. 28
    C. 30

D. 20

E. 4

10. *Which of the following frames sees the target and the source of the frame as the same host?*

A. ARP request, opcode 1

B. ARP reply, opcode 2

C. RARP request, opcode 3

D. RARP reply, opcode 4

E. RARP opcode 1

FREE RESPONSE

1. *State in your own words why ARP requests are broadcast rather than unicast.*

2. *Why does the ARP cache reduce network traffic and improve network performance?*

The Internet Layer and IPv4

EXAM OBJECTIVES

5.1 IPv4 Address Classes, Netmasks, and the Broadcast Address

5.2 Subnetting

5.3 The IPv4 Datagram Header and Datagram Fragmentation

5.4 Classless Inter Domain Routing (CIDR)

5.5 The Netmasks File

5.6 Variable Length Subnet Masks (VLSM)

5.7 Configuring a Network Interface

After completing this chapter, you will be able to meet the following Network Administration Exam objectives:

- Describe IP addressing, broadcast address, netmask, datagram, and IP fragmentation.
- Explain how subnetting works.
- Describe classless inter domain routing (CIDR).
- Identify the file used to set netmasks.
- Identify the features and benefits of the variable-length subnet masks (VLSM).
- Configure a network interface.

To help you meet these objectives, this chapter covers the following topics:

- the five IPv4 address classes, subnet masks, the broadcast address, and special IP address formats
- subnets and how to implement them
- the structure of the IPv4 datagram and header
- how an IPv4 datagram gets fragmented
- how classless inter domain routing works
- the Solaris /etc/inet/netmasks file

- the practical uses of variable-length subnet masks
- how to configure an interface

5.1 IPv4 Address Classes, Netmasks, and the Broadcast Address

The Internet Protocol (IP) is fundamental to TCP/IP, as it carries nearly all traffic passed down the stack by TCP, and UDP, and most applications. IP is a *homogeneous* layer in that it is the only protocol operating at the Internet layer that performs the function of IP datagram routing based on a destination IP address.

There is no alternative to IP in the TCP/IP family of protocols. That is, only the IP protocol offers a datagram routing service to upper-layer protocols. We know that Internet Control Message Protocol (ICMP) also functions at this layer, but it is actually encapsulated in IP and is not an alternative to IP. ICMP is not able to route IP datagrams. Figure 5-1 shows where IP operates in the Sun TCP/IP 5-layer model that we delineated in Chapter 1.

If we could look out across the Internet's webbed shores, we would see IP's great homogeneous cloak, an ocean of byte barges all en route to an electronic harbor in some distant port.

IPv4 Address Classes A, B, C, and D

Understanding IP addresses is fundamental to a good understanding of several other IP-related topics, such as routing and subnetting. IP as a

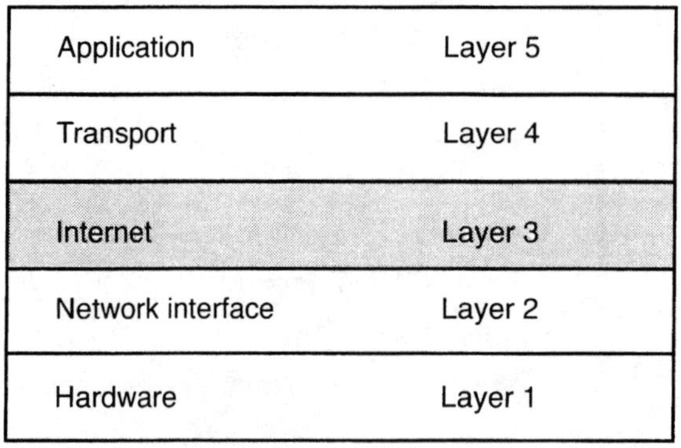

Application	Layer 5
Transport	Layer 4
Internet	Layer 3
Network interface	Layer 2
Hardware	Layer 1

Figure 5–1   *IP functioning at Layer 3 of the Sun TCP/IP 5-layer model*

protocol is responsible for routing IP datagrams (discussed later in this chapter) and for fragmenting datagrams when necessary. The IP address is the fundamental piece of information that enables IP to route the datagrams and is found in the header of every IP datagram or fragment. The IP header occupies a minimum of 20 bytes and contains (among other things) the source and destination address of the datagram. IP operates at the Internet layer (3) of the Sun TCP/IP stack.

The Internet Protocol version 4 address, or *IPv4 address*, is a 32-bit (4 byte) address, normally represented in dotted decimal notation (also called *dotted quad notation*) as shown in the following example:

```
194.168.85.51
```

IPv4 addresses contain a *network number* and a *host number*. Put another way, an IPv4 address is made up of a network component, shared by all systems on that network, and a host component that is unique to a particular system, enabling that system to be addressed individually.

The IPv4 address class determines the number of hosts allowed on a given network. There are four basic classes of IPv4 address: A, B, C, and D. All classes use 32-bit addresses. The number of bits used to identify the host and network number portions of an IPv4 address is what differentiates one class from another. The importance of IPv4 classes has been eroded somewhat by classless inter domain routing (CIDR) and classless routing (to be explained shortly), but they are still relevant and must be understood by the network administrator. Let us examine the four classes of IPv4 addresses (A through D) and see how fixed bits in the first octet force an IPv4 address to belong to a specific class.

The class of an IP address is determined by fixing specific bits in the first octet at a value of either 0 or 1. Remember, only in the first octet are bits fixed in order to determine a given class range. The values in the second, third, and fourth octets have a range of 0 to 255 for all four classes.

Figure 5-2 shows how fixing specific bits determines whether an IPv4 address is assigned to class A, B, C, or D and defines a minimum and a maximum value (a valid range of addresses) for each class.

The following, Figure 5-2, shows the high order octet, the minimum and maximum allowed value, and also the first octet range of each class.

	Bit	128	64	32	16	8	4	2	1
Class A min value 0		0							
Max value 127		0	1	1	1	1	1	1	1
1st octet range 0–127									

	Bit	128	64	32	16	8	4	2	1
Class B min value 128		1	0						
Max value 191		1	0	1	1	1	1	1	1
1st octet range 128-191									

	Bit	128	64	32	16	8	4	2	1
Class C min value 192		1	1	0					
Max value 223		1	1	0	1	1	1	1	1
1st octet range 192–223									

	Bit	128	64	32	16	8	4	2	1
Class D min value 224		1	1	1	0				
Max value 239		1	1	1	0	1	1	1	1
1st octet range 224–239									

Figure 5–2 *Classes A–D, first octet fixed bits and range in binary*

Note The *higher order bits* are at the 128-bit end of the binary bit range. The *lower order bits* start at the 1-bit end of the range.

Class A Networks and Addresses

Figure 5-3 shows the range of binary bit values for class A network addresses. As you can see, even if bits 64, 32, 16, 8, 4, 2, and 1 all have a value of 1, the maximum attainable value in the first octet is 127. Add 64, 32, 16, 8, 4, 2, and 1 together and you get a maximum value of 127, which ensures that the first octet is valid for the class A range. Class A network and host addresses cannot exceed 127 because the 128 bit is fixed at 0.

Possible class A networks are few in number: only 128 total including 0. Each class A network, however, theoretically has 24 bits for hosts, which translates to approximately 16 million possible hosts. Within its range of valid addresses, each network consumes one address as a broadcast and one that represents the network itself.

For example, 10.0.0.0 is a valid class A network address (number) because it is within the valid range for a class A address (0.0.0.0 to 127.255.255.255). An example host address is 10.34.23.4, which is a valid class A host address on network 10.0.0.0. Like address classes, network addresses have a range of valid addresses, which are used primarily for hosts connected to the network. When the default netmask is applied, network 10.0.0.0 has the address range 10.0.0.0 to 10.255.255.255. The importance of the netmask in determining network and host bit ranges within a class will be examined shortly.

Here is a summary of the important points to remember about our sample class A network address and related addresses:

- valid range of addresses for class A: 0.0.0.0 to 127.255.255.255
- sample class A network address: 10.0.0.0
- sample class A host IP address: 10.34.23.4
- unique host portion of sample host address: 34.23.4
- broadcast address for sample network: 10.255.255.255

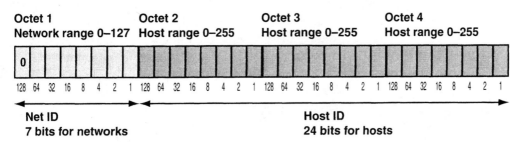

| Octet 1
Network range 0–127 | Octet 2
Host range 0–255 | Octet 3
Host range 0–255 | Octet 4
Host range 0–255 |

Net ID
7 bits for networks

Host ID
24 bits for hosts

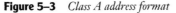

Figure 5–3   *Class A address format*

Notice that one address within the valid range (10.0.0.0) represents the network itself and that a separate address (10.255.255.255) represents the broadcast address. That is, for each network address, at least two addresses—namely, the network address itself and the broadcast address—cannot be used for host IP addresses.

EXAM NOTES

KEY LEARNING POINTS

- Class A networks use 7 bits of the first octet for networks.
- Class A network addresses use 24 bits for hosts.
- Each class A network uses one address for broadcasting.
- Each class A network uses one address for the network itself.
- Class A networks have a first octet that ranges from 0 to 127.
- Class A IP addresses range from 0.0.0.0 to 127.255.255.255.

Class B Networks and Addresses

Class B network addresses are more abundant than class A network addresses. Each class B network theoretically has 16 bits for hosts, which translates to approximately 64,000 possible hosts. Each class B network consumes one address as a broadcast address, and one additional address represents the network address itself.

Figure 5-4 shows the permitted range of binary values for class B network and host addresses. Notice that class B network addresses are identified by a first-octet range of 128 through 191 and that the second octet is included in the class B network address range. Only the last two octets are available for hosts on class B networks.

As you can see, even if bits 128, 32, 16, 8, 4, 2, and 1 all have a value of 1, the maximum attainable value is 191 and the minimum value is 128 because bit 128 is fixed by the IP software. That is, even if you add 128, 32, 16, 8, 4, 2, and 1 together because they all have a binary value of 1, you still only achieve a total value of 191, which ensures that the first octet is valid for a class B network range of addresses. Both the first and second octets are used by the class B network, with a second octet network value range of 0 to 255.

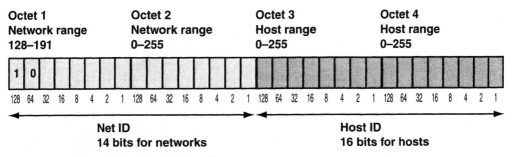

Figure 5–4 *Class B address format*

For example, assume that 129.156.0.0 is a valid class B network address and that 129.156.23.4 is a valid host. Sample addresses might then look like this:

- class B network number: 129.156.0.0
- valid range of addresses: 129.156.0.0 to 129.156.255.255
- IP address: 129.156.23.4 (an example host address from range)
- network address: 129.156.0.0
- host portion of network: 23.4

EXAM NOTES

KEY LEARNING POINTS

- Class B networks use 14 bits for networks and 16 bits for hosts.
- Each class B network uses one address for broadcasting.
- Each class B network uses one address for the network itself.
- Class B networks have a first octet that ranges from 128 to 191.
- Class B IP addresses range from 128.0.0.0 to 191.255.255.255.

Class C Networks and Addresses

Possible class C networks are in even greater abundance than class B, with up to 16 million network addresses available. Each class C network has only 8 bits for hosts, giving it a maximum of 254 hosts. Each network consumes one address as a broadcast address and another for the network itself. Figure 5-5 shows the range of binary bit values for class C network addresses.

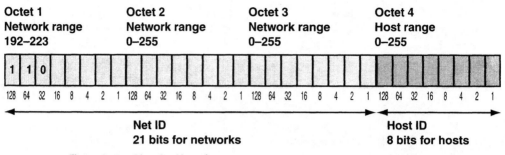

Figure 5–5   *Class C address format*

As you can see from the figure, even if bits 128, 64, 16, 8, 4, 2, and 1 of the first octet have a value of 1, the maximum value attainable is 223. That is, adding together 128, 64, 16, 8, 4, 2, and 1 gives the sum of 223, thus ensuring that the first octet is valid for the class C range of network addresses. The first, second, and third octet are used by the class C network, with a range of 0 to 255 available for both the second and third octet.

For example, assume that 194.168.85.0 is a valid class C network address and that 194.168.85.51 is a host address on that network. Sample addresses might then look like this:

- valid range of addresses: 194.168.85.0 to 194.168.85.255
- IP Address: 194.168.85.51
- network: 194.168.85.0
- broadcast: 194.168.85.255
- host portion: 51

EXAM NOTES

KEY LEARNING POINTS

- Class C network addresses use 21 bits for networks.
- Class C network addresses use 8 bits for hosts.
- Each class C network uses one address for broadcasting.
- Each class C network uses one address for the network itself.
- Class C networks have a first octet with values that range from 192 to 223.
- Class C IP addresses range from 192.0.0.0 to 223.255.255.255.

Class D Multicast Identifiers and Multicast Groups

Class D is different from classes A, B, and C in that its addresses identify multicast groups rather than networks and individual hosts on those networks. Therefore, a multicast address identifies one or more hosts that belong to the multicast group. Addresses for classes A, B, and C, as we have seen, identify either a single host (unicast) or all hosts on a given network (broadcast). Figure 5-6 shows the available range of values for class D addresses.

In summary, a multicast group address is the combination of the first octet—4 high-order bits of 128, 64, 32, and 16 fixed at binary value 1110, respectively—and the multicast group ID identified by the last 28 bits. The last 28 bits are not fixed and may be set at 1 or 0, which gives us a large range of possible multicast group IDs. The resulting multicast address range is 224.0.0.0 to 239.255.255.255.

If the 4 high-order bits of the first octet (128, 64, 32, 16) have fixed binary values of 1110, they have a minimum value of 224. That is, add 128, 64, and 32 together to yield 224. The 4 nonfixed low-order bits of the first octet (8, 4, 2, 1) are available to identify multicast groups, as are all the bits of octets 2, 3, and 4, which total 28 bits. It is important to observe that class D addresses do not identify networks and the hosts on the networks as did class A, B, and C IPv4 addresses. Class D addresses are multicast groups using 4 bits from the first octet and 24 bits from the last three octets, yielding 28 bits for a multicast address range. IPv4 multicast addresses map onto pseudo MAC addresses, as you will see in Chapter 6 when we examine the **in.rdisc** routing daemon that uses the multicast addresses 224.0.0.1 and 224.0.0.2.

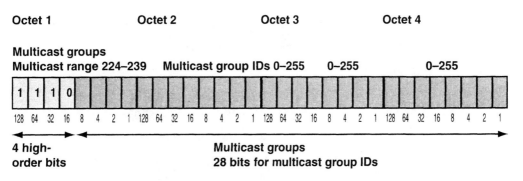

Figure 5–6   *Class D address format*

For example, assume that 224.0.0.1 is a valid multicast group address (ID). Sample addresses might then look like this:

- multicast group address: 224.0.0.1
- high-order 4 bits: 224.0.0.0

We explore multicasting further in Chapter 6.

EXAM NOTES

KEY LEARNING POINTS

- Class D networks use 28 bits for multicast groups.
- A host group listens to a particular multicast group address.
- The class D high-order bits range in values from 224 to 239.
- Multicast addresses map onto pseudo-Ethernet addresses (are assigned to an existing Ethernet card).
- Multicast addresses are shared by one or more hosts.

So, in summary, to identify which class an IP address belongs to, it is sufficient to look at just the first octet. To identify the network portion of an IP address and consequently identify the network of a host, however, we need to know the netmask value. In the next section, we examine the netmask, which allows us to differentiate between network bits and host bits for addresses in classes A through D.

Table 5.1 summarizes the address ranges of the classes we have examined. Be aware that class E addresses are not used at this time but may be reserved for future use.

Table 5.1 *Address Ranges of the Five Different Classes of Internet Addresses*

CLASS	RANGE
A	0.0.0.0 to 127.255.255.255
B	128.0.0.0 to 191.255.255.255
C	192.0.0.0 to 223.255.255.255
D	224.0.0.0 to 239.255.255.255
E	240.0.0.0 to 247.255.255.255

KEY LEARNING POINTS

- IP was originally designed to allow some networks to have few hosts (class C) and others to have millions (class A).
- Inspection of the first octet is sufficient to identify an IPv4 address class.
- Address classes A, B, and C allow systems with unique IP addresses to share networks and a broadcast address.
- Class D allows for a group of systems to share a group address.

Netmask (Subnet Mask)

It is critical for network administrators to be able to identify the network portion of an IP address and to differentiate that from the host portion of the address. The *netmask* is what makes such differentiation possible. Each class of IP address has a default netmask, which is sometimes referred to as the *subnet mask*. Essentially, the netmask identifies (masks) network bits, thus determining which bits in an address are network bits as opposed to host bits. Table 5.2 shows the default netmask values for the four address classes A, B, C, and D.

Table 5.2 *Default Netmasks for IP Address Classes A, B, C, and D*

CLASS	DECIMAL	HEXA-DECIMAL	BINARY
A	255.0.0.0	ff:00:00:00	11111111.00000000.00000000.00000000
B	255.255.0.0	ff:ff:00:00	11111111.11111111.00000000.00000000
C	255.255.255.0	ff:ff:ff:00	11111111.11111111.11111111.00000000
D	240.0.0.0	f0:00:00:00	11110000.00000000.00000000.00000000

We can express the netmask value in any number base. Decimal, hexadecimal, and binary are most commonly used, and their equivalent expressions of netmask values appear in Table 5.2.

Truth Tables, Binary Logic, and the Netmask Value

Before looking at the details of how the netmask functions, we need to be familiar with the logical AND, OR, and NOT operations. A *truth table*, which shows the organizational logic of an operation, can help us. The purpose of a truth table is to demonstrate binary logic in a visual format. We specifically focus on the AND, OR, and NOT binary logic operations as they are relevant to our subject.

In binary logic, there are only two possible values, namely 1 to represent TRUE and 0 to represent FALSE. Binary logic operations are easier to demonstrate using a truth table, where a value of 1 means TRUE and a value of 0 means FALSE. Here, we examine the AND operation, then OR and NOT. There are other logic operations that are not relevant to the context of this book and therefore will not be covered.

First we examine the logical AND. With logical AND, combinations of two bits are compared. Only a combination of two 1s can produce a result of TRUE. Any other combination of two bits produces a result of FALSE. So,

- FALSE and FALSE is FALSE
- FALSE and TRUE is FALSE
- TRUE and FALSE is FALSE
- TRUE and TRUE is TRUE

Figure 5-7 shows the binary logic of the AND operation graphically.

With this understanding of the logical AND operator, you can now appreciate the logic of the netmask:

- If the bit in the IP address has a value of 1 and the corresponding bit in the netmask also has a value of 1, then that IP address bit is a network bit (selected by mask).
- Bits that are neither masked nor selected by the mask are therefore host bits.

AND	0	1
0	FALSE (0)	FALSE (0)
1	FALSE (0)	TRUE (1)

Figure 5–7 *Logical AND operations*

Computing the Network Number Using the Netmask Rule

Let us demonstrate the significance of the netmask using an example of a network address. We will use example network 10.0.0.0 (a class A address) to illustrate how to compute a network number with the help of the netmask.

When calculating the network portion of an IP address, we compare bits in the IP address with the netmask. The bits in the same binary position of the netmask and the IP address are referred to as *corresponding bits*. That is, they represent the same binary value and are therefore both in the same binary column or position.

In the sample address 10.34.23.4 in Figure 5-8, the first octet's bit 8 and bit 2 both have a binary value of 1, which adds up to 10—hence the 10 in the first octet. In effect, the netmask bits 8 and 2 have masked bits 8 and 2 in the IP address, making them network bits. In this context, you can think of masking as similar to selecting.

Here are our example values from which we can compute the network number:

- IP address (decimal): 10.34.23.4
- IP address (binary): 00001010.00100010.00010111.00000100
- Class A netmask in decimal notation: 255.0.0.0
- Netmask, binary notation: 11111111.00000000.00000000.00000000

Figure 5-8 shows the result of using a logical AND for IP address 10.34.23.4 and the netmask 255.0.0.0. The corresponding bits that have a value of 1 in both the netmask and IP address 10.34.23.4 appear in

Applying the logical AND operator

IP address (decimal)	10	34	23	4
IP address (binary)	00001010.00100010.00010111.00000100			
Netmask (binary)	**11111111.00000000.00000000.00000000**			
Network (binary)	00001010.00000000.00000000.00000000			
Network (decimal)	10	0	0	0

Figure 5–8 *Calculating the network number using a netmask*

italic for easy reference. The corresponding bits that both have a value of 1 are network bits.

As you can see, the network number is 10.0.0.0, meaning that this host is number 34.23.4 on network 10.0.0.0. The host's complete IP address, then, is 10.34.23.4. We will elaborate further on the significance of the netmark in the sections of this chapter where we explore subnetting.

EXAM NOTES

KEY LEARNING POINTS

- The netmask identifies (masks) bits in an IP address as network bits.
- The netmask identifies the network.
- The netmask reveals host bits by not masking (selecting) them.
- The netmask has default values for classes A, B, C, and D.

The Broadcast Address

IPv4-based network traffic may be directed at three types of IP addresses:

- a single host (unicast address)
- a group of hosts (multicast address)
- all hosts on a logical network (broadcast address)

We have already discussed IP address classes; here, our concern is with broadcast addresses. We can calculate the broadcast address for any given IP address by using the netmask. Remember that the broadcast address is essentially the network bits plus all possible host bits with a value of 1.

Before examining how to calculate the broadcast, let us review the truth tables for logical OR and NOT, because the OR and NOT logical operations are integral to the process of calculating broadcast addresses. With logical OR operations, combinations of two bits are compared, and only two 0s produce a FALSE. Any other combination of two bits produces a TRUE. With logical NOT operations, on the other hand, bits are not compared as with AND and OR logic operations, but simply inverted or flipped. (To flip a bit, simply change 0 to 1 and 1 to 0.)

OR		
	0	1
0	FALSE (0)	TRUE (1)
1	TRUE (1)	TRUE (1)

Figure 5–9   *The logical OR truth table*

NOT	
	Result
0	TRUE (1)
1	FALSE (0)

Figure 5–10   *The logical NOT truth table*

Figure 5-9 shows the truth table for the logical OR operation, and Figure 5-10 shows the truth table for the logical NOT operation.

The results of the OR truth table are:

- FALSE and FALSE is FALSE
- FALSE and TRUE is TRUE
- TRUE and FALSE is TRUE
- TRUE and TRUE is TRUE

The results of the NOT truth table are:

- FALSE is TRUE
- TRUE is FALSE

To compute the broadcast address, perform the following steps. Please refer to Figure 5-11 to see the results of calculating each step using the class A address previously discussed as an example.

1. Perform a logical NOT operation on the bits in the netmask, which converts the zeroes to ones and the ones to zeroes. The netmask in binary was 11111111.00000000.00000000.00000000, but after the NOT operation, it becomes 00000000.11111111.11111111.11111111.
2. Convert the decimal network address to binary. Decimal 10.0.0.0 becomes binary 00001010.00000000.00000000.00000000.
3. Perform a logical OR of the binary netmask (which has now been NOT'd) and the binary network address bits. The result of the

Example IP address	10.34.23.4
Network	10.0.0.0.
Host portion	34.23.4
Netmask	255.0.0.0

Netmask (binary)	11111111.00000000.00000000.00000000
IPv4 network (binary)	00001010.00000000.00000000.00000000
NOT'd netmask	**00000000.11111111.11111111.11111111**
Result of OR operator	00001010.11111111.11111111.11111111

Figure 5–11 *Calculating the broadcast address from the netmask and network address*

OR operation, shown here in binary notation, becomes 00001010.11111111.11111111.11111111 and is the calculated broadcast address.

4. Simply convert to decimal notation to see the normal decimal representation of the broadcast address, 10.255.255.255.

Special-Case IP Addresses

In addition to each IP address having a particular broadcast address, there are additional special broadcast addresses as shown in Table 5.3. In this table, a value of 0 denotes a field that contains all bits with values of 0, and a value of 1 denotes a field that contains all bits with values of 1. *Net ID* represents the network portion of an IP address, *Host ID* represents the host portion of an IP address, and *Subnet ID* is the subnet identifier when we have subnetted an IP address (an explanation of the subnetting process appears later in this chapter).

Table 5.4 shows some sample addresses and sample explanations based on the information in Table 5.3. Addresses that are allowed to be source addresses only use a designation of (source). Addresses that are allowed to be destination addresses only use a designation of (destination). A star character (*) indicates that the address can be both a source and a destination address. The sections that follow explain some of the special broadcast address types.

Table 5.3 *Special IP and Broadcast Addresses*

| IP ADDRESS | | | CAN APPEAR AS | | |
NET ID	SUBNET ID	HOST ID	SOURCE?	DESTINATION?	DESCRIPTION
0		0	OK	Never	This host on this net
0		Hostid	OK	Never	Particular host on this net
127		0.0.1	OK	OK	Loopback address
1		1	Never	OK	Limited broadcast
Netid		1	Never	OK	Net-directed broadcast
Netid	Subnetid	1	Never	OK	Subnet-directed broadcast
Netid		1	Never	OK	All-subnets-directed broadcast

Table 5.4 *Sample Special IP and Broadcast Addresses*

ADDRESS	INTERPRETATION
0.0.0.0	Some unknown host (source)
255.255.255.255	Any host (destination)
129.156.1.5	Host number 1.5 in network 129.156 (*)
129.156.0.0	Network 129.156 (destination)
129.156.255.255	All hosts in network 129.156.0.0 (destination)
0.0.0.5	Host number 5 on *this network* (source)
127.0.0.1	This host (local host address) (*)

Special Broadcast Address Types

Special broadcast address types include the limited broadcast, the net-directed broadcast, the subnet-directed broadcast, and the all-subnets-directed broadcast.

THE LIMITED BROADCAST ADDRESS

The address 255.255.255.255 is known as the *limited broadcast address*. A limited broadcast address can be only a destination address, never a source address, and it should never be forwarded. It is typically used when a host that has no knowledge of its own network attempts to learn its own IP address and subnet mask.

THE NET-DIRECTED BROADCAST ADDRESS

A *net-directed broadcast address* like the one in Table 5.4 is the broadcast address used by a host that knows its own IP address and wishes to contact all hosts on its own logical network. On network 194.168.85.0 with a standard netmask, for example, address 194.168.85.255 is the net-directed broadcast, which, as we discussed previously in this chapter, is the network address plus all host bits set to 1.

THE SUBNET-DIRECTED BROADCAST ADDRESS

The *subnet-directed broadcast address* is in principle identical to the net-directed broadcast but requires knowledge of the netmask. This is because the IP address range has been subnetted, with the consequence that the broadcast address will be different on the subnets.

THE ALL-SUBNETS-DIRECTED BROADCAST ADDRESS

The *all-subnets-directed broadcast address* is one that includes all subnets in a subnetted scheme. If 129.156.1.0 to 129.156.255.0 were our range of subnets, the all-subnets-directed broadcast address would be 129.156.255.255 to include all subnets. Were the IP network address 129.156 not subnetted, the broadcast address 129.156.255.255 would be a net-directed broadcast address. It is the same as the broadcast address of the non-subnetted network but simply has a different name when used in the subnetted environment.

EXAM NOTES

KEY LEARNING POINTS

- The broadcast address applies to all systems on the logical network.
- The broadcast address includes all the network bits plus all host bits set to 1.

- The net-directed broadcast address is the highest address on the network.
- The subnet-directed broadcast address requires knowledge of the net-mask value.
- The all-subnets-directed broadcast address is the same as the broadcast address of the primary network but has a different name in the subnetted enrivonment.

5.2   Subnetting

Subnetting is a process that splits a single network address into multiple network addresses, thus making more efficient use of the primary network address. Before examining exactly how to subnet, you should appreciate why you might choose to subnet your IP network address.

Why Subnet?

Subnets are networks within networks. Subnetting offers several advantages, including:

- creation of multiple logical networks from a single network address
- traffic and protocol isolation
- increased security
- delegated subnet administration

Let us examine each of these advantages in detail.

Creating Multiple Logical Networks from a Single Network Address

Subnetting allows multiple networks to be created from a single network address. This is the primary reason for subnetting in most cases.

Traffic and Protocol Isolation

Selected network traffic can be restricted to its own subnet, which is an idea we now explore using Figure 5-12. If we put PCs using non-TCP/IP protocols on subnet 1, for example, router 1 would block the protocol from passing through it to subnets 2 and 3. In addition, broadcast traffic generated from within a subnet is blocked by the router from spreading to the other subnets. Routers usually do not allow broadcast traffic to pass through them.

Increased Security

Subnetting makes it possible to add extra layers of security. Each subnet is protected by a router. In addition, the router can be replaced by a firewall system acting as a router. This enables excellent protection for the hosts behind the router on a given subnet.

Delegated Subnet Administration

Subnetting also offers advantages in terms of sharing staff workload. Responsibility for a given subnet and its range of addresses can be delegated to specific departments. Departments within colleges and universities, for example, often manage their own subnet.

How Subnetting Works

In this section, we will explain the mechanics of subnetting using a sample class B network address of 129.156.0.0. As Figure 5-12 shows, we have three networks within this network address:

- 129.156.1.0
- 129.156.2.0
- 129.156.3.0

The original class B address of 129.156.0.0 has been used in all three subnetworks, but we are using the third octet of the address to identify a network within 129.156. The rest of this section explains how to achieve the subnetting shown in the figure.

Subnetting allows us to change the default use of bits within an IP address in terms of how many bits of an address are used to identify networks versus how many bits identify hosts. Subnetting includes the process of extending the netmask to designate additional network bits and, therefore, more networks. The disadvantage of subnetting is that the IP address now has three subcomponents, rendering it more complex to route. In addition, each subnet has fewer bits available for hosts when compared with the main network. This occurs because each subnetted

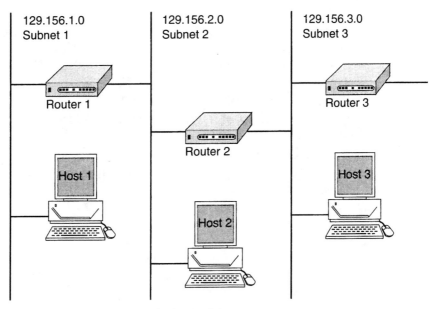

Figure 5–12   *Subnetted network 129.156.0.0*

IP address is composed of the main network, the subnet, and the host address all within a single IP address.

The three components of a subnetted address are

- network number
- subnet number
- host number

The default netmask for our example network is 255.255.0.0. This default netmask identifies the last two octets as hosts.

By default the netmasks for our example network are as follows:

- netmask (default) 255.255.0.0
- network 129.156.0.0

The default netmask for this network, 255.255.0.0, identifies the last two octets as hosts. We choose, however, to use the first three octets for networks and only the last octet for hosts, by changing the netmask on the systems in question to 255.255.255.0. Notice that the revised netmask now includes the the third octet in its entirety (255).

So, how many subnets can we achieve? The third octet consists of eight bits; therefore, we can obtain 2^8 (2 to the power of 8) subnets beneath network 129.156, or 255 subnets. The netmask now designates all the bits of the first, second, and third octets as network bits, giving us subnets in the range 129.156.1.0 to 129.156.255.0. This is because the third octet's minimum value is a binary 00000000 (decimal 0) and its maximum binary value is 11111111 (decimal 255).

Having created several subnets, let us next examine a valid address on one of them. We will use address 129.156.1.5 as our example, which is a valid IP address on subnet 129.156.1.0. Address 129.156.1.5 is a valid class B subnet host address.

To know how a subnet was specified, only the netmask and IP address need be known; the broadcast address can be calculated from the netmask and IP address. The following details show the parameters related to subnet 129.156.1.0, IP address 129.156.1.5, and the netmask that identifies this subnet:

- IP Address: 129.156.1.5
- Netmask: 255.255.255.0
- Network (subnet): 129.156.1.0
- Host portion: 0.0.0.5

Figure 5-13 shows how the netmask 255.255.255.0 masks or selects the bits in the first three octets of the IP address 129.156.1.5 that have a value of 1 and designates 129.156.1.0 as the subnet.

For this example, notice that the netmasked bits are selected because bit 1 is set to 1 in both the netmask of 255.255.255.0 and the address of 129.156.1.5. The masked bits (bits at one in both mask and IP

	Octet 1	Octet 2	Octet 3	Octet 4
	128 64 32 16 8 4 2 1	128 64 32 16 8 4 2 1	128 64 32 16 8 4 2 1	128 64 32 16 8 4 2 1
129.156.1.5	1 0 0 0 0 0 0 1	1 0 0 1 1 1 0 0	0 0 0 0 0 0 0 1	0 0 0 0 0 1 0 1
255.255.255.0	1 1 1 1 1 1 1 1	1 1 1 1 1 1 1 1	1 1 1 1 1 1 1 1	0 0 0 0 0 0 0 0
Masked	1 1	1 1 1 1	1	
Subnet	129	156	1	0
Host bits	0	0	0	5

Figure 5–13 *Example Class B subnet 129.156.1.0*

address) identify subnet 129.156.1.0. The bits with a value of 1 in the address 129.156.1.5 that are not selected by the netmask are therefore host bits. In Figure 5-13, only bits 1 and 4 of the fourth octet are not selected by the netmask. Add the 4 and the 1 together to identify a host value of 5. The IP address is 129.156.1.5, but the last octet, which has a value of 5, is the host-specific octet on subnet 129.156.1.0.

Subnetting on a Non-Byte Boundary

Let us examine the case of a class C address that we need to subnet because we want to create multiple logical networks from a single address. Using a netmask of 255.255.255.224, we are able to designate the three high-order bits of the fourth octet (128, 64, and 32, which when added together yield 224) as network bits. Table 5.5 shows the eight possible subnets available when we use the three high-order bits of the fourth octet.

As you can see, you can calculate the subnet addresses by working out all the possible values of bits 128, 64, and 32 in the fourth octet. The number of subnets is eight because 2^3 (2 to the power of 3) is eight. Table 5.5 shows what happens when we manipulate the 128, 64 and 32 bits in terms of subnet numbers. In this table, the high-order bits start at bit 128, and the low-order bits start at bit 1.

Table 5.5 *Subnet Numbers Possible Using Three High-Order Bits*

SUBNET NUMBER (FOURTH OCTET)	TOP THREE (HIGH-ORDER) BITS		
	128	64	32
0	0	0	0
32	0	0	1
64	0	1	0
96	0	1	1
128	1	0	0
160	1	0	1
192	1	1	0
224	1	1	1

In order to select the last three bits of the fourth octet, we need to use the following mask:

- 255.255.255.224: decimal notation
- ff:ff:ff:e0: hexadecimal notation
- 11111111.11111111.11111111.11100000: binary notation

Having chosen a netmask of 255.255.255.224 (decimal), we need to examine the subnets, host address ranges, and broadcast addresses of each subnet. Table 5.6 shows the subnet address, host address range within the subnet, and the broadcast address on each subnetwork. Notice that the broadcast address is the highest-numbered address on each subnet because it includes the subnet itself plus all possible host bits for that subnet with a value of 1.

Table 5.6 *Three Example Subnets*

SUBNET	HOST ADDRESS RANGE	BROADCAST ADDRESS ON SUBNET
194.168.85.0	194.168.85.1–30	194.168.85.31
194.168.85.32	194.168.85.33–62	194.168.85.63
194.168.85.64	194.168.85.65–94	194.168.85.95
194.168.85.96	194.168.85.97–126	194.168.85.127
194.168.85.128	194.168.85.129–158	194.168.85.159
194.168.85.160	194.168.85.161–190	194.168.85.191
194.168.85.192	194.168.85.193–222	194.168.85.223
194.168.85.224	194.168.85.225–254	194.168.85.255

Figure 5-14 shows a network using only three of the possible valid subnets for class C network address 194.168.85.0 when a netmask of 255.255.255.224 is applied.

Let us take as an example a host address on one of the class C subnets. We shall choose IP address 194.168.85.137. Looking at Figure 5-14, it is apparent that a host with a fourth octet value of 137 is a host on subnet 194.168.85.128, where the host addresses range from 129 to 158 with a broadcast address of 194.168.85.159. A host with a fourth octet of 137 is on subnet 194.168.85.128, which has a host address range of 194.168.85.129 to 194.168.85.158. The subnet itself is 194.168.85.128, which has a broadcast address of 194.168.85.159. Put simply, 137 falls between 128 and 159, the value range that determines the subnet to which it must belong.

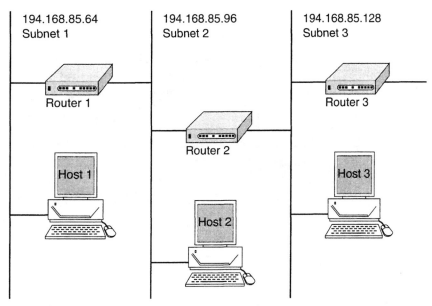

Figure 5–14   *Subnetted network with three subnets of 194.168.85.0*

One of our valid class C IP addresses in the sample network is 194.168.85.137. It includes the following addresses:

- IP address: 194.168.85.137
- netmask: 255.255.255.224
- network (subnet): 194.168.85.128

Figure 5-15 shows that IP address 194.168.85.137, when masked by 255.255.255.224, is on subnet 194.168.85.128 and that the host-specific bits are 0.0.0.9.

Given the netmask of 255.255.255.224, it is apparent that, because the value 255 appears in the first three octets of the mask, the first three octets of any IP address will be network bits and not hosts. The fourth octet has the non-standard mask and therefore demands a closer look. Notice in Figure 5-16 (which examines the fourth octet of the IP address, which is 137 and the fourth octet of the netmask, which is 224) that bit 128 is the only bit with a value of 1 in both the netmask and the IP address. Applying a logical AND operation as we discussed earlier in this chapter, we find that bit 128 is a network bit because both the mask's bit 128 and the IP address's bit 128 both have a value of 1. From this

	Octet 1								Octet 2								Octet 3								Octet 4							
	128	64	32	16	8	4	2	1	128	64	32	16	8	4	2	1	128	64	32	16	8	4	2	1	128	64	32	16	8	4	2	1
194.168.85.137	1	1	0	0	0	0	1	0	1	0	1	0	1	0	0	0	0	1	0	1	0	1	0	1	1	0	0	0	1	0	0	1
255.255.255.0	1	1	1	1	1	1	1	1	1	1	1	1	1	1	1	1	1	1	1	1	1	1	1	1	1	0	0	0	0	0	0	0
Masked	1	1					1		1		1		1					1		1		1		1	1							
Subnet				194								168								85								128				
Host bits				0								0								0								9				

Figure 5–15   *Example Class C subnet 194.168.85.137*

194.168.85.137			Octet 4					
Binary values	128	64	32	16	8	4	2	1
Octet of mask (224)	1	1	1	0	0	0	0	0
Fourth octet of IP (137)	1	0	0	0	1	0	0	1
Network bits	1	0	0	0	0	0	0	0

Figure 5–16   *The fourth octet for subnet 194.168.85.137*

information, we draw the conclusion that because bits 8 and 1 in the fourth octet of 137 are not masked by 224, they are host identifiers. Therefore, our subnet is 194.168.85.128 and our host is 0.0.0.9. Our host's IP address is 194.168.85.137, of course, but it is the 9 (8+1 bit) that is unique to it on its subnet of 194.168.85.128. Host 194.168.85.137 is therefore a valid host on subnet 194.168.85.128.

KEY LEARNING POINTS

- Subnets are logical networks within networks.
- Subnets are created by extending the default netmask by one or more bits so that it selects more network bits when it is compared with an IP address and performs its masking function.
- Subnetted IP network addresses use a nonstandard netmask.
- Extending the netmask changes IP's designation of the net and host bit division within a given class. More bits are available for networks when the netmask is extended, leaving fewer host bits per subnetwork.

5.3   The IPv4 Datagram Header and Datagram Fragmentation

The IPv4 datagram carries or encapsulates the data of upper-layer protocols, as you saw in Chapter 1. The maximum size of the datagram is 64 KB, although it usually needs to be fragmented, as shown in the next section. IP routes the datagrams across the Internet or network to the destination IP address found in the IPv4 header.

The IPv4 Header

To understand the datagram, we need to examine the IP header, a diagram of which appears in Figure 5-17. Table 5.7 shows the header in tabular format.

IPv4 Header Fields

We describe the fields of the header in the following sections. There is no need to remember the specific fields for the Sun certification exam, but you will be better prepared to answer some questions correctly if you have a good understanding of the header.

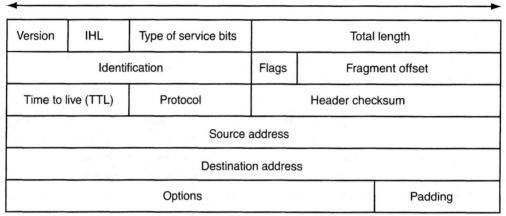

Figure 5–17   *The IPv4 header*

Table 5.7   *Breakdown of the IP Header*

FIELD	BITS	DESCRIPTION
Version	4	4
Header length	4	Length of header
Type of service	8	Service level
Length	16	Total length of IP datagram
Identification	16	Unique value assigned by sender for reassembly of fragments
Flags	3	For fragmentation control
Fragment offset	13	For fragment reassembly
Time to live	8	Time to live (hops)
Protocol	8	What higher level protocol is being encapsulated
Header checksum	16	Checksum
Source IP	32	Source IP
Dest IP	32	Destination IP
Options	Variable	Might not be present

VERSION

This field is 4 bits in size and contains the IP version number, which is currently 4.

HEADER LENGTH

The header length field indicates the length of the IP header itself. The minimum header size is 20 bytes, and the maximum header size is 60 bytes.

TYPE OF SERVICE

This field, which is 8 bits (1 byte) in length, describes the type of service (TOS) desired for the datagram. Valid properties of the IP service include

- minimize delay
- maximize throughput
- maximize reliability
- minimize monetary cost

LENGTH

This field is 16 bits (2 bytes) long and specifies the total length of the datagram in octets. Please note that this length includes the header.

IDENTIFICATION (ID)

The identification field occupies 16 bits (2 bytes) and contains an identifying value that the IPv4 protocol uses to associate fragments of a datagram. The combination of this identification value plus the protocol field makes the identity of a given datagram unique. We will examine IPv4 fragmentation shortly.

FLAGS

This field, 3 bits in length, specifies whether fragmentation is allowed and whether a given fragment is the last fragment or more fragments are to follow.

FRAGMENT OFFSET

This field, together with a portion of the flags field, specifies the numerical position of a datagram fragment relative to the beginning of the data carried by the original datagram. The fragment offset is always a multiple of 8 bytes, except for the last fragment, which might not be.

TTL

The TTL field indicates the maximum amount of time a datagram is permitted to remain in the Internet. (If there were no limiting mechanism, a datagram could get into a routing loop and circulate forever on the Internet.) Each gateway (router) that forwards the datagram decrements the value of this field by 1. The default value of TTL is 256.

PROTOCOL

The protocol field occupies 8 bits of the IP header and indicates which higher layer protocol IP is carrying. The field permits IP to pass its datagram up through the protocol stack to the correct upper layer protocol. You can find the valid protocol values for this field in the Solaris file /etc/inet/protocols.

HEADER CHECKSUM

The checksum is calculated and inserted into the IP header by the source (sender) of the datagram and is checked by the receiving (destination) host. If the checksum is in error (which will be detected by the destination host), the datagram has been corrupted and is discarded. Please note that the IP checksum covers only the IP header, not its data. The higher-layer protocols checksum their own headers and data, thus making it unnecessary for IP to perform this function. This means that the header checksum covers only the IP header itself.

SOURCE IP, DESTINATION IP

These two fields, 32 bits in length each, identify the source address and destination address, respectively, of the datagram. The destination address enables IP to route the datagram to the correct destination.

OPTIONS

This field can be of variable length and is not always present. It contains additional options, most of which are not used today and so will not be discussed further. Note that if an option (or more than one) is used, the options field is padded as necessary with bytes that have a value of 0.

Padding is sometimes required, as the IPv4 protocol demands that the IPv4 header end on a 32-bit boundary.

KEY LEARNING POINTS

- The datagram is IP's unit of data.
- The IP header has a minimum size of 20 bytes and a maximum size of 60 bytes.
- The maximum size of a single datagram is 64 KB (65,535 bytes).
- The IPv4 header must end on a 32-bit (4-byte) boundary.
- Datagrams are not acknowledged by the receiving IP layer.

Datagram Fragmentation

Fragmentation of datagrams occurs when the MTU of the Network Interface layer technology (refer to Chapter 3) cannot accommodate a complete datagram or fragment. As you have seen, the IP header contains fields that enable a datagram to be fragmented and then reassembled at the IP layer on the receiving end of the communication. The fields that accomplish defragmentation and reassembly are the flags and fragment offset fields.

Figure 5-18 shows a network in which router A connects an FDDI and an Ethernet LAN. Ethernet and FDDI have different MTUs:

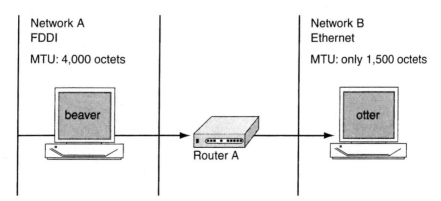

Figure 5–18 *Network forcing fragmentation to occur*

Ethernet has an MTU of 1,500 bytes, while FDDI has an MTU of 4,000 bytes. This means that FDDI can carry a larger sized datagram than Ethernet, as will be seen in the example to follow. Datagrams traveling from the FDDI network (beaver) therefore require fragmentation when they pass through router A on the way to the Ethernet network (otter) because the MTU of an Ethernet network is only 1,500 bytes; the IP datagram carried in the FDDI frame is too large to fit into the Ethernet frame's much smaller data field.

Be aware that the number of octets carried in a datagram is always a multiple of eight. The fragment offset field is therefore always a multiple of eight except for the last fragment, which can contain fewer than eight bytes.

The four-part Figure 5-19 shows a 4000-byte datagram both before fragmentation has occurred and as it is broken down into three fragments. Figure 5-19a shows the datagram as it is on the FDDI side of Figure 5-18, where FDDI's large MTU permits the datagram to travel unfragmented. Figures 5-19b, c, and d show how router A fragments the datagram for transmission across the Ethernet en route to otter.

Notice the Length field is 4000 octets. The data is 4000 octets and the 20-byte (20-octet) IP header makes a datagram of 4020 octets.

Our datagram on reaching router A, traveling from beaver on the FDDI net to otter on the Ethernet network, would be fragmented by the router as follows.

The single datagram would be fragmented into *three* fragments because it is too big to fit into a single Ethernet frame.

You should note the following significant facts about the breakdown of the datagram:

- The more frags (MF) bit is set in the first and second fragment, indicating that additional fragment(s) are to follow.
- The third fragment's MF bit is set to 0 because it is the last fragment.
- The fragment offset is measured from the beginning of the original datagram.
- The length of the header (L) is set to the length of the data plus its header.

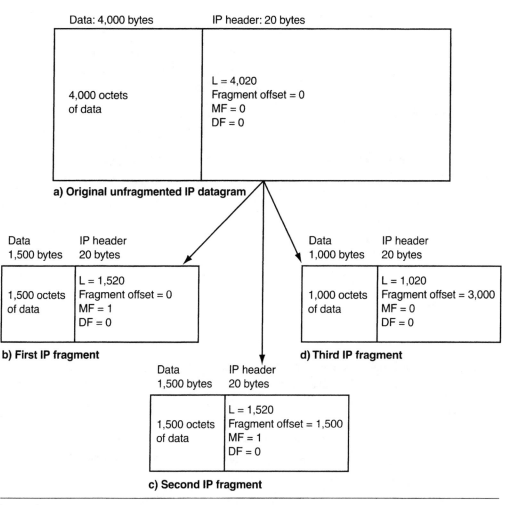

a) Original unfragmented IP datagram

b) First IP fragment

c) Second IP fragment

d) Third IP fragment

Legend:

L	Length of datagram (fragment plus IP header)
MF	More frags bit
DF	Don't fragment bit
Fragment offset	This value is used by IP to reassemble the fragments in the correct order as they arrive at the destination hosts. The fragment offset number indicates the position of the first byte of the fragment (and hence the entire fragment) in the overall datagram.

Figure 5–19   *A datagram before and after fragmentation*

- The length is always a multiple of eight (except for the last fragment). In our example, dividing 1520 by 8 yields 190.

Also be aware that datagrams are not usually reassembled en route; they are assembled at the end of their journey, at the destination host specified in the IP header. There are three good reasons why reassembly en route is not performed:

- We cannot guarantee that all datagrams will pass through the same router.
- If IP reassembled the datagram en route and then encountered a smaller MTU later on closer to the destination, it would have to fragment the data again.
- To reassemble data en route, it would be necessary to buffer all the packets, which would prove unnecessarily memory intensive and time consuming.

EXAM NOTES

KEY LEARNING POINTS

- Fragmentation is performed by an IP router if it receives a datagram to route which is larger than the MTU of its outboard interface permits. If necessary, a fragment may be fragmented several times as it passes through multiple routers.
- Datagrams are fragmented if the Network Interface layer demands it.
- A router encountering an IP datagram with the don't fragment (DF) bit set to 1 will discard the datagram if fragmentation is required.
- The fragmentation offset is always measured from the start of the original, unfragmented datagram.
- Datagrams are reassembled at the destination, not en route.

5.4   Classless Inter Domain Routing (CIDR)

Classless inter domain routing (CIDR), defined in 1992, came about primarily because of the exhaustion of available class B addresses, which in turn led to the allocation and subsequent heavy use of class C networks. The routing table explosion began about 1992, when Internet routing tables became too full owing to the continuing allocation of and use of class C network addresses. (A *routing table* is a memory-based structure that the IP protocol uses to determine how to route an IP datagram; Chapter 6 looks at routing in detail.) Companies that previously would have used a single class B network address were allocated multiple class Cs instead. This led to congested routing tables, a problem that CIDR was designed to solve.

The CIDR solution deals efficiently with the allocation of class C network addresses. The principle of CIDR is simply that multiple network addresses share a single entry in the routing table. The class C addresses to be allocated must, however, conform to certain features for this block allocation or *aggregation* to work:

- Network addresses must share the same high-order bits.
- Routing tables and algorithms must base their decisions on 32-bit IP addresses and 32-bit netmasks.
- Routing protocols must carry the 32-bit netmask in addition to the 32-bit address.

For example, the address range 194.0.0.0 to 195.255.255.255 represents 65,536 networks, all of which are allocated to European network providers by an organization called Repository for IP addresses in Europe (RIPE). (The American Registry for Internet Numbers [ARIN] handles the allocation of IP addresses in America, and Asia Pacific Network Information Center [APNIC] handles the allocation of IP addresses in Asia.) Every address in the range 194.0.0.0 to 195.255.255.255 shares the same high-order 7 bits: All 65,536 networks could be routed to the main European routers using the address 194.0.0.0 (0xC2000000) and a mask of 254.0.0.0 (0xFE000000). Once the IP traffic is routed to Europe, the other bits from the seven high-order bits allow for further routing that may take place.

RIPE has contiguous blocks of class C addresses that it can allocate to service providers and other such organizations. Once RIPE has allocated a contiguous block to a Local Internet Registry (LIR), a single routing table entry will enable all the LIR's IP traffic to be routed to its network. See the Web site http://www.ripe.net for more information.

We use the term *classless* when referring to CIDR, because networks that use the CIDR address schema no longer neatly fit into A, B, and C classes but instead use a 32-bit network address and a 32-bit mask expressed as in the following example:

```
194.168.64/18
```

This translates into a netmask address of 255.255.192.0.

KEY LEARNING POINTS

- CIDR enables a single routing table entry to route to multiple networks, thus reducing the size of routing tables.
- CIDR blocks are often based on geography.
- CIDR is intended mainly for class C addresses.

5.5   The Netmasks File

The Solaris file /etc/inet/netmasks stores the permanent network and netmask pairs, which are permanent in the sense that they are retained across a reboot. The contents of the /etc/inet/netmasks file is read by the **ifconfig** command, whose task is to plumb in interfaces at system boot time.

The **ifconfig** command is called by several shell scripts—initially by /etc/rcS.d/S30network.sh and later by /etc/rc2.d/S69initinet and /etc/rc2.d/S72inetsvc. **Ifconfig** configures the systems interface(s) at boot time by acquiring the correct IP address(es) and other interface parameters for each interface from the files /etc/inet/netmasks and /etc/inet/hosts.

Let us look at an example IP address and netmask to see how they are specified in the relevant files. Assume that we are looking at the netmasks file on host 129.156.1.1, which we examined previously in the context of the discussion on subnetting. Recall that the host with IP address 129.156.1.1 was on subnet 129.156.1.0 and had a netmask of 255.255.255.0. In the output samples that follow, the # symbol denotes a comment line.

The /etc/inet/netmasks file for host 129.156.1.1 on subnet 129.156.1.0 would contain

```
# field 1          field 2 in decimal
129.156.0.0        255.255.255.0
```

You can also express the netmask in hexadecimal if you prefix the netmask by `0x` as shown next.

```
# field 1          field 2 in hexadecimal
129.156.0.0        0xffffff00
```

Notice that the network address (field 1) is not the subnet the machine is actually on (129.156.1.0), but rather the original non-subnetted class B network address of 129.156.0.0. Field 2 is the netmask. The **ifconfig** command configures interface(s) at boot time using the values in the /etc/inet/netmasks file to apply the correct mask to each of the system's interfaces.

Note also that interfaces using a default netmask as described earlier in this chapter need not have their interfaces defined in the /etc/inet/ netmasks file, because IP as a protocol knows the default netmask values to apply to IP addresses in classes A through D.

EXAM NOTES

KEY LEARNING POINTS

- In Solaris 8, netmasks are stored in the /etc/inet/netmasks file.
- The **ifconfig** command reads /etc/inet/netmasks at boot time.
- The netmask can be entered in decimal or hexadecimal notation.

5.6   Variable Length Subnet Masks (VLSM)

Variable length subnet masks (VLSM) make possible the recursive division of the network address space, with the result that many layers of subnets within subnets can be created. With VLSMs, the routing tables at each layer are greatly reduced, and the address space is divided efficiently. Figure 5-20 shows an example VLSM scheme in which we have subnetted class A network number 10.0.0.0. Note that the subnet ranges shown are not complete; only the start of the range is shown as example subnets in the VLSM scheme. Network 10.1.0.0, for example, would have an address range of 10.1.0.0 to 10.255.0.0, as the whole of the second octet is available for subnets.

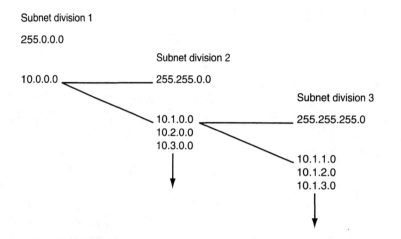

Figure 5–20 *Possible VLSM scheme for network 10.0.0.0*

At the uppermost layer (subnet division 1), a mask of 255.0.0.0 is applied. At subnet division 2, a mask of 255.255.0.0 is applied. And at the third division, a mask of 255.255.255.0 is applied.

There are two primary advantages of using VLSM to subnet a subnet:

- Multiple subnet layers make possible more efficient use of an IP network address.
- Multiple subnet layers permit better aggregation of routing information; routing information is more evenly spread across multiple routers.

You should be aware that only certain routing protocols, for example, Open Shortest Path First (OSPF), understand VLSM. OSPF is supplied with **gated**, a routing daemon that understands five routing protocols including OSPF. **Gated** is available through Cornell University, where it was developed (refer to the Web site http://www.cornell .edu. It is not bundled with Solaris 8.

EXAM NOTES

KEY LEARNING POINTS

- VLSM allows for the creation of subnets within subnets.
- VLSM makes efficient use of the IPv4 address space.

5.7 Configuring a Network Interface

Network interfaces on Solaris are configured primarily by the **ifconfig** command. Shell scripts call the **ifconfig** command during system boot. In this section we examine the use of the **ifconfig** command. Table 5.8 shows the Solaris shell scripts that call the **ifconfig** command and the run state in which they are called. The scripts call the **ifconfig** command, which configures the interfaces.

> Run states in Solaris relate to the number of processes running on the Solaris host. Run state 1 is known as a single-user run state in which few processes are running and only minimal networking is configured. It is in effect a maintenance state, in which the administrator (the single user) is able to log in at the system console and carry out maintenance operations. Run state 2 is a multiuser state in which most processes are running and the system is fully functioning. Networking is fully functioning, although NFS servers are not enabled until the system reaches run state 3.

Table 5.8 *Interface Configuration Scripts*

RUN STATE	SCRIPTS THAT RUN IFCONFIG
1	/etc/rcS.d/S30network.sh
2	/etc/rc2.d/S72inetsvc

Solaris interfaces are automatically configured at boot time by the **ifconfig** command, which is called by the shell script /etc/rcS.d/ S30network.sh. For each system interface that needs to be automatically configured at system boot, the administrator needs to create a file called /etc/hostname.*interface*, where *interface* is the name of the interface to be configured and plumbed in. For example, if the interfaces hme0, qfe0, and qfe1 exist and require autoconfiguring at boot time, we will have files called:

- /etc/hostname.hme0
- /etc/hostname.qfe0
- /etc/hostname.qfe1

In effect, each interface has its own configuration file.

For example, to have **ifconfig** automatically configure the interface qfe0 at boot time, create a file called /etc/hostname.qfe0. In this file, enter the name to be associated with the interface and ensure that the same name and an IP address are entered in the /etc/inet/hosts file. The /etc/inet/hosts file creates a mapping between a system's IPv4 address and its name, as shown in this example:

```
# cat /etc/hostname.hme0
wilde
```

```
# cat /etc/inet/hosts
127.0.0.1          localhost
194.168.85.51      voyager loghost
10.1.1.1           wilde  mailhost
```

When the interface qfe0 is automatically configured at boot time by **ifconfig**, the IP address for wilde (10.1.1.1) will be associated with the interface.

To view an interface's configuration, type **ifconfig** followed by the interface name, for example:

```
# ifconfig qfe0
```

Ifconfig responds with

```
qfe0: flags=1000843<UP,BROADCAST,RUNNING,MULTICAST,IPv4> mtu
1500 index 3
inet 10.1.1.1  netmask ff000000 broadcast 10.255.255.255
ether 8:0:20:ba:e1:c1
```

Table 5.9 shows the analysis of the output of **ifconfig**.

Types of Solaris 8 Interfaces

Solaris 8 features three types of interfaces:

- *Standard interfaces:* These are associated with a NIC card, for example, hme0, qfe0, qe0, le0.
- *Virtual interfaces:* Interfaces that are associated with a standard interface. We examine this type later in this chapter.
- *Loopback interfaces:* Packets addressed to this type of interface never enter the network but instead are internally *looped back* on the sending (source) machine. All Solaris systems have a loopback interface; the data addressed to the loopback interface is

never transmited onto the bus, so the fact that all loopback interfaces have the same IP address of 127.0.0.1 is not a problem.

Having now listed the three types of Solaris interface—standard, virtual, and loopback—we need to examine the **ifconfig** command and look at examples of configuring each interface type. Table 5.9 shows some of the parameters that the **ifconfig** command displays frequently, some of which are configurable.

Table 5.9 Ifconfig *Output Parameters*

PARAMETER	DESCRIPTION
mtu	Indicates the interface MTU (Maximum Transmission Unit)
flags	A numerical representation of the flags set
index	Indicates the number of the interface card. Each interface card has a unique index.
inet	The IP (inet family) address
netmask	The interface's current netmask value shown in hexadecimal (ff:ff:ff:00) or in decimal notation, 255.255.255.0
broadcast	The interface's current broadcast address
ether	The interfaces Ethernet (MAC) address
UP	Indicates that the interface is enabled
BROADCAST	Indicates that the interface supports broadcasts
RUNNING	Indicates that the kernel recognizes the interface
MULTICAST	Indicates that the interface supports multicasting
IPv4	Indicates that the interface is configured for IPv4 rather than IPv6

Configuring the Three Types of Solaris Interfaces

All three types of interfaces can have numerous parameters applied to them; refer to Table 5.10 and the examples that follow. Each example in Table 5.10 describes a *state* or current configuration of an interface, and the descriptive sample scenarios that follow show the commands needed to achieve the state and effect described.

Table 5.10 *Examples of Configuring Ethernet Interfaces*

EXAMPLE NUMBER	DESCRIPTION OF STATE	EFFECT
1	Plumbed in	The interface is now known to the kernel, but not enabled
2	Enabled (up)	The interface is now enabled in the kernel
3	Disabled (down)	The interface is disabled, but not yet removed
4	Unplumbed	Removed from the kernel/system
5	Using DHCP	Assign an address using DHCP
6	Add a virtual interface	Method 1: Add a second address to an interface
7	Add a virtual interface	Method 2: Add a second address to an interface

Example 1

In this scenario, we plumb in the interface, assign an IP address, apply a nonstandard netmask, and ask the system to calculate the broadcast based on the netmask value:

```
# ifconfig hme0 plumb 194.168.85.51 netmask 0xffffff00
broadcast +
```

We have now plumbed in the interface with the selected parameters. We can check that it has been correctly configured with the following command, which displays the current state of the interface:

```
# ifconfig hme0

hme0: flags=1000843<BROADCAST,RUNNING,MULTICAST,IPv4> mtu
1500 index 2
inet 194.168.85.51 netmask ffffff00 broadcast 194.168.85.255
ether 8:0:20:b1:ed:cf
```

Example 2

Here, we enable (bring up) the interface hme0:

```
# ifconfig hme0 up
```

We have now enabled (brought up) the interface called hme0. We can ensure that it has been correctly enabled with the following command, which displays the current state of the interface. Notice the UP in the list of <> enclosed parameters.

```
# ifconfig hme0

hme0: flags=1000843<UP,BROADCAST,RUNNING,MULTICAST,IPv4> mtu
1500 index 2
inet 194.168.85.51 netmask ffffff00 broadcast 194.168.85.255
ether 8:0:20:b1:ed:cf
```

The two operations shown in examples 1 and 2 can be combined in a single command as follows:

```
# ifconfig hme0 plumb 194.168.85.51 netmask 0xffffff00
broadcast + up

hme0: flags=1000843<UP,BROADCAST,RUNNING,MULTICAST,IPv4> mtu
1500 index 2
inet 194.168.85.51 netmask ffffff00 broadcast 194.168.85.255
ether 8:0:20:b1:ed:cf
```

Example 3

Here, we disable (take down) the interface hme0:

```
# ifconfig hme0 down
```

We can confirm that the interface is down by using the following command. Notice in the output that the word UP is missing from the angle bracket (<>) list. This means that the interface is disabled (down):

```
# ifconfig hme0

hme0: flags=1000842<BROADCAST,RUNNING,MULTICAST,IPv4> mtu
1500 index 2
inet 194.168.85.51 netmask ffffff00 broadcast 194.168.85.255
ether 8:0:20:b1:ed:cf
```

Example 4

In the example that follows, we *unplumb* the interface, thus removing it from the list of available interfaces.

```
# ifconfig hme0 unplumb
```

We can check the list of known interfaces:

```
# ifconfig hme0
```

```
hme0:  bad interface
```

This means that the interface is now unavailable.

Example 5

We can assign an IP address to an interface using the Dynamic Host Configuration Protocol (DHCP), providing a DHCP server is available. (Refer to Chapter 9 for more information about DHCP.) The address 194.168.85.88 in this example is assigned by the DHCP server.

```
# ifconfig hme0 dhcp
```

We can now confirm that the interface was DHCP configured by using the following command:

```
# ifconfig hme0
```

```
hme0: flags=1000843<BROADCAST,RUNNING,MULTICAST,IPv4,DHCP> mtu
1500 index 2
inet 194.168.85.88 netmask ffffff00 broadcast 194.168.85.255
ether 8:0:20:b1:ed:cf
```

Notice the DHCP in the angle bracket (<>) list. This means that the interface was indeed assigned an IP address by a DHCP server.

Example 6

A virtual interface simply means an interface that is not physical. Solaris enables us to add many IP addresses (up to 256 by default) to the same physical interface.

Following are two examples of when a virtual interface might be useful. The first scenario is simple. The second requires more thought and a good understanding of the rest of this chapter.

First we describe the two example scenarios and then look at the commands needed to plumb in and enable virtual interfaces. We see how to enable temporary virtual interfaces (lost on a reboot) and permanent virtual interfaces, which are retained across reboots.

VIRTUAL INTERFACE SCENARIO 1: WEB SERVER WITH VIRTUAL INTERFACES

Assume that a Web server needs to offer dedicated IP addresses to several Web sites, but that the server has only a single Ethernet NIC. By using virtual addresses, the Web server becomes able to offer each site a dedicated IP address. Figure 5-21 shows a Web server with multiple virtual *interfaces* on a single NIC.

VIRTUAL INTERFACE SCANARIO 2: TWO LOGICAL IP NETWORKS SHARING THE SAME PHYSICAL NETWORK

The following scenario is fairly involved, but it clearly demonstrates an excellent, if not obvious, use of virtual interfaces. It also forces you to consider in detail the significance of IP addresses in terms of being the source and destination address as found in IP headers. Refer to Figure 5-22.

In our scenario, several systems are sharing a single Ethernet LAN behind a Sun firewall that filters traffic to and from the two network address ranges sharing the LAN. These address ranges are:

- 194.168.85.0 (class C), an internal network
- 62.254.198.0 (class A subnet), also an internal network

The Sun Stealth Packet Filter (SPF) firewall is invisible and has interfaces with no IP address—hence its "stealthy" architecture.

The important point to observe about the Sun stealth firewall is that it is not a router, unlike some firewalls that function as packet-filtering routers. The Cisco router in Figure 5-22, therefore, is on the same logical network (194.168.85.0) as workstations B and C. The significance of this fact is that workstation B and workstation C can directly address packets to the Cisco router and use it as their default router for outbound packets.

hme0: Interface 194.168.85.50

Web server with multiple IP addresses
hme0:1 www.domainshop.co.uk   194.168.85.220
hme0:2 www.domainbank.co.uk   194.168.85.221

Figure 5–21 *Web server with virtual interfaces*

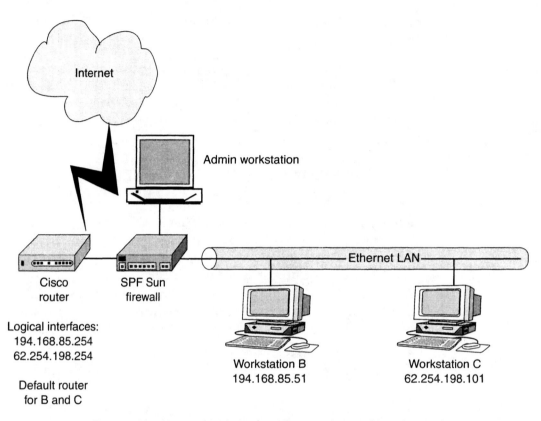

Logical interfaces:
194.168.85.254
62.254.198.254

Default router
for B and C

Figure 5–22   *A network with two firewall-protected internal logical networks*

The problem that we confront arises because there is no internal router. Workstations B and C cannot use the Cisco router to route packets to each other; the Sun firewall's anti-spoofing rules would block the traffic between the workstations.

What is spoofing? Imagine that a hacker has configured a system outside the firewall to use workstation B's IP address in the IP headers it generates. The act of using another system's IP address for hacking purposes is called *IP spoofing*. Say, for example, that workstation C trusts workstation B in terms of file sharing. If the hacker's system (outside the firewall) can fool workstation C into believing that the hacker's system is workstation B, it can share workstation C's files and break security. The biggest problem for the hacker is how to get the packets routed back to it successfully.

So, the Sun firewall's *anti-spoofing* rules would prevent workstation B from routing packets to workstation C through the Cisco router. This is because anti-spoofing rules on the firewall prevent an internal system from being the source of packets that enter the firewall on its external interface. Think back to earlier in this chapter, where we examined the IPv4 header. A packet from workstation B to workstation C using the Cisco as a default router would have source and destination addresses on the same logical network.

As you can see in Figure 5-22, the IP traffic as seen by the Cisco and the Sun firewall has a source and destination IP address that are both inside the firewall (internal). That seems innocent enough, but from the firewall's perspective, internal systems should route internally and should not need to be rerouted back in by the Cisco. Internal systems should never be the source of inbound packets traveling up the firewall's protocol stack when those inbound packets have entered the firewall through an external interface but originated from an internal address. Internal systems may be the recipients of inbound packets that have originated on an external network if the firewall permits traffic to pass through them.

Figure 5-23 shows that IP datagrams that originate from host 194.168.85.51 cannot travel out through the Sun SPF firewall to the Cisco router and then make a U-turn back through the SPF firewall on their journey to intended destination 62.254.198.101. The Sun SPF firewall would block the inbound packets because the source IP address (194.168.85.51) is not allowed to be the source of IP datagrams traveling inbound though the external interface. Hosts on networks 194.168.85.0 and 62.254.198.0 can be the source of IP datagrams as they travel out through the SPF firewall but can never be the source of inbound packets. Notice that the SPF firewall blocks the U-turning traffic.

Although the two hosts (workstations B and C) are in the same switch, they cannot reach each other over TCP/IP, as they do not share an interface on a common network. That is, although they are on the same physical network, they are not on the same logical network address. Workstation B is on network 194.168.85.0, while workstation C is on network 62.254.198.0. This is a real-world problem.

We can solve the routing issue by creating a virtual interface on workstation C or B, which in effect makes that system a router between the two logical networks, although through a single Ethernet interface. We will create virtual interface hme0:1.

The addition of hme0:1 on workstation C allows workstation B to route packets directly to C, as they now both have interfaces on logical network 194.168.85.0. Figure 5-24 shows that now B may route to C

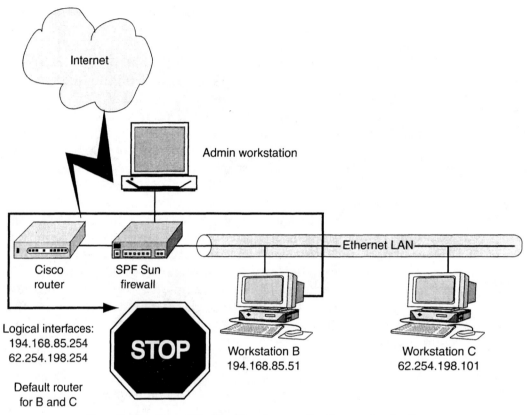

Figure 5–23   *Firewall blocking IP packets traveling from workstation B to workstation C through the Cisco and firewall*

through interface hme0:1 with address 194.168.85.51, and C may route to B, through virtual interface hme0:1 with address 194.168.85.200.

In summary, the creation of the virtual interface on workstation C (hme0:1) allows for communication between B and C because they both have interfaces on 194.168.85.0. That is, they now share a logical network.

As we described in example 6 of the virtual interface scenarios, virtual interfaces are useful because they permit the addition of multiple IP addresses to a single physical Ethernet interface. We can add virtual interfaces either as a temporary measure (in which case they are lost upon reboot) or permanently.

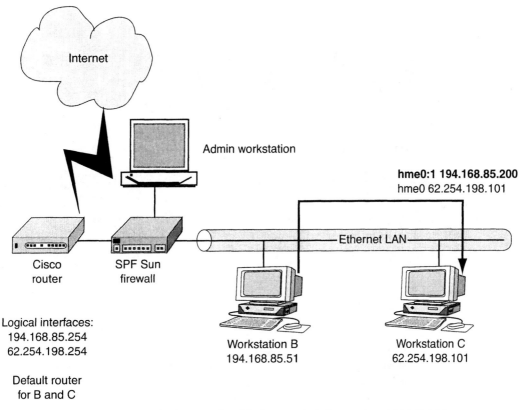

Figure 5–24   *Workstations C and B sharing a logical network on 194.168.85.0*

Plumbing in a Temporary Virtual Interface

A temporary virtual interface is one that is removed from memory during reboot. Following are the steps needed to add a temporary virtual interface. In our example, we add the virtual interface *194.168.85.200* as *hme0:1 to hme0*, the primary interface.

1. Plumb in the virtual interface:

   ```
   #  ifconfig hme0:1 plumb
   ```

2. Assign an address to the virtual interface, set the netmask and the broadcast address, turn off trailer encapsulation, and bring up the virtual interface:

   ```
   # ifconfig hme0:1 194.168.85.200 netmask 0xffffff00
   broadcast + -trailers up
   ```

3. To display the virtual interface, type:

```
# ifconfig hme0:1
hme0:1:
flags=1000863<UP,BROADCAST,NOTRAILERS,RUNNING,MULTICAST,IPv
4>mtu 1500
index 2    194.168.85.200 netmask ffffff00 broadcast
194.168.85.255
```

Creating a Permanent Virtual Interface

The problem with creating temporary virtual interfaces is that they are lost upon system reboot. We can make virtual interfaces permanent by creating configuration files that reestablish the virtual interfaces at boot time.

Following are the steps needed to ensure that a virtual interface is plumbed in during reboot. The virtual interface in our example is hme0:1 and the address is 194.168.85.200.

1. First, update the /etc/inet/hosts file with the chosen hostname and IP address of the virtual interface you are adding. Here we add virtual interface hme0:1, which has an IP address of 194.168.85.200 and hostname pluto-virtual:

```
#cat /etc/inet/hosts
127.0.0.1               localhost timehost
62.254.198.101          pluto     loghost
194.168.85.200          pluto-virtual
```

2. Solaris requires that each interface that is to be automatically plumbed in at boot time have a file called /etc/hostname.*interface*, where *interface* is the literal name of the interface. We are plumbing in virtual interface hme0:1, so the file we create must be called /etc/hostname.hme0:1. Using an editor, create the file /etc/hostname.hme0:1 and enter the name pluto-virtual in the file:

```
# cat /etc/hostname.hme0:1
pluto-virtual
```

The foregoing two steps will ensure that the interface is plumbed in during a reboot.

KEY LEARNING POINTS

- Three types of interfaces exist: physical, virtual, and loopback.
- Each physical hardware interface has a unique index number.
- A virtual interface is so called because it shares a network interface with another IP address.
- The loopback interface address, known as the localhost (address 127.0.0.1) is never seen on the LAN.
- Each interface has a /etc/hostname.interface file.
- The **ifconfig** command configures interfaces at boot time.
- Solaris supports 256 virtual interfaces by default. With **ndd**, we can increase this number to 8,192.

SUMMARY

In this chapter we examined IP address classes, observing how the IPv4 address scheme was designed for small and large networks. We also examined the significance of the netmask, which identifies network bits, leaving host bits to identify systems on the network.

Next, we explored subnetting, which allows a single network address to represent multiple networks, and the broadcast address, which allows all hosts on a given network to be the target of network traffic.

We then investigated the IPv4 header and discovered how IP datagrams can be fragmented and reassembled should the Network Interface layer demand it. The flexibility and robustness of the IPv4 protocol was further revealed through our examination of CIDR, which grew out of IPv4 address exhaustion, and VLSM, which stemmed from a desire to further subdivide the IPv4 address space into an even more hierarchical address space. The need to introduce these extensions to the original IPv4 reveals both the inflexibility and an inherent weakness of the protocol. This weakness was solved by IPv6, the next generation of IP, which we examine in Chapter 13.

Finally, we looked at the practical side of turning a Sun workstation into an IP router and at the files and commands involved in this process. We examined how to manipulate Solaris interfaces and create virtual interfaces, which are so useful when multiple IP addresses are needed on a single physical interface. IPv4 is a powerful protocol that is evolving to meet the changing needs of a demanding and rapidly growing Internet, with IPv6 the result (thus far) of the evolutionary process.

TEST YOURSELF

MULTIPLE CHOICE

1. *The first octet of a class B address has what possible range of values?*
   A. 128 to 191
   B. 0 to 127
   C. 192 to 223
   D. 224 to 239
   E. 1 to 100

2. *The first octet of a class A address has what possible range of values?*
   A. 128 to 191
   B. 0 to 127
   C. 192 to 223
   D. 224 to 239
   E. 1 to 100

3. *The first octet of a class C address has what possible range of values?*
   A. 128 to 191
   B. 0 to 127
   C. 192 to 223
   D. 224 to 239
   E. 1 to 100

4. *How many bits of a non-subnetted class A address identify hosts?*
   A. 20
   B. 192
   C. 16
   D. 14
   E. 24

5. *How many bits of a nonsubnetted class C address identify hosts?*

    A. 8

    B. 16

    C. 24

    D. 4

    E. 32

6. *What type of address is 194.168.85.255?*

    A. Netcast

    B. Unicast

    C. VLSM

    D. Broadcast

    E. Anycast

7. *When datagrams are fragmented, it is for what reason?*

    A. IP runs over TCP, which requires fragmentation.

    B. IP's MTU needs to be reduced for greater speed of transmission.

    C. UDP demands fragmentation of all IP packets.

    D. The MTU of the Network Interface layer demands fragmentation.

    E. Routers demand that IP packets be as small as possible.

8. *Which Solaris 8 file holds netmask values?*

    A. /etc/inetmasks

    B. /etc/inet/netmasks

    C. /etc/ipmasks

    D. /etc/ipnodes

    E. /etc/tcpnodes

9. *What type of interface is hme0:88?*

    A. Loopback

    B. Multicast

    C. Virtual

    D. Surreal

    E. Unicast

10. *From which file does **ifconfig** get an interface's IP address?*

    A. /etc/inetd.conf

B. /etc/services

C. /etc/hostname.hme0

D. /etc/inet/hosts

E. /etc/netmasks

FREE RESPONSE

1.   *Why are datagrams sometimes fragmented?*

2.   *If an IP datagram is fragmented, when are the fragments reassembled?*

FURTHER READING

Stevens, W. Richard. *TCP/IP Illustrated, Volume 1: The Protocols.* ISBN 0-201-63346-9. Reading, MA: Addison-Wesley, 1994.

Tannenbaum, Andrew S. *Computer Networks,* 2nd ed. ISBN 0-13-166836-6. Englewood Cliffs, NJ: Prentice Hall, 1988.

Routing over TCP/IP with Solaris 8

EXAM OBJECTIVES

6.1   IP Routing—An Introduction

6.2   Solaris 8 Routing Protocols and Daemons

6.3   Solaris 8 Router Configuration Files and Their Functions

6.4   Configuring a Solaris 8 System as a Router

6.5   Administering the Solaris 8 Routing Table Using the **route** and **netstat** Commands

After completing this chapter, you will be able to meet the following Network Administration Exam objectives:

- Identify the Solaris 8 daemons, which implement routing protocols.
- Identify the files used to configure routing.
- Specify the purpose of the files used to configure routing.
- Administer the routing table.

To help you meet these objectives, this chapter covers the following topics:

- the basics of IP routing
- Solaris 8 routing protocols and daemons and how to use them
- Solaris 8 router configuration files
- how to configure a Solaris 8 system as a router
- how to administer the Solaris 8 routing table

6.1   IP Routing—An Introduction

IP routing is the process of forwarding IP datagrams between networks. The *inbound* datagrams enter a system through an interface and are passed up the protocol stack to the Internet layer. At the Internet layer, the datagram is either passed further up the stack (if the datagram's destination address matches one of the addresses of the receiving host) or is passed down the stack (if the receiving host is configured as a router). The datagram then becomes *outbound* toward the destination address. If a nonrouter receives a datagram that is not addressed to it, it will refuse to route the datagram and will reject it.

The fundamental role of an IP router is to connect networks and facilitate the passage of IP datagrams between them. A router can be either a dedicated hardware device (such as those produced by Hewlett-Packard and Cisco, described in Chapter 2), or a Sun Solaris system configured as and acting as a router, also called a *router host* or *multihomed host*. Sun uses the term *multihomed host* to describe a system that connects to more multiple networks (or homes).

If routing fails, client and server applications using the transport protocols (TCP and UDP) will also fail. The transport protocols have no routing capability and therefore rely completely on the IP layer to perform the routing function.

The behavior of router hosts is quite different from that of non-router hosts, in that the former is prepared to forward IP packets for other hosts, whereas the latter will not forward or route any datagrams on behalf of other hosts.

Non-router Host Behavior

A *non-router host* is one that cannot forward packets on behalf of other systems and is capable only of sending its own datagrams. If it receives a datagram from another system and the datagram requires routing, the non-router host simply declines to forward it.

The routing process for a non-router host is simple. There are two possible cases, depending on the destination address of the datagram:

- If a host is sending an IP datagram to a system on the same logical network as itself, it simply encapsulates the IP datagram in a *link-*

level frame (a Network Interface layer frame, typically Ethernet) and transmits it, having set the destination link layer (MAC) and destination IP address to that of the directly accessible host.

- If the host is sending an IP datagram to a nonlocal system that is accessible only through a local router, it encapsulates the IP datagram in a link-level frame and transmits it, having set the destination IP address to that of the targeted host but the link-layer (MAC) address to that of the next-hop router. A non-routing host should never forward or attempt to route IP datagrams for other systems.

A non-router host accepts packets destined for its Ethernet address and sends them up the protocol stack. It accepts certain broadcast and multicast packets also, but it never forwards to another host any datagrams it receives.

RFC 1122 describes the expected behavior of a non-router host. This RFC is accessible on many official servers, including http://info.internet.isi.edu.

Router Host Behavior

A Solaris host configured as a router (*router-host*) accepts IP datagrams and attempts to route them based on the IP destination address in the IP datagram header. Its *routing table* enables it to make a routing decision. The Solaris routing table is a memory-based structure that contains routes or paths to destinations that are accessible through the routers specified in that table. Those routers act as gateways to the destinations. Later in this chapter, we examine the Solaris routing table and how it is propagated and maintained.

The routing mechanism involves receiving inbound datagrams and passing them up the protocol stack to the Internet layer (3), where the routing decision is made regarding the forwarding path (also called the *next hop*) for the datagram(s). Routing takes place at the Internet layer (3) of the stack. At this layer, if the destination address is examined and is found to be directly accessible (that is, on the same logical network as the router), the router acquires the link-layer (MAC) address that corresponds to the destination IP address, encapsulates the IP datagram in an Ethernet frame, and transmits it on the Ethernet bus. The host usually uses the ARP protocol that you learned about in Chapter 4 to acquire the Ethernet address of the destination. If, on the other hand, the IP header's destination address is not on a directly accessible network, the router host forwards it to the next-hop router based on information in its own routing table. The outbound datagram is sent in a frame whose destination link layer (MAC) address is that of the next-hop router.

RFC 1009 describes the behavior expected of a router host.

An administrator can prevent a Solaris router from forwarding IP datagrams by setting the *ip_forwarding* kernel parameter to 0 using the **ndd** command as follows:

```
# ndd -set /dev/ip ip_forwarding 0
```

A Routing Example

Figure 6-1 shows how IP datagrams pass up to the third layer of the protocol stack on the router (nexus in this case), where a routing decision is made. In the example shown in the figure, IP datagrams sent from satori to moon enter router nexus at interface hme0 (address 192.168.20.1) and are passed up the stack to the Internet layer (3). As a non-router host, satori decides to use nexus as its next-hop router, acquires nexus's Ethernet address using ARP (as seen in Chapter 4) and encapsulates its outbound IP datagrams in Ethernet frames destined for the MAC address of nexus.

The details of the routing and routing decision process in the example proceed as in the following steps.

1. The Ethernet frames are detected by nexus, which copies them off the bus and into interface hme0.
2. They travel up the stack on nexus.
3. At layer 3 of the stack, the IP datagrams are examined and found to be destined for host moon, whose address is not on the same logical network as nexus.
4. Examining its routing table, nexus calculates that moon is accessible through blade.
5. Nexus then encapsulates a datagram in an Ethernet frame targeted at blade's Ethernet address and sends it out through interface qfe0. The packet's direction is now outbound.
6. Blade's hme0 interface detects the Ethernet frame from nexus targeted at blade's Ethernet address. It copies the inbound Ethernet frame off the bus and up the stack to the Internet layer (layer 3), where blade will make an IP routing decision. Blade's routing table

indicates that moon, the destination of the datagram, is directly accessible through qfe0 on network 10.2.1.0.

7. Blade acquires moon's Ethernet address using ARP (if it does not have this address already) and encapsulates the datagram in an Ethernet frame. This frame will travel in an outbound direction onto network 10.2.1.0 through interface qfe0, whose IP address is 10.2.1.1.

8. Moon detects the frame through interface hme0 (IP address 10.2.1.2), and copies it off the Ethernet bus and up the stack. The datagram has now reached its final destination, which is 10.2.1.2.

To summarize, IP datagrams enter an interface and are passed up the protocol stack. At the Internet layer (3) of the stack, the datagram's header is examined. If the packets are addressed to one of the router's own IP addresses, the IP header is removed and the data is passed up the protocol stack to the upper layer protocol identified in the protocol field of the IP header (see Chapter 5).

The IP header contains a protocol number (as seen in Chapter 5) that indicates whether the data encapsulated in the IP datagrams is destined for protocol 6 (TCP), protocol 17 (UDP), or protocol 0 (ICMP). See the file /etc/protocols, which contains a full list of protocols and their associated numbers. If the IP datagrams do not contain any of the

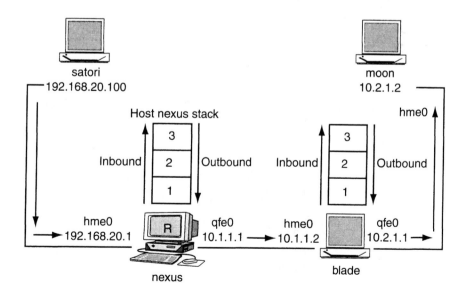

Figure 6–1   *Routing taking place at the Internet layer (3)*

routers' IP addresses, the routing table is consulted and the datagram is routed according to the routing table.

As you have already seen, expected behavior differs for a router and a non-router host. A router is expected to receive packets not necessarily addressed to one of its IP addresses, and to forward them on behalf of the source host.

EXAM NOTES

KEY LEARNING POINTS:

- Non-routers are not expected to forward datagrams for other hosts.
- Non-routers attempt to route only their own IP datagrams.
- Router hosts are expected to forward packets on behalf of other (external) hosts.
- You can turn off a router's ability to forward datagrams by using the **ndd** command to set the kernel parameter *ip_forwarding* to 0.
- At the Internet layer of the stack, the host's IP protocol makes a routing decision.

6.2   Solaris 8 Routing Protocols and Daemons

The IP routing mechanism is *table driven*, which means that routing information is held in a table in system memory. The table of routing information, called the *routing table*, can be added to either statically or dynamically. Figure 6-2 shows the protocols, files, and daemons that can update the routing table.

The routing table contains only three types of routes:

- A *host route* is a route whose destination is an individual host or IP address, not a network. Hosts usually have few routes of this type in their routing table; we will see shortly how these routes are added.
- A *network route* is one whose destination is a network and, therefore, a range of IP addresses. Such routes are common on Solaris and usually constitute most of the routes in the routing table.
- A *default route* is a route used when the routing table has no explicit host or network route to a destination to which it is trying to send datagrams. If a datagram is addressed (in the IP header) to an IP address that is not accessible through a host or

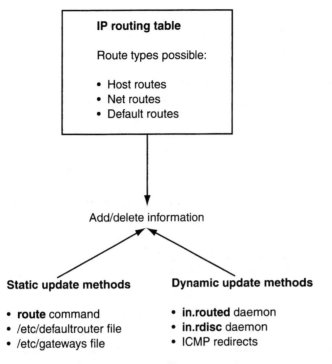

Figure 6–2 *Static and dynamic methods for updating the kernel's IP routing table*

network route that is in the routing table, the default route serves as a catch-all for all unlisted destinations.

These three types of routing table entry may be added to the routing table through files, commands, and dynamically by Solaris routing daemons. In this section we examine *dynamic routing*, which means that the routing table is updated automatically by Solaris daemons based on changes detected in the network environment.

Several of each type of route may exist in a host's routing table simultaneously. For each type of route, remember that the route in the table represents a destination to which IP datagrams may be directed and that the routing table lists the router (or gateway) that will act as a go-between to that destination. Entries in the routing table include both a destination and the router that leads to that destination.

For example, a host could be trying to send an IP datagram to host 192.20.20.1. A routing table entry might indicate that distant network 192.20.20.0 (which host 192.20.20.1 is on) is available by sending the datagrams through local router 194.168.85.254. The sending host (the source) is connected to network 194.168.85.0, the network to which our first-hop router is connected. Network 192.20.20.0 is *distant* because the datagrams we send will pass through many routers and networks before they reach the ultimate destination.

In this section we examine the two main Solaris routing daemons, namely **in.routed** and **in.rdisc.**

Two routing daemons, **in.routed** and **in.rdisc**, implement dynamic routing in Solaris 8. Table 6.1 shows the two Solaris routing daemons and the options that determine whether they run in client or server mode. The mode in which they run determines whether they actively advertise their routes to other hosts (server mode) or passively listen for advertisements from other routers (client mode). First we explore the Solaris **in.routed** daemon, which implements the Routing Information Protocol (RIP). We then examine the Router Discovery Protocol (RDP), as implemented by the Solaris daemon **in.rdisc.** We will discuss the files that start the routing daemons later in the chapter. Here, we examine the routing daemons themselves and the protocols they implement.

Table 6.1 *Solaris Routing Daemons*

ROUTING PROTOCOL	DAEMON NAME	CLIENT MODE	SERVER MODE
Routing Information Protocol (RIP)	**in.routed**	Option –q	Option –s
Router Discovery Protocol (RDP)	**in.rdisc**	Option –s	Option –r

The Routing Information Protocol (RIP)

Solaris offers two main routing daemons that implement two different routing protocols. The RIP protocol (the older of the two) is implemented by the **in.routed** daemon, and when running in server mode, it advertises routes to distant networks using broadcast addressing.

The RDP protocol is chronologically younger than RIP, and it uses a multicast address rather than a broadcast address. The RDP protocol advertises default routers, unlike RIP, which advertises routes to distant networks. This means that RDP communicates only with other hosts running **in.rdisc**, which share the same multicast addresses. Let us explore the two protocols, starting with RIP.

Systems configured to advertise their routing table using RIP run **in.routed** with the **–s** (server) option. These systems are RIP routers that propagate their routing table every 30 seconds. Clients of these systems or non-router hosts simply listen on UDP port 520 for the server's RIP advertisements. They never advertise and are said to be passive. Clients run **in.routed** with the **–q** (quiet) option.

RIP Features

Here is an overview of the general features of the RIP routing protocol:

- It is implemented on Solaris by the **in.routed** daemon.
- RIP version 1 has no understanding of subnetting.
- RIP version 2 understands subnetting and VLSM.
- It uses broadcasting to propagate the routing table.
- It uses UDP port 520.
- RIP routers advertise their routes every 30 seconds.
- RIP routers consider destinations that are more than 15 hops away as *unreachable* or *infinite*.
- The protocol uses UDP for speed and low overhead.
- It advertises routes to networks.
- It is an interior routing protocol, suitable for use by companies to maintain routes between routers within their own intranets.

The RIP Routing Process

Figure 6-3 shows how RIP propagates its routing information using a broadcast address. RIP servers run **in.routed –s** to broadcast their routes to immediate neighbors—those that are within reach of the broadcast traffic. RIP servers are said to be active because they broadcast their routing information. The RIP clients, on the other hand, run **in.routed –q** and simply listen for updates from the servers. They process traffic targeted at their broadcast address and pass any RIP packets they receive up to UDP port 520 where their in.routed is listening. They are said to be passive because they only listen for RIP traffic, but never advertise.

RIP routers use broadcasting to advertise their routes to their immediate or *same net* neighbors. The advertisement uses the local network broadcast address and so is audible only to systems on the router's local network(s). This is an important concept to remember.

Another important concept is *metric count*, also known as *hop count*, which is important to consider before we look at a concrete example of how a router might advertise its routes. RIP uses a *distance-vector algorithm*, which means that it calculates best routes based on how many

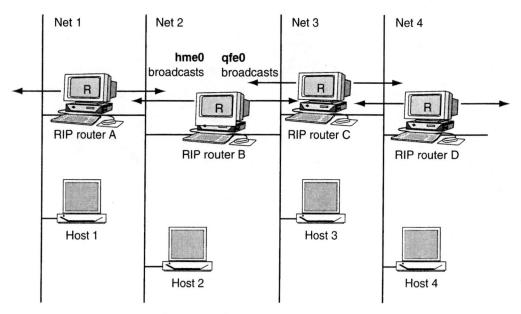

Figure 6–3 *How RIP advertisements are propagated*

routers (hops) an IP datagram would have to go through to reach its destination; one router equals one hop. It is important to realize that

- the hop to the network a system is connected to is 1 hop
- the hop count from a machine to itself is 0 hops

Table 6.2 contains several examples of hop count analysis.

Table 6.2 *Hop Count Analysis*

PATH	HOP COUNT (METRIC)
From router A to router B	1
From router A to router A	0
From router A to router C	2
From router A to host 1	1
From router A to host 2	1
From router A to host 3	2
From router A to host 4	3

Let us now look at a concrete example of how a router might broadcast routes. Table 6.3 shows an example RIP broadcast from router B in terms of the routes router B would advertise and on which network. Router B would know these routes because of its own plumbed-in interfaces; it has not learned these routes from another router. (Once router B has been running for awhile, it will learn additional routes from other routers, but for the moment we are not interested in learned routes.) As you can imagine, RIP routes take some time to filter or propagate through the network, because RIP routers advertise using a broadcast address that is heard only by their immediate neighbors. If two routers, for example, are separated by 10 networks, and the routers are advertising every 30 seconds, a route could theoretically take up to five minutes to propagate through all 10 networks.

Note

If a system receives a route to a destination that is greater than 15 hops away, it is classed as unreachable or infinite.

Table 6.3 *Router B Advertising Scope*

ROUTER B INITIAL ADVERTISEMENTS	ADVERTISED ON NET?	WHO WILL HEAR?	METRIC
A route to net 2 on net 3, through qfe0	Net 3	Router C and Host 3	1
A route to net 3 on net 2, through hme0	Net 2	Router A and Host 2	1

Stability Properties of RIP

The following features of RIP are considered stability features. RIP (currently in version 2) has been around since the early days of the Internet and so is a highly mature protocol.

HOP COUNT LIMIT

As stated previously, RIP as an interior routing protocol is limited in range and is therefore used primarily for inter-company routing. RIP's hop count limit helps prevent routing loops, which would unnecessarily burden network traffic. Protocols such as the Exterior Gateways Protocol (EGP) and the Border Gateway Protocol (BGP) are designed for greater distances and communication between the routers of different organizations.

SPLIT HORIZON

Let us use the network shown in Figure 6-3 as the basis of our next two RIP scenarios. In a hypothetical scenario involving three routers, Router A must route through Router B to reach Router C. When Router A advertises, then, it is pointless for A to inform B about C, as B is A's router to C and is presumed to be closer to the target. A knows of B's proximity to C because A's own routing table uses B to reach C. For that reason, A will not advertise to B its route to C through B. This feature is called *split horizon* because the router interface can "see" in two directions (two horizons) and treats each direction differently in terms of the advertisements it sends to each.

SPLIT HORIZON WITH POISONOUS REVERSE

In this variation, rather than A not advertising to B that it can see C through B, Router A advertises the route as unreachable with a metric of 16 (infinite), thus ensuring that Router B and other systems beyond B never use A's path to C when B clearly has the shortest path. This feature is called *split horizon with poisonous reverse* because Router A "poisons" the route through itself by discouraging Router B from using it.

COUNTDOWN TO INFINITY

Countdown to infinity process occurs as the outcome of a routing loop and broken links, whereby the metric to one or more destinations increases with every advertisement until infinity (16 hops) becomes the metric for the route. At that point, the destination is considered an unreachable, infinite route and is marked for deletion from the routing table.

TRIGGERED UPDATES

Triggered updates occur when is it necessary to quickly propagate routing table changes throughout the network. Usually routing advertisements take place every 30 seconds. A wait of 30 seconds after certain events occur, however, is considered too long. An important event can trigger immediate routing table propagation. For example, the timeout of a router table entry, which occurs if a route is considered to have become unavailable or bad, triggers an immediate update or advertisement.

HOLD-DOWN STATE

The term *hold-down state* describes a router's ability to hold back from reintroducing a bad route to its routing table. In practice, it plays out as follows. A router learns through a triggered update that a route has gone bad, so it marks the route as *infinite* in its routing table. Shortly afterward, it receives an update indicating that the same route is now good. Given this conflicting information, it holds back the reinstatement of the bad route until it has more update information, allowing it to make a more informed decision. Essentially, it waits for more news of the route, which will enable it to adjust its routing tables more accurately. Over a period of minutes, the routing tables should stabilize and reach a state called *convergency*, which describes a condition in which all routers are in agreement about which routes are good and bad. Remember that a RIP router's definition of convergency is based on knowledge of routes and routers that are within 15 hops of it; beyond 15 hops, everything is considered infinite and unreachable.

The Router Discovery Protocol (RDP)

The Router Discovery Protocol (RDP) is implemented on Solaris 8 by the **in.rdisc** daemon. RDP uses a multicast address (not a broadcast address like RIP) and primarily advertises routes to systems that are configured as *default routers*—routers (and their associated routing table entries) that a host can use when a destination that the host is attempting to reach is not explicitly contained in the routing table. Routes discovered by **in.rdisc** are added dynamically to the routing table as default routes. Solaris 8 allows for multiple default routers and spreads the load equally across all defined default routers. A *default route* in the routing table does not lead to a specific destination but is rather used for all destinations for which an explicit entry does not exist.

Note the following characteristics of the RDP routing protocol:

- RDP's **in.rdisc** daemon uses multicast network address 224.0.0.0.
- **In.rdisc** clients and routers use multicast group addresses.
- Clients use 224.0.01, which specifies all hosts on the current network.
- Routers use 224.0.0.2, which specifies all routers on the current network.
- **In.rdisc** clients run **in.rdisc –s**.
- **In.rdisc** routers (servers) run `in.rdisc -r`.

- The protocol uses ICMP for the sake of speed and low overhead.
- Servers advertise themselves as available default routers.
- RDP does not advertise routes to other networks as RIP does, but rather routes to available default routers.

Table 6.4 shows how **in.rdisc** functions on Solaris 8. As you can see, the client solicits for a router on multicast address 224.0.0.2, where the server listens. The server advertises on 224.0.0.1, where the client listens. Essentially, **in.rdisc** uses two multicast addresses for better communication between client and router. The use of multicast addresses means that only those listening on the multicast address will hear the advertisements.

Note

Hosts will add a default router to their routing tables only if the router (discovered through RDP) is on the same network as the host. That is, when hosts receive an advertisement on multicast address 224.0.0.1 and learn of potential routers, they add only those with whom they share a network. More than one default router can be added in this fashion.

Table 6.4 *Multicast Addresses Used by RDP*

TYPE OF RDP SYSTEM	LISTEN ON	ADVERTISE OR SOLICIT ON
Client **in.rdisc –s**	224.0.0.1	224.0.0.2
Server (router) **in.rdisc –r**	224.0.0.2	224.0.0.1

In the course of our discussion of broadcast addresses in Chapter 5, we observed that the problem with using the broadcast address is that all systems listening on the IP broadcast address receive the packet. Figure 6-4 shows that Ethernet frames are examined by the interface card, and if the Ethernet address belongs to the card or is a broadcast Ethernet address, the frame is copied off the bus. Otherwise, it is ignored. If the Ethernet frame checksum (CRC) is incorrect, the frame is immediately discarded. If the frame looks correct, it is passed up the stack to the Ethernet driver. Next, the Ethernet driver examines the frame, and if it identifies a supported, upper layer protocol (such as IP, ARP, or RARP), it will be passed up to that protocol; otherwise, it is discarded. Most packets are addressed to IP, of course. At the IP layer, if the datagram identifies a supported upper layer protocol, such as TCP, UDP, or ICMP, the transport header and data are again passed up to the stack; otherwise, it is discarded. (We concern ourselves only with UDP because TCP never uses a broadcast

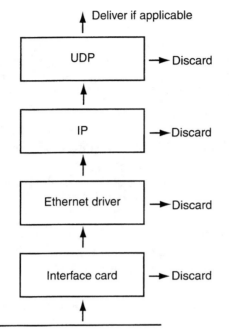

Figure 6–4 *Filtering upward through the protocol stack when a frame is received*

address to deliver data.). Finally, at the Transport layer, if the application identified in the port field of the UDP protocol header is not actually running, the datagram is discarded. If the application is running on the host, the data is passed up to the process. **In.routed** is one example of a process that uses UDP and broadcast addressing.

The load on the host can become considerable, as you might imagine. The solution to this potential load problem is to use multicasting. Let us examine how multicasting differs from broadcasting and the benefits it offers.

Building the MAC Address for a Multicast Group

Multicasting uses class D addresses (examined in Chapter 5) and allows us to address a group of hosts. A total of 28 bits of the class D address range is used to identify multicast groups. A *host group* is identified as a set of hosts listening to a particular multicast address, such as 224.0.0.1. Certain IP multicast addresses are reserved by the Internet Assigned Number Authority (IANA), the organization that coordinates the assignment of Internet numbers across the world; these reserved addresses are known as *permanent host groups.*

For example, address 224.0.0.1 identifies such a permanent group and specifies all hosts on this subnet, whereas the address 224.0.0.2 identifies all routers on this subnet. But how does Solaris 8 map these multicast addresses, which are used by **in.rdisc**, onto an Ethernet address?

IANA, as an organization, owns Ethernet block 00:00:5e. This is comprised of the high-order 24 bits of the Ethernet address, meaning that this block includes addresses in the range 00:00:5e:00:00:00 through 00:00:5e:ff:ff:ff. IANA allocates 50 percent of this block specifically to multicasting. An additional IANA rule states that the first byte of any Ethernet address used for multicasting must be set at 01. That is, 00:00:5e becomes 01:00:5e. The entire IANA block allocated to multicasting, then, actually ranges from 01:00:5e:00:00:00 to 01:00:5e:7f:ff:ff. This is a considerable range of addresses.

IANA provides guidelines to use when forming pseudo-Ethernet addresses from multicast addresses. All multicast addresses (class D addresses, as you saw in chapter 5) have the top four high-order bits set to 1110.

In addition, the next five bits of the multicast group ID are not used when forming the pseudo-MAC address used by the multicast group. That means that of the 32 bits potentially available, 9 bits (bits 0 through 8 in the figure) are not used when calculating a pseudo Ethernet address. This leaves 23 bits that are actually used in the calculation. To form the Ethernet address to be used for **in.rdisc**, we take the low-order 23 bits of 224.0.0.1 (bits 9 to 31), which is 0.0.1 (00:00:01 in hexadecimal notation), and, given that IANA dictates that all pseudo-Ethernet addresses used as multicasts must begin with 01:00:5e, we form the Ethernet address 01:00:5e:00:00:01. Address 01:00:5e:00:00:01 is the pseudo-Ethernet address that is associated with 224.0.0.1, which is the address used by **in.rdisc**.

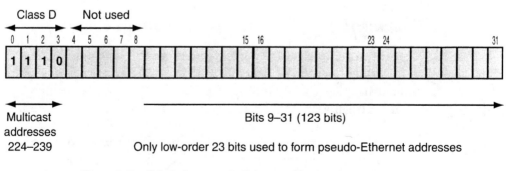

Multicast
addresses
224–239

Bits 9–31 (123 bits)

Only low-order 23 bits used to form pseudo-Ethernet addresses

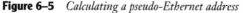

Figure 6–5   *Calculating a pseudo-Ethernet address*

Figure 6-5 shows the bits used in calculating the pseudo-Ethernet address.

KEY LEARNING POINTS

- Solaris has two main IPv4 routing daemons: **in.rdisc** and **in.routed**.
- These two daemons implement dynamic routing.
- The **in.routed** daemon implements the RIP routing protocol.
- The RIP protocol is broadcast-based and advertises to its immediate neighbors.
- **In.rdisc** implements the Router Discovery Protocol (RDP).
- RDP is multicast-based and advertises to a multicast host group.
- RIP advertises routes to distant networks.
- RDP advertises routers that hosts add to their routing tables as default routers. Hosts select from the RDP advertisements default routers that are directly reachable and therefore on their own network.
- RDP (**in.rdisc**) uses multicast addresses and pseudo-MAC addresses.
- Solaris supports a client having multiple default routers.
- Solaris maps multicast addresses on pseudo-Ethernet addresses.

6.3 Solaris 8 Router Configuration Files and Their Functions

As we have stated earlier, there are essentially three types of routes found in the Solaris routing table:

- *Host-specific routes* are always checked first by IP when it is attempting to deliver IP datagrams. That is, if the destination address in the IP header matches a host in the destination field of the routing table, the packet is sent to the IP address defined as the gateway to that host, which is usually (although not always) the host itself. As you might imagine, including host-specific routes to all possible target hosts would be difficult and is rarely done.
- *Network-specific routes* work as follows. Assume that we wish to route to all machines on a given class C network, which, as we saw in Chapter 5, would be 254 possible hosts. We could either

add 254 individual entries in the routing table (one host-specific entry for each host we need to route to) or simply add one routing table entry to the network where the 254 hosts are located. The latter strategy is obviously preferable. When IP attempts to send an IP datagram, in the absence of a host-specific route, it then checks for the next best thing, which is a network-specific route. That is, IP calculates the network portion of the IP address it is trying to route to by applying the netmask (the default mask for the class if a specific mask is unknown), and then checks for a routing table entry that matches the network the destination host is on. The end result is that if we send the IP datagram to the network the final destination IP is on, it will reach the host. So for all 254 hosts, we need only a single routing table entry. Network-specific routes are in common use because each one leads to all machines on the given network.

- *Default routes*, as explained previously, are used if the intended IP destination matches neither a host-specific nor a network-specific route. A default route and associated router are used for all routing destinations that are not explicitly included in the routing table as host- or network-specific routes.

All three types may be added to a routing table statically or dynamically. In this section we explore the Solaris configuration files that configure both dynamic and static routing. Keep in mind that most datagrams are aimed at a specific IP, which is the destination address in the IP datagram header. A small percentage of IP datagrams is aimed at a broadcast or multicast address and therefore either at a group of hosts (multicast) or at all hosts on the network (broadcast), but most are aimed at a specific IP address.

Static routing revolves around the act of manually adding routes, using UNIX commands or configuration files that hold routing information, which are read at boot time. The following files are used to configure routing on Solaris:

- /etc/defaultrouter
- /etc/gateways

Let us examine these files in greater detail using Figure 6-6 as a reference.

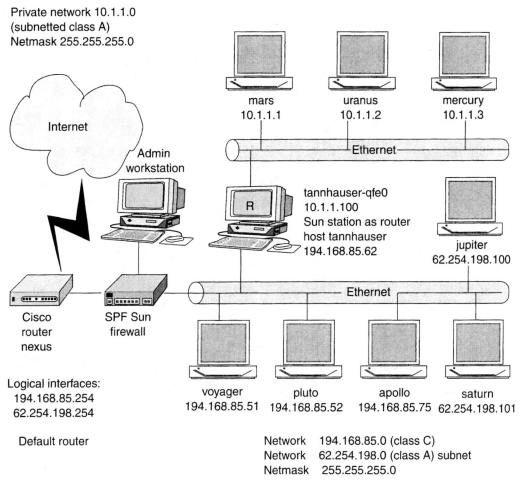

Private network 10.1.1.0
(subnetted class A)
Netmask 255.255.255.0

Internet

Admin
workstation

mars
10.1.1.1

uranus
10.1.1.2

mercury
10.1.1.3

Ethernet

tannhauser-qfe0
10.1.1.100
Sun station as router
host tannhauser
194.168.85.62

R

jupiter
62.254.198.100

Ethernet

Cisco
router
nexus

SPF Sun
firewall

Logical interfaces:
194.168.85.254
62.254.198.254

Default router

voyager
194.168.85.51

pluto
194.168.85.52

apollo
194.168.85.75

saturn
62.254.198.101

Network   194.168.85.0 (class C)
Network   62.254.198.0 (class A) subnet
Netmask   255.255.255.0

Figure 6–6 *Basic example network*

Adding Default Routes through the /etc/defaultrouter File

A default router is the preferred router for destinations for which there
is no explicit route in the routing table. You can use the /etc/
defaultrouter file (as its name suggests) to add one or more default routers to the routing table at boot time. At the same time, this file disables
dynamic routing and prevents the routing daemons we have just discussed from starting up.

The content of the /etc/defaultrouter file is simply the IP address or resolvable name of the default router. Host mars in Figure 6-6 would use 10.1.1.100 (tannhauser) as its default router because tannhauser will allow mars to see the Internet through Cisco router nexus.

To set up mars to use tannhauser as its default router, first use the command **uname –n** to identify the current host:

```
# uname -n

mars
```

The output just shown reveals that mars is the current host. Next, examine the content of the file /etc/defaultrouter to reveal the default router used by mars:

```
# cat /etc/defaultrouter

tannhauser-qfe0
```

We see from the output that tannhauser –qfe0 is the default router used by host mars.

You may determine whether tannhauser is in the /etc/inet/hosts file by searching for lines containing the word *tannhauser*, using the UNIX **grep** command to display the appropriate lines. If you add a system name rather than just an IP address to the /etc/defaultrouter file, be sure to add the name to the /etc/inet/hosts file as well:

```
# grep tannhauser /etc/inet/hosts

194.168.85.62 tannhauser       #is a Solaris 8 router
10.1.1.100        tannhauser-qfe0  #interface on net 10.0.0.0
```

The output shows that tannhauser has two addresses and is, in fact, a router.

If you need to add multiple default routers, which is allowed, add one per line to the /etc/defaultrouter file. Solaris 8 will round-robin between the alternative default routers.

The default router(s) you choose need to be available as direct routes and on the same subnet. Using the network in Figure 6-6 as our example, host mars should use tannhauser-qfe0 (10.1.1.100) as its default router because it is the only available router on subnetted network 10.1.1.0. Cisco router nexus is not available to mars because it is not directly reachable.

The existence of an /etc/defaultrouter file automatically prevents Solaris from running the in.routed and in.rdisc daemons at boot time.

Direct and Indirect Routing

Direct routing occurs when a host sends traffic to hosts on its own logical network. If traffic needs to be directed through a router to reach the destination, such a route is said to be *indirect*.

In the network depicted in Figure 6-6, for example, the route from mars to mercury is a direct route, whereas the route from mars to nexus is indirect. Traffic traveling in the mars-to-nexus direction would need to pass through tannhauser in order to reach nexus and other Internet destinations.

Put another way, an indirect route is reachable only through a router, whereas a direct route does not require a router. Table 6.5 shows some example routes and identifies them as direct or indirect based on their relationship to Figure 6-6.

Table 6.5 *Examples of Direct and Indirect Routes*

SOURCE OF IP DATAGRAM	DESTINATION	ROUTE TYPE	NEXT HOP FROM SOURCE	IP ADDRESS OF NEXT HOP
mars 10.1.1.1	nexus	indirect	tannhauser-qfe0	10.1.1.100
apollo 194.168.85.75	nexus	direct	nexus	194.168.85.254
jupiter 62.254.198.100	mercury	indirect	tannhauser	194.168.85.62

Be aware that the Sun Stealthy Packet Filter (SPF) firewall is invisible because its Ethernet interfaces have no IP addresses. By extension, then, it cannot be a router. Routers must by definition be visible and accessible at their IP address by the hosts that use them.

When routing to systems on its own logical network, a host performs an ARP broadcast to acquire the MAC address of the destination, as you saw in Chapter 4. When using a router to send datagrams, it is the router's Ethernet address we need to acquire, as the router is the next hop.

Working with the /etc/gateways File

You can use the /etc/gateways file for several purposes, including adding static routes and controlling RIP behavior. In this section we will explore some examples of these uses.

Using /etc/gateways is another way of adding static routes at system boot. You have seen previously how to use the /etc/defaultrouter file to add one or more static routes of the default type. With the help of this same file, you can add routes of type net and default and, in addition, control whether RIP traffic is allowed through the interfaces. The syntax of the file is as follows:

```
[net | host ] value gateway value metric value
[passive|active]
```

Example 1: Adding a Network Route to the Routing Table on Host Voyager

In the following example, we examine the contents of the /etc/gateways file on host voyager when adding certain routes. Voyager's /etc/ defaultrouter file currently points to nexus. We use /etc/gateways to add additional static routes to subnet 10.1.1.0 through router tannhauser and to control the direction of RIP packets through interfaces.

In this first example, we add a static route of type net to subnet 10.1.1.0 through router tannhauser, using the /etc/gateways file. The new static route will be added to the file at boot time. We use the **cat** command to show the contents of the /etc/gateways file.

```
# cat /etc/gateways

net 10.1.1.0 gateway 194.168.85.62 metric 1 passive
```

The foregoing output communicates the following:
- It adds a network-specific route to the routing table.
- The network 10.1.1.0 is accessible via router 194.168.85.62.
- The router is 1 hop away.
- The router does not advertise the route and is therefore passive.
- The route is a passive one and so will not be dropped from the routing table, if gateway 194.168.85.62 (tannhauser) fails to advertise it.

Example 2: Adding a Default Route to the Routing Table Using the /etc/gateways File

In the next example, we use the UNIX **cat** command to examine the file /etc/gateways. The command reveals a line of code that adds a default route (the `0.0.0.0` designates the route type as default) to the routing table when the system boots. The IP address of the new default router is 194.168.85.254.

```
# cat /etc/gateways

net 0.0.0.0 gateway 194.168.85.254 metric 1 active
```

The foregoing snippet communicates the following:

- It adds a default route; `net 0.0.0.0` means default router.
- The default router (gateway) is 194.168.85.254.
- The router is 1 hop away.
- The router should advertise, meaning that it is active.
- The route should be dropped from the routing table if it fails to advertise itself for approximately 180 seconds (six times the normal scheduled RIP advertisement period).

We can use the /etc/gateways file not only to add routes but also to control the direction of RIP packets through a Solaris interface, as we will show in the examples yet to come.

Example 3: Preventing RIP from Entering or Leaving an Interface

The examples given thus far show how you may use the /etc/gateways file to add static routes to the routing table. Keep in mind that the /etc/gateways file is read by the **in.routed** daemon (which implements RIP) when the system boots.

You can also use the /etc/gateways file to issue further instructions to the **in.routed** daemon regarding which interfaces the RIP protocol will be permitted to pass through. You can configure the /etc/gateways file to control the direction of RIP packets, as is shown in the following examples. The syntax is:

```
norip      <interface>
noripin    <interface>
noripout   <interface>
```

The following line in /etc/gateways tells the current host to prevent RIP packets from entering interface hme0. We display the desired line from /etc/gateways by using the **cat** command:

```
# cat /etc/gateways

noripin hme0
```

The next example line in the /etc/gateways file prevents RIP from either entering or leaving the hme0 interface. The effect of this line is to block RIP completely from the hme0:

```
# cat /etc/gateways

norip hme0
```

Now that you have seen examples of how to use the /etc/defaultrouter and /etc/gateways files to add static routes to the Solaris routing table and control the behavior of RIP, it is time to examine the steps that are needed to configure a Sun system running Solaris 8 as a router.

EXAM NOTES

KEY LEARNING POINTS

- Routes are said to be direct or indirect.
- Direct means reachable without a router (this net).
- Indirect means the route is only reachable through a router.
- /etc/gateways allows for the adding of additional static routes.
- /etc/gateways may be used to add network and default routes.
- 0.0.0.0 in /etc/gateways means default.
- /etc/gateways may be used to filter RIP traffic on interfaces.

6.4   Configuring a Solaris 8 System as a Router

In this section, we again make use of the example network in Figure 6-6 to explain the steps necessary to make a Solaris system act as a router. Specifically, we review the steps necessary to create router tannhauser, which has addresses 194.168.85.62 on interface hme0 and 10.1.1.100 on interface qfe0. It is a router that connects subnet 10.1.1.0 to subnet 194.168.85.0. (Refer back to Chapter 5 to learn more about subnets.)

In the following steps, we configure a Solaris host (tannhauser) as a router that connects two networks. This process involves extending the host's connectivity by adding and configuring a second interface (qfe0) on tannhauser, assigning the new interface the correct name and IP address, and editing the appropriate files so that the changes and interface parameters are stored in files and retained across reboots.

Assume that at this point in time, we have shut down tannhauser and physically plugged in the new quad Ethernet card qfe. Our first step in the process of configuring tannhauser as a router is to boot tannhauser with the –**r** option. This forces Solaris to build the device names for the new interface. Let us get started:

1. Shut down Solaris with no grace (-g0) to run level 0 (-i0) and instruct it to answer its own questions with a yes (-y):

   ```
   # shutdown -i0 -g0 -y
   ```

2. Once the system is shut down, open the case and add the new interface card.

3. When the card is added, boot the system using the –**r** (reconfigure) option. At the OpenBoot prompt, type the following command to ensure that Solaris builds the device name for the new Ethernet card. This is important because if the card has no device name, later steps will fail, and the card will be reported as having a bad address:

   ```
   ok  boot -r
   ```

4. Your next step is to create an entry for tannhauser-qfe0 in the /etc/inet/hosts file on tannhauser. Log in as `root` and create an entry in the /etc/inet/hosts file for the name `tannhauser-qfe0`, the name assigned to the new interface. Be sure to leave the entry for hme0, the existing interface, in the /etc/inet/hosts file:

   ```
   # grep -i  tannhauser /etc/inet/hosts
   194.168.85.62  tannhauser       loghost
   10.1.1.100     tannhauser-qfe0  #new interface
   ```

   The second interface name of this host in our example actually contains the string `qfe0`. In a real-world situation, you can call the interface whatever you choose, providing the name is available.

   ```
   # cat /etc/hostname.hme0
   tannhauser
   ```

Note

To configure Solaris to plumb in and assign the correct address to `qfe0` at boot time, you must create a file name called /etc/hostname.qfe0 that contains the name tannhauser-qfe0. Leave the existing interface name that was created at the time of initial system installation. (The initial interface on tannhauser in this case was hme0 and will be stored in the file /etc/hostname.hme0, which will contain the name tannhauser.)

5. The /etc/hostname.qfe0 file must contain the name we are assigning to the interface (qfe0). The existence of this file causes the **ifconfig** command to configure the interface at boot time. Use the following simple redirected **echo** command to create the one-line file:

```
# echo tannhauser-qfe0 > /etc/hostname.qfe0
```

6. Having created the file, check its content by using the **cat** command, which displays the file's content:

```
# cat /etc/hostname.qfe0
tannhauser-qfe0
```

7. Add the network 10.0.0.0 and netmask 255.255.255.0 to the file /etc/inet/netmasks, which is read by **ifconfig** at system boot. Edit the file using a text editor such as **vi** and add the following lines, or, if your netmasks file already has content, add the following lines to the bottom of the file:

```
# cat /etc/inet/netmasks
10.0.0.0          255.255.255.0
```

8. Now use the **reboot** command. The new interface (qfe0) should be automatically plumbed in and configured. Proceed to step 9. Alternatively, you could test the file's syntax without rebooting by inputting the following code, which will plumb in the new interface. Note that you must use the back quote syntax (`` `cat /etc/hostname.qfe0` ``) to test the name correctly.

```
# ifconfig qfe0 plumb `cat /etc/hostname.qfe0' netmask
255.255.255.0 broadcast + up
```

9. Now check the new interface using the **ifconfig** command. The **ifconfig** command should automatically add a routing table entry for the new interface when it is plumbed in, either during a system reboot or if **ifconfig** is used to plumb the interface in manually (as in the alternative to step 8).

```
# ifconfig qfe0
qfe0:
flags=1000843<UP,BROADCAST,RUNNING,MULTICAST,IPv4> mtu
1500 index 4
inet 10.1.1.100 netmask ffffff00 broadcast 10.1.1.255
ether 8:0:20:7b:33:a4
```

10. Run **netstat –r** to ensure that **ifconfig** actually added the routing table entry. Use the **grep** command to filter out unwanted lines, as you are only interested in the route associated with the 10.1.1.100 interface.:

```
# netstat -rn    |   grep 10.1.1.100

Destination Gateway      Flags Ref Use  Interface
----------- ----------   ----- --- ---  ---------
10.1.1.0    10.1.1.100   U     1   10   qfe0
```

11. Make tannhauser forward IP packets by setting the *ip_forwarding* variable to 1 (a value of 0 tells the system not to forward IP packets):

```
# ndd -set /dev/ip ip_forwarding 1
#  ndd /dev/ip ip_forwarding
1
```

If you have rebooted tannhauser, the *ip_forwarding* variable will be automatically set to a value of 1 because tannhauser now has more than one physical interface. In addition, you may create an empty file called /etc/notrouter, which has the effect of turning off IP packet forwarding (*ip_forwarding* is set to 0), even on systems with multiple physical interfaces.

12. This last step is optional if you wish to enable dynamic routing on tannhauser. Restart **in.routed** and **in.rdisc** in router mode as we described earlier in this chapter. Because tannhauser now has more than one physical interface, the routing daemons will automatically start on a reboot unless the existence of a /dev/defaultrouter prevents them from starting.

Configuring the router is now complete. The remainder of this chapter illustrates how to administer the routing table.

6.5   Administering the Solaris 8 Routing Table Using the route and netstat Commands

So far in this chapter, we have examined several aspects of the Solaris routing process. You have learned about the two routing daemons, **in.routed** and **in.rdisc**, which add and delete routes dynamically. You have also seen how to use files such as /etc/gateways and /etc/defaultrouter to add additional routes.

But there is a third way to add and delete host, network, and default routes, namely by using the **route** command. The workings of this command is the subject we will explore now.

Adding and Deleting Routes Using the route Command

You can add and delete static routes with the **route** command either by manually adding and deleting them on the UNIX command line or by automating the task in a shell script. In the examples that follow, we once again reference the example network shown in Figure 6-6. We also use the command-line headers with each example to identify each component of the **route** command.

Example 1: Adding a Network-Specific Route on mars

In this example, we add a network-specific route on host mars, enabling it to route packets to 194.168.85.0 through local router tannhauser-qfe0 (10.1.1.100):

```
Command   Action  Type   Destination    Gateway       Metric
# route    add     net    194.168.85.0   10.1.1.100    1
```

These instructions tell mars

- to add a route of type network
- that the destination network is 194.168.85.0
- that it is using router (gateway) address 10.1.1.100
- that the gateway is 1 hop away (metric)

Example 2: Adding a Network-Specific Route on pluto

In the next example, we are adding a network-specific route on host pluto, enabling it to route packets to subnet 10.1.1.0 through local router tannhauser (194.168.85.62). We specifically include a netmask for the routing table entry because 10.1.1.0 is a subnet and uses a nondefault mask.

```
Command Action Type Destination  Gateway       Netmask value
Metric
# route add     net  10.1.1.0     194.168.85.62 –netmask 255.255.255.0 1
```

These instructions tell pluto

- to add a route of type network
- that the route has a destination address of 10.1.1.0
- that the router (gateway) address is 194.168.85.62
- that the router netmask is 255.255.255.0
- that the gateway is 1 hop away

Alternatively, you can add the same route using the following command and expressing the route mask as follows:

```
Command    Action  Type Destination  Gateway       Metric
#   route  add     net  10.1.1.0/24  194.168.85.62  1
```

These instructions tell pluto

- to add a route of type network
- that the destination network is 10.1.1.0
- that the router (gateway) is 194.168.85.62
- that the route netmask is 255.255.255.0

The foregoing entry expresses the 24-bit mask 255.255.255.0 as /24. These characters must be placed immediately after the destination as shown.

Example 3: Adding a Default Route on voyager

In the next example, we add a default type route on voyager:

```
Command Action  Type     Gateway        Metric
# route add     default  194.168.85.254  1
```

These instructions tell voyager

- to add a route of type default
- that the router (gateway) is nexus at 194.168.85.254

Notice that the destination column is not needed when you add a default router. This is because the default router is not for a specific destination, but rather is used for all destinations for which there is not a specific router available, according to routing table information.

Example 4: Deleting the Network-Specific Route Added in Example 1

In addition to adding routes to the routing table with the **route** command as you saw in the previous examples, you may delete them. In the following example, we use the **route** command on host mars to delete the routing table entry to network 194.168.85.0, which is accessible through gateway 10.1.1.100:

```
Command  Action  Type  Destination  Gateway
# route  delete  net   194.168.85.0 10.1.1.100
```

The foregoing **route** command instructions tell mars

- to delete a route of type network
- to delete the route to destination network address 194.168.85.0
- that the router (gateway) is 10.1.1.100

Notice that the metric (hop count) is not needed when you are deleting a route.

Example 5: Deleting the Network-Specific Route Added in Example 2

In the following example, we use the **route** command on host pluto to delete the routing table entry to subnet 10.1.1.0, which is accessible through gateway 194.168.85.62. The destination network we are deleting is a subnet of class A address 10.0.0.0—specifically, subnet 10.1.1.0, which requires that we specify the correct subnet netmask (see Chapter 5). The network address 10.1.1.0 uses 24 bits (the first three octets). We must therefore delete the route using a 24-bit netmask, as shown in the command that follows:

```
Command Action  Destination Gateway       Netmask
# route delete net  10.1.1.0    194.168.85.62  -netmask
255.255.255.0
```

These instructions tell pluto

- to delete a route of type network
- that the destination network is 10.1.1.0
- that the router (gateway) address is 194.168.85.62
- that the netmask for the route was 255.255.255.0

Failing to specify the route-specific netmask will lead to the error message `route not in table`. Notice that the hop count is not needed when you are deleting a route.

Example 6: Deleting the Default Route on voyager Added in Example 3

In the next example, we use the **route** command on host voyager to delete the routing table entry to default gateway 194.168.85.254:

```
Command Action    Type         Gateway
# route delete    default      194.168.85.254
```

These instructions tell voyager
- that it is deleting a route of type default
- that the router (gateway) address is 194.168.85.254

Notice that the hop count is not needed when you are deleting a route. Also notice that no specific destination is not given when deleting a default router, because (as you saw in Example 3) when adding a default router, you do not enter a specific destination.

Continuously Monitoring Routing Information Using the route Command

The route command is also useful for network administrators who wish to debug and monitor live routing changes on the network as they occur. You use the **monitor** parameter of the **route** command as in the following example to continuously monitor and report any changes to the routing information base, such as routing lookup *misses* (a miss is an unsuccessful search for a route) or suspected network partitioning:

```
# route monitor

got message of size 124RTM_ADD: Add Route: len 124, pid:
29153, seq 1, errno 0, flags:<UP,GATEWAY,DONE,STATIC>locks:
inits:sockaddrs: <DST,GATEWAY,NETMASK>
10.1.1.0 tannhauser gateway 255.255.255.0
```

To summarize, **route monitor** has detected an inbound router advertisement packet of size 124 bytes, which, when added to the routing table, creates an entry of length 124 bytes. The packet is of type RMT_ADD (add route), which means that it contains one or more routes that may safely be added to the current host's routing table. The PID (UNIX process id) of the listening **route monitor** process is 29153, and the packet is the first in a possible sequence, It contains no detectable errors. We are instructed to add a route of type static to a gateway that is available (UP, STATIC GATEWAY,DONE), as indicated by the flags.

The <DST, GATEWAY, NETMASK> string indicates that we should add a destination (DST) to 10.1.1.0 through gateway (GATEWAY) tannhauser, using the nonstandard netmask (NETMASK) of 255.255.255.0. Gateway tannhauser has offered a route to destination subnet 10.1.1.0, which we may add to the routing table. Address 10.1.1.0 is a subnet with netmask 255.255.255.0.

Getting Routing Information and Displaying on Standard Output

In this next example, we use **route get** to acquire the route to mars from voyager, the current host. The **route get** command lets us determine what the current host's routing table believes are routes to 10.1.1.1 (host mars). The flags indicate that the gateway is available (UP) and that the route is of type static. You can **get** only those routes that exist in the routing table.

```
# route get 10.1.1.1
route to: mars
destination: 10.1.1.0
mask: 255.255.255.0
gateway: tannhauser
interface: hme0
flags: <UP,GATEWAY,DONE,STATIC>
```

The gist of these instructions is that the current host voyager should send packets to mars through gateway tannhauser. We can confirm that this is correct and in the routing table on voyager by using the **netstat** command:

```
# netstat -rn | grep 10.1.1.0
10.1.1.0    194.168.85.62           UG        1        1
```

As you can see, tannhauser is in fact designated as the router to subnet 10.1.1.0 according to the routing table on voyager.

Viewing the Routing Table with netstat

The **netstat** command enables the administrator to examine the IP routing table on Solaris systems. In the following examples, the **netstat** command is run on a host called *hercules*. When we look at IPv6 in Chapter 13, we will also explore IPv6-specific routing table entries. For now, we are only examining IPv4 routing.

The command **uname** checks that the current host is actually hercules:

```
# uname -n
hercules
# netstat -r
Destination    Gateway                Flags Ref   Use
Interface
-----------    -------------------    ----- ---   ------    ----
194.168.85.0   hercules.gvon.co.uk U     5     57416995 hme0
10.1.1.0       tannhauser             UG    9     6382
default        nexus                  UG    0     276765
224.0.0.0      hercules.gvon.co.uk U     5     0         hme0
localhost      localhost              UH    0     3830782  lo0
```

Let us examine this output one line at a time, showing the column headings in each example for easy reference. Please note as we look at these examples that *gateway* means router; Sun uses the word "gateway" for historical reasons.

Line 1

```
Destination    Gateway                Flags Ref   Use
Interface
194.168.85.0 hercules.gvon.co.uk U     5     7416995 hme0
```

The interface hme0 connects hercules to its local Ethernet. Hercules is the gateway to the destination 194.168.85.0, the class C network to which hercules is directly connected. We know it is directly connected because we know that we are on system hercules.

If we were not actually on hercules, a capital G would appear in the flags column because hercules would be the gateway to network 194.168.85.0, and from our perspective, hercules would be a remote router. Conversely, when the **netstat –r** command is run on a host that is the gateway to a given destination, a G is not shown for that route in the routing table.

From the output we also see that the route is up, as identified by the U flag. This route is an example of a network-specific route.

Line 2

```
Destination Gateway       Flags  Ref   Use   Interface
10.1.1.0    tannhauser    UG     9     6382
```

The interface is not shown in this line because this route uses gateway tannhauser, as indicated by the G flag. This flag emphasizes that the gateway for the route is not the host on which the **netstat –r** command is running, but rather a different host. We are running the command on hercules, but tannhauser is the gateway for this particular routing table entry. That is, to reach destination 10.1.1.0 a router must be used, namely tannhauser. The U flag indicates that the route is available.

Line 3

```
Destination   Gateway   Flags  Ref        Use      Interface
default       nexus     UG     0          276765
```

Line 3 shows that this is the default route for all IP destinations for which we do not have specific routing table entries. The default router itself is nexus. Again, remember that the G flag indicates that nexus is not the host we are running the **netstat –r** command on. A default router is important, but it is used only when host- or network-specific routes do not exist in the routing table for the destination to which the host is attempting to route packets. Most systems are configured to use one or more default routers, but have network-specific routes for directly connected networks, which Solaris automatically adds to the routing table as interfaces are enabled (brought up), plus static routes to specific internal networks. In addition, Solaris automatically adds a host-specific route to localhost through IP address 127.0.0.1.

Line 4

```
Destination Gateway               Flags  Ref  Use
Interface
224.0.0.0   hercules.gvon.co.uk    U      5    0       hme0
```

Line 4 shows us that the destination is multicast network 224.0.0.0. The host the **netstat –r** command is run on will always identify itself as the router to this particular destination, as long as multicasting is supported by the host's primary interface, in this case hme0.

Line 5

```
Destination    Gateway      Flags  Ref  Use      Interface
localhost      localhost     U      H   03830755  lo0
```

This line is a *host specific* entry, hence the H flag. That is, the destination to this particular destination, namely localhost, is a host rather than a network. Notice that the interface is lo0, the loopback interface.

Using netstat –rn

The **netstat** command can be run as **netstat –rn**. The use of this switch prevents *address-to-name translation*, the process of translating IP addresses to names:

```
# netstat -rn

Destination    Gateway      Flags  Ref  Use       Interface
-----------    -------------  -----  ---  ----      --------
--
194.168.85.0   194.168.85.60  U      5    57416995  hme0
10.1.1.0       10.1.1.100     UG     9    6382
Default        194.168.85.254 UG     0    276765
224.0.0.0      194.168.85.60  U      5    0         hme0
127.0.0.1      127.0.0.1      UH          03830782  lo0
```

The output from the **netstat** command, when using the –r option, contains a flags field. Several flags were seen in the previous examples, which we summarize in Table 6.6.

Table 6.6 netstat *Flag Summary*

FLAG	DESCRIPTION
H	Indicates that the destination is a host.
U	Route is available (up).
G	The destination in the destination column is reachable through the gateway (router) in the Gateway column.
D	The route was added by ICMP.
M	The route was modified by ICMP.

Additional in.routed Options

Having examined the RIP protocol, which is implemented by the Solaris **in.routed** daemon, we need to examine other capabilities of this daemon. We have seen that the command **netstat** is able to display the routing table, to which the daemon adds. Before leaving **in.routed** behind, as we continue our sojourn through Solaris routing, it is worth examining a few other features of this flexible program.

The **in.routed** command, which also starts the daemon of the same name, has several useful *trace and debug options*. Trace and debug options are used to produce output that is usually not displayed, although it is related to the detailed functioning of the protocol or command. Tracing implies the act of observing to learn more about how a protocol functions and the events that are taking place, whereas debugging implies the need to obtain more output in order to troubleshoot a problem. The relevant options include

- –v—verbose mode, prints additional details
- –q—suppress all output and simply listen as client (passive)
- –t—write to standard output (stdout)
- –s—run as a router, advertising routes (active)

Following are some examples showing how you might use these options in real-world situations.

Capturing Routing Information in a Log File

In the first example, we trace **in.routed** packets on UDP port 520 and save them to a log file, in this case /var/tmp/riplog:

```
# in.routed  -q -v   /var/tmp/riplog
```

You can view the contents of the log file with a standard editor like **vi**, the venerable UNIX interface.

```
# cat /var/tmp/riplog

June 30 14:49:19 ADD dst 62.0.0.0 via 194.168.85.1 metric 2
if hme0:55 state CHANGED
```

The output shows that the current host has heard from 194.168.85.1 that destination 62.0.0.0 is up and available two hops (metric) away. The result of this advertisement would be a new entry in the routing table on the current host, like this:

```
# netstat -rn | grep 62
62.0.0.0                194.168.85.1              UG       1
7
```

We now have a route to network 62.0.0.0, through gateway 194.168.85.1. The route is up (U), and 194.168.85.1 is the gateway through which this host may reach it. The G indicates that 194.168.85.1 is a gateway, but not the current host. If the current host were the gateway, a G would not appear in the flags field, as G means that the gateway is at least 1 hop away in routing terms.

Capturing Routing Information and Displaying on Standard Output

In the next example, we use **in.routed** to capture RIP (UDP port 520) traffic and write it to the display (technically, to the shell's output channel, known as *standard out* and abbreviated as *stdout*). The running **in.routed** command must first be killed to avoid possible port contention problems (only one **in.routed** command may listen or advertise on UDP port 520 at any one time).

We can kill the running **in.routed** daemon with the **pkill** command:

```
# pkill in.routed
```

Now, the way is clear to start **in.routed** with the –s and –t options, which force the daemon to listen for routing information while advertising its own routes and to generate trace information to standard output:

```
# in.routed -s  -t

RESPONSE from 62.254.198.253.520: dst 194.168.85.0  metric
1
RESPONSE from 194.168.85.51.520:  dst 62.0.0.0       metric
1
RESPONSE from 62.254.198.5.520:   dst 62.254.198.0  metric
1
                                  dst 194.168.85.0  metric
1
Interrupted with CTRL-C
#
```

KEY LEARNING POINTS

- The **route** command can add and delete static routes.
- The **route** command can add host, network, and default type routes.
- The **route monitor** command listens for router advertisements.
- The **route get** command uses the routing table to calculate a route.
- The **netstat –rn** command displays the current routing table.

SUMMARY

In this chapter we explored the routing protocols RIP and RDP as they are implemented on Solaris 8, discovering that Solaris routing is table driven and composed on direct and indirect routes, which are added dynamically or statically. We contrasted RIP (implemented by the **in.routed** daemon), which uses a broadcast address, with RDP (implemented by the **in.rdisc** daemon), which uses multicast addresses and is therefore more selective in nature and scope.

We examined configuration files such as /etc/defaultrouter and /etc/gateways, which allow the administrator to add additional static routes as specified within the files. The configuration files are usually read at boot time.

Finally, we saw how to configure a Solaris host as a router, as well as how to manipulate the routing table using the **route** command.

TEST YOURSELF

MULTIPLE CHOICE

1. *Which of the following are routing table entry types? Choose three.*
   A. Default
   B. Primitive
   C. Network
   D. Host
   E. Ethernet

2. *Which of the following daemons implements the RIP protocol?*
   A. **in.rdisc**
   B. **in.routed**
   C. **inetd**
   D. **in.netstatd**
   E. **in.routingd**

3. *What type of address does RDP use?*
   A. Broadcast
   B. Unicast
   C. Multicast
   D. Anycast
   E. Routecast

4. *RIP servers who wish to advertise routes must use which one of the following options when they run in.routed?*
   A. **-s**
   B. **-r**
   C. **-q**
   D. **-t**
   E. **-m**

5. *Which **netstat** option allows the routing table to be viewed?*
   A. **netstat -a**
   B. **netstat -m**
   C. **netstat -r**
   D. **netstat -p**
   E. **netstat -i**

6. *Which two multicast addresses does the **in.rdisc** routing daemon use? Choose two.*
   A. 224.0.0.1
   B. 233.1.1.0
   C. 233.1.1.1
   D. 224.0.0.2
   E. 244.9.9.1

7. *The /etc/gateways file does what?*

A. Configures the **in.rdisc** daemon

B. Configures the **in.routed** daemon

C. Allows one to add more static routes

D. Allows one to delete unwanted static routes

E. Enables multicast routing

8. *An indirect route is one that specifically requires what?*

A. The /etc/gateways file

B. The /etc/defaultrouter file

C. A router

D. The **in.rdisc** daemon to be running

E. The **in.routed** daemon to be running

9. *How else can the destination network 10.1.1.0, with a netmask of 255.255.255.0, be expressed using network/mask notation?*

A. 10.1.1.0/24

B. 10.1.1.0/255/255/255

C. 10.1.1.0/255.255.255

D. 10.1.1.1/0.0.0.0

E. 10.1.1.1/24.0.0.0

10. *The forwarding of IP packets is disabled by setting which kernel parameter to 0?*

A. *ip-forwarding*

B. *ip_forwarding*

C. *ip_forwarding_tcp*

D. *ip_forewarding_ip*

E. *ipforwarding*

FREE RESPONSE

1. *Why is routing so fundamentally important in networking terms?*

2. *Describe the advantages and disadvantages of dynamic routing as opposed to static routing.*

FURTHER READING

Heutema, Christian. *Routing in the Internet.* Upper Saddle River, NJ: Prentice-Hall, 1995. ISBN 0-13-022647-5.

7

The Transport Layer Protocols

EXAM OBJECTIVES

7.1 TCP Encapsulation, Header, and Features

7.2 UDP Encapsulation, Header, and Features

7.3 Comparison of TCP and UDP

7.4 The IP Interface to the Transport Layer

A fter completing this chapter you will be able to meet the following Network Administration Exam objectives:

- Identify the features of the Transmission Control Protocol (TCP) and the User Datagram Protocol (UDP).

- Define the terms *connection oriented*, *connectionless*, *stateful*, and *stateless*.

- Describe the relationships between port numbers, network services, and **inetd**.

To help you meet these objectives, this chapter covers the following topics:

- TCP encapsulation, the components of the TCP header, and TCP features

- UDP encapsulation, the components of the UDP header, and UDP features

- a comparison of TCP and UDP

- the IP interface to the Transport layer protocols and what happens when IP datagrams are fragmented or arrive out of order

7.1   TCP Encapsulation, Header, and Features

The TCP and UDP protocols operate at the Transport layer (4) of the protocol stack. Figure 7-1 shows where they operate in the TCP/IP 5-layer model that we discussed in Chapter 1. These two protocols offer a delivery service to upper-layer (layer 5) applications and protocols but use IP to route their data. Both TCP segments and UDP datagrams encapsulate their applications data and are themselves encapsulated by IP datagrams for routing purposes.

In this section we explore the TCP protocol and its header in detail. You will learn how the protocol *sequences* (numbers) the bytes it delivers and how, through a feature called *positive acknowledgment with retransmission*, it is able to offer upper-layer applications and protocols a guaranteed delivery service. You will also learn about the most important features of TCP; we will simply list the less important features for completeness so that we can compare TCP to UDP later in this chapter.

TCP Encapsulation

TCP's unit of data is a *segment*, which contains both the TCP header and data. The header is overhead because it contains no data that TCP is delivering for an application but only information that TCP needs to perform its function.

Application	Layer 5
Transport	Layer 4
Internet	Layer 3
Network interface	Layer 2
Hardware	Layer 1

Figure 7–1   *TCP and UDP protocols functioning at layer 4 of the TCP/IP 5-layer model*

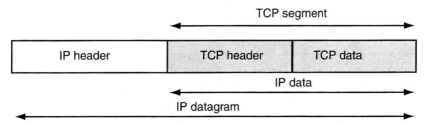

Figure 7–2   *Encapsulation of a TCP segment within an IP datagram*

Figure 7-2 shows how TCP's segment is encapsulated within an IP datagram (refer back to Chapter 5 to learn more about the IP datagram and header). Notice that

- TCP's segment consists of the TCP header plus the TCP data.
- The TCP segment makes up IP's data content.

By the end of this chapter, we will have covered IP, TCP, and UDP in detail. That will be the appropriate point at which to examine what happens in two not uncommon scenarios:

- when the fragments of an IP datagram arrive at the destination host in the wrong order, and
- when, upon reassembly, the fragments of an IP datagram are passed up to TCP in the wrong order.

The TCP Header

If you know a little about the organization of the TCP header, you can more easily understand and appreciate the features of the TCP protocol itself. You need not memorize the fields of the TCP header for the exam; this information is being presented for your edification only.

The TCP header is a minimum of 20 bytes in size; the addition of options will lengthen it further. The TCP header as shown in Figure 7-3 reflects the organization set forth by RFC 793. Table 7.1 presents the same information in tabular format for easy reference. What follows is a look at each field of the IPv4 header.

Source and Destination Port Numbers

The first two fields of the TCP header give the 16-bit source and destination port numbers, respectively. The purpose of the port numbers is

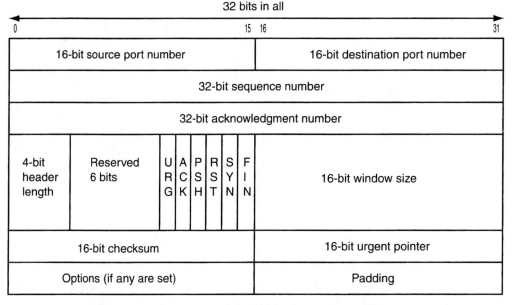

Figure 7–3   *Organization of the TCP header according to RFC 793*

to identify the upper-layer protocols with which a TCP connection is associated (see Chapter 8). Remember that data traveling up the stack is passed or *demultiplexed* to different applications based on the destination port number, as shown in Figure 7-4. (Demultiplexing involves separating inbound data into different data streams and feeding each stream to the correct destination port number specified in the TCP header of the arriving TCP segment.) TCP uses this port number so it knows which application should receive the data in the segment.

> **Note**
>
> The TCP transport protocol forms a virtual connection between two hosts, which must be established before the application using TCP is allowed to send a single byte of data. TCP endpoints are pairs of integers, such as host.port, where *host* is the IP address of a host and *port* is a TCP port on the host. For example, the endpoint 194.168.85.51.80 describes host IP address 194.168.85.51 and port 80 on that host.
>
> From TCP's perspective, then, when a connection is established between two hosts at the Transport layer (peers), we have what is referred to as an *association* or what was originally referred to as a *socket*.

When data is passed to TCP by a sending application (for delivery), TCP encapsulates the data in one or more outbound segments (TCP data plus TCP header). It then passes the data to IP, having filled the TCP header with the appropriate information in terms of source and destination ports, sequence number, and so on.

Table 7.1 *Fields of the TCP Header*

HEADER	SIZE OF FIELD (BITS)	DESCRIPTION OF FIELD CONTENTS
Source port	16	The source port number is stored in this field. Both the client and the server are the sources of different traffic. For example, if the client sends the server a segment, the client is the source. When the server sends the acknowledgment segment, it is the source of the traffic to the client.
Destination port	16	The destination port number is stored in this field. Both the client and the server are the destinations of different traffic. For example, if the client sends the server a segment, the server is the destination. When the server sends the acknowledgment segment to the client, the client is the destination.
Sequence	32	Starting byte number of this segment, which is the sequence number of the first byte in the segment
Acknowledgment number	32	Contains a number that is one value larger than the byte sequence number of the last byte successfully received from the other end. This number reveals the byte number of the last successfully acknowledged byte, in that it indicates the next byte expected (but not yet received). The number is significant only if the ACK control bit (also in the TCP header) is also set.
Header length in 32-bit words	4	The length of the TCP header; this field typically has a value of 5, indicating five 32-bit words (20 bytes), the normal header length
Control bits	64	Various flags (ACK, SYN, FIN, RST, URG, PSH) to be explained in the course of this chapter
Window	16	Number of bytes the receiving host is able or willing to receive
Checksum	16	Calculated for each segment by the sending host and recalculated by the receiving host

32-Bit Sequence Number

The Sequence field contains a number that uniquely identifies each TCP segment to support sequenced and reliable delivery. TCP transmits a byte-stream across a TCP connection and numbers each byte with a sequence number. The sequence number field in a given segment identifies the first byte in that segment. The purpose of the sequence numbers is to ensure that the stream of data is delivered to the destination by TCP in the exact byte-order it left the source.

The sequence number field specifies the number of the first byte in each segment. The sequence number is therefore a byte count, not a segment count.

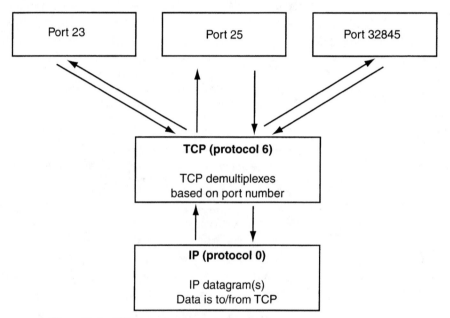

Figure 7–4   *TCP interface to ports*

32-Bit Acknowledgment Number

The two systems involved in a TCP connection use the Acknowledgment number field to inform one another that bytes have been received or *acknowledged*. The acknowledgment number is the sequence number of the last successfully received byte plus 1. So, for example, if the acknowledgment number is 100, then all bytes up to and including 99 have been received. The next byte expected (identified by its acknowledgment number) is 100. This does not imply that the first byte in the byte stream segmented and delivered by TCP was byte 1. The TCP ISN may start anywhere between 1 and 4294967296 (2^{32}), as the sequence number is a 32-bit field.

The Acknowledgment field must always contain a value, as it forms part of the header in all TCP packets. Therefore, no overhead is involved in setting this field in every segment, even if the field is full of padding (zeros).

There is a field in the control bits (also called *type of service* bits) called the Acknowledgment flag (ACK) bit. If the ACK flag is not set, the 32-bit Acknowledgment number field is ignored.

4-Bit Header Length

The purpose of the Header Length field is to indicate the number of 32-bit words (4 bytes each) in the TCP header. The minimum TCP header length is 20 bytes, but it can be bigger (up to a maximum of 60 bytes) if options such as MSS or SYN are set in the TCP header. The 4-bit Header Length field limits the header size to a maximum length of 60 bytes because 4 bits in binary is

```
8  4  2  1
1  1  1  1  =  15
```

which means 15 lots of 32-bit words. Remember that 32 bits is 4 bytes (8 bits per byte), which means 15 times 4 bytes, which equals 60 bytes. When we have the minimum TCP header size of 20 bytes, the bits in this field are set to

```
8  4  2  1
0  1  0  1  =  5
```

This translate to 5 times 4 bytes, equalling 20 bytes.

Control Bits

This field carries control information that helps to establish, maintain, and terminate a connection. There are six possible flag bits:

- URG—This flag refers the receiving TCP to the Urgent pointer field of the TCP header, to be discussed shortly.
- ACK—This flag appears in the field when the Acknowledgment number is valid or significant.
- PSH—The PSH control bit indicates to TCP that each character typed must be pushed or passed to the application immediately. Interactive programs such as **rlogin** and **telnet** use this bit.
- RST—This flag tells the receiving TCP to reset the connection.

- SYN—This flag is set only during the three-way handshake (connection establishment, synchronize sequence numbers) and means that a connection is required. (See the "TCP Features" section of this chapter.)
- FIN—This flag is issued only by a system that is ready to close a TCP connection. Either the sending or the receiving system can signal to the other the desire to finish a communication, but usually the client issues the initial FIN, to which the server complies with a FIN of its own to show mutual agreement.

Among these flags, SYN and ACK are the most important; we will examine these in greater detail than the others.

Window Size

The Window field indicates the number of data octets, starting with the one in the Acknowledgment field, that the sender of the current TCP segment is willing to accept. Remember that the Acknowledgment field shows one number higher than the last byte received thus far and therefore shows the number of the next byte expected. So, for example, if the Acknowledgment field is set to 100 and the Window field is set to 50, the sending host is prepared to accept 50 bytes at this time, numbered from 100 to 150 (because 100 is the sequence number of the next expected byte).

Each end of the TCP connection advertises its preferred window size. Later in this chapter, we will see how adjustment of this field and the use of the sliding window protocol together manage flow control.

Checksum

The Checksum field is calculated from and therefore includes both the TCP header and TCP data; it is calculated by the sender and checked by the receiver. The purpose of the checksum is to ensure that the data has arrived at the correct transport layer (TCP or UDP) and at the correct host, and also that the data in the segment has not changed in any way and has therefore maintained its integrity.

To compute the checksum, the sending system's TCP layer prepends a pseudo header to the TCP header, pads the segment (using an octet of zeros) to an exact multiple of 16 bits, and then computes a checksum of the entire object. Note that while the checksum is being computed, the header checksum field itself is replaced with zeros. This is the header field where the checksum is stored once it is calculated.

Note that the pseudo header and padding are not actually transmitted by TCP but are merely included in the checksum calculation. The checksum is transmitted in the TCP header. To understand this, we need to look at the pseudo header itself. Figure 7-5 shows the content of the pseudo header. The 0–31 represents a width of 32 bits (and the pseudo header has a size of 96 bits). The number in each field represents the length of that field in bits. Here is a description of each field in the pseudo header:

- *Source IP Address* is the sending system's IP address.
- *Destination IP Address* is the destination's IP address.
- *Protocol* contains the TCP/IP protocol type code for TCP, which is 6 (see /etc/inet/protocols)
- *Zero*. This field is passed with zero bits if needed (up to 1 byte) to make the total segment length an exact multiple of 16 bits.
- *TCP Length* is the length of the entire segment (TCP header plus data) but does not include the pseudo header itself.

The system receiving the TCP segment recalculates the checksum in the following order of steps:

1. It extracts the IP address from the IP header of the datagram that is carrying the TCP segment. In effect, IP passes this information to TCP. Note that both the source address and destination address are important to TCP because it must use them to identify the connection to which the segment belongs.
2. The receiving system then builds the pseudo header (as did the sending system) and recalculates the checksum.
3. The receiving system then compares the checksum it has computed to the one in the received segment, and if they are identical, the seg-

0	32 bits in all	31
	15 16	

Source IP address (32)		
Destination IP address (32)		
Zero (8)	Protocol (8)	TCP length (16)

Figure 7–5   *The TCP pseudo header*

ment has been delivered to the correct system and protocol and is considered valid. Its data integrity has been maintained.

Because the pseudo header checksum contains the IP addresses of the source and destination systems, it will fail to compute if the TCP segment is delivered to the wrong system. It will also fail if it is delivered by or to the wrong protocol, which is also referenced in the checksum calculation. This means of computing a checksum is also used by UDP, covered later in this chapter. If the checksum is incorrect, the segment is discarded. The sending system will timeout waiting for the ACK of the lost segment and will retransmit.

Urgent Pointer

An application can indicate that certain data is especially urgent and that TCP should transmit the data without delays. This instruction is valid only if the Urgent pointer flag (URG) is set. It is a positive offset that must be added to the sequence number field of the segment to yield the sequence number of the last byte of urgent data. Put another way, it points to the sequence number of the octet following urgent data.

Options

The Options field contains additional items not already specified in the TCP header. The most commonly used option is Maximum Segment Size (MSS), which specifies the maximum size segment the sender is prepared to accept or receive. The two ends of the TCP connection advertise this value during the initial three-way handshake or connection phase when the SYN bit is set. We will examine the MSS in detail when we look at the TCP three-way handshake later in this chapter.

Padding

The purpose of the Padding field is to ensure that the TCP header ends and the data begins on a 32-bit boundary.

TCP Data

The TCP data follows the header but is not part of it. Together, the TCP header and data comprise the TCP segment.

TCP Features

The major features of the TCP protocol are

- connection establishment and release
- sequenced delivery
- virtual circuit
- multiplexing of several TCP connections
- positive acknowledgment with retransmission
- flow control through a sliding window protocol

Of these six features, the four most important are the TCP three-way handshake, Maximum Segment Size (MSS) negotiation, positive acknowledgment with retransmission, and the sliding window protocol. We examine these important TCP features next.

Connection Establishment and Release

TCP, like other connection-oriented protocols, must provide for the stages of connection, reliable data transfer, and disconnection. Such a connection-oriented protocol is considered *stateful* because the current state of the connection is known by both ends of the connection.

TCP THREE-WAY HANDSHAKE

Before the TCP client and server application may send data to one another, a connection must be established at the Transport layer. TCP uses a three-way handshake to establish a connection. Before we look at the three-way handshake in detail, some general points are worth stressing. The purpose of the three-way handshake is to allow both ends to

- agree to the connection (SYN bit flag set)
- exchange a starting byte number, known as the initial sequence number (ISN)
- agree on a Maximum Segment Size (MSS) for transmitted data
- acknowledge one another's ISN numbers (ACK field value and ACK bit flag set)

The most important point to remember is that the connection is being established by the transport protocol, not by the application. For example, a **telnet** between two systems would use TCP, but before a single byte of **telnet** data can travel between the two systems, TCP must first establish a connection at the transport layer. You should also keep in mind that during the handshake, the two systems also agree upon an MSS, which determines the maximum amount of data transmitted per TCP segment.

For the purpose of the following description, we will refer to the initiating end of the connection as the client and to the other end as the server. In real-world scenarios, what usually causes a connection to be required is a client connecting to the server side of that application.

The major steps of the three-way handshake follow in this sequence:

1. The client TCP sends segment 1 indicating a desire to connect.
2. The server TCP responds and sends segment 2, agreeing to a connection.
3. The client TCP replies and sends segment 3, during which the connection is established.

Here is how these steps look in detail (refer to Figure 7-6). In the steps, we refer to the side requesting the connection as the client TCP because although a client application typically forces establishment of a TCP connection, it is the TCP protocol at the Transport layer that we are examining here. We are looking at a TCP Transport-layer handshake,

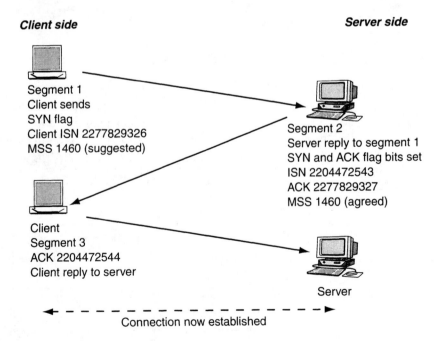

Client side   **Server side**

Segment 1
Client sends
SYN flag
Client ISN 2277829326
MSS 1460 (suggested)

Segment 2
Server reply to segment 1
SYN and ACK flag bits set
ISN 2204472543
ACK 2277829327
MSS 1460 (agreed)

Client
Segment 3
ACK 2204472544
Client reply to server

Server

Connection now established

Figure 7–6   *Phases of the TCP three-way handshake (connection establishment segments)*

not an Application-layer handshake. We refer to the client as the TCP client because we are referring to the TCP protocol on the host on which the client application resides.

1. The client TCP sends an initial packet. In this segment, the SYN (synchronize) bit, the Initial Sequence Number (ISN), and the Maximum Segment Size (MSS) bits are all set. This packet (segment 1) consumes a single client-side sequence number, which is 2277829326 as shown in Figure 7-5. Notice that 2277829326 is the ISN, that is, the number of the first byte sent.

2. The server's TCP layer responds by sending segment 2. In this segment's header, the SYN is set as well as the server's calculated ISN which is 2204482543. The TCP layer also acknowledges the TCP client's ISN plus 1 (2277829326 + 1 = 2277829327). In segment 2, it sets the ACK control bit because its Acknowledgment field is significant. In addition, it agrees or disagrees with the client's suggested MSS. If it agrees, it sends back the same MSS value that the client suggested in segment 1, which was MSS=1460, or it sends its own suggested MSS. In our example, the server agrees in segment 2 to the suggested MSS of 1460. So, in summary, this packet is segment 2, which consumes a single server-side sequence number.

3. Finally, the client replies and sends the final segment of the three-way handshake, which is segment 3. In segment 3, the client acknowledges the server's initial segment (segment 2) by setting the Acknowledgment field to 2204472543 plus 1 (the server's ISN + 1 = 2204472544). In effect, the client is saying that all bytes from the server's ISN up to the Acknowledgment field to 2204472544 – 1 have been received successfully. This means that only byte number 2204472543 has been received so far, which is correct. The client also sets the header ACK control bit, as the Acknowledgment number in this segment is significant.

The connection at the Transport Layer is now established. The host that initiates the connection (usually the client TCP) by sending the first SYN is said to perform an *active open*. The system that responds is said to perform a *passive open*.

The details of the three-way handshake illustrate that the TCP protocol must establish a connection before the application layer process can use the service of TCP as a transport. Please note that the sequence numbers appearing in Figure 7-6 are merely examples and have no specific significance other than their relationship to one another.

In summary, the goal of the three-way TCP handshake is to allow the client and server TCP layers to exchange initial sequence numbers (ISNs) from which they number the bytes they transmit, and also to acknowledge one another's ISNs. As you can see, TCP requires an elaborate handshake prior to client and server data exchange. TCP also requires a four-way close to the connection, so as a protocol it has significant overhead, which is the price paid for guaranteed delivery.

MAXIMUM SEGMENT SIZE NEGOTIATION

Prior to sending its initial segment of data to IP, TCP calculates a Maximum Segment Size (MSS). The MSS is based on the MTU of the Network Interface layer as IP reports it to TCP. TCP aims to send segments that will not require fragmenting when they are encapsulated by IP and then further encapsulated at the Network Interface layer (commonly one of Ethernet, ATM, or FDDI). The MSS is set during the three-way handshake.

Let us take a look at captured TCP packets showing the headers we have just discussed. It is not necessary to examine **snoop** packets for all features of TCP, but it is instructive to view the headers for at least one TCP operation—the critical three-way handshake and MSS negotiation, which epitomizes TCP's connection-oriented nature.

In the following examples, Ether and IP header components have been removed so that you may focus on the TCP header. The packets captured using **snoop** show a **telnet** from host hercules to host auriga.

1. We first issue the **snoop** command and specify that the output should go into a file called netdata, and that we are interested only in packets between hercules and auriga:

   ```
   # snoop -o  netdata hercules auriga
   ```

2. Next, in another Solaris window (leaving **snoop** running), we **telnet** from hercules to auriga, which forces a TCP connection to be established at the Transport layer. Consequently, we are able to capture the three-way handshake (described earlier) as it occurs. On hercules, we issue the following **telnet** command:

   ```
   # telnet auriga
   ```

   and the output showing the connection is as follows:

   ```
   Trying 194.168.85.1...
   Connected to auriga.
   Escape character is '^]'.
   ```

```
SunOS 5.8

login:
```

At this point, the **telnet** connection to auriga is complete and the
TCP three-way handshake must have occurred because the application **telnet** has connected to auriga. We know we are connected to
auriga because we see the login prompt from auriga, and part of the
output reads "Connected to auriga." We need not actually enter a
login name and password at the login prompt from auriga, because
we have now captured the packets of interest, namely, the three-way
TCP handshake.

3. We may now terminate **snoop** and examine the captured packets.
Enter Ctrl-D, which terminates **snoop** but leaves the data in a file
called netdata, as we specified in step 1. You may now read the
snoop data by issuing the following command, which reads the captured data file (netdata) into **snoop,** which will then display it:

```
# snoop -v -i   netdata
```

Note

The netdata file is in a special format that only snoop can read. You can, however, also
dump the snoop data file (netdata) into text and then read it with any text editor by
entering the following (we are using the text editor vi in our example):
```
# snoop -v -i netdata > netdata.text
```
In this command, we have captured the snoop output (using the redirection symbol >) into
a file called netdata.txt, which is created automatically. Now, you may read the netdata.text
file with any text editor of your choice.

Next, here is the code pertaining to the first step in the three-way
handshake; line numbers have been added for reference.

```
TCP:   ----- TCP Header -----
TCP:
TCP:   Source port = 44623                                    1
TCP:   Destination port = 23 (TELNET)                         2
TCP:   Sequence number = 2277829326                           3
TCP:   Acknowledgment number = 0
TCP:   Data offset = 24 bytes
TCP:   Flags = 0x02
TCP:           ..0. .... = No urgent pointer
TCP:           ...0 .... = No acknowledgment
TCP:           .... 0... = No push
TCP:           .... .0.. = No reset
TCP:           .... ..1. = Syn
4
```

```
TCP:         .... ...0 = No Fin
TCP:   Window = 8760
TCP:   Checksum = 0x2566
TCP:   Urgent pointer = 0
TCP:   Options: (4 bytes)
TCP:      - Maximum segment size = 1460 bytes
5
TCP:
TELNET:    ----- TELNET:     -----
TELNET:
TELNET:    " "
TELNET:
```

LINE 1 • TCP: Source port = 44623

In line 1, the client TCP is initiating a connection on behalf of client application using port 44623. You will learn in this chapter that client applications are typically allocated an arbitrary high-numbered port, unlike servers (which usually use a well-known fixed port number).

LINE 2 • TCP: Destination port = 23 (TELNET)

The destination port that client port 44623 is attempting to connect to is well-known server port 23.

LINE 3 • TCP: Sequence number = 2277829326

Line 3, the client's first segment, contains the client's ISN. The client will number the bytes it transmits starting at this number.

LINE 4 • TCP: .... ..1. = Syn

This packet is part of the three-way handshake, so the SYN bit is set. The SYN bit is never set except in the three segments that make up the three-way handshake.

LINE 5 • TCP: - Maximum segment size = 1460 bytes

In Line 5, the client is suggesting a MSS of 1,460 bytes. This is because the MTU over Ethernet is 1,500 bytes, and the client is using Ethernet. The IP datagram, therefore, will transmit a maximum datagram of 1,500 bytes, so TCP calculates that setting a segment size of 1,460 will leave 40 bytes in the datagram for the 20-byte IP header and the 20-byte TCP header. Keep in mind that TCP wishes to send segments that IP can transmit in a single datagram, because doing so is more efficient and avoids unnecessary data reassembly.

Next, we examine segment 2 of the three-way handshake, the reply to segment one. Once again, some lines are numbered so that we can refer back to them in the discussion that follows.

```
TCP:    ----- TCP Header -----
TCP:
TCP:    Source port = 23                            1
TCP:    Destination port = 44623                    2
TCP:    Sequence number = 2204472543                3
TCP:    Acknowledgment number = 2277829327          4
TCP:    Data offset = 24 bytes
TCP:    Flags = 0x12
TCP:        ..0. .... = No urgent pointer
TCP:        ...1 .... = Acknowledgment         5
TCP:        .... 0... = No push
TCP:        .... .0.. = No reset
TCP:        .... ..1. = Syn                    6
TCP:        .... ...0 = No Fin
TCP:    Window = 24820
TCP:    Checksum = 0xce53
TCP:    Urgent pointer = 0
TCP:    Options: (4 bytes)
TCP:       - Maximum segment size = 1460 bytes  7
TCP:
TELNET: ----- TELNET:    -----
TELNET:
TELNET:    " "
```

LINE 1 • TCP: Source port = 23
Line 1 identifies the server's port as 23, which is **telnet.** Refer to the
Solaris /etc/inet/services file for a list of well-known ports; we will return
to the subject of well-known ports in Chapter 8.

LINE 2 • TCP: Destination port = 44623
The server is responding to the client, who, as we saw in segment 1, is
using port 44623.

LINE 3 • TCP: Sequence number = 2204472543
In Line 3, the server's ISN is set. Notice that the server ISN has no relationship to the client ISN.

LINE 4 • TCP: Acknowledgment number = 2277829327
Here, the server is acknowledging the client's ISN of 2,277,829,326.
Notice that the acknowledgment number is one higher than the client's
ISN because we next expect a byte numbered 2,277,829,327.

LINE 5 • TCP: ...1 .... = Acknowledgment
In line 5 the ACK bit is set, so the acknowledgment number is significant.

LINE 6 • TCP: .... ..1. = Syn
Here, the SYN bit is set, as this segment is part of the three-way handshake.

LINE 7 • TCP: - Maximum segment size = 1460 bytes

Finally, the server agrees to the MSS of 1,460 bytes proposed by the client. Next, we examine the third segment of the three-way handshake.

```
TCP:   ----- TCP Header -----TCP:
TCP:   Source port = 44623                              1
TCP:   Destination port = 23 (TELNET)                   2
TCP:   Sequence number = 2277829327                     3
TCP:   Acknowledgment number = 2204472544               4
TCP:   Data offset = 20 bytes
TCP:   Flags = 0x10
TCP:        ..0. .... = No urgent pointer
TCP:        ...1 .... = Acknowledgment                  5
TCP:        .... 0... = No push
TCP:        .... .0.. = No reset
TCP:        .... ..0. = No Syn
TCP:        .... ...0 = No Fin
TCP:   Window = 8760
TCP:   Checksum = 0x24cd
TCP:   Urgent pointer = 0
TCP:   No options
TCP:
TELNET:   ----- TELNET:    -----
TELNET:
TELNET:   " "
```

LINE 1 • TCP: Source port = 44623
In Line 1, the client port is indicated as 44,623.

LINE 2 • TCP: Destination port = 23 (TELNET)
The client is communicating with server port 23, which is **telnet**.

LINE 3 • TCP: Sequence number = 2277829327
The start byte number of the third segment is 2,277,829,327.

LINE 4 • TCP: Acknowledgment number = 2204472544
This acknowledgement number represents the server's ISN number plus one. That is, by sending an acknowledgment value of 2204472544, the client is confirming to the server that it has safely received all bytes from the server's ISN up through this acknowledgment number minus one— the last byte acknowledged was 2204472543. Note that a SYN segment consumes only one sequence number.

LINE 5 • TCP: ...1 .... = Acknowledgment
In line 5, the client is acknowledging the server's segment 2. The next byte that the server sends should therefore be numbered 2,204,472,544.

Note that during the three-way handshake, segments were acknowledged by the combination of the ACK bit, plus the setting of the acknowledgment number.

Positive Acknowledgment with Retransmission

TCP's reliability as a protocol is accomplished through a mechanism called *positive acknowledgment with retransmission*. This term describes the TCP mechanism whereby each byte received is acknowledged by the receiving end, which sends an acknowledgment number (in a segment's header) that represents the next byte expected. This number implies that all previous bytes have now been acknowledged. Retransmission of a segment occurs when the receiving end fails to acknowledge its arrival, which is accomplished by sending an acknowledgment for the received segment back to the sender. This leads to a timer expiring at the sending end, which is then forced to retransmit the segment. Figure 7-7 shows how all bytes are acknowledged.

Not every byte warrants an individual ACK packet; a byte is acknowledged only when a byte numbered higher than itself is acknowledged. For example, assume we have a connection that started with an ISN of 2,000 and has since successfully transmitted a further 1,000 bytes. The receiver

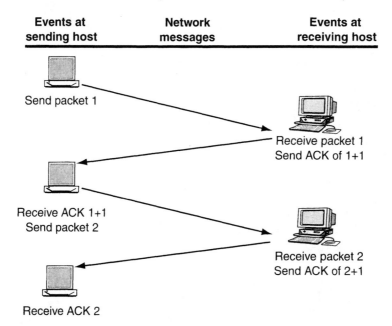

Events at sending host	Network messages	Events at receiving host

Send packet 1

Receive packet 1
Send ACK of 1+1

Receive ACK 1+1
Send packet 2

Receive packet 2
Send ACK of 2+1

Receive ACK 2

Figure 7–7 *Positive acknowledgment of transmitted data*

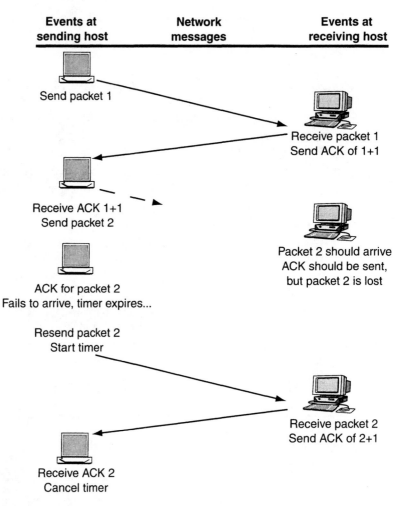

| Events at sending host | Network messages | Events at receiving host |

Send packet 1

Receive packet 1
Send ACK of 1+1

Receive ACK 1+1
Send packet 2

Packet 2 should arrive
ACK should be sent,
but packet 2 is lost

ACK for packet 2
Fails to arrive, timer expires...

Resend packet 2
Start timer

Receive packet 2
Send ACK of 2+1

Receive ACK 2
Cancel timer

Figure 7–8   *Positive acknowledgment with retransmission*

may send a single ACK packet back to the sender containing an ACK field of 3,001, indicating that all bytes from the ISN and up through 3,000 have been received and the next one expected (but so far not acknowledged) is 3001. In summary, then, a single ACK normally amounts to the acknowledgment of the range of bytes in a successfully received frame.

Figure 7-8 illustrates what happens when a frame is lost. If a segment fails to arrive as expected, a timer expires on the sending host, which then retransmits the segment. Segments received are *positively acknowledged*, which means that the receiving end tells the sending end that it has received the segment.

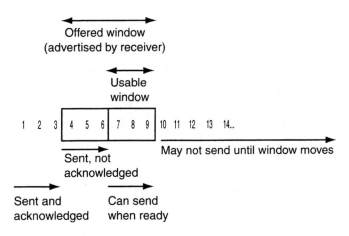

Figure 7–9 *Visualization of the TCP sliding window*

Sliding Window Protocol

TCP uses a *sliding window protocol.* This mechanism allows a system to send the amount of data that is currently within a "window" and to advance ("slide") that window over an additional group of bytes that the system may then send once the destination system acknowledges bytes already received. Figure 7-9 illustrates the principle of the sliding window.

The window is currently over six bytes numbered 4 through 9. Bytes 4, 5, and 6 have been sent, but unlike bytes 1, 2, and 3, they have not been acknowledged. Bytes 7, 8, and 9 (the usable window) are in the window and so may be sent immediately. We cannot yet send bytes 10 and beyond because we have not yet received acknowledgments for 4, 5, or 6. Once byte 4 is acknowledged, the window will move forward by one and advance over byte 10, which may then be transmitted. This simplified example illustrates the sliding window protocol mechanism, but note that in reality the window encompasses a much greater number of bytes and that ACK segments are sent that acknowledge whole segments worth of bytes at a time.

EXAM NOTES

KEY LEARNING POINTS

- **TCP's minimum header is 20 bytes.**
- **TCP as a protocol has significant overhead.**
- **TCP's unit of data is the segment.**

- TCP's segment is its header plus data.
- The SYN bit is set during the three-way handshake.
- The acknowledgment number gives the next expected sequenced byte.
- TCP uses positive acknowledgment with retransmission.
- TCP's sliding windows manage flow control of data.

7.2   UDP Encapsulation, Header, and Features

UDP is a transport protocol and offers a connectionless datagram delivery service to upper layer applications and protocols. In this section we explore the UDP protocol in detail, including UDP encapsulation and the UDP header. In contrast to TCP, the UDP datagrams are individual units that are not sequenced (numbered) in any way. Applications that use UDP can impose reliability over UDP, but UDP itself is non-guaranteed and has only a simple checksum, which is often turned off. As a transport protocol, UDP is very fast. It has extremely low overhead because of its simple header and its lack of reliability features. Unlike TCP, UDP does not need to form a connection at the Transport layer; it simply sends data when it is ready.

UDP Encapsulation

Whereas the unit of data for the TCP protocol is the segment, for UDP it is the datagram (discussed in Chapter 5 as it pertains to IP). The term datagram applies to both the UDP's and IP's unit of data, but note that the two types of *datagram* headers are quite different, with the IP header being far more complex. In addition, IP (layer 3) offers a datagram routing service to upper layer protocols such as UDP and TCP, whereas UDP simply offers a delivery service to applications, using port numbers to identify each application.

The UDP datagram contains both the UDP header (which is overhead) and data. The header is overhead because it is not data that UDP is delivering for an application, but simply information that UDP needs to perform its function. Notice that

- UDP's datagram is made up of the UDP header and UDP data, and
- IP's data is the UDP datagram.

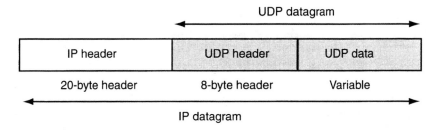

Figure 7–10   *UDP datagram encapsulated in IP*

Figure 7-10 shows the encapsulation of the UDP datagram in an IP datagram.

Having seen how the UDP datagram is encapsulated within an IP datagram, we now need to explore the UDP header itself, which is delightfully simple when compared with the TCP header.

The UDP Header

Although it is not necessary to memorize the fields of the UDP, IP, and TCP headers for the purpose of Sun certification, it is instructive to examine the header fields to gain a solid appreciation for the features of the protocol. Figure 7-11 shows the UDP header, which is notably simple when compared to its TCP counterpart—the UDP header size is a significantly smaller 8 bytes in length. The numbers above the header diagram in the figure indicate a header width of 32 bits (4 bytes). Table 7.2 shows the header in tabular format for easy reference.

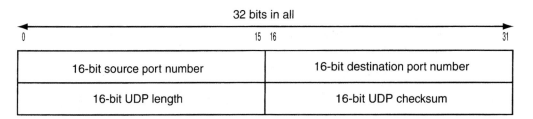

Figure 7–11   *The UDP header*

Table 7.2 *Fields of the UDP Header*

HEADER FIELD	SIZE OF FIELD IN BITS	DESCRIPTION OF FIELD CONTENTS
Source port	16	The client-side application port number on the source host
Destination port	16	The server-side application port number on the destination host
UDP length	16	Length of the UDP datagram
UDP checksum	16	Checksum of the UDP header plus its data (the datagram)

Source and Destination Port Fields

The Source and Destination Port fields contain the port numbers for the client and server applications using UDP, which are typically running on different hosts, as peers. The purpose of the port numbers is to identify the upper layer protocol using UDP, such as RIP or DNS.

The UDP Length Field

This 8-byte field is used to show the length of the UDP header plus the data. The length of a UDP datagram may also be calculated by subtracting 20 bytes from the IP datagram length field of the IP datagram that is carrying a given UDP datagram. That is, the length of an IP datagram with an encapsulated UDP datagram is equivalent to the length of the IP datagram minus the IP header.

The UDP Checksum Field

The checksum is optional and is often not enabled by default. It is controlled by the kernel parameter called **udp_do_checksum.** In Solaris 8, we enable the checksum feature using **ndd**. A value of 0 turns checksum off, and a value of 1 means that the checksum feature is enabled.

To get the current value, type the following at the prompt:

```
# ndd -get /dev/udp udp_do_checksum
0
#
```

In the foregoing example, the checksum is turned off. To enable it, type

```
# ndd -set /dev/udp udp_do_checksum     1
1
#
```

The UDP checksum is calculated exactly as the TCP checksum is calculated—through the use of a pseudo header that is prepended to the appropriate Transport layer header. The structure of the 12-octet UDP pseudo header is as shown in Figure 7-12.

Here is a summary of each field in the pseudo header:

- Source IP address is the sending system's IP address.
- Destination IP address is the destination's IP address.
- Zero (to round out the pseudo head plus the transport header plus the data to a multiple of 16 bits)
- The Protocol field contains the TCP/IP protocol type code for UDP, which is 17 (see the /etc/inet/protocols file).
- UDP length is the length of the entire datagram, not including the pseudo header.

The process of calculating the UDP checksum is identical to that of calculating the TCP checksum, which has already been covered earlier in this chapter.

UDP Features

UDP provides a connectionless transport service and has the following characteristics:

- It provides high speed transport but does not guarantee delivery.
- No Transport layer connection is required.
- Its overhead is low.

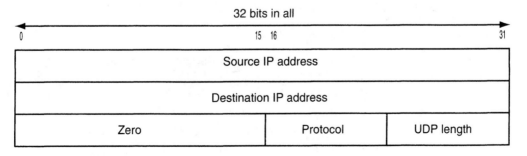

Figure 7–12   *Structure of the UDP checksum pseudo header*

- It does not provide for acknowledgment of received bytes.
- It adds port addressing capability to IP.
- It is datagram based like IP.
- Checksum is optional but should be turned on for optimum data integrity.

UDP is to application processes what IP is to UDP and TCP—namely, a datagram-based service. IP and UDP differ, however, in that IP routes datagrams between hosts based on IP addresses, whereas UDP can differentiate between application processes based on port numbers but relies on IP to actually route packets based on a destination IP address.

In addition, UDP is not reliable or at least does not guarantee delivery. Applications using UDP must therefore accept full responsibility for handling problems related to reliability, including message loss, duplication, delay, and out-of-order delivery.

UDP epitomizes a *stateless* protocol, which means that no connection is necessary between the parties involved. A stateless connection also implies that the UDP datagrams are not related in any way to each other through, for example, identification numbers (as used by IP) or sequence numbers (as used by TCP), and that the UDP protocol peers at each end of the communication are not keeping a record of UDP datagrams sent.

Do not misunderstand this point. UDP datagrams *are* related to each other in that they may be destined for the same host IP address and port number, but they are not transmitted as a numbered sequence of datagrams, because the header has no means of identifying a sequence of datagrams. An application using UDP may impose data ordering, as NFS version 2 does, by using a higher layer protocol (RPC and XDR in the case of NFS) to impose order, handle error checking, and impose a degree of reliability. In other words, UDP may be used reliably, but only if the application does the error checking. Interestingly, NFS version 3 uses TCP so that reliability can be imposed at the Transport layer and not merely by the application.

With TCP, the data stream is chopped up into sequence segments that have no natural boundaries. UDP datagrams, however, have natural boundaries in that each datagram is distinct from the next and not related to its neighbors in terms of the header content.

Figure 7-13 illustrates that when datagrams are lost, UDP does not know and simply transmits the next datagram. An application might notice the loss of data and ask for the UDP client application to retransmit (as did NFS version 2), but UDP itself is oblivious to this.

One advantage of UDP's lack of guaranteed delivery is that much less overhead is needed than with TCP. In effect, we are trading reliability for speed and low overhead, which suits some applications well.

The Routing Information Protocol (RIP), for example, uses UDP (refer back to Chapter 6). RIP servers advertise their routing tables every 30 seconds using the broadcast address to ensure that all listening systems on the same subnet hear the routing table broadcasts. Imagine what would happen if **in.routed** had to establish and de-establish a connection for all same-subnet systems (as TCP does) every 30 seconds! The overhead would be unacceptable and inefficient.

Clearly, UDP is better suited to applications that regularly send smaller chunks of data to several hosts and for which a missed packet does not have disastrous consequences. Domain Name Service (DNS) queries also tend to use UDP for the same reason. The DNS resolver (client) packets tend to be small, and so UDP suits it well. Simple Network Management Protocol (SNMP) also uses UDP. Applications such as DNS clients, therefore, do not wish to incur the overhead that TCP

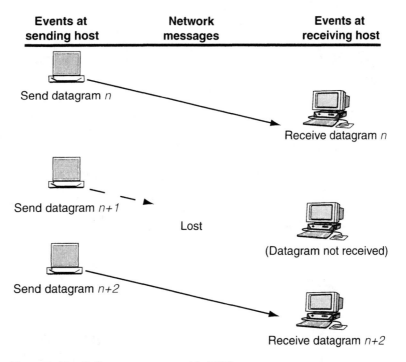

Figure 7–13   *Delivery not guaranteed by UDP*

would impose on them and so favor the simplicity and low overhead of the UDP protocol.

Following are sample DNS packets captured using **snoop.** In the example, we see the DNS server auriga.gvon.co.uk replying to a lookup of www.sun.com, indicating that the information is about sun.com. Some of the lines in the captured output are numbered for easy reference in the discussion that follows. Focus on the fields of the UDP header.

```
UDP:    ----- UDP Header -----
UDP:
UDP:   Source port = 53                              1
UDP:   Destination port = 1190                       2
UDP:   Length = 278
UDP:   Checksum = 5D1F
UDP:
DNS:    ----- DNS Header -----
DNS:
DNS:   Response ID = 1
DNS:   RA (Recursion Available)
DNS:   Response Code: 0 (OK)
DNS:   Reply to 1 question(s)
DNS:   Domain Name: www.sun.com.
```

Line 1

```
UDP:   Source port = 53
```

Line 1 indicates that the source port number of the UDP datagram is 53.

Line 2

```
UDP:   Destination port = 1190
```

Line 2 indicates that the destination port number is 1190. As you can see, the UDP protocol is simple indeed, with only port numbers being of any significance in the header.

EXAM NOTES

KEY LEARNING POINTS

- UDP's header is a fixed 8 bytes in length.
- UDP as a protocol has no overhead other than an optional checksum.
- UDP's unit of data is the datagram.

- UDP datagrams use port numbers to identify applications.
- UDP is encapsulated in IP's datagram.

7.3 Comparison of TCP and UDP

Table 7.3 contains a list of protocol features and indicates which are available to UDP, TCP, or both

Table 7.3 *Comparison of TCP and UDP Features*

FEATURE	UDP	TCP
Connection oriented		x
Message boundaries	x	
Data checksum	Optional	x
Positive acknowledgments		x
Timeout and retransmission		x
Duplicate detection		x
Sequencing		x
Flow control		x

7.4 The IP Interface to the Transport Layer

Thus far, we have seen that IP routes data in units called datagrams. It fragments its datagrams if the Network Interface layer technology over which it travels (such as Ethernet) demands it.

When IP datagrams deliver UDP datagrams as encapsulated data, the process at the receiving end is simple. If the IP datagram that is routing a UDP datagram (as encapsulated data) is fragmented, the IP layer at the destination end reassembles the IP datagram into a whole IP datagram and delivers a complete UDP datagram up the stack. The UDP protocol at the receiving end is completely unaware that the original UDP datagram was fragmented inside multiple IP datagrams (fragments) and then reassembled by the receiving host's IP layer. UDP datagrams are not related to each other, so they are not reordered by UDP. They are distinct units with little header information and no numbering sequence.

TCP is different. Recall that TCP units are called segments and that they are encapsulated in IP datagrams. Unlike UDP datagrams, however, the TCP segments are related to each other through a byte sequence number stored in the segment header, which allows TCP to send a stream of related bytes in multiple sequenced segments that can be reordered at the destination end.

An important point about this process needs to be stressed. If an IP datagram (carrying a segment) is fragmented en route, it is IP (not TCP) that reassembles the IP fragments at the destination end. At the Transport layer, TCP receives only complete segments (already reassembled) from IP. IP datagrams can be passed up to TCP in the wrong order, however. If they arrive at the destination end in the wrong order, they are also passed to TCP in the wrong order, but as whole datagrams. In such cases, it is TCP (not IP) that reorders the now deencapsulated TCP segments, relying on the sequence numbers to reorder the byte sequence. Once the segmented data is reordered by TCP, it sends that data up to the application, which (if fragmentation did occur) is oblivious to the whole process of IP reassembly and TCP segment reordering.

Exam Notes

Key Learning Points

- IP reassembles IP fragments at the destination end before it passes the de-encapsulated data (UDP datagrams or TCP segments) up to the appropriate Transport layer protocol.
- TCP reorders segments that are out of sequence.
- UDP receives only whole UDP datagrams from IP, which are not numbered or sequenced in any way. The Application layer might be ordering the UDP datagrams in some ways, but that is neither known nor managed by the UDP protocol itself.

Summary

This chapter focused on the Transport layer protocols, TCP and UDP, whose headers we examined. Both protocols are encapsulated in IP, and both offer a service to the Application layer. We explored the concepts of connection-oriented (stateful) and connectionless (stateless) protocols, and discovered that while TCP offers a guaranteed service, it is costly in terms of overhead, whereas UDP, although not guaranteed, offers lower overhead and is therefore fast and better suited to broadcast-type applications and applications that send small discrete packages.

We used **snoop** to examine sample headers of these two protocols, clearly revealing the far more complex nature of TCP with its 20-byte minimum header in contrast to the 8-byte header of UDP. Both protocols use checksums, and both prepend a pseudo header to their payload when calculating the checksum. We also examined the sliding window mechanism that TCP uses to handle flow control, in contrast to UDP, which has no such mechanism.

Next, in Chapter 8, we examine client and server applications and how port numbers identify the clients and servers.

TEST YOURSELF

MULTIPLE CHOICE

1. *The TCP segment is made up of what components?*
   A. IP datagram plus IP header
   B. TCP header plus IP datagram
   C. TCP header plus TCP data
   D. TCP datagram plus TCP header
   E. TCP header plus IP data

2. *What is the length of the TCP header source port field?*
   A. 20 bits
   B. 40 bits
   C. 16 bits
   D. 8 bits
   E. 4 bits

3. *The TCP MSS is which of the following?*
   A. The maximum segment size
   B. The minimum segment size
   C. The master segment size
   D. The minimum source size
   E. The maximum source size

4. The TCP three-way handshake's first two segments must set which of the following two flag bits? ~~Choose two.~~
   - A. URG
   - B. PSH
   - C. RST
   - D. SYN
   - E. FIN

5. What is the minimum size of the TCP header?
   - A. 24 bytes
   - B. 20 bytes
   - C. 8 bytes
   - D. 12 bytes
   - E. 16 bytes

6. What is the minimum size of the UDP header?
   - A. 24 bytes
   - B. 20 bytes
   - C. 8 bytes
   - D. 12 bytes
   - E. 16 bytes

7. What is the size of the ~~UDP~~ *TCP* destination port field?
   - A. 24 ~~bytes~~ bits
   - B. 20 ~~bytes~~ bits
   - C. 8 ~~bytes~~ bits
   - D. 12 ~~bytes~~ bits
   - E. 16 ~~bytes~~ bits

8. What is the size of the UDP pseudo header?
   - A. 24 bytes
   - B. 20 bytes
   - C. 8 bytes
   - D. 12 bytes
   - E. 16 bytes

9. What is TCP's protocol number as stated in the /etc/inet/protocols file?
   - A. 6
   - B. 0

      C. 17

      D. 1

      E. 10

10.   *What is UDP's protocol number as stated in the /etc/inet/protocols file?*

      A. 6

      B. 0

      C. 17

      D. 1

      E. 10

FREE RESPONSE

1.   *Why might an application developer choose UDP if TCP is so reliable?*

2.   *Describe what happens when TCP segments arrive out of order in IP fragments that have likewise arrived out of order. Describe the process from the point at which the IP fragments arrive at the destination machine.*

FURTHER READING

Stevens, W. Richard. *TCP/IP Illustrated, Volume 1: The Protocols.* Reading, MA: Addison-Wesley, 1994. ISBN 0-201-63346-9.

The Client-Server Model

EXAM OBJECTIVES

8.1 Servers, Clients, and Services

8.2 Configuring Solaris 8 Servers

8.3 Monitoring Services and Servers

After completing this chapter, you will be able to meet the following Solaris Network Administration Exam objectives:

- Explain the terms *client*, *server*, and *service*.
- Administer Internet services and RPC services.
- Collect information about services configured on hosts.

To help you meet these objectives, this chapter covers the following topics:

- servers, clients, and services, including XDR, TLI, sockets, NFS, and NIS/NIS+
- types of Solaris 8 servers (socket-based and XDR/RPC-protocol based) and how to administer them
- using the **netstat** and **rpcinfo** commands to monitor servers and services

229

8.1   Servers, Clients, and Services

UNIX has always been rich in networking tools and client/server communication, even in the early days of UNIX—the platform upon which TCP/IP was developed. Sun's Solaris UNIX has added significantly to the traditional server/client technology base by developing a completely distributed networking environment called ONC+, which we investigate in this chapter.

Solaris 8 servers, clients, and services are a crucial and an integral part of Solaris 8, which is highly focused on distributed computing of the highest order. No other operating system or version of UNIX on the market offers such stability and reliability as Solaris 8, which helps account for its great popularity.

In this chapter we focus on how to configure Solaris 8 native clients and servers, exploring both the server processes (usually referred to as server *daemons*) and their configuration files. Having configured the servers and enabled the respective services, we need to ensure that they are running correctly using the **netstat** and **rpcinfo** commands, which display the status of Solaris 8 clients and servers.

Previous chapters examined the underlying, lower level protocols such as Ethernet, TCP, UDP, and IP. Our journey has taken us up the stack on our protocol tour, and at last we reach the vast ocean of applications. It is now time to investigate the applications that ride the waves of the protocol surf, such as **telnet, ftp**, and many others.

Client/Server Applications: An Overview

A client uses a service made available by a server. A *client* is a process running on the system of a user who connects to a server. Under Solaris, a *server* can be one of two things:

- a complete system configured to offer a specific service and dedicated to that task—as, for example, mail servers and Web servers—or
- an individual process offering a service, such as the **in.ftpd** daemon, which offers an ftp service.

When we refer to a client or server in this chapter, we are referring specifically to a server process—such as **in.ftpd** or **in.telnetd**—which offers a specific service—such as **ftp** or **telnet**—to connecting clients.

ONC+ Applications

Open network computing (ONC) + is a distributed computing environment pioneered and developed by Sun Microsystems. It is essentially a suite of tools and technologies related to client and server computing. Let us examine some of the Sun client/server computing applications now.

Figure 8-1 shows the interrelationships of some of the components to be described in this section. As you can see, applications that make use of the Remote Procedure Call (RPC) are at the Application layer. RPC client and server sessions are managed through the use of RPCs, which operate at the Session layer.

Note that eXternal Data Representation (XDR) is used to standardize the RPC server and client headers so that they are not specific to any operating system. For this reason, several platforms can communicate with one another using ONC+ technologies. For example, Sun's Network File System (NFS) technology is found on several platforms, including UNIX, Windows, OS/2, and VMS.

Interestingly, ONC+ introduces presentation and session layer protocols, which fit into the OSI 7-layer networking model examined in Chapter 1. The OSI networking model designates specific layers for presentation and session protocols, but the TCP/IP networking model does not—yet Sun provides applications that use these layers nonetheless.

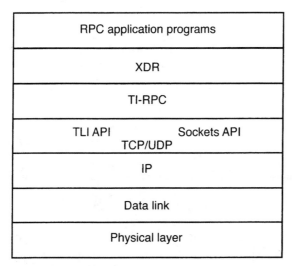

Figure 8–1   *Relationships among ONC+ protocols*

Table 8.1 shows where the ONC+ technologies fit within the OSI networking model. XDR, RPC, TLI, and sockets are shown at specific layers of the stack.

Table 8.1 *ONC+ Technologies and the OSI Model*

LAYER (NUMBER)	ONC+ POSITION IN STACK
Application (7)	RPC-based application servers such as NIS/NIS+ and NFS (these applications make use of the RPC protocol, which functions at the Session layer)
Presentation (6)	XDR
Session (5)	RPC
Transport (4)	TCP, UDP, Sockets, TLI
Network (3)	IP
Datalink (2)	Ethernet, Token Ring, FDDI, and others
Physical (1)	Fiberoptic, wire, and others

Table 8.2 shows where the ONC+ technologies fit within the Sun TCP/IP networking model. XDR, RPC, TLI, and sockets are shown at specific layers of the stack.

Table 8.2 *ONC+ Technologies and the TCP/IP Model*

LAYER (NUMBER)	ONC+ POSITION IN STACK
Application (5)	RPC-based applications such as NIS/NIS+, NFS. XDR and RPC also function at this layer.
Transport (4)	TCP, UDP, TLI, Sockets
Internet (3)	IP
Network (2)	Ethernet, Token Ring, FDDI, and others
Physical (1)	Fiberoptic, wire, and others

eXternal Data Representation (XDR)

eXternal Data Representation (XDR) is an architecture-independent specification for data representation and the backbone of Sun's RPC-based server technology. Applications that use XDR can exchange data across heterogeneous networks and hardware.

As a data representation and coding standard, XDR transfers data between different computer architectures and handles the presentation of several data types as well as their alignment across multiple architectures. See RFC 1832 for more details.

Transport Layer Interface (TLI)

AT&T introduced the Transport Layer Interface (TLI) in 1986 with System V, release 3 UNIX as a Transport layer API. TLI was modeled after the ISO Transport Service Definition (TSD) and provides an API between the OSI Transport and Session layers. With TLI, applications can run over both UDP and TCP without being hard-coded to any given Transport layer protocol.

Sockets

The *socket* is the Berkeley Software Distribution (BSD) method for accomplishing interprocess communication (IPC). A socket acts as an endpoint of a communication, which allows processes to communicate, typically across a network.

The Berkeley UNIX socket interface to network protocols was originally developed at the University of California at Berkeley in 1983. The XNS 5 (UNIX98) version of sockets, which is slightly different from BSD sockets, is also available on Solaris.

Network File System (NFS)

The Network File System (NFS), developed by Sun in 1984, provides transparent access to remote file systems (directories and files) in a mixed or heterogeneous environment, allowing for data sharing between different operating systems and platforms that support NFS. In this context, *transparent access* means that the data appears to be local to the NFS client even though it is remote and on the NFS server. NFS version 2 uses UDP, and the current version 3 uses TCP.

Network Information Service (NIS/NIS+)

NIS and NIS+ are naming services that provide information about hosts, users, and other network service information. Servers provide this information in the form of maps (in the case of NIS) or tables (in the case of NIS+). Both versions are configurable to support nonstandard maps, such as a phone number table or map. Both NIS and NIS+ are what Sun calls *enabling technologies*, which means that they allow for the creation and support of nonstandard maps (in the case of NIS) and nonstandard tables (in the case of NIS+). One such map or table could be a company-wide phone directory made available through NIS/NIS+ to clients.

For a further comparison of naming services, including NIS/NIS+ and Domain Name Service (DNS), see Chapter 11.

EXAM NOTES

KEY LEARNING POINTS

- ONC+ technologies provide a distributed networking environment.
- XDR provides a standard, architecture-independent way of presenting data across a network.
- RPC offers a Session layer service.
- NIS and NIS+ provide information about hosts, users, and other network service information.
- NFS provides a transparent means of sharing files and directories.
- ONC+ technologies use both TCP and UDP.

8.2   Configuring Solaris 8 Servers

Solaris 8 basically has two categories of servers and clients:

- Traditional TCP/IP socket-based clients and servers
- RPC clients and servers, which always use TLI and are commonly referred to as TI-RPC clients and servers

The difference between these two types of servers lies in the technologies they employ. For the purposes of this chapter we will call the first type *traditional* servers, because they were the original servers bundled with UNIX. Although they might use TLI, they tend to simply use TCP/UDP sockets (ports) but not XDR or RPC. The second type of server we shall refer to as *TI-RPC* servers. They are transport independent (TI) in that they are not tied to a given transport protocol. On Solaris 8, TCP/UDP are the only relevant transport protocols. They often use XDR at the Presentation layer of the OSI networking model (see Figure 8-1) and always use RPC at the Session layer.

Starting Servers

There are two main ways in which servers may be started: by means of startup scripts or through a server configuration file. In the following sections, we examine how to start both traditional and TI-RPC servers using startup scripts (as *standalone servers*) or through a server configuration file called /etc/inet/inetd.conf, which is read by the super daemon **inetd**.

Starting Standalone Servers

Standalone servers are so called because they are processes that are not started by the Solaris daemon **inetd**. Standalone daemons (processes) are started as either

- *single standalone*—One process is started initially, but child processes are forked (started) as required; or
- *multiple standalone*—Multiple copies are started initially, and more are forked (started) if needed.

STARTING SINGLE STANDALONE SERVERS

Standalone daemons are started by shell scripts at boot time, not by the **inetd** daemon. A classic example of a standalone daemon is **sendmail**, which is started by the shell script /etc/rc2.d/S88sendmail seen running here:

```
# ps -ef | grep sendmail | grep -v grep
root 14710 1 0 Jan 4 ? 85:74 /usr/lib/sendmail -bd -q15m
#
```

In the foregoing example, the parent **sendmail** daemon (a non-TLI/RPC-based standalone daemon) starts or forks a child **sendmail** as inbound e-mail needs to be dealt with. In the specific case of **sendmail**, Simple Mail Transport Protocol (SMTP) traffic is delivered to port 25, where, as we shall see later in this chapter, **sendmail** listens. In short, it is not unusual to see multiple copies of **sendmail** running.

Mountd is an example of a standalone TI-RPC server; it is needed on NFS servers. The **mountd** daemon responds to the client mount requests and so is critical to the correct functioning of the NFS service.

Mountd is started on NFS servers by the shell script /etc/rc3.d/ S15nfs.server, which is automatically run when the system transitions to run State 3. To check it is running, use the following **ps** command:

```
# ps -ef | grep mountd | grep -v grep
  root 26104 1 0 20:52:27 ? 0:00 /usr/lib/nfs/mountd
```

STARTING MULTIPLE STANDALONE SERVERS

In some cases, multiple copies of a daemon are started because of a predicted load. They are started before they are needed so that they are ready as and when the demand increases.

The Apache Web server approach (apache is bundled with Solaris 8) is to start multiple copies of the apache Web server daemon called **httpd**. The daemon starts when apache starts, typically at boot time. The administrator, through the main configuration file httpd.conf, specifies the number of daemons to start using the apache StartServers directive:

```
StartServers 5
```

The next example shows the running **httpd** daemons but filters out the **grep** itself in the process list using the **-v** switch. If more **httpd** daemons are required, apache forks more child processes to deal with the spike or additional load.

```
#  ps -ef | grep httpd | grep -v grep
root   6300   1  0   Apr 23 ?
0:12 /usr/local/apache/bin/httpd -DSSL
nobody 23188 6300  0 15:05:08 ?  0:00 /usr/local/apache/
bin/httpd -DSSL
nobody 23467  6300  0 15:16:25 ? 0:00 /usr/local/apache/
bin/httpd -DSSL
nobody 23125  6300  0 15:03:08 ? 0:00 /usr/local/apache/
bin/httpd -DSSL
nobody 23068  6300  0 15:00:37 ? 0:00 /usr/local/apache/
bin/httpd -DSSL
nobody 22525  6300  0 14:40:40 ? 0:00 /usr/local/apache/
bin/httpd -DSSL
nobody 23456  6300  0 15:15:55 ? 0:00 /usr/local/apache/
bin/httpd -DSSL
nobody 23289  6300  0 15:09:39 ? 0:00 /usr/local/apache/
bin/httpd -DSSL
```

Note

The -DSSL switch appears in the foregoing example because my own apache Web server is configured to run ApacheSSL (Secure Sockets Layer).

Starting Services through inetd

As you have seen, standalone daemons are Solaris server daemons that are started either when the system boots or manually after the boot. They are started by shell scripts and are not dependent on another server daemon starting them.

In contrast, the Internet **inetd** daemon starts other server processes. It can start both traditional, socket-based Internet services—such as **ftp** and **telnet**—and TI-RPC servers. With traditional services, clients and servers communicate using addresses known as ports or sockets, which are addresses in the kernel that are associated with a given service. The **inetd** daemon starts server daemons on demand, not necessarily at boot time. Note that **inetd** starts a server daemon only when it is required by a communicating client that contacts one of the server ports on which **inetd** is listening.

inetd reads the following two files to discover which ports to listen to and which services are enabled:

- */etc/inetd.conf*—This file is symbolically linked to the /etc/inet/ inetd.conf file, which determines whether a service is enabled or disabled and provides **inetd** with sufficient configuration information for it to start both traditional and TI-RPC servers.
- */etc/inet/services*—**inetd** acquires each server's well-known port number from this file. This applies only to non-TLI/RPC servers. TI-RPC servers acquire their port number from a daemon called **rpcbind,** explained later in this chapter.

Let us examine the contents of the two files, starting with /etc/inet/ inetd.conf, with a view to learning how **inetd** can start both traditional and TI-RPC servers. The /etc/inet/inetd.conf file identifies which services **inetd** is to offer and provides other parameters relating to the type of server and how to start the service.

The initial lines of inetd.conf in Solaris 8 (lines 1 through 90) refer to traditional Internet services using either TCP or UDP routed across IPv4 or IPv6 networks. The latter part of the file (lines 91 through 184) refers to TI-RPC servers, which also run over TCP or UDP. Both types of server run over TCP/IP, but the TI-RPC servers use RPC and often XDR, which the traditional Internet servers do not.

For a more complete explanation of the file /etc/inetd.conf, see section 4 of the online Solaris manual pages, which covers the format and syntax of Solaris 8 files.

DEFINING TRADITIONAL SOCKET-BASED SERVERS IN /ETC/INET/INETD.CONF

The /etc/inet/inetd.conf file defines two main types of Solaris servers—traditional, non-RPC-based servers (lines 1 through 90) and RPC servers (lines 91 through 184). First, we will examine the traditional socket-based servers and the syntax needed to define them. Our starting point is the syntax of the /etc/inet/inetd.conf file, which is defined in the Solaris manual pages. To view the manual page that shows the syntax of the inetd.conf file, type:

```
# man -s  4 inetd.conf
```

The syntax of inetd.conf traditional server lines is

```
service_name socket_type proto flags user server_pathname
args
```

Let us take a look at each of these fields.

SERVICE NAME • The service name is the first field in /etc/inet/inetd.conf and must exactly match the first field of a line in /etc/inet/services where the service port number on which **inetd** will listen is identified. Field one must therefore be the name of a valid service listed in the /etc/inet/services file.

SOCKET_TYPE • The socket_type field uses a number of possible keywords:
- stream—used by TCP-based services and servers
- dgram—used by UDP-based services and servers
- tli—used for all TLI endpoints

PROTO • This field stands for protocol. The protocol must be one of the following: tcp (IPv4), tcp6 (IPv6), udp (IPv4), or udp6 (IPv6). When a proto value of tcp6 or udp6 is specified for a service, **inetd** will pass the appropriate daemon an AF_INET6 socket. The following services have been modified to be able to accept AF_INET6 sockets on Solaris 8:

- ftp
- telnet
- shell
- login
- exec
- tftp
- finger
- printer

FLAGS • The flags field determines whether more than one instance of the service may run at any one time. Two values are possible here: wait or nowait. Wait means that only one instance of a given daemon (service) may run at any one time. Nowait means that multiple copies may be started by **inetd** up to the maximum allowed by the kernel.

USER (UID) • This field specifies the user ID under which the server should run. This allows servers to run with access privileges other than those of the system administrator, who is called the *root user*.

SERVER_PATHNAME • The server_pathname field contains either the absolute pathname of a server program to be invoked by **inetd** to perform the requested service, or the word internal if **inetd** itself provides the service. Simple servers, such as echo and discard, are built into **inetd** and are not separate programs.

ARGS • The args field specifies which arguments are to start the server program defined in the server_pathname field.

We next look at some examples of traditional socket-based service lines from the /etc/int/inetd.conf file. Refer back to the explanations of field variables just given for the significance of specific field values.

EXAMPLE 1: DISABLING A PARTICULAR SERVICE • To disable a traditional service using **inetd**, hash out the appropriate line by starting the line with a hash character (#), as in the following example:

```
# ftp stream tcp6 nowait  root /usr/sbin/in.ftpd in.ftpd
```

The hash character informs the **inetd** daemon not to listen on that particular port address, which effectively disables the service. Each service—**ftp,** for example—is associated with a specific port address.

Please note that changes to the inetd.conf configuration file require that **inetd** reread the file inetd.conf, which you may force the daemon to do by sending it the SIGHUP signal (abbreviated as HUP) as follows:

```
# pkill -HUP inetd
```

EXAMPLE 2: ENABLING AN IPv4 SERVICE USING TCP • To enable a service, simply ensure that the line does not begin with a hash character (#), as in the following example:

```
ftp stream tcp nowait root /opt/sfw/bin/in.ftpd in.ftpd -
adl
```

This **ftp** line we have added to replace the standard Solaris ftp service that we disabled in the previous example. On the Companion CD-ROM that is shipped with Solaris 8, Sun provides a more secure, more flexible version of **ftp** called **WUFTP,** which was developed by Washington University. Notice that we start **in.ftpd** with certain options, namely **–adl.** The **in.ftpd** daemon will behave differently when started with the following options:

- **-a**—Lock the user in the directory to which they log in via ftp to prevent them from roaming around the ftp server.
- **-l**—Turn on logging.
- **-d**—Turn on debugging.

EXAMPLE 3: ENABLING AN IPv4 SERVICE USING UDP AS THE TRANSPORT PROTOCOL • To enable a service, simply ensure that the line does not begin with a hash character (#). In the following example, notice that the server we enable uses the UDP transport protocol (dgram udp), whereas the server we enabled in example 2 used TCP as its transport protocol (stream tcp):

```
talk dgram udp wait root /usr/sbin/in.talkd in.talkd
```

Be aware that only one instance of **in.talkd** is allowed at any one time. This limitation is enforced by the wait option.

We have now seen how to enable and disable the traditional, non–TI-RPC servers. Next, we examine how to use **inetd** to start the second category of server, namely, TI-RPC servers.

DEFINING TI-RPC CLIENTS AND SERVERS IN /ETC/INET/INETD.CONF

We now look at the syntax of the inetd.conf file in relation to TI-RPC servers. Our example line is for the Solaris remote execution service. Focus on the format and refer back to it as we explore the fields:

```
rexd/1 tli rpc/tcp wait root /usr/sbin/rpc.rexd rpc.rexd
```

The full syntax of inetd.conf TI-RPC server lines is as follows:

```
rpc_prog/vers endpoint-type rpc/proto flags user pathname args
```

Let us briefly explain each of the fields this syntax uses.

RPC_PROG/VERS • The `rpc_prog/vers` field gives the RPC server name and version number. In our example, they are `rexd/1`, indicating that the RPC server is **rexd**, version 1.

ENDPOINT-TYPE • The `endpoint-type` field can contain one of three values:

- `tli`—either TCP or UDP
- `stream`—TCP
- `dgram`—UDP

In our `rexd` example line above, the endpoint-type is `tli` because **rexd** may use either TCP or UDP.

RPC/PROTO • This field is literally `rpc` followed by a transport protocol to show whether the rpc server uses TCP or UDP. In our `rexd` example line above, the rpc/proto field is

```
rpc/tcp
```

which indicates that `rexd` is an RPC server using TCP in this instance.

FLAGS • The `flags` field determines whether more than one instance of the service may run at any one time. `Wait` means that only one instance of a given daemon (service) may run at any one time, and `nowait` means that multiple copies may be started by **inetd** to the maximum number allowed by the kernel. In our `rexd` example, the flags field value is `wait`, indicating that only one instance of `rexd` may run at any one time.

USER (UID) • This field specifies the user ID under which the server should run. This allows servers to run with access privileges other than those for root. In our `rexd` example, the `user(uid)` field is `root`, indicating that the service is started with root user privileges.

SERVER_PATHNAME • This field specifies either the absolute pathname of a server program to be invoked by **inetd** to perform the requested service, or the word internal if **inetd** itself provides the service. Simple servers, such as echo and discard, are built into **inetd** and are not separate programs. In our rexd example above, the server_pathname is

```
/usr/sbin/rpc.rexd
```

This pathname allows **inetd** to locate the **rpc.rexd** server daemon in order to start (execute) it.

ARGS • The args field specifies the arguments that will start the specified server program (see the **ftp** example discussed previously). In our rexd example, the args field value is rpc.rexd, indicating that we should start it without options.

We now look at some examples of TI-RPC service lines from the inetd.conf file. Refer back to the foregoing explanations for the significance of individual field values.

EXAMPLE 1: DISABLING AN RPC SERVICE (SPRAYD) • The spray server is used primarily for testing. In this example we disable it. The example runs onto two lines but is a single entry.

```
#sprayd/1 tli rpc/datagram_v wait root /usr/lib/netsvc/
spray/rpc.sprayd      rpc.sprayd
```

Please note once again that changes to the inetd.conf configuration file require that **inetd** reread the file inetd.conf, which you may force the daemon to do by sending **inetd** the SIGHUP signal.

EXAMPLE LINE 2: ENABLING RUSERD • The **ruserd** service allows remote systems to query which users are logged into the system running the **ruserd** server. For this reason, it is often commented out (using the hash character #) and disabled. In the next example, the **ruserd** service is enabled (not hashed out).

```
rusersd/2-3 tli rpc/datagram_v,circuit_v wait root /usr/
lib/netsvc/rusers/rpc.rusersd rpc.rusersd
```

Note that if you start a TI-RPC server through the inetd.conf file, it registers with a server process called **rpcbind,** which maintains a database of running TI-RPC servers. You will learn more about **rpcbind** shortly.

Allocating Port Numbers to Traditional and TI-RPC Servers

Port numbers identify services. The transport protocols have a `port` field in their headers that enables them to pass their data up to the correct application server or client listening on the identified port. When the IP protocol passes data up the stack that is destined for the transport protocols TCP or UDP, the `protocol` field in the IP header (see Chapter 7) enables IP to pass the data up to the correct transport protocol.

In this section we examine two means of allocating port numbers, where a port number (or address) is a number associated with a service. Both clients and servers use port numbers to communicate. The client port is *arbitrary* (random) because it is is allocated to the client by the kernel, is known only by the client and kernel, and need not be a well-known or reserved port. When the client first contacts the server, it passes along its arbitrary port number so that the server may communicate with the client.

The server port number, unlike the client port number, must be well known and available; otherwise, the client has no means of making the initial contact with the server. The server ports are allocated using one of two different mechanisms depending on the server type:

- Traditional, non-TI-RPC servers acquire their port numbers through the /etc/inet/services file.
- TI-RPC servers receive their port numbers through **rpcbind** server. TI-RPC servers use dynamic allocation.

Let us examine each of these methods individually.

Port Allocation to Traditional Servers via /etc/inet/services

The range of port numbers available from the /etc/inet/services file extends from 0 through 65,535 because the `port` field in the UDP and TCP header is a 16-bit field (2^{16} power). Ports 0 through 511 are officially assigned by the Internet Assigned Numbers Authority (IANA), but port numbers 512 and above are deemed unofficial. In addition, ports 0 through 1,024 are started with *root privilege*—as though by the system administrator, who may execute any command without restriction—and are referred to as *privileged* ports.

Let us examine just a small section of the /etc/inet/services file:

```
# cat /etc/inet/services
#ident   "@(#)services 1.24  99/07/18 SMI" /* SVr4.0 1.8 */
#
# Copyright (c) 1999 by Sun Microsystems, Inc.
```

```
# All rights reserved.
#
# Network services, Internet style
#
tcpmux          1/tcp
echo            7/tcp
echo            7/udp
discard         9/tcp       sink null
discard         9/udp       sink null
systat          11/tcp      users
daytime         13/tcp
daytime         13/udp
netstat         15/tcp
chargen         19/tcp         ttytst
sourcechargen   19/udp         ttytst source
ftp-data        20/tcp
ftp             21/tcp
telnet          23/tcp
smtp            25/tcp         mail
. . . . .
```

The syntax of the lines in /etc/inet/services is as follows:

```
Service-name    port/protocol    aliases
```

Within this syntax, each field has a special significance:

- Service-name specifies the official Internet name of the service, for example, **telnet** or **ftp**.
- Port/protocol describes both the port number and the protocol that provides the service, such as 512/tcp.
- Aliases is a list of alternate (i.e., unofficial) names by which the service might be requested. This field is optional and so can be blank.

An example line from the /etc/inet/services file follows. We use the **grep** command to extract the telnet line and display it:

```
# grep telnet /etc/inet/services
telnet              23/tcp
```

This line shows that the service called **telnet** uses port 23 and the TCP transport protocol.

Please note that some services use both TCP and UDP protocols, depending on which function of the application is running. DNS is an example of one such application. The DNS entry reads as follows and shows that both transport protocols are used by DNS:

```
domain              53/udp
domain              53/tcp
```

Port Allocation to TI-RPC Servers via **rpcbind**

TI-RPC servers are started either as standalone daemons or through the /etc/inetd.conf mechanism. When TI-RPC servers start, they contact a daemon called **rpcbind** that always listens on UDP and TCP port 111. Please note that **rpcbind** is also called the *portmapper*, which was its previous name under SunOS, Sun's pre-Solaris BSD-based version of UNIX. (Also keep in mind that TI-RPC servers have a fixed program number, which is not to be confused with the port number. We examine the program numbers of TI-RPC servers in the next section of this chapter.)

Here are the steps by which TI-RPC servers receive their port allocations:

1. The **rpcbind** daemon runs at boot time and creates a TCP end point (an address pair consisting of a port plus an IP address), performing a *passive open* on TCP port 111. A port on which a passive open has been performed indicates that the server (**rpcbind** in this case) has started automatically at boot time rather than as a response to receiving a TCP packet with the SYN bit set in the TCP header, and the server simply listens on a port, waiting for client requests. On the other hand, when a client connects to the **rpcbind** port (port 111), it is said to perform an *active open* because it sends the first TCP segment with the SYN bit set, actively seeking a connection.

2. The **rpcbind** daemon also creates a UDP end point and waits for a UDP datagram to arrive for UDP port 111.

3. As RPC servers start, they create a TCP end point and a UDP end point for each version of the program they support. (A given RPC program can support multiple versions. The client specifies which version it wants when it calls a server procedure.) It does not matter whether the TCP port number is the same as or different from the UDP port number. The server registers each program, version, protocol, and port number by making a remote procedure call to the portmapper's PMAPPROC_SET procedure.

4. When the RPC client program runs, it calls **rpcbind**'s PMAPPROC_GETPORT procedure to obtain the server's port number for a given protocol, program, and version number.

5. The client sends an RPC message to the port number returned in the previous step. If UDP is being used, the client just sends a UDP datagram containing an RPC request to the server's UDP port number.

6. The server responds by sending a UDP datagram that contains an RPC reply back to the client.

If TCP is being used, the client performs an active open on the RPC server's TCP port (the port acquired from **rpcbind** in step 4), which forces a TCP connection to be established at the transport layer. The RPC client and server may now send messages over the TCP connection.

We have now examined how traditional servers acquire port numbers though the /etc/inet/services file and how TI-RPC servers acquire a dynamic, ephemeral port from the **rpcbind** portmapper. RPC servers also have a specific program number, which we discuss next.

TI-RPC Server Program Numbers

All RPC servers have a program number, which you should not confuse with their port number. The program numbers of RPC servers are listed in the Solaris 8 file /etc/rpc. Organizations that create TI-RPC services may have their TI-RPC service officially recognized and assigned an official program number though IANA, which manages the official numbering of TI-RPC servers.

When RPC clients contact the **rpcbind** daemon, they supply the program number of the TI-RPC server they wish to contact, along with the version number and transport protocol.

Here are the first 16 lines from the /etc/rpc file:

```
#ident "@(#)rpc 1.12 99/07/25 SMI" /* SVr4.0 1.2 */
#
# rpc
#
rpcbind 100000 portmap sunrpc rpcbind
rstatd 100001 rstat rup perfmeter
rusersd 100002 rusers
nfs 100003 nfsprog
ypserv 100004 ypprog
mountd 100005 mount showmount
ypbind 100007
walld 100008 rwall shutdown
yppasswdd 100009 yppasswd
etherstatd 100010 etherstat
rquotad 100011 rquotaprog quota rquota
sprayd 100012 spray
```

Let us look more closely at two example lines. Here is the first, which identifies the **rpcbind** server itself.

```
rpcbind 100000 portmap sunrpc rpcbind
```

In this example,

- `rpcbind` is the TI-RPC server's name,
- `100,000` is its program number (not port), and
- `portmap` and `sunrpc` are aliases of **rpcbind**.

Here is the second example showing the NFS server daemon **mountd**:

```
mountd 100005 mount showmount
```

In this line,

- `mountd` is the TI-RPC server's name,
- `100,005` is the program number, and
- `mount` and `showmount` are aliases.

EXAM NOTES

KEY LEARNING POINTS

- Standalone server daemons do not use the **inetd** mechanism but are instead started by a script or by the administrator.
- The **inetd** daemon starts servers enabled by the /etc/inet/inetd.conf file by listening for client connections on server ports specified in the /etc/inet/services file.
- TI-RPC servers register with the **rpcbind** server.
- The **rpcbind** server allocates an ephemeral, dynamic port number to TI-RPC servers that register with it.
- RPC servers do not have fixed port numbers, but they do have fixed program numbers that are listed in the /etc/rpc file.
- Both socket-based and RPC servers may be started by the **inetd** daemon.

8.3   Monitoring Services and Servers

So far we have seen that servers start either as standalone daemons or through the **inetd** mechanism. In the remaining portion of this chapter, we discuss how to monitor which servers (both traditional socket-based and TI-RPC) are currently running. The tools for this purpose are the **netstat** and **rpcinfo** commands, which allow administrators to check the port and program numbers for running servers.

Server Monitoring with the netstat Command

The command **netstat –a** displays a list of active sockets for each protocol and other parameters relating to the status of the ports. If a stand-alone server or **inetd** is listening on a port, we can view its status with **netstat –a**. The –a option makes the **netstat** command display the status of active sockets.

    The output for the **netstat –a** command consists of two main sections. The first section has UDP-related information, while the second provides TCP-related information. The following code represents the request for the first 30 lines (the UDP information) followed by the actual output. We use the **–P udp** option to force netstat to display just udp information:

```
# netstat -a -P udp | head -30

UDP: IPv4
   Local Address         Remote Address         State
-------------------- --------------------- -------
*.sunrpc Idle
*.*     Unbound
*.32771 Idle
*.*                                         Unbound
*.*                                         Unbound
*.name                                      Idle
*.time                                      Idle
*.echo                                      Idle
*.discard                                   Idle
*.daytime                                   Idle
*.chargen                                   Idle
*.32772                                     Idle
*.32773                                     Idle
*.*                                         Unbound
*.*                                         Unbound
*.*                                         Unbound
*.*                                         Unbound
*.*                                         Unbound
*.*                                         Unbound
```

```
*.32776                                    Idle
*.lockd                                    Idle
*.1023                                     Idle
*.1022                                     Idle
*.syslog                                   Idle
*.*                                        Unbound
```

In analyzing the foregoing output, notice that there are three columns of information: local address information on the left, remote-address information in the middle, and state information on the right. Local addresses show IP addresses on the same host on which **netstat** is being run; remote addresses are those that have connected from other hosts.

The local address information is preceded by a star character (*), as in the example

```
*.syslog                              Idle
```

In this example, the service **syslog** is available on all local IP addresses, as shown by the wildcard star character. Please note that in the example, no remote host has yet connected, so the remote address field in the middle of the line remains blank. The star character (*) refers to any IP address associated with the current host: *.syslog means that syslog is listening on all addresses. But on which port? To check the port number for syslog, query the /etc/services file:

```
# grep syslog /etc/services
```

The **grep** command responds showing that **syslog** uses server port 514 and the UDP transport protocol:

```
syslog      514/udp
```

The whole purpose of the /etc/services file is to dictate to servers which port they should use (in the case of **syslog**, port 514 and UDP). The administrator has the benefit of examining this configuration information.

At this point, you can run **netstat –a** and **grep** for port 514 to confirm that the syslog service is listening on the port:

```
# netstat -an | grep 514
*.514                                      Idle
```

When the characters *.* appear in the first column (which they do in several of the lines quoted in our examples), they indicate that a socket is available to listen on any of the local systems' IP addresses and any local port.

The column for remote address information is always empty when UDP is being used because UDP is a connectionless service. Remote addresses are associated with remote connections, as you will see when we examine the output for the portion of the **netstat –a** command that pertains to TCP.

The third and last column of the output is status-related information and contains one of two possible values:

- *Unbound* indicates that a socket is available for any service.
- *Idle* indicates that a particular service is listening on the port but is not responding to a client request and is therefore idle.

Next, we examine a selection of output lines from the **netstat –a** command related to TCP services. Please note that the actual output from this command is 300 lines, so most were omitted. In the output lines, the **uname** command (with option **–n**) shows the current host's name, which is centauri. We will refer to this host as either the current host or the local host, depending on the context. The **netstat** command displays the status of local and remote TCP endpoints (sockets) and any available connection information. The **–P** option (with tcp as the parameter) forces **netstat** to display only TCP protocol information.

```
# uname -n
   centauri
# netstat -a -P tcp
TCP: IPv4
```

Local Address	Remote Address	Swind	Send-Q	Rwind	Recv-Q	State
.	*.*	0	0	24576	0	IDLE
*.sunrpc	*.*	0	0	24576	0	LISTEN
.	*.*	0	0	24576	0	IDLE
*.ftp	*.*	0	0	24576	0	LISTEN
*.telnet	*.*	0	0	24576	0	LISTEN
*.time	*.*	0	0	24576	0	LISTEN
*.echo	*.*	0	0	24576	0	LISTEN
*.discard	*.*	0	0	24576	0	LISTEN
*.daytime	*.*	0	0	24576	0	LISTEN
*.chargen	*.*	0	0	24576	0	LISTEN
*.33926	*.*	0	0	24576	0	LISTEN
*.nfsd	*.*	0	0	24576	0	LISTEN
centauri.33927	alpha.telnet	32768	0	24820	0	ESTABLISHED

Let us examine the final line of the output pertaining to centauri because a **telnet** session is established on it. First we examine the local and remote address columns. The data in the remote address column, alpha.telnet, means that a remote system called alpha has a server called **telnet** (port 23 defined in the /etc/services file) running on it, which is connected to local host centauri via client port 33,927 (shown in the local address column). Because **telnet** is a well-known service and is defined in the /etc/services file, it follows that 33,927 on the local host is a telnet client. Clients are usually given high-numbered ports (33,927 in this case) because well-known servers occupy the lower numbered ports. The higher numbered ports are available and will not clash with server ports.

The last five columns of data (Swind, Send-Q, Rwind, Recv-Q, State) give the sizes of the TCP send and receive window and queue in bytes:

```
32768       0 24820       0 ESTABLISHED
```

Let us take a look at each of the columns and their significance:

- swind—This column represents the TCP window size of the sending TCP port. Centauri is the sending machine from the perspective of the local host (see Chapter 7 to review the details of the sliding window protocol).

- Send-Q—This column represents the real-time bytes in the queue waiting to be sent. This value is usually 0, which indicates that everything has been sent without congestion.

- Rwind—This field gives the window size that the local host has received from the other end of the TCP connection (the **telnet** server running on alpha in this case).

- Recv-Q—This field is the receive queue. A value of 0 means that all inbound bytes have been processed.

- State—This is the most important field of the five. There are several possible **state** values for TCP sockets: BOUND, CLOSED, CLOSING, ESTABLISHED, LISTEN, CLOSE_WAIT, FIN_WAIT_1, FIN_WAIT_2, IDLE, LAST_ACK, SYN_RECEIVED, SYN_SENT, and TIME_WAIT. See the Solaris manual page for **netstat** for further details. You do not need to know these states for the purposes of the Sun exam.

In the State column of our example line, ESTABLISHED means that a TCP connection has been established at the Transport layer. The send (swind) and receive window sizes are adjusted as traffic passes across the transport connection. (See Chapter 7 for more details about TCP and window sizes.)

Other lines in the same section of output indicate that a server is listening on a port waiting for a connect. Following is an example.

```
Local Address    Remote Address    Swind Send-Q Rwind    Recv-Q  State
*.ftp            *.*               0     0      24576    0       LISTEN
```

In this example, **ftp** (well-known port 21 in the /etc/services file) is listening on all local IP addresses (as signified by the first star character, *) and will accept a connection from any remote address and any remote port, as indicated by the characters *.* in the Remote Address column. Because no remote client has connected yet, the port is in a LISTEN state. A more exact explanation is that **inetd** is listening and will start up the **ftp** server on demand.

The netstat command has some other useful options, which appear in Table 8.3.

Table 8.3 *Important* netstat *Options*

OPTION	FUNCTION
−a	Shows currently active services
−s	Shows protocol statistics
−r	Displays the IP routing tables
−m	Displays kernel buffers
−p	Displays the ARP cache
−i	Displays interface parameters

Server Monitoring with the rpcinfo Command

In section 8.2, we examined the two types of Solaris server—traditional TCP/IP socket-based servers and RPC (TI-RPC) servers. The **netstat** command allows us to examine the status of sockets used by traditional TCP/IP socket-based servers. We next examine the **rpcinfo** command, which probes the **rpcbind** TI-RPC server daemon and forces it to display the status of all TI-RPC servers that have registered with **rcpbind.**

Recall from section 8.2 that TI-RPC servers register with **rpcbind** (also known as the portmapper) as they start up. We saw how **rpcbind** performed a passive open on UDP and TCP ports 111 and then listened for TI-RPC servers to register with it. Once registered, the servers listen on the dynamic port number allocated to them by **rpcbind.**

In the following command, we run **rpcinfo –p**, which forces **rpcbind** to display the TI-RPC servers that are running and have registered with it. We feed the output from the **rpcinfo** command to **egrep** (extended **grep**) because we wish to search for lines that contain the specific words "rpcbind" and "mountd." The command line output for **rpcinfo –p** is piped to the **egrep** command. Egrep then examines the lines piped to it (its input) and displays only those that contain the words rpcbind and mountd in brackets.

```
# rpcinfo -p  | egrep '( rpcbind | mountd )'
```

Following is the output from the foregoing command, which shows only lines that contain the words rpcbind and mountd at least once, as required by the **egrep** command:

```
program vers proto    port   service
100000  4    tcp      111    rpcbind
100000  3    tcp      111    rpcbind
100000  2    tcp      111    rpcbind
100000  4    udp      111    rpcbind
100000  3    udp      111    rpcbind
100000  2    udp      111    rpcbind
100005  1    udp    32783    mountd
100005  2    udp    32783    mountd
100005  3    udp    32783    mountd
100005  1    tcp    32790    mountd
100005  2    tcp    32790    mountd
100005  3    tcp    32790    mountd
```

rpcbind *Fields*

The output fields for the **rpcbind** lines deserve further explanation. We will refer to the first line of output in the foregoing section as our example line. Here it is again:

```
100000   4     tcp      111    rpcbind
```

PROGRAM

The program field shows that TI-RPC servers have program numbers, which should not be confused with the port number. The program number of **rpcbind** itself is 100000. All official TI-RPC servers are registered with an organization called IANA (see http://www.iana.org). On Solaris, the /etc/rpc file contains a list of the TI-RPC servers and their fixed program number. Program numbers are passed by the TI-RPC client when it asks the **rpcbind** server (on port 111) for the location of the TI-RPC server is it seeking.

VERS

Solaris runs several versions of the same TI-RPC server for backward compatibility. In our example line, the version number is 4.

PROTO

This field represents the protocol. TI-RPC servers use both TCP and UDP at the Transport layer. In our example line, the protocol is tcp.

PORT

The port number is allocated to the TI-RPC server by **rpcbind**. In this case, we are actually looking at the **rpcbind** server itself. That is, **rpcbind** (unlike other TI-RPC servers) always allocates to itself the same port number 111 to ensure that other TI-RPC servers can always locate it.

SERVICE

This field gives the name of the service as listed in the Solaris 8 /etc/rpc file. The first seven lines of the **rpcinfo -p** command shown previously show that six instances of the rpcbind service are running simultaneously. This is because there are three versions running, and each version is running both TCP and UDP. The six relevant lines are:

```
program     vers   proto   port   service
100000      4      tcp     111    rpcbind
100000      3      tcp     111    rpcbind
100000      2      tcp     111    rpcbind
100000      4      udp     111    rpcbind
100000      3      udp     111    rpcbind
100000      2      udp     111    rpcbind
```

mountd *Fields*

Next, we briefly examine the **mountd** lines, also shown in the **rpcinfo –p** command discussed previously. We need not examine them in as much detail as we did the lines pertaining to **rpcbind**, because the meaning of all the lines produced by **rpcinfo –p** are the same even though the content of each line is different.

Notice, first of all, that **mountd** is program number 100005, which is again found in the Solaris file /etc/rpc. Three versions of **mountd** are running, each using both TCP and UDP. Six **mountd** TI-RPC servers therefore appear in the **rpcinfo** command output. The port number 32783 is used by the udp instance of the **mountd** server, and port number 32790 is used by the tcp version of the **mountd** TI-RPC server.

Note The TI-RPC server port numbers are not fixed, but rather have been dynamically allocated by the rpcbind server and might be different on different hosts running mountd. They can even differ on the same host if mountd is stopped and started and so forced to reregister with the rpcbind server.

The /etc/rpc File

We mentioned the Solaris 8 file /etc/rpc server several times in the foregoing discussion. It is now time to view its contents, which will show us where some of the **rpcinfo** values are derived from. The /etc/rpc file lists the official TI-RPC servers' names and their program numbers. The TI-RPC servers must use the program numbers listed in this file.

We can use the **cat** and **head** commands to extract just the first 10 lines of the file, as shown in the following command:

```
# cat /etc/rpc | head -10
```

Here is the output from the command:

```
#ident "@(#)rpc 1.12 99/07/25 SMI" /* SVr4.0 1.2 */
#
# rpc
#
rpcbind 100000 portmap sunrpc rpcbind
rstatd  100001 rstat   rup perfmeter
rusersd 100002 rusers
nfs     100003 nfsprog
```

```
ypserv   100004 ypprog
mountd   100005 mount    showmount
```

The first few lines are simply comments in the file and may be ignored. We shall examine the syntax of the last line of the /etc/rpc file, and we shall see how **rpcinfo**'s "mountd" output correlates with the contents of the /etc/rpc file:

```
mountd   100005 mount showmount
```

Official Server Name

The first field is the server's official name. In our example line, the server's official name is mountd.

Program Number

The next field gives the TI-RPC server's official program number. The **mountd** program number is always 100005.

The official program number is not a port number. TI-RPC servers have a fixed program number but an rpcbind-allocated, dynamic port number.

Aliases

All values that follow the program number (mount and showmount in our example line) are aliases for the official service name, shown in the first field.

TI-RPC servers should not simply be killed with the Solaris **pkill** command. Please ensure that you first deregister them with the **rpcbind** server to ensure the correct and smooth functioning of the system. In this next example we see how to correctly deregister a TI-RPC server, in this example **mountd**. Note that each version must be deleted individually. Here we delete all three versions that we know are running, based on our examination of **mountd** in the previous example:

```
# rpcinfo -d 100005 2
# rpcinfo -d 100005 3
# rpcinfo -d 100005 4
```

The command has no output. We may ensure that **mountd** has indeed been deregistered by using the **rpcinfo** command to print out the **rpcbind** registered server list, and then searching for lines that contain **mountd**. We should see none:

```
# rpcinfo -p | grep mountd
```

The output shows that **mountd** is no longer registered with **rpcbind**, which is what we expect.

Comparing inetd and rpcbind

Table 8.4 summarizes the similarities and differences between **inetd** and **rpcbind** server daemons. Most of the items in the table should be familiar if you have read the previous discussions.

Table 8.4 *Comparing the* inetd *and* rpcbind *Server Daemons*

THE INETD SERVER	THE RPCBIND SERVER
Listens on many ports for all the servers that are configured and enabled in the /etc/inet/inetd.conf file. The port numbers for servers are acquired from the /etc/services file.	Simply allocates an ephemeral port number to TI-RPC servers that register with it but only listens on port 111. The TI-RPC servers that register with **rpcbind** listen on the port **rpcbind** allocates to them.
Services typically have well-known ports listed in the /etc/inet/services file. The non TI-RPC servers on which **inetd** predominantly listens have no RPC program number, as they are not RPC based.	TI-RPC servers do not have well-known ports. TI-RPC servers register with **rpcbind** using program numbers from /etc/rpc for identification.
Largely socket based; can be TLI based.	TI-RPC based, often uses XDR as well.
Clients are allocated a random (next available) port number.	Clients are allocated a random (next available) port number

EXAM NOTES

KEY LEARNING POINTS

- The **netstat –a** command shows the status of sockets and ports.
- The **rpcinfo –p** command dumps a database of TI-RPC servers that have registered with **rpcbind**.
- Traditional socket-based servers typically have well-known ports.
- TI-RPC servers are dynamically allocated ports to listen on by **rpcbind**.
- TI-RPC servers have fixed program numbers.
- TI-RPC program numbers are listed in the file /etc/rpc.
- The **rpcbind** daemon is also known as **sunrpc** or as the portmapper.

SUMMARY

This chapter explored both traditional, socket-based servers and the chronologically more recent TI-RPC servers, pioneered by Sun as part of their ONC+ environment.

We examined the role played by the super daemons **inetd** and **rpcbind**, which facilitate client and server communication on the Solaris platform. We discovered how to enable and disable services and how some daemons are standalone and always listening on a port, while others are started by **inetd**. We also discussed how to use the **netstat** and **rpcinfo** commands to examine running processes and query the status of active ports. Finally, we contrasted **rpcbind** and **inetd**, which, although offering different services, both offer a mechanism through which clients and servers communicate.

TEST YOURSELF

MULTIPLE CHOICE

1. *Which of the following is at the Session layer of the OSI 7-layer model?*
   A. XDR
   B. RPC

   C. TCP

   D. UDP

   E. IP

 2. *What is a standalone server? Choose two.*

   A. One that is started by **inetd**

   B. One that is started by **rpcbind**

   C. One that is started by a client request

   D. One that is started by a shell script

   E. One that is started by the administrator

 3. *The **inetd** daemon reads which file to discover how to start servers?*

   A. /etc/services

   B. /etc/inetd.conf

   C. /etc/conf.inetd

   D. /etc/rpc

   E. /etc/rpc.conf

 4. *Which file lists TI-RPC server program numbers?*

   A. /etc/services

   B. /etc/inetd.conf

   C. /etc/conf.inetd

   D. /etc/rpc

   E. /etc/rpc.conf

 5. *Which file supplies port numbers to the traditional category of server?*

   A. /etc/services

   B. /etc/inetd.conf

   C. /etc/conf.inetd

   D. /etc/rpc

   E. /etc/rpc.conf

 6. *Which daemon allocates ephemeral port numbers to TI-RPC servers?*

   A. **inetd**

   B. **rpcbind**

   C. **portbind**

   D. **mountd**

   E. **rpcinfo**

7.   *Which command checks for running TI-RPC servers?*
     A. mount
     B. rpcinfo
     C. portinfo
     D. netstat
     E. pstat

8.   *XDR functions at which layer of the OSI stack?*
     A. Session
     B. Presentaion
     C. Transport
     D. Application
     E. Network

9.   *On which port number does the **rpcbind** daemon always listen?*
     A. 111111
     B. 100000
     C. 100
     D. 111
     E. 1000

10.   *What do the characters* *.* *mean in the output of the* **netstat –a** *command?*
     A. Any port.Any IP address
     B. Any IP address.Any port
     C. Any local.Any remote
     D. Any remote.Any local
     E. Any port.Any port

FREE RESPONSE

1.   *Describe the senses in which a port can be said to be ephemeral.*

2.   *Use the analogy of a receptionist to describe the way **rpcbind** works.*

Dynamic Address Allocation with DHCP

EXAM OBJECTIVES

9.1 Overview of DHCP

9.2 DHCP Configuration Files

9.3 Administering DHCP Clients and Servers

9.4 The DHCP Server Daemon in.dhcpd

After completing this chapter, you will be able to meet the following Network Administration Exam objectives:

- State the benefits of Dynamic Host Configuration Protocol (DHCP).
- Identify DHCP configuration files.
- State the purpose of DHCP configuration files.
- Administer DHCP clients and servers.

To help you meet these objectives, this chapter covers the following topics:

- DHCP terminology, allocation modes, and advantages and disadvantages of using DHCP
- DHCP configuration files, examples, symbols, and macros
- commands for creating and administering DHCP clients and servers
- the DHCP server daemon and its debugging and verbose options

9.1 Overview of DHCP

Dynamic Host Configuration Protocol (DHCP) makes it possible to allocate IP addresses to hosts automatically. It provides a framework for passing network configuration information to hosts on a TCP/IP network. DHCP client- and server-side software was introduced into the Solaris distribution with Solaris 7, with functionality extended in Solaris 8. You should be aware that although DHCP is a standard protocol, the commands and range of features supported by specific vendors of UNIX will vary. In this chapter, we focus on DHCP as supported and implemented by Sun's Solaris 8.

DHCP is an extension of the Bootstrap protocol (BOOTP), as defined in RFC 2131 and RFC 2132. In addition to offering BOOTP capability, it offers reusable IP addresses through a time-based leasing scheme. Through this scheme, IP addresses are leased for a period of time and may then be leased to another host when the current host's lease expires. We will take a closer look at this feature later in this chapter.

To lay the groundwork for our exploration of DHCP, we will first define some general DHCP terminology and identify the broad advantages and disadvantages of using DHCP for IP address management.

DHCP Terminology

The following terms are used by the DHCP protocol and need to be defined in the context of DHCP:

- client
- server
- BOOTP relay
- DHCP binding
- DHCP lease

DHCP Client

A DHCP client is usually a host but can be another network device (such as a network printer) using DHCP to obtain interface configuration parameters such as an IP, netmask, or broadcast address from a DHCP server. Clients can also use DHCP to learn information relating to DNS, Network Time Protocol (NTP), and network routers. In essence, almost any network parameter can be passed from server to client through the DHCP infrastructure.

In section 9.3 we will see how to configure a Solaris DHCP client. DHCP clients rely on DHCP servers, which we describe next.

DHCP Server

A DHCP server is a host that returns DHCP parameters to DHCP clients that request them through the DHCP service. You can configure DHCP to return a wide range of client parameters. The main pieces of information that pass from the DHCP server to the DHCP client are the IP, netmask, and broadcast addresses that you learned about in chapter 5. In section 9.3, you will learn how to configure a Solaris DHCP server.

When DHCP server and clients are on the same logical network, they can communicate using both unicast and broadcast addresses. A fundamental problem occurs, however, when the DHCP client and server are on different networks. This is because data addressed to a network's broadcast address and does not usually pass though a network's IP router, as you will recall from Chapter 5.

By design, much of the DHCP server and client network traffic is broadcast based, meaning that DHCP client requests on one network are not heard by DHCP servers on other networks. In most cases, this is desirable. When communication between remote networks is desired, DHCP offers a means by which the DHCP traffic can be relayed through routers, so that local DHCP clients can reach remote DHCP servers. For example, there might be only one DHCP server but four different networks with DHCP clients. Setting up a DHCP server for each network that has DHCP clients could be a painful process. The solution is to set up BOOTP relays, which we briefly explore next.

BOOTP Relay

Recall from Chapter 6 that broadcasts do not pass through Solaris routers. To work around this dilemma, a BOOTP relay server relays communication packets between DHCP clients and servers that exist on different networks, thus eliminating the need for DHCP servers to reside on every network where DHCP clients exist. The BOOTP relay listens for DHCP packets and relays them between DHCP client and server. In section 9.3 we see how to configure a Solaris DHCP server and BOOTP relay.

Once a client has found a DHCP server and is using that server, the client is said to be *bound* to the server. Binding between DHCP client and server is the next term we examine.

DHCP Binding

A *binding* is a collection of configuration parameters (at minimum, an IP address) that is associated with or bound to a DHCP client and allocated or provided by a DHCP server. The status of this binding is known by both DHCP client and server. The client and server write this information to files, which implies that the information is remembered across a reboot. A binding implies that a relationship exists between client and server, whereby the client uses information and resources—such as an IP address—made available by the DHCP server.

Lease

The term *lease* describes the period of time during which the DHCP server allows a DHCP client the use of an allocated IP address from the said DHCP server's pool of currently available addresses. The DHCP client asks for an IP address to use (usually when it boots up), and the DHCP server provides an IP address from its available IP addresses, but it restricts the use of this address to a finite period of time—typically three days. The network administrator may change the default lease period. It is this feature that allows the DHCP server to share a fixed set of IP addresses among several client hosts. On expiration of the lease, DHCP can allocate the IP address to another client, or the IP address may become available in the pool once again if the DHCP client relinquishes it. This leasing capability of DHCP makes the protocol different from BOOTP.

Note A DHCP client usually acquires its IP address and other network parameters at boot time. It is possible, however, to use DHCP to assign an IP address and other parameters to an interface by using ifconfig as follows:

```
# ifconfig qfe0    DHCP
```

Advantages of Using DHCP

From the client's point of view, there are both advantages and disadvantages to using DHCP. The benefits of DHCP relate primarily to the automated provision of host-related parameters that DHCP servers make available to clients. We will discuss in this chapter all of the following advantages:

- automatic allocation and deallocation of IP addresses to client hosts
- reuse of IP addresses released by DHCP clients and returned to the DHCP server pool, where they become available for other clients
- passing of other useful information, such as domain name server information, between client and servers (Domain Name Service [DNS] is covered in Chapter 11)
- IP address sharing by nomadic nodes that connect to the network at different times
- host relocation eased by auto-assignment of a valid IP address through DHCP when a DHCP client connects to a new network
- use of BOOTP relays to allow clients to talk to servers on different subnets

Disadvantages of Using DHCP

DHCP also has some disadvantages:

- There is the risk of an intruder being autoallocated an IP address if a means of connecting to the network is found.
- Specialized DHCP training is needed by network administrators.
- DHCP needs to be monitored.

Although the dynamic allocation of an IP address reduces the work of the network administrator, it has the disadvantage that human intervention is not required for an IP address to be allocated to an intruder's rogue client. Many companies have network access panels (floor patch panels); an intruder could theoretically merely plug a PC or other mobile device into the floor panel access point and immediately be allocated an IP address by the DHCP server.

In addition, to manage DHCP, the network administrator needs to understand how DHCP servers and clients operate and interact, particularly when problems occur. Initially, DHCP needs to be installed, configured, and tested.

Following installation, DHCP requires monitoring to ensure the detection of problems such as the deletion of a server's IP address pool, client binding problems, the presence of rogue clients, clients using the wrong IP address, or clients refusing to release an IP address. As with any network service, the logs are critical with respect to troubleshooting and monitoring.

Some of these disadvantages can be overcome by limiting DHCP IP address assignment to known Ethernet addresses (see section 9.3 on configuring a DHCP server). Additionally, SNMP-managed devices such as hubs and switches can be programmed to recognize an allowed list of Ethernet addresses that are assigned to the device. When an unknown Ethernet address is detected on the network, the device can sound an alert or inform the administrator through e-mail, for example.

DHCP IP Address Allocation Modes

DHCP supports three modes or mechanisms for allocating IP addresses to DHCP clients:

- *automatic allocation*—permanent, nonspecific IP addresses
- *dynamic allocation*—nonspecific IP addresses leased for a fixed time period
- *manual allocation*—permanent, specific IP addresses

A *permanent* IP address is one that is allocated for an infinite amount of time and is not subject to a time-based lease. A *leased* IP address, on the other hand, is one that is allocated to a client for a finite amount of time. The amount of time is measured in seconds and calculated as an integer that represents the number of seconds from January 1, 1970 (UNIX Epoch day) to the present day, plus the length of the lease. The lease period represents a finite number of seconds, which if added to January 1, 1970, would reach a time chronologically ahead of the time the lease was started by the length of the lease in seconds.

The term *specific*, as it applies to a DHCP-leased IP address, means a predetermined IP address that is reserved and allocated only to a particular client. We can also describe this type of address as *static* or *fixed*.

The following discussion introduces and briefly describes each of the three allocation modes. In later sections of this chapter, you will learn how to configure a DHCP server to deploy each of the three modes.

Automatic Allocation of Permanent IP Addresses

Automatic allocation means that the DHCP server assigns an IP address to a DHCP client when the host connects to the network without administrator intervention or manual configuration. The IP address is assigned on a permanent basis, is not subject to lease for a finite period of time, and cannot be revoked by the DHCP server. The IP address itself is usually automatically selected from the DHCP server's pool of available IP addresses and is not a predetermined or specific IP address. (With the manual mode of allocation, an administrator can preassign IP addresses to systems based on the system's Ethernet address.)

Dynamic Allocation of IP Addresses

With *dynamic allocation*, the DHCP server assigns an IP address to a client for a limited period of time, which is measured in seconds. The client may explicitly relinquish its need for the IP address or request an extension of the lease, and this renewal of the lease may occur repeatedly or be denied by the DHCP server.

The lease of a dynamically allocated IP address has a time limit imposed on it, even though that time period may be years in length. Like automatic allocation, the dynamic allocation method does not require administrator intervention. It is dynamic in that, compared with automatic allocation, there is far greater negotiation between client and server, which may result in IP addresses and other network-related parameters changing in real time.

Only the dynamic allocation mode allows for the automatic reuse of an IP address that is no longer required by the client to which it was allocated. Thus, dynamic allocation is particularly useful for assigning addresses to clients that will be connected to the network for a short period of time, or for sharing a limited pool of IP addresses among a group of nomadic clients that do not need permanent IP addresses. For example, nomadic salespeople who use their laptops to plug into the office LAN during fleeting onsite visits are excellent candidates for dynamic allocation.

Manual Allocation of IP Addresses

With *manual allocation*, a client's IP address is preassigned by the network administrator in the DHCP configuration files, and DHCP is used simply to convey the assigned address to the client, usually when the client boots. Network administrators may choose to mix automatic, dynamic, and manual DHCP modes.

Allocating a Specific Address to a DHCP Client

You may have wondered why the network administrator might wish to allocate a specific address to a given client. There are many possible reasons, and the explanations for some of them are extensive, security-related, and beyond the scope of the Sun exam. But here is a brief description of them for your information:

- *Monitoring and logging purposes*—Administrators might choose to monitor and log a given client closely, especially if there is suspicion of foul play or other questionable network activity.

- *Restrictive server*—Administrators might wish to restrict the use of some servers and services (for example, Web, e-mail, DNS, news, ftp servers) to permitted IP addresses.

- *Firewall security/blocking IP addresses*—A firewall's main role is to block inbound network traffic that is attempting to enter an intranet, or to block outbound traffic that is leaving an intranet. Administrators can, for example, create firewall rules that block specific employee IP addresses from sending outbound network packets or that monitor the Internet use of each employee.

- *Firewall security/network address translation (NAT)*—Firewalls (and other devices such as routers) have the ability to translate outbound and inbound IP addresses as found in IP datagram headers. You should recall from Chapter 5 that if a company uses IP addresses that have not been assigned "officially" by APNIC, ARIN, and RIPE, these are considered "private" or unofficial addresses that cannot be used on the public Internet. Many companies use such unofficial IP address ranges, however. If a DHCP server is configured to allocate addresses from unofficial ranges, administrators can allow DHCP clients to "see" the Internet by using the firewall's capability to map specific IP addresses onto a legal IP address through NAT.

KEY LEARNING POINTS

- DHCP is an enhancement of BOOTP.
- DHCP manages the autoallocation of IP addresses to DHCP clients that use DHCP to acquire an IP address and other important network parameters.
- DHCP uses BOOTP to relay DHCP information between or through routers.
- Leases of IP addresses are time-based and measured in seconds.
- Automatic allocation assigns a permanent, nonspecific IP address.
- Dynamic allocation assigns a nonspecific address that is leased for a finite period of time.
- Manual allocation assigns a permanent, specific IP address.

9.2 DHCP Configuration Files

DHCP has several configuration files that require editing. In this section, we examine the purpose and content of each DHCP-related configuration file. In section 9.3 of this chapter, we examine the commands available to modify the contents of these files.

The DHCP configuration files are:

- /etc/dhcp/inittab
- /var/dhcp/*dhcp_network*, where dhcp_network is generic and replaced by the actual network address, with full stops (.) replaced by underscore characters (_). For example, for network 194.168.85.0, the corresponding file would be called /var/dhcp/ 194_168_85_0.
- /var/dhcp/dhcptab
- /etc/dhcp.*interface*, where interface is symbolic. For example, for interface hme0, the corresponding file would be called /etc/ dhcp.hme0.
- /etc/default/dhcp
- /etc/default/dhcpagent

The /etc/dhcp/inittab File

The purpose of the /etc/dhcp/inittab file is to define options for data objects that pass between DHCP server and client. This file is available on both DHCP servers and clients. It does not usually require much modification and acts as a text-based database of options for DHCP programs and processes.

Five categories of supported options are found in the file. Each option category has a specific *scope*, which indicates whether the options are local to one company's network(s) or global and not specific to any one site. The five option categories are:

- STANDARD
- SITE
- VENDOR
- FIELD
- INTERNAL

In the pages that follow, we will discuss examples of options from each category. The total list of options is extensive and need not be covered for purposes of the Sun exam. For a complete list of DHCP options, see RFC 2132. RFC 2131 is a general introduction to DHCP and is also worth a read. In addition, the Solaris manual pages have extensive information about the contents of this file. Run the following command at the Solaris command prompt:

```
#  man -s 4 dhcp_inittab
```

to display the format of the /etc/dhcp/inittab file.

Most options describe parameter information that is passed from DHCP server to client in a specific format, such as IP address, octet, or ASCII. Most lines in the file have the same fields regardless of category, so once having examined examples of options, there is no need to examine all five categories in detail. Differences in line content among the five category types will be stressed as we discuss each category.

Warning

The /etc/dhcp/inittab file should not be modified except to add support for optional SITE and VENDOR options. Existing STANDARD options should not be modified.

Option Type STANDARD

The STANDARD option type is administered by the Internet Assigned Numbers Authority (IANA); it is universal among all DHCP clients and servers and should therefore not be modified. Following are several example lines from the file /etc/dhcp/inittab. Using the **cat**, **grep**, and **head** command line shown next, we may display the first six STANDARD options.

```
# cat /etc/dhcp/inittab | grep STANDARD | head -6

Subnet      STANDARD,    1,    IP,            1,    1,    sdmi
UTCoffst    STANDARD,    2,    SNUMBER32,1,         1,    sdmi
Router      STANDARD,    3,    IP,            1,    0,    sdmi
Timeserv    STANDARD,    4,    IP,            1,    0,    sdmi
IEN116n     STANDARD,    5,    IP,            1,    0,    sdmi
DNSserv     STANDARD,    6,    IP,            1,    0,    sdmi
```

The purpose of the last of these six lines (option DNSserv) is to define DNS servers, whose IP addresses are passed from DHCP server to client. Using this line as an example, we can divide the information in each line into seven fields as follows:

```
Field 1    Field 2    Field 3   Field 4   Field 5  Field 6
Field 7
DNSserv    STANDARD,  6,        IP,       1,       0,
sdmi
```

We can gain insight into the information in and structure of the /etc/dhcp/inittab file by looking closely at each of the seven fields.

FIELD 1: IDENTIFIER

```
DNSserv
```

The first field describing an option is a user-friendly mnemonic identifier for the option's number, which is shown in the third field (6 in this example line).

FIELD 2: OPTION CATEGORY TYPE

```
STANDARD
```

The second field in an option line describes the category type, in this case STANDARD. This field determines the scope of the option.

FIELD 3: OPTION NUMBER

6

The third field identifies the option number. All options in the /etc/dhcp/inittab file have a unique identifying number. Field 1, DNSServ, is a mnemonic for option number 6.

FIELD 4: DATA FORMAT

IP

Field 4 reveals the data format type of an option. The field given here as an example specifies that when option 6 (DNSserv) data is passed from server to client, the data in the DHCP protocol packet must be an IP address. The complete list of possible data types includes the following:

- Ascii—A printable character string
- Octet—An array of bytes
- Unumber8—An 8-bit unsigned integer
- Snumber8—An 8-bit signed integer
- Unumber16—A 16-bit unsigned integer
- Snumber16—A 16-bit signed integer
- Unumber32—A 32-bit unsigned integer
- Snumber32—A 32-bit signed integer
- Unumber64—A 64-bit unsigned integer
- Snumber64—A 64-bit signed integer
- Ip—An IP address

FIELD 5: GRANULARITY

1

Field 5 is the granularity field, which indicates how many items of the type described in field 4 (data format) make up a whole value. In this example, the value is 1, indicating that a single IP address is a complete value.

FIELD 6: COUNT ALLOWED

0

This field indicates how many units of the data type described in field 4 are allowed in a DHCP packet being passed from a client to a server. A value of 0, as in the example of DNSserv shown here, indicates that there is no maximum limit.

FIELD 7: VISIBILITY

smdi

Visibility determines which programs may make use of this line of information (i.e., the current option). Currently, **smdi**, **smi**, **id**, and **dm** are understood by the **dhcpinfo** command, examined in section 9.3.

Option Type SITE

Options in the SITE category are site specific: Within a site, the meaning of these options is agreed upon, but beyond the confines of that site, the meaning of the same option may be different. By default, no SITE options are in the Solaris 8 /etc/dhcp/inittab file.

Option Type VENDOR

The DHCP vendor, such as Sun Microsystems, may define up to 254 options specific to its own products. Following are four example lines from the Solaris 8 /etc/dhcp/inittab file. We may use the **cat** command with **grep** and **head** to display the first four lines containing the word VENDOR:

```
# cat /etc/dhcp/inittab | grep VENDOR | head -4
```

```
SrootOpt    VENDOR,    1,    ASCII,    1,    0,    smi
SrootIP4    VENDOR,    2,    IP,       1,    1,    smi
SrootNM     VENDOR,    3,    ASCII,    1,    0,    smi
SrootPTH    VENDOR,    4,    ASCII,    1,    0,    smi
```

Notice that in the foregoing example, the fields are almost identical in format to the ones in the STANDARD option that we have already discussed. There is one exception: the last field, smi. This simply identifies Sun Microsystems Incorporated as the vendor.

Option Type FIELD

The FIELD category allows the fixed fields within a DHCP packet to be aliased to a mnemonic for use with the **dhcpinfo** command, which we explore further in section 9.3. Here, as an example, are the first four lines containing the word FIELD in the Solaris 8 /etc/dhcp/inittab file:

```
# cat /etc/dhcp/inittab | grep FIELD | head -4
```

```
Opcode   FIELD,           0,      UNUMBER8,  1,   1,      id
Htype    FIELD,           1,      UNUMBER8,  1,   1,      id
HLen     FIELD,           2,      UNUMBER8,  1,   1,      id
Hops     FIELD,           3,      UNUMBER8,  1,   1,      id
```

In the example just given, Opcode (category type FIELD) is an 8-bit unsigned integer as indicated by the fourth (data format) field, which contains the value UNUMBER8.

Option Type INTERNAL

The INTERNAL category is used internally by Sun. Unfortunately, the Sun manual says that no information may given about type INTERNAL. We may use the **cat** command with **grep** and **head** to display the first four lines in the /etc/dhcp/inittab file that contain the word FIELD:

```
# cat /etc/dhcp/inittab | grep INTERNAL | head -4
```

```
Hostname   INTERNAL,       1024,    BOOL,      0,   0,      dm
LeaseNeg   INTERNAL,       1025,    BOOL,      0,   0,      dm
EchoVC     INTERNAL,       1026,    BOOL,      0,   0,      dm
BootPath   INTERNAL,       1027,    ASCII,     1,   128,    dm
```

These options are used internally by Sun's implementation of DHCP and must not be modified.

In summary, the purpose of the /etc/dhcp/inittab file is to provide STANDARD, VENDOR, SITE, FIELD, and INTERNAL options, as defined in RFC 2132. The options define parameters and a data field. The data stored in the option may be passed by the server to the client.

The /var/dhcp/*dhcp_network* File

The purpose of the /var/dhcp/*dhcp_network* file is to identify a pool of IP addresses and the server that allocates them to DHCP clients. Each line in the file ends with a string or identifier that associates the line to macros defined in the file /var/dhcp/dhcptab. Those macros, as we shall see when we examine the /var/dhcp/dhcptab file, define a list of parameters to associate with the client.

The first point to stress is that the actual filename of the /var/dhcp/dhcp_*network* file depends on the network it contains. For example, if the network the DHCP server is serving is network 194.168.85.0, the file would be called /var/dhcp/194_168_85_0. Notice also that the filename uses underscores, not dots.

The /var/dhcp/*dhcp_network* file is created by the **dhcpconfig** command (see section 9.3) and is essentially a simple text-based database. This database is located by the DHCP server at runtime upon receipt of a DHCP request. The DHCP network databases can exist as either NIS+ tables or ASCII files. The database should be managed by the **pntadm** command (see section 9.3), as its format can change, so manual editing is not recommended.

Following is an example of the file's content. Unlike the /etc/dhcp/inittab file, the /var/dhcp/*dhcp_network* file varies greatly from DHCP server to server, as it contains network-specific information. We use the UNIX **cat** command to display its contents:

```
# cat  /var/dhcp/194_168_85_0

010800207B33A4 00 194.168.85.180 194.168.85.51 1009397309 gvonnet1
0100008627A032 03 194.168.85.181  194.168.85.51  -1        gvonnet1
00        00        194.168.85.182  194.168.85.51  0        gvonnet1
00        00        194.168.85.183  194.168.85.51  0        gvonnet1
00        00        194.168.85.184  194.168.85.51  0        gvonnet1
00        00        194.168.85.185  194.168.85.51  0        gvonnet1
00        00        194.168.85.186  194.168.85.51  0        gvonnet1
00        00        194.168.85.187  194.168.85.51  0        gvonnet1
00        00        194.168.85.188  194.168.85.51  0        gvonnet1
00        00        194.168.85.189  194.168.85.51  0        gvonnet1
```

Please note that *dhcp_network* is a generic filename and that the actual name, following the configuration of DHCP for a given network, is based on the network ranges configured. In the example, the file is actually called /var/dhcp/194_168_85_0 because the network address range being managed by DHCP is 194.168.85.0.

Let us now explain the generic format and the fields of lines in the /var/dhcp/*dhcp_network* file using a line from the foregoing sample output. The information on each line can be separated out into six fields:

```
Field 1          Field 2 Field 3         Field 4         Field 5      Field 6
010800207B33A4 00         194.168.85.180 194.168.85.51 1009397309 gvonnet1
```

FIELD 1: CLIENT IDENTIFIER

```
010800207B33A4
```

The variable *client_ID* must be unique within the database and is usually composed of something unique to the client, such as the Ethernet address plus other general information. On Solaris, the *client_ID* is 01 and is usually simply suffixed to the client's Ethernet address to form a unique *client_ID*. Each line will begin with a unique *client_ID* value.

FIELD 2: FLAGS

```
00
```

Field 2 has predefined values that are used across all Solaris DHCP implementations. These are shown in Table 9.1.

Please note that field values may be combined. For example, a Field 2 value of 03 indicates that the IP address in question is both manual and permanent.

Table 9.1 *Flag Field Types and Codes*

NAME OF ENTRY TYPE	CODE	MEANING
Dynamic	00	The lease is negotiable if the LeaseNeg macro value is set to 1.
Permanent	01	The lease is permanent.
Manual	02	The IP address is fixed.
Unusable	04	ICMP has reported that the IP address is in use and so unusable.
Bootp	08	The IP address is reserved for BOOTP clients, not DHCP clients.

FIELD 3: CLIENT_IP

194.168.85.180

Field 3 holds the IP address of the system and must be unique, as only one system may be assigned a given IP address.

FIELD 4: SERVER_IP

194.168.85.51

This field holds the address of the server that must allocate the IP address in the *Client_IP* field.

FIELD 5: LEASE

1009397309

Field 5 holds an absolute lease expiration time, which is expressed in seconds starting at UNIX epoch day (January 1, 1970). A value of -1 in this field indicates a permanent lease. A value of 0 indicates that the IP address in the line is still available.

FIELD 6: MACRO

gvonnet1

This ASCII field uses a macro that is defined in the dhcptab file. In so doing, this field associates the values of the dhcptab macro with the IP address in this dhcp_network entry. We will see how to create the macros when we examine the dhcptab file shortly.

In the foregoing example, the macro is gvonnet1. Field 6 acts as a link field to the next file we examine, which is called /var/dhcp/dhcptab.

The /var/dhcp/dhcptab File

The purpose of the /var/dhcp/dhcptab file is to define macros and the symbols used in macros. The macros defined in this file are used in the /var/dhcp/*dhcp_network* file. The example macro given in the previous section was **gvonnet1**, which is defined in the following /var/dhcp/dhcptab file:

```
# cat /var/dhcp/dhcptab
gvonnet1   m  :GvonstatRt=10.1.1.0  194.168.85.62:\
Include=Locale:  :Timeserv=194.168.85.51:LeaseTim=259200:\
DNSdmain=gvon.com::DNSserv=194.168.85.1 194.168.85.2:\
LeaseNeg:
```

The /var/dhcp/dhcptab file has the following format:

```
Name |  Type |  Value
```

Following is an elucidation of these three fields.

Name

The `Name` field serves as an index into the /var/dhcp/*dhcp_network* file, linking it with the /var/dhcp/dhcptab file. In the example just given, gvonnet1 is a macro, hence the *m* that follows the word *gvonnet1*.

Type

The `Type` field specifies the record type of the `Value` field that follows it. At present, there are only two legal record type values: *s* (symbol) and *m* (macro). Once defined, a symbol can be used in macro definitions. Actual defined symbols and macros are stored in the `Value` field.

Value

The `Value` field contains the contents of a macro if the `Type` field contains a value of *m* for macro. If the `Type` field contains a value of *s*, the `Value` field contains a symbol. Let us look at an example of each.

SYMBOL CHARACTERISTICS

A symbol consists of a series of fields, each separated by a comma (,). The syntax of a symbol includes five fields:

- context
- code
- type

- granularity
- maximum

In order for a new symbol to be recognized, you must add it to the Solaris 8 file /etc/dhcp/inittab. Having done so, you may use it in macro definitions.

Here is an example symbol called GvonstatRt to illustrate this syntax in context:

```
GvonstatRt   s      SITE,130,IP,2,0
```

CONTEXT • The context is GvonstatRt, the name of the symbol.

CODE • The code is 130, indicating that it is a SITE-specific option. Recall that the codes for options are STANDARD (values 1 through 127), SITE (values 128 through 254), and VENDOR (values 1 through 254).

TYPE • IP is the field type in our example. Other legal values include ASCII string, BOOLEAN value, or NUMBER (unsigned integer).

GRANULARITY • The granularity determines how many values of the specified type make up this symbol. The value is 2 in our example because GvonstatRt is made up of two IP addresses.

MAXIMUM • In the case of GvonstatRt, the maximum value is zero because the symbol may contain an infinite number of pairs of IP addresses.

MACRO CHARACTERISTICS

A macro consists of a series of symbol=value pairs, each separated by a colon (:) character. Here is a macro defined using the symbol we created in the foregoing paragraphs:

```
gvonnet1  m   :GvonstatRt=10.1.1.0  194.168.85.62:
```

This macro would be associated with the lines that reference the macro gvonnet1 in the /var/dhcp/194_168_85_0 file discussed previously. The contents of the macro gvonnet1 would be passed to all DHCP clients whose entries in the /var/dhcp/194_168_85_0 file contains gvonnet1 in the last (macro) field.

A fuller gvonnet1 macro definition in dhcptab might look like this:

```
gvonnet1  m  :GvonstatRt=10.1.1.0  194.168.85.62:\
Include=Locale: :Timeserv=194.168.85.51:LeaseTim=259200:\
DNSdmain=gvon.com::DNSserv=194.168.85.1 194.168.85.2:\
LeaseNeg:
```

Notice that other symbols are in use in this macro, including Timeserv, LeaseTim, DNSdmain, DNSserver, and Leaseneg. To learn more about building symbols and macros, see the Solaris manual page that describes the dhcp file. Check the pages by using the Solaris command

```
# man dhcptab
```

In our example, the gvonnet1 value (a macro) is spread over two lines. As you can see, it contains symbols that include information about DNS (DNSdmain), routing (GvonstatRt), time servers (Timeserve), and lease negotiation parameters. The lease is negotiable (LeaseNeg is present), and the duration of the lease is 259,200 seconds, or three days.

Please note that although the lease is shown in the /var/dhcp/dhcptab file as 259,200 seconds, in the /var/dhcp/194_168_85_0 file (the dhcp_network file), it is represented as the number of seconds since January 1, 1970 to the exact point in time when the lease will expire. The lease time was calculated by the DHCP server at time T0 as the number of seconds from January 1, 1970 to time T0, plus the number of seconds the lease is to run. Time T0 is the time from which the DHCP server starts the lease. If you refer to Figure 9-1, where we explore the concept of the DHCP client time states graphically, you will see that DHCP client 194.168.85.180 has a lease that will expire in 1,009,397,309 seconds from January 1, 1970.

Lease Negotiation

Two predefined symbols used in the macros just discussed are of special significance. They are LeaseTim and LeaseNeg.

LEASETIM

The LeaseTim symbol is shown as the lease time in seconds, so a three-day lease would appear in dhcptab as LeaseTim=259200. We can see this in the definition of the macro gvonnet1. The IP address line in /var/dhcp/194_168_85_0 would show a line like this:

```
010800207B33A4 00 194.168.85.220 194.168.85.51\
1009397309 gvonnet1
```

LEASENEG

The LeaseNeg parameter indicates that the lease is negotiable and may be renegotiated by the client as it nears its expiration time. The parameter is a

Boolean value. If it exists, then the lease is negotiable. If it does not, the lease is nonnegotiable.

If the macro does contain the LeaseNeg parameter, how far into the lease time can the client contact the server and ask for an extension? If, following the negotiation of an existing lease request, the client knows the address of the DHCP server, it will send unicast packets to the server. If the client does not know the server's IP address following the initial negotiation, it will broadcast while searching for a DHCP server. Certain messages from the client (such as DHCPDECLINE, used by a client to decline a server's offer) are always broadcast based so that other DHCP servers are aware that the client has declined the initial offer and is still looking for a DHCP server.

RFC 2131 explains how the client renegotiates an existing lease. Figure 9-1 represents this process.

Note On Solaris 8, a host configured as a DHCP client that fails to locate a DHCP server when first booted as a DHCP client, will boot using the old IP address found in the /etc/inet/ hosts file. If no current IP address is found in the /etc/inet/hosts file, it will continue to attempt to acquire a leased IP address.

At boot time, the client broadcasts a DHCPDISCOVER and might successfully acquire an IP address. If the client does not acquire an address, it can continue to broadcast its search for a DHCP server that will lease it an IP address. We refer to this process of broadcasting for a DHCP server who will lease an IP address to a DHCP client as *state INIT*, which occurs at time T (refer back to Figure 9-1).

We say that the DHCP client is bound to a DHCP server when it has acquired an IP address from it. In terms of the DHCP client timeline, this time is known as *T0*.

When 50 percent of the lease time has elapsed, the DHCP client has reached *time T1*. At this point, it will attempt to extend the current lease and is said to be in a RENEWING state. The client sends a DHCPREQUEST to its current server's unicast address, asking for an extension of the lease. It includes an xid number to identify its request and also includes its current IP address. If the server responds with a DHCPACK reply that matches the client's outstanding request (one with the same xid number), the client remains in a BOUND state and continues to use the IP address. It is at time T0 once again.

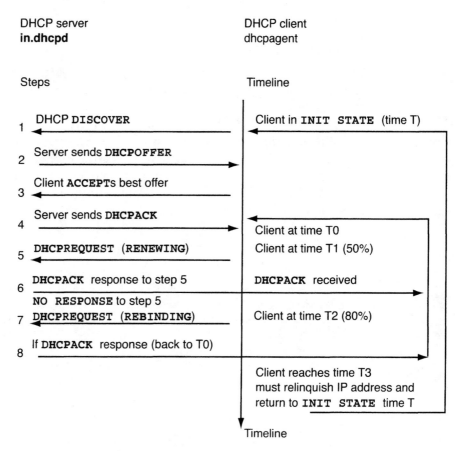

Figure 9–1   *The DHCP client time states*

If, however, the client does not receive a DHCPACK from the current
server and eventually reaches time *T2* (80 percent through the current
lease period), it enters a REBINDING state but still attempts to renew its
current IP address from the current server.

If the lease is not offered despite several DHCPREQUESTS, the client
returns to a state called INIT and time T. It now attempts to acquire a
new IP address and locate a DHCP server using its broadcast address. It
now has no current IP address, which makes this INIT state different
from the RENEWING or REBINDING states already discussed.

The /etc/dhcp.interface File

During the installation of Solaris 8, the installer is asked whether DHCP should be used to acquire an IP address for the installing client. If the installer chooses to enter an IP address manually, but later chooses to make the host a DHCP client, how can the host be converted? To configure a Solaris 8 system to attempt to acquire a lease at boot time, simply use the **touch** command to create the empty file /etc/dhcp.*interface*, where the actual interface name is substituted for the generic name `interface`. Our DHCP client's primary interface is called hme0, so the corresponding DHCP client file must be called /etc/dhcp.*hme0*. The /etc/dhcp.hme0 file acts as a simple trigger. Its existence means that the client is to use DHCP to acquire an IP address.

Use **touch** as follows to create the empty file:

```
# touch /etc/dhcp.hme0
```

At boot time, this system will now attempt to use DHCP to lease an IP address from a DHCP server for interface hme0. You can prevent this behavior by removing the /etc/dhcp.hme0 file.

In summary, the purpose of the /etc/dhcp.interface file is simply to act as a switch that makes the host a DHCP client.

The /etc/default/dhcp File

The dhcp file resides in the directory /etc/default and contains parameters for specifying the type and location of DHCP service databases as well as DHCP service daemon default settings. Some example lines from the file follow:

```
# cat /etc/default/dhcp

RUN_MODE=server
RESOURCE=files
PATH=/var/dhcp
```

Most settings from the dhcp file are variables with values and use the format

```
VARIABLE=value
```

For example,

```
RUN_MODE=server
```

indicates that the host is a DHCP server. The line

```
RESOURCE=files
```

indicates that dhcptab is an ASCII file, not a NIS+ table. And the line

```
PATH=/var/dhcp
```

indicates that the dhcptab and *dhcp_network* files are in the /var/dhcp directory on this dhcp server.

In summary, the purpose of the /etc/dhcp/dhcp file is to hold general-information DHCP parameters that both client and server use.

The /etc/default/dhcpagent File

The /etc/default/dhcpagent file contains tunable parameters that are used by the **dhcpagent** daemon. The **dhcpagent** daemon handles communications between the **ifconfig** command and DHCP, using **ifconfig** to manipulate the interfaces configured through DHCP.

This **dhcpagent** file contains a number of default variables, which are user customizable. Following are some excerpts from the /etc/default/dhcpagent file to serve as examples.

Example 1

```
PARAM_REQUEST_LIST=1,3,12,43
```

This parameter indicates which options (as defined in the /etc/dhcp/inittab file) the DHCP client attempts to acquire from the DHCP server through the DHCP agent daemon. Our examination of the /etc/dhcp/inittab file revealed that each option has a uniquely assigned number. The options in the listing for this example (defined in the inittab file) are

- 1—netmask
- 3—router
- 12—hostname
- 43—vendor options

Example 2

```
ARP_WAIT=1000
```

When a DHCP client is offered an IP address by a DHCP server, it uses ARP to make sure the IP address is not is use, sending out an ARP request for the Ethernet address. If it receives a reply to the ARP request, the IP address is already in use, and the DHCP client declines the DHCP server's offer of the address. The ARP_WAIT parameter determines (in milliseconds) how long the client should wait for a response to its ARP request.

The parameters in the /etc/default/dhcpagent file may be modified by either the administrator or DHCP commands examined in the next section. The configuration files we have explored are usually manipulated by DHCP commands, which we examine next. The administrator can modify the files with an editor, such as **vi,** but this method is not recommended, as hand editing of such complex files can be prone to error and cause problems.

EXAM NOTES

KEY LEARNING POINTS

- DHCP servers have several key configuration files.
- The /etc/dhcp/inittab file contains key DHCP options.
- DHCP macros and symbols are defined in the /var/dhcp/dhcptab file.
- Macros are associated with clients through the /var/dhcp/dhcptab file.
- Server IP address pools for network 194.168.85.0 are listed in the file /var/dhcp/194_168_85_0.
- The /etc/dhcp.hme0 trigger file causes the booting client to be a DHCP client.
- The /etc/default/dhcp file holds some general variables used by DHCP, such as whether the server should log, and the location of the path to the DHCP network file.
- The /etc/default/dhcp file specifies which parameters are used by the **dhcpagent** daemon, which manipulates interfaces on the client that are configured for DHCP.

9.3   Administering DHCP Clients and Servers

Several commands exist for administering the Solaris 8 implementation of DHCP. Table 9.2 summarizes their names and uses. We discuss each command in detail in the following sections.

Table 9.2 *Commands Used to Configure DHCP*

COMMAND NAME	DESCRIPTION
Dhcpconfig	Performs a basic installation of the DHCP server from the command line.
Dhcpmgr	This GUI-based X program creates an initial setup of DHCP.
Pntadm	Manages and configures the /var/dhcp/*dhcp_network* file.
Dhtadm	Manages and configures the /var/dhcp/dhcptab file.

DHCP Server Installation Using dhcpconfig

Use the **dhcpconfig** command to perform the initial setup of the DHCP server and produce the initial set of server files. Once DHCP has been installed, you can use the **pntadm** and **dntadm** commands to modify the server files.

The **dhcpconfig** command invokes a menu. The options chosen for the following example produced the files shown in the previous section on configuring DHCP files. In our example, we use **dhcpconfig** to configure host voyager (the current host) to serve IP addresses 194.168.85.180 through 194.168.85.189 by running **dhcpconfig** at the Solaris command line:

```
# dhcpconfig
```

The following menu appears in response:

```
DHCP Configuration ***
Would you like to:
1) Configure DHCP Service
2) Configure BOOTP Relay Agent
3) Unconfigure DHCP or Relay Service
4) Exit
```

From this menu, we choose option 1, `Configure DHCP Service`, for our example.

The following lines show the interactive installation process. Our input is shown at the end of each line. Notice you can press Return if you simply wish to accept the default choice shown in square brackets []:

```
Would you like to stop the DHCP service? (recommended)
([Y]/N):y
### DHCP Service Configuration ###
### Configure DHCP Database Type and Location ###
Enter datastore (files or nisplus) [nisplus]: files
Enter absolute path to datastore directory [/var/dhcp]:
### Common daemon option setup ###
Would you like to specify nondefault daemon options (Y/
[N]):n
### DHCP server option setup ###
Would you like to specify nondefault server options (Y/
[N]):n
### Initialize dhcptab table ###
Enter default DHCP lease policy (in days) [3]:
Do you want to allow clients to renegotiate their leases?
([Y]/N):y
### Select Networks for BOOTP/DHCP Support ###
Enable DHCP/BOOTP support of networks you select? ([Y]/N):y
### Configure Local Networks ###
Configure BOOTP/DHCP on local LAN network: 194.168.85.0?
([Y]/N):y
Do you want hostnames generated and inserted in the files
hosts tables? (Y/[N]):y
What rootname do you want to use for generated names?
[voyager-]:
Is Rootname voyager- correct? ([Y]]/N):y
What base number do you want to start with? [1]:
Enter starting IP address [194.168.85.0]: 194.168.85.180
Enter the number of clients you want to add (x <255): 10
Disable (ping) verification of 194.168.85.0 address(es)?
(Y/[N]):y
0% Complete. 10 entries for network: 194.168.85.0
```

Next, you are asked if you wish to support remote networks. In the example shown here, the choice is not to support them.

```
### Configure Remote Networks ###
Would you like to configure BOOTP/DHCP service on remote
networks? ([Y]/N):n
Would you like to restart the DHCP service? (recommended)
([Y]/N):y
*** DHCP Configuration ***
```

At this point, we choose exit (option 5) to exit the menu. Our server is ready.

The configuration files examined in section 9.2 were produced from the interactive installation process just shown, where we configured the current host, voyager, to serve IP addresses from 194.168.85.180 through 189.

This **dhcpconfig** command has set up network file /var/dhcp/dhcp/194_168_85_0. Before we examine the **pntadm** command, it would be useful to delete this file, as we need to demonstrate how to create it with **pntadm.** Usually, once the administrator has created the file with **dhcpconfig, pntadm** need not be used for this purpose.

Use the command **rm** to delete the file:

```
# rm /var/dhcp/194_168_85_0
```

The file is now deleted. We will recreate it with the **pntadm** command.

Managing the/var/dhcp/dhcp_network File with the pntadm Command

The **pntadm** command manages the /var/dhcp/*dhcp_network* file and the macros and symbols found in the file. The command has seven main options, of which at least one must be used with each **pntadm** command line. The options must not be combined. Table 9.3 shows these options.

We will now survey the most important options and examine examples of using the **pntadm** command. For further examples, see the online UNIX manual, using the following UNIX command:

```
# man pntadm
```

Table 9.3 pntadm *Command Options*

OPTION	DESCRIPTION
–c	Creates the DHCP /etc/dhcp/dhcp_network table file.
–a	Adds entries to the /etc/dhcp/dhcp_network file.
–m	Modifies entries in the /etc/dhcp/dhcp_network file.
–d	Deletes entries in the /etc/dhcp/dhcp_network file.
–p	Displays the contents of the /etc/dhcp/dhcp_network file.
–r	Removes the /etc/dhcp/dhcp_network file completely.
–l	Lists the network numbers that have /etc/dhcp/dhcp_network files.

Let us examine examples of using **pntadm** and some of its many options. In our examples, the specific *dhcp_network* file will be /var/dhcp/ 194_168_85_0.

The –c Option

This option creates a new *dhcp_network* file called 194_168_85_0 in this example. Enter the command

```
# pntadm   -C 194.168.85.0
```

to create the empty file /var/dhcp/194_168_85_0.

The –a Option

This option creates a new client entry (194.168.85.191 in this example) in a *dhcp_network* file called 194_168_85_0, using resource files. The path to the dhcp_network file is /var/dhcp, and the network file to which we are adding is 194_168_85_0. Here is the command to enter:

```
# pntadm -A 194.168.85.191   -r files -p /var/dhcp/194_168_85_0
```

As a result of using this command, the following line is added to the file /var/dhcp/194_168_85_0:

```
00        00       194.168.85.191   194.168.85.51    0   UNKNOWN
```

Notice the UNKNOWN in the last field. This tells us that so far no macro entry is associated with the server-managed IP address 194.168.85.91. We will modify this next using the –m option.

The –m Option

The –m option modifies an existing entry in a *dhcp_network* file, such as /var/dhcp/194_168_85_0. We modify IP address entry 194.168.85.191 using the command

```
# pntadm -M 194.168.85.191 -m gvonnet1 -f  'BOOTP'
194.168.85.0
```

The command causes the following line to be added to 194_168_85_0:

```
00      08   194.168.85.191   194.168.85.51   0        gvonnet1
```

Notice that the flags -f   'BOOTP' in the command result in the value 08 appearing in the flags field. Also notice that the entry -m gvonnet1 in the command results in the new gvonnet1 field, which, as we discussed in section 9.1 of this chapter, is used as an index into the /var/dhcp/dhcptab file.

The –d Option

The –d option deletes an entry completely and should therefore be used with caution. Here is the command we use for our example:

```
# pntadm -D 194.168.85.191 194.168.85.0
```

The result is that the line for IP address 194.168.85.191 is deleted from the /var/dhcp/194_168_85_0 file.

The –p Option

This option displays the contents of /var/dhcp/*dhcp_network* files. For our example case, we are using the command **grep** to filter and display lines that contain the string gvonnet1:

```
# pntadm -P 194.168.85.0  | grep  gvonnet1
```

The resulting line appears as follows:

```
00      08  194.168.85.191  194.168.85.51  0  gvonnet1
```

The –r Option

The –r option removes the named *dhcp_network* table completely and should therefore be used with caution. Typing the example command

```
# pntadm -R  files 194.168.85.0
```

deletes the file /var/dhcp_194_168_85_0.

The –l Option

The –l option simply lists the networks that are configured, as in the following example command:

```
# pntadm -l
```

As you can see from the result, only network 194.168.85.0 is configured:

```
194.168.85.0
```

Managing the /var/dhcp/dhcptab File with the dhtadm Command

The **dhtadm** command configures the /var/dhcp/dhcptab file. As Table 9.4 shows, this command has five main options. One option must be used with each **dhtadm** command; you cannot combine multiple options.

In the following sections, we provide examples of how to use each option. For further examples of how to use the **dhtadm** command, refer to the online UNIX manual pages by invoking the following UNIX command:

```
# man dhtadm
```

Table 9.4 dhtadm *Command Options*

OPTION	DESCRIPTION
–C	Creates a new dhcptab file.
–A	Adds a macro or symbol to the dhcp table.
–M	Modifies the definition of an existing macro.
–D	Deletes the definition of an existing symbol.
–R	Removes the dhcptab file or NIS+ table.

The –C Option

The –C option creates a new dhcptab file and uses the following syntax:

```
#   dhtadm    -C
```

The –A Option

The –A option adds a new macro or symbol to the table of an existing dhcptab file. In the example that follows, we create a new symbol called NewSym:

```
# dhtadm -A -s NewSym  -d 'Vendor=SUNW.PCW.LAN,20,IP,1,0' \
-r files -p /var/dhcp
```

As a result, the following line is added to the dhcptab file:

```
NewSym s          Vendor=SUNW.PCW.LAN,20,IP,1,0
```

The following command is a second example of using the –A option. In this example, we create a new macro called sunmacro1:

```
# dhtadm -A -m sunmacro1 -d \
':Timeserv=194.35.252.7:DNSserv=194.168.85.1 194.168.85.2:'
```

This command results in the following line being added to the dhcptab file:

```
sunmacro1     m
:Timeserv=194.35.252.7:DNSserv=194.168.85.1 194.168.85.2:
```

The –M Option

Once a macro exists, you can use the –M option to modify it. In the following example, we rename the dhcptab-defined macro sunmacro1 to sunmacro2:

```
#   dhtadm -M -m sunmacro1 -n sunmacro2
```

The –D Option

The –D option deletes a symbol or macro that already exists in the dhcptab file. In the following example, we delete the symbol NewSym:

```
#   dhtadm -D -s NewSym
```

The –R Option

The –R option deletes the entire dhcptab file; please use this command with caution. Here is the syntax for deleting the dhcptab file:

```
# dhtadm -R -r files
```

Note Solaris 8 has an X-based graphical user interface (GUI) called dhcpmgr. This GUI may be used to install and configure some of the DHCP files. It is not included in the Solaris exam and is therefore not covered in this book.

9.4 The DHCP Server Daemon in.dhcpd

The DHCP server daemon **in.dhcpd** listens for DHCP client requests and handles communications from the DHCP server. It also handles other functions such as logging and debugging, but only if it is configured to do so. The daemon normally runs in quiet mode, not revealing its interaction with clients. You can run the DHCP daemon in debug mode, however, to reveal the interaction between client and server. Debug mode is especially useful when you need to troubleshoot. To observe the interaction between a DHCP client and server, and to observe problems that might occur during the client's boot or renegotiation of a lease, run the DHCP daemon in debug mode using the following steps:

1. First, stop the DHCP server daemon **in.dhcpd** using the script /etc/init.d/dhcp and passing the *stop* parameter. You need to do this because the daemon normally runs without debugging enabled. To enable debugging, you must first stop it and then restart it with the appropriate options:

   ```
   # /etc/init.d/dhcp stop
   ```

2. Next, start the DHCP server in debug and verbose modes (using the –**d** and –**v** options) and boot the client:

   ```
   # /usr/lib/inet/in.dhcpd -d -v
   ```

   The output from the daemon follows, indicating that the server is listening for DHCP clients (author's comments are prefixed with a *** to provide commentary about what is happening):

   ```
   Daemon Version: 3.3
    Maximum relay hops: 4
    Run mode is: DHCP Server Mode.
   ```

```
***The system is a DHCP server.

 Datastore: files
 Path: /var/dhcp
 DHCP offer TTL: 10
 Ethers compatibility enabled.
 ICMP validation timeout: 1000 milliseconds, Attempts:
 2.
 Read 4 entries from DHCP macro database on Tue Apr 10
 18:14:51 2001
 Monitor (0005/hme0) started...

***The server is listening on interface hme0.

 Thread Id: 0005 - Monitoring Interface: hme0 *****
 MTU: 1500      Type: SOCKET
 Broadcast: 194.168.85.255
 Netmask: 255.255.255.0
 Address: 194.168.85.51
```

***At this point, the server is ready and listening for
clients. The server has IP address 194.168.85.51 and is
listening on broadcast address 194.168.85.255.

```
 Datagram received on network device: hme0
```

***A datagram has been received from a DHCP client on
hme0. The server ensures that its first available IP
address is definitely not in use. The IP address is
194.168.85.181.

```
 Started ICMP thread 7 to validate IP 194.168.85.181,
 PENDING
```

*** The server is using ICMP to ensure that
194.168.85.181 is not in use.

```
 ICMP thread 7 exiting, IP: 194.168.85.181 = plp-
 >d_icmpflag: AVAILABLE...
```

*** ICMP has suggested that address 194.168.85.181 is
not in use and is therefore AVAILABLE.

```
 Using ICMP validated address: 194.168.85.181
 Unicasting datagram to 194.168.85.181 address.
```

```
*** The server will allocate 194.168.85.181, as it has
been validated.

 Adding ARP entry: 194.168.85.181 == 0800200DC77C

*** Next, the server adds an ARP entry for
194.168.85.181 and associates it with the client's
Ethernet address, which it has received from the
client.

 Added offer: 194.168.85.181
 Datagram received on network device: hme0
 Found offer for: 194.168.85.181
 Client: 010800200DC77C maps to IP: 194.168.85.181

*** The client has accepted the offer and the server
has updated its dhcptab file.
```

The following line was added to the DHCP server's /var/dhcp/
194_168_85_0 file after the client has accepted the offer of address
194.168.85.181:

```
010800200DC77C    00        194.168.85.181  194.168.85.75
987182346         gvonnet1
```

The address 194.168.85.181 has now been allocated, as you can see
from the updated /var/dhcp/194_168_85_0 file. This concludes our
examination of DHCP as implemented on Solaris 8.

EXAM NOTES

KEY LEARNING POINTS

- The **in.dhcpd** daemon may be stopped and started using the /etc/init.d/ dhcp script with the *stop* or *start* parameter.
- Running **in.dhcpd –d –v** runs the daemon in debug mode, revealing DHCP client and server communication.
- When a client accepts a server's offer of an address, it updates the /var/ dhcp/*dhcp_network* file.

SUMMARY

In this chapter we explored DHCP, a protocol that reduces the network administrator's work by enabling DHCP servers to automatically allocate IP addresses and other parameters to DHCP clients requesting them. DHCP is an enhancement of the BOOTP protocol and introduces the facility of the leased IP address, which is leased for a period of time measured in seconds from the January 1, 1970.

We explored the DHCP configuration files, their content, and the meaning of the lines in each. We then examined the commands **dhcpconfig**, **ptmadm**, and **dhtadm**, which configure the DHCP files, and their main options, which enable a number of operations to be carried out on the files.

Finally, we explored the **in.dhcpd** daemon and how to run it in debug mode, which is so useful when you need to monitor the communication between DHCP server and client.

TEST YOURSELF

MULTIPLE CHOICE

1. *If DHCP servers and clients are on different networks, what specialized server type permits them to communicate?*
   A. DHCP relay
   B. BOOTP relay
   C. DHCP server
   D. DHCP client
   E. BOOTP client

2. *When a DHCP client is using a DHCP server, it is said to be what?*
   A. linked
   B. sourced
   C. bound
   D. locked
   E. attached

3. *Identify the three types of IP allocation modes. Choose 3.*
   A. dynamic

B. automatic

C. serial

D. binding

E. manual

4. *In which of the following modes is a fixed IP address always allocated?*

A. dynamic

B. automatic

C. serial

D. binding

E. manual

5. *In which of the following modes is an address allocated from a pool of addresses for an infinite period of time?*

A. dynamic

B. automatic

C. serial

D. binding

E. manual

6. *In which of the following modes is an address allocated from a pool of addresses on a leased basis and for a finite amount of time?*

A. dynamic

B. automatic

C. serial

D. binding

E. manual

7. *Which of the following commands can be used to set up the Solaris DHCP server?*

A. **ptmadm**

B. **dtmadm**

C. **dhcpconfig**

D. **catdhcp**

E. **dhcpcat**

8. *Which of the following DHCP files would list the pool of available IP addresses for network 194.168.85.0?*

A. /etc/dhcp/inittab_194_168_85_0

B. /var/dhcp/194_168_85_0

      C. /var/dhcp/dhcp_194_168_85_0

      D. /etc/dhcp/inittab

      E. /etc/default/dhcp

9. *Which of the following DHCP flags found in the file /etc/dhcp/inittab means that the IP address is unusable?*

      A. 00

      B. 04

      C. 03

      D. 08

      E. 01

10. *Which DHCP command is used to configure the dhcptab file?*

      A. **dhcpconfig**

      B. **dhcpmgr**

      C. **dhtadm**

      D. **ptmadm**

      E. **catdhcp**

FREE RESPONSE

1. *What types of network environments are not suitable for DCHP?* H C

2. *How does DHCP differ from BOOTP? Why is it considered an enhancement?*

REFERENCES

The RFCs on the subject of DHCP are superb. See http://www.rfc.org.uk to acquire them.

RFC 2131 Dynamic Host Configuration Protocol. R. Droms. March 1997. (Format: TXT=113738 bytes) (Obsoletes RFC1541) (Status: US:) (Status: DRAFT STANDARD)

RFC 2132 DHCP Options and BOOTP Vendor Extensions. S. Alexander, R. Droms. March 1997. (Format: TXT=63670 bytes) (Obsoletes RFC1533) (Status: US:) (Status: DRAFT STANDARD)

Network Management Using SNMP

EXAM OBJECTIVES

10.1 Network Management: An Overview

10.2 Introduction to the Simple Network Management Protocol (SNMP)

After completing this chapter, you will be able to meet the following Network Administration Exam objectives:

- Identify tools that use the Simple Network Management Protocol (SNMP).
- Describe the Simple Network Management Protocol (SNMP).

To help you meet these objectives, this chapter covers the following topics:

- software and devices used by network administrators in the context of enterprise management
- SMI, the OID tree, SNMP functions, and Sun SNMP-based enterprise management products

10.1   Network Management: An Overview

Network management is a complex topic, owing to the vast range of SNMP-based products that today's networks employ. In this chapter we look at the organizations involved in network management and at definitions of network management according to the International Standards Organisation (ISO). Next, we briefly explore Simple Network Management Protocol (SNMP), a network management protocol used by tools such as Sun Microsystems' Solstice Enterprise Manager and other SNMP-based management applications.

Our focus for this chapter is very specific. It is necessary to have a basic understanding of SNMP and the Object Identifier (OID) Global tree, which makes it possible to locate an object within a distributed SNMP database. We explore the functions of SNMP, such as **get**, **set**, and **trap**, and we examine SNMP's use of the User Datagram Protocol (UDP) as a Transport protocol. These aspects of the subject are the ones covered by the Sun exam. This chapter does not look at any particular Sun application in detail, because such knowledge is not a requirement of certification. The focus of this chapter will be on a basic understanding of SNMP as a protocol and the infrastructure in which it operates.

Network Management as Defined by ISO

Network management involves several protocols and may be described in several ways depending on which organization provides the description. Sun, like most other organizations, adopts the ISO definition of network management. The ISO concept covers five main aspects of network management including:

- *configuration management*—monitoring and maintaining the current state of the network
- *fault management*—detecting, isolating, and correcting abnormal conditions
- *performance management*—ensuring that network performance is optimized and functioning within acceptable performance thresholds as defined by network management teams
- *accounting management*—enabling charges to be established for the use of network resources
- *security management*—providing authorization, access control, encryption, and key management

Network Management Tools

Network management tools include everything from basic Solaris commands such as **ifconfig, netstat,** and **ping** (discussed in Chapter 5) to tools that check the quality of cables, signal strength, and network packets. They can also include more complex SNMP-based network management solutions. Listed here are a few tools that classify as network management tools:

- *Digital voltmeter*—A voltmeter measures continuity, which checks for cable problems such as electrical faults (shorting out).
- *Time-domain reflectometer*—This device sends pulses along cables and is able to measure cable length, detect signal weakening (usually called *attenuation*), and test certain types of cable, such as CAT 4 and CAT5 (discussed in Chapter 3).
- *Oscilloscope*—An oscilloscope measures signal voltage over a unit of time and other electrical properties.
- *Protocol analyzer*—Also known as *sniffers* or *network analyzers*, this device performs real-time network packet capturing and can also capture data to a log file for later analysis. A protocol analyzer can be a dedicated hardware device or a software product. Some examples of the latter are **snoop** or **tcpdump. Snoop** is bundled with Solaris, and **tcpdump is** available from http://www.sunfreeware.com.
- *Network monitor*—This process tracks and monitors parts or all of a given network and is usually specific to a given operating system.
- *Network management station*—Usually run on UNIX hosts, a network management station uses SNMP to manage network entities such as hubs, switches, and routers. The entities so managed are explored later in this chapter.

This chapter does not examine any specific management solutions, but the following are popular examples in use today:

- Sun Microsystems' Enterprise Manager
- Cabletron Spectrum
- HP Openview
- IBM Netview

Next, we briefly examine the SNMP protocol, its functions, and its features. For a full treatment of SNMP, please see the publications referenced at the end of this chapter.

KEY LEARNING POINTS

- ISO has defined several aspects of network management.
- Per ISO, network management encompasses network configuration, fault, performance, accounting, and security.
- There are several management tools on the market, ranging from cable testers to time-domain reflectometers and network sniffers such as **snoop**.
- Many corporations, including Sun, HP, Cabletron, and IBM produce network management software solutions.

102 Introduction to the Simple Network Management Protocol (SNMP)

Although the word *simple* is part of the protocol's name, SNMP is far from a simple protocol. In what follows, we take a brief look at the main functions of SNMP. At the end of this chapter we reference publications that explore the SNMP protocol more thoroughly.

As a protocol, SNMP functions at the application layer (5). SNMP is simply another upper layer protocol, although it is involved with network management itself. Figure 10-1 shows where SNMP operates within the TCP/IP 5-layer model that we explored in Chapter 1.

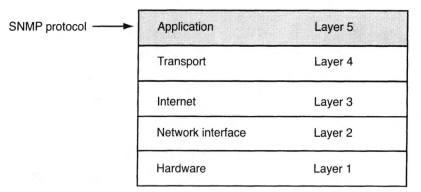

Figure 10–1 *SNMP functioning at Layer 5 of the TCP/IP 5-layer model*

SNMP uses UDP because of its low overhead and speed of operation. You might imagine that the TCP protocol would be a better choice for SNMP because of TCP's superior reliability, but this is not necessarily the case. In congested networks, especially when a problem has developed, TCP might have trouble establishing a transport connection (which is necessary, as we discussed in Chapter 7) between a managed device and the manager of that device. In such a case, management of the device could fail. UDP, however, does not need to form a transport connection and can therefore be used by SNMP without delay and without overloading the network with unnecessary handshaking segments. In a congested, troubled network, speed and low overhead are critical factors that decide in favor of using UDP.

Important features of SNMP include

- the SNMP functions **get**, **set**, and **trap**
- structure of management information (SMI)
- object identifier (OID)

We devote the remainder of this chapter to exploring each feature briefly.

SNMP Functions: get, set, and trap

SNMP management performs the following important functions, which facilitate communication between management device and managed device:

- **get**—The **get** function retrieves data from a managed device by way of its SNMP agent. Network management stations often poll managed devices periodically and perform SNMP **get**s to update a graphic display—usually a map that shows the status of the managed device(s). If a given device fails to respond, the map graphic displays a warning that the device has a problem.
- **set**—The **set** function changes data on a managed device by way of the SNMP agent. A device can be instructed to change parameters, such as its IP address or netmask. Before implementing such changes, it is vital to consider carefully their consequences and their effects on the client. The client might become unreachable following modifications to its network parameters.
- **trap**—The **trap** function sends an unsolicited message to the management station. SNMP traps are often used by network devices to report on network link failures, device reboots, and other critical events.

SNMP **get** and **set** operations retrieve data from or place data into objects identified through the Object Identifier (OID) tree, which we examine next. OIDs are defined in the Structure of Management Information, popularly referred to as the SMI. OIDs are stored or identified through the use of the OID tree, our next subject.

Structure of Management Information (and the OID Tree)

The SMI for TCP/IP-based networks is defined in RFC 1155 and RFC 1156. These documents describe how managed objects contained in a management information base (MIB) are defined.

RFC 1155 states that "an Object Identifier (OID) is a sequence of integers which traverse a global tree. This tree consists of an unlabelled root connected to a number of labeled nodes via edges. Each node may, in turn, have children of its own which are labeled." The OID tree enables us to identify an object defined by a string of numbers, which serves as a means of indexing the OID tree. Figure 10-2 shows the OID tree as described by the RFCs just cited. Please note that the figure is not complete, but rather shows only a part of the tree.

To use the OID, an SNMP manager constructs a path of objects that points to an object within the tree. For example, to construct a path that identifies the Sun HostID, SNMP would have to do a **get** using the following OID:

```
iso.org.dod.internet.private.enterprise.sun.sunMib.sunSystem.h
ostID
```

Alternatively, an SNMP manager could do an SNMP **get** that looks like this:

```
1.3.6.1.4.1.42.3.1.2
```

SNMP-based network management software can index into the tree using a string of tree labels or by creating a path consisting of integers, which together form a complete path to the object to which access is sought. In the examples just given, the path `1.3.6.1.4.1.42.3.1.2` points to the hostID(2) object. Tree objects can include organizations (such as ISO), manufacturers such as Sun, and specific objects such as hubs, routers, and even a Sun system's hostID. The objects themselves are further defined in the Management Information Base (MIB), which we explore next.

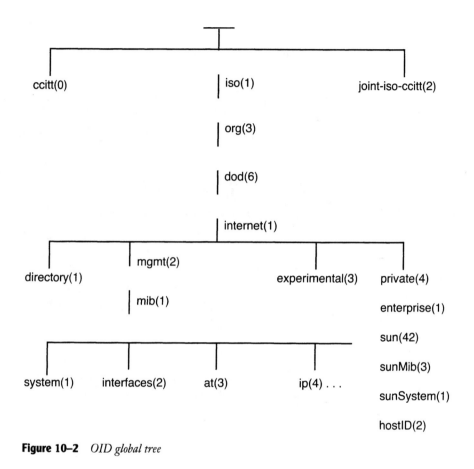

Figure 10–2 *OID global tree*

Management Information Bases (MIB) and ASN

RFC 1156, "Management Information Base for Network Management of TCP/IP-based Internets," defines the managed objects contained in the MIB using the syntax known as Abstract Syntax Notation One (ASN.1). ASN.1 is set forth in ISO standard number 8824 and defines a means of describing devices in an abstract, generic fashion.

The object groups defined in RFC 1156 include both protocols (such as IP and TCP) and hardware devices such as interfaces and systems. These object groups include

- system
- interface
- address translation

- IP
- ICMP
- TCP
- UDP
- EGP

Each of the object groups just listed includes objects that must also be described. RFC 1156 includes guidelines that make it possible to define generically any object that can be known (defined and used) by the MIB. These specifications include:

- *Object*—The object is a textual name, termed the *object descriptor*, for the object type, along with its corresponding object identifier.
- *Syntax*—The abstract syntax for the object type is presented using ASN.1. This must resolve to an instance of the ASN.1 type object syntax defined in the Structure of Management Information (SMI).
- *Definition*—A definition consists of a textual description of the semantics of the object type. Implementations should ensure that their interpretation of the object type fulfills this definition, as the MIB is intended for use in multivendor environments. It is therefore vital that object types have consistent meaning across all machines.
- *Access*—Access is a read-only, read-write, write-only, or not-accessible value.
- *Status*—This is a mandatory, optional, or obsolete value.

Vendors can write their own specific MIB extensions to take advantage of their products' features.

As stated previously in this chapter, there are many vendors in the marketplace who use SNMP, OID, and the SMI base as the bases of their products and software. The following section shows Sun Microsystems' offerings in terms of tools that use the SNMP protocol.

Sun's SNMP-Based Management Tools

The following list summarizes Sun Microsystems' SNMP-based management applications, which suit networks of different sizes. The tools are graphical and scale to meet the needs of either a single site or the global enterprise.

- Sun's Solstice Site Manager
- Sun's Solstice Domain Manager

- Sun's Solstice Enterprise Manager
- Sun's Sun Management Center

A network management application, such as Sun's Domain Manager or HP's Openview, has a GUI-based admin console to facilitate management. The admin console shows a graphical representation of the network's topology and includes log file analysis tools for problem solving and troubleshooting scenarios. Typically, one or more management stations monitor and control network devices, which can be simple devices such as hubs or more complex devices such as host stations or routers.

In practice, a management station is frequently split into two systems: a management station that performs the network management tasks and a separate system that displays network maps and the GUI for the network management application.

The device being managed deploys SNMP, which is usually implemented through the use of agents that run on the managed device. The agents in turn communicate with the management station and are also monitored by the management station. There are two RFCs that relate to this subject; they are referenced at the end of the chapter.

Network managers need not buy all of their vendor SNMP management products and agents; free SNMP-based utilities are available for download over the Internet. One of the best known is an SNMP product from the University of California at Davis, which you may acquire from http://ucd-snmp.ucdavis.edu and which may be extended.

EXAM NOTES

KEY LEARNING POINTS

- **SNMP functions at the Application layer(5) of the protocol stack.**
- **SNMP uses the UDP Transport protocol to take advantage of its speed and low overhead.**
- **The three most important SNMP functions are get, set, and trap.**
- **The SNMP OID makes it possible to locate an object in the distributed SNMP database.**
- **The Structure of Management Information (SMI) is defined in RFC 1155 and defines the use of Abstract Syntax Notation One (ASN.1) for defining Management Information Bases (MIBs).**
- **Protocols and solid objects like hubs and interfaces are defined by MIBs.**
- **Sun offers several Solstice applications that are SNMP-based.**

SUMMARY

This chapter examined briefly the subject of network management, focusing mainly on ISO's definition of what constitutes network management and the SNMP protocol itself, which dominates this sphere. SNMP, the Simple Network Management Protocol, has many functions including **get, set,** and **trap**, and it accesses objects through an Object Identifier Tree known as the OID Tree. We explored the Structure of Management Information (SMI) in which Management Information Bases (MIBs) define the object group types. We further explored the ANS.1 notation, which is used to define the objects themselves. Finally, we reviewed Sun's Solstice family of management products that use SNMP for site, domain, and enterprise management.

TEST YOURSELF

MULTIPLE CHOICE

1. *At which layer of the protocol stack does SNMP operate?*
   A. Application
   B. Transport
   C. Internet
   D. Network Interface
   E. Hardware

2. *Which of the following are SNMP functions? Choose all that apply.*
   A. Get
   B. Set
   C. Push
   D. Place
   E. Trap

3. *What does OID stand for?*
   A. Oriented Illumination
   B. Object Identifier
   C. Object Interlocutor
   D. Oriented Identifier
   E. Object Interfaces

4. *What does ASN stand for?*

    A. Abstract Symbol Notation

    B. Abstract Syntax Number

    C. Abstract Symbol Numerator

    D. Abstract Syntax Notation

    E. Almost Sane Narrator

5. *Which one of the following is not one of the eight SNMP object groups defined by RFC 1156?*

    A. interfaces

    B. ICMP

    C. network

    D. EGP

    E. IP

6. *Which two organizations are at the very top of the OID tree?*

    A. Sun

    B. HP

    C. CCITT

    D. ISO

    E. DOD

7. *Which of the following Sun products use SNMP? Choose all that apply.*

    A. Solstice Disksuite

    B. Solstice Backup

    C. Solstice Site Manager

    D. Solstice Enterprise Manager

    E. Solstice Adminsuite

8. *Why does SNMP use UDP rather than TCP as a transport protocol? Which of the following statements are true? Choose all that apply.*

    A. UDP is more secure than TCP.

    B. UDP has a faster startup than TCP.

    C. UDP has less overhead than TCP.

    D. UDP is faster than TCP.

    E. UDP has a checksum in the header.

9. *What, according to the RFC 1155, is a "sequence of integers that traverse a global tree"?*
    A. An OID
    B. An ASN
    C. An SMI
    D. An SNMP agent
    E. An SMTP IP address

10. *Which of the following are network management tools? Choose all that apply.*
    A. Time Domain Reflectometer
    B. Snoop
    C. Cable Tester
    D. Oscilloscope
    E. SNMP

FREE RESPONSE

1. *Why does SNMP use UDP?*

2. *What does the SNMP OID allow you to do, compared with what a Web address allows you to do in DNS? Is there a similarity?*

REFERENCES

Mauro, Douglas R. and Kevin J. Schmidt. *Essential SNMP.* Sebastopol, CA: O'Reilly Press, 2001. ISBN 0-59600-020-0.

Rose, M.T. and K. McCloghrie. RFC1155, "Structure and identification of management information for TCP/IP-based internets," May 1, 1990.

Rose, M.T. and K. McCloghrie. RFC1156, "Management Information Base for network management of TCP/IP-based internets," May 1, 1990.

Domain Name Service (DNS)

EXAM OBJECTIVES

11.1 DNS: The Glue of the Internet

11.2 DNS and Berkeley Internet Name Domain (BIND) Software

11.3 The DNS Namespace

11.4 Types of DNS Servers

11.5 The Main Configuration File /etc/named.conf

11.6 The Zone Database Files and the Resource Record (RR) Format

11.7 Creating a DNS Server and Client Step by Step

11.8 DNS Debugging and Dumping the DNS Cache

After completing this chapter, you will be able to meet the following Network Administration Exam objectives:

- Identify the purpose of DNS.
- Describe address resolution and reverse address resolution.
- Identify the correct Resource Record syntax.
- Explain the steps needed to configure DNS.
- State the purpose of DNS configuration files.

To help you meet these objectives, this chapter covers the following topics:

- the relationship between DNS and BIND with reference to Solaris 8
- the architecture of the DNS namespace
- the five types of DNS servers and their properties
- working with the main DNS configuration file
- zone files and the Resource Record (RR) format
- how to configure a DNS server and client
- debugging DNS
- dumping the DNS cache

11.1   DNS: The Glue of the Internet

The Domain Name Service (DNS) is the glue that binds the many services of the Internet together. DNS forms a transparent layer between the friendly world of familiar Web names and the opaque arena of IP addresses and the TCP/IP tapestry that we have studied in this book. The role of DNS, although crucial, is a mysterious one, not understood by most Internet users, even though it is more important than almost any other piece of the Internet puzzle.

It is thanks to DNS that we can employ user-friendly site names (such as www.sun.com) with our Web browsers and user-friendly mail addresses (such as rick@gvon.com) with our e-mail clients. These two types of human-friendly text address strings actually resolve to numeric IP addresses as required by the software that deals with e-mail and Web traffic. A Web address (www.sun.com in our example) resolves to a Web server's IP address, and an e-mail address (rick@gvon.com in our example) resolves to a numeric address for the mail server for the gvon.com domain. But it is DNS that allows the user-friendly, text-based names to communicate with the less familiar and relatively opaque world of IP addresses and TCP/IP.

The purpose of DNS—to perform the mapping service that *resolves* (translates) host names to IP addresses and IP addresses back to host names—is actually simple in principle. Most humans prefer to use familiar text-based names and find them easier to remember (and to type!) than IP addresses. DNS is said to be a *naming service* because it allows names to be used and because it is built upon the foundation of Berkeley Internet Name Domain (BIND) software.

Here's a real-world example. The name of Gvon's Web server—www.gvon.com—is easier to remember than its IP address, which is 194.168.85.51. With the advent of IPv6 addresses, which are 128 bits (16 bytes) in length (see chapter 13), using names rather than addresses will become even more important, as the new breed of IPv6 addresses will be four times as long and twenty times as hard to remember.

DNS is a distributed database, global in scope and implemented across untold numbers of DNS servers (mainly UNIX because of its reliability) around the world. It manifests itself as a hierarchical tree of domain names that end in the now familiar suffixes com, net, org, co.uk, and others that we will explore in this chapter.

Throughout the remaining pages of this chapter we will explore essential DNS terms such as *domain, zone, namespace, Top Level Domain (TLD)*, and *distributed database* and explore in detail the Solaris files through which DNS, a true Internet giant, is configured.

EXAM NOTES

KEY LEARNING POINTS

- DNS maps IP addresses to host names and names to IP addresses.
- DNS is a naming service, built from BIND libraries.
- DNS is a globally distributed, text-based database.
- DNS is a giant among Internet services and of critical importance.

11.2 DNS and Berkeley Internet Domain Name (BIND) Software

DNS is built from the Berkeley Internet Domain Name (BIND) software libraries and is considered to be an implementation of BIND. DNS is bundled with most versions of UNIX and is considered a core UNIX service. Three versions of the Berkeley Internet Domain Name (BIND) software are currently in use on the Internet:

- version 4 (current version 4.1.9)
- version 8 (current version 8.1.12)
- version 9 (current version 9.2)

The differences among the various versions relate to security and performance enhancements. Most DNS servers are running versions 4 and 8, as version 9 is extremely new.

Solaris 8 Version of DNS and BIND

Solaris 8 is shipped with BIND version 8.1.2. Table 11.1 shows the versions of BIND bundled with the three most recent releases of Solaris.

Table 11.1 *BIND Versions Shipped with Solaris 2.6 through 8*

VERSION OF SOLARIS	BIND VERSION SHIPPED	MAIN BOOT FILE
2.6	4.1.6	/etc/named.boot
2.7	8.1.2	/etc/named.conf
8	8.1.2	/etc/named.conf

One suggested way to discover the version of BIND you are running is to locate the DNS server daemon (always **in.named** on Solaris), run the **strings** and **grep** commands, and search for the word BIND, as follows.

```
# strings /usr/sbin/in.named | grep BIND
```

The output from the **strings** command reports that the version of BIND is 8.1.2.

```
@(#)in.named BIND 8.1.2 Wed Dec 22 00:01:15 PST 1999
Generic-5.8-February 2000
in.named BIND 8.1.2 Wed Dec 22 00:01:15 PST 1999
BIND 8.1.2
```

The main DNS configuration file on Solaris (known as the *bootfile*) is /etc/named.boot on version 4.x of BIND and /etc/named.conf on version 8.x of BIND. Important differences in syntax exist between the main boot files /etc/named.boot and /etc/named.conf. When we explore how to set up DNS servers, we will examine the /etc/named.conf file in great detail. But first, we will review the various name services available on Solaris, of which DNS is the most significant on the world stage.

To find out more about BIND and to download the latest version of BIND, visit http://www.isc.org.

Solaris Name Services: A Comparison

As Table 11.2 shows, Sun offers several naming services, but only DNS offers a global namespace shared by thousands of organizations worldwide. The term *namespace* describes the hierarchical tree of names that DNS servers manage and to which we will refer throughout this chapter.

The term *global in scope* that appears in the table implies not only that the service can be accessed anywhere in the world through the Internet but also that the organizations using it share a common namespace—the

Table 11.2 *A Comparison of Naming Services*

NAME SERVICE	GLOBAL IN SCOPE?	LOCAL TO COMPANY?
/etc/inet/hosts	No	No
Domain Name Service (DNS/BIND)	Yes	Can be local with private DNS
Network Information Service (NIS)	No	Yes
Network Information Service+ (NIS+)	No	Yes
Lightweight Directory Access Protocol (LDAP)	No	Yes

namespace is not used privately within a single organization. As you can see by a comparison with other naming services, DNS is really the only service that is global in visibility and scope, in that unrelated organizations share a common global namespace through the 13 root-level servers that we discuss later in this chapter.

This common namespace is a crucial feature of the Internet infrastructure. The World Wide Web, for example, is a collection of Web servers and Web pages, but it is DNS that allows us to access them easily without being forced to remember the IP addresses of individual Web sites we wish to visit. If the Internet is a library of Web sites and Web pages, DNS is the indexing system that provides us with a means of identifying within that great sea of names the particular Web server whose pages we are attempting to access. IP routes the data, but DNS usually provides the IP address to route to.

Note

Interestingly, most ISPs do not restrict which DNS clients (IP addresses) may use their DNS servers, so you can actually configure your client to point to another ISP's DNS servers. It makes much more sense to configure your system to use your own ISP's DNS servers, but with many ISPs it is not compulsory to do so.

Each company or organization is ultimately responsible for maintaining only its own part of the namespace and usually pays an ISP to do this. Technical companies that have permanent Internet access (leased lines) may choose to host their own DNS domains on their own DNS servers. Companies such as Sun, HP, and IBM, for example, maintain their own DNS servers.

What differentiates DNS from services like NIS and NIS+ is that with DNS, an organization must maintain only its own small part of the namespace (its own domains). With NIS and NIS+, however, the company manages the namespace in its entirety. Companies do not share their NIS or NIS+ information with other organizations.

EXAM NOTES

KEY LEARNING POINTS

- BIND is a set of libraries from which DNS is built and developed.
- There are several versions of BIND: Versions 4, 8, and 9. Versions 4 and 8 are currently the most poplular, as BIND 9 is very new.
- Solaris 8 ships with Version 8.1.2 of DNS (BIND).
- The master configuration file for BIND 8.1.2 is /etc/named.conf.
- The Solaris DNS server daemon is **in.named**.

11.3 The DNS Namespace

DNS is a distributed database of *domains* (or zones), which are managed by a large number of organizations and DNS administrators. The total aggregate of domain names is referred to as the *namespace tree* (or just the *namespace*); it forms the space within which the names operate and are used. In this part of the chapter, we look at domain names and examine the basic rules that govern them.

Domain Name Basics

A *domain name* is a string made up of one or more words, which may include alphabetical characters, numerics, and the hyphen (dash) character. The words (technically called *labels*) are separated by the full stop (.), which acts as a separator or *delimiter*. In Solaris path names such as /etc/named.conf, the forward slash (/) acts as a delimiter, separating etc from named.conf. In DNS domain names, the (.) acts as a delimiter between the labels of the domain name.

The domain name acts like a key in a database; it allows DNS servers to index into the namespace and extract information relating to a given name, such as an IP address or mail relay information. Later in this chapter, when we explore resource records and the files that actually store domain information, we will examine how DNS stores information, how servers perform lookups, and the mechanism by which servers can return to clients (or other DNS servers) the domain information required.

Fully Qualified Domain Names (FQDN) versus Relative Domain Names (RDN)

A *fully qualified domain name* (FQDN) is one that describes the domain name completely from the base label to the top label, where a *label* is a string between the dot (.) characters. For example, sun.com is a domain with two labels, namely sun and com, which are separated by the dot delimiter. Another example is sun.co.uk, which is comprised of three labels.

If, however, we refer to just the domain "sun," we are discussing a *relative domain name* (RDN). The single label is relative because several domains called "sun" may exist within the DNS namespace, just as Solaris has several files called passwd (/bin/passwd, /etc/passwd, /etc/default/passwd, to name just a few). To help you understand the difference between FQDNs and RDNs, we can compare absolute pathnames (/etc/passwd) with relative pathnames (passwd), which are very familiar to all UNIX administrators. DNS's FQDN sun.com is analogous to an absolute pathname, while the RDN sun is analogous to a relative pathname. Here is a summary of rules that govern domain names:

- FQDNs may not exceed 255 characters in total length.
- A single-label RDN (the label between the dot delimiters) must not exceed 63 characters.
- Alphabetical characters, numerics, and the hyphen (or dash) are the only characters permitted.
- Domain names are not case sensitive.

Top Level Domains (TLDs)

The top level of the DNS namespace is ultimately managed by an organization called the Internet Corporation for Assigned Names and Numbers (ICANN). ICANN delegates parts of the top level to other organizations to manage. For example, the top-level domain *edu* is managed by Network Solutions Incorporated (NSI), and the country code top-level domain *uk* is delegated to an organization called Nominet UK Ltd., which operates in Oxford, England. We explore the subject of delegation further in this section and then again when we explore the DNS server's configuration files.

The DNS namespace is normally represented as an inverted, hierarchical treelike structure (inverted because the root level is at the top). There are literally millions of domains in today's actual namespace on the Internet, with thousands being added daily. In addition to the millions of live domains in use, there are countless millions purchased but not actually in use (these are usually referred to as *parked* or *dormant domains*).

The top level of the namespace includes two types of domain name: One type is called *generic* and the other *geographical*. The generic domains are broad enough to encompass vast numbers of organizations of different types under a single branch of the tree, such as .com, .org, or .net, for example. The geographical type uses country codes. Figure 11-1 shows the generic names within the top layer of the DNS tree. It is possible to show all the generic top-level domains (gTLDs), as they are few in number (com, net, org, edu, mil, gov, arpa, biz, info), but there are more than 80 country codes—far too many to display on a small diagram. Geographical top-level domains that use country codes are referred to as ccTLDs. In Figure 11-1, we have shown just four ccTLDs (uk, us, ca, and de), which are further described in Table 11.3.

The null or root domain is found at the very top (root) of the namespace tree and indicates the absolute beginning of all DNS names. Remember that although DNS names are read from left to right, the start of all names is at the rightmost part of the name. Technically, the full DNS path, sun.com. (notice the trailing dot indicating the root domain) is called a Fully Qualified Domain Name or FQDN.

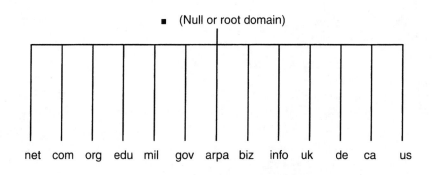

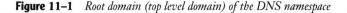

Figure 11-1   *Root domain (top level domain) of the DNS namespace*

Table 11.3 lists the generic domains (and a few of the geographical ones) possible within the TLD and gives a brief description of each.

Table 11.3 *TLDs Including Generic Top-Level Domains (gTLDs) and Country Code Top-Level Domains (ccTLDs)*

DOMAIN	DESCRIPTION
net	Networking organizations, ISPs, network providers
com	Commercial companies trading for profit
org	Organizations, often non-profit making
edu	Educational institutions, primarily US-based
mil	US military (restricted to the USA military)
gov	US government (restricted to the USA government)
arpa	IP address-to-name resolution
biz	Business and companies
info	Unrestricted use
coop	Cooperatives (not yet live)
name	For individuals (not yet live)
aero	Air-transport industry (not yet live)
pro	Professionals (not yet live)
museum	Museums (not yet live)
uk (ccTLD)	United Kingdom (county code)
us (ccTLD)	United States (country code)
de (ccTLD)	Germany (country code)
ca (ccTLD)	Canada (county code)

Of the seven recently established gTLDs (biz, info, aero, coop, pro, museum, name) only biz and info are live at the time this book goes to press. See www.icann.org for further information and www.domain-shop.co.uk to preorder the new domains.

For more information about the full list of country codes, see www.iana.org/cctld/cctld-whois.htm. For more information about the top-level domains and who manages them, see www.icann.org, www.iana.org, and www.internic.net.

ICANN, which has ultimate control over each top-level domain, delegates management of ccTLDs to a single organization within each country. For example, Nominet UK, based in Oxfordshire, England, manages all domains ending in uk, the most popular being co.uk, which accounts for 95 percent of all names registered that end in uk. For a complete list of country codes, as approved by the Internet Assigned Number Authority (IANA), see http://www.iana.org/cctld/cctld-whois.htm.

Countries often split their own namespace into multiple subdomains. Beneath the ccTLDs, the organization managing that branch of the namespace tree can choose to create official subdomains and allow organizations and individuals to register domains beneath those. A *subdomain* is a domain that is a child of a parent domain. Later in the chapter, we will see how to setup DNS servers to support this hierarchy.

Take the UK namespace, for example. (Please note that different countries organize their subdomains differently and do not all use the same model as the United Kingdom.) Figure 11-2 shows the UK namespace as an example of how a county might choose to create official subdomains.

Table 11.4 shows how management of the domains within the UK is apportioned among various organizations. Some domains are managed by the UK naming registry Nominet UK, which may be found at http://www.nic.uk. UKERNA, another UK organization, manages two of the domains beneath UK, namely ac.uk and gov.uk, and it may be contacted at www.ukerna.ac.uk.

In Table 11.4, we see that several subdomains exist beneath uk, but how are these child domains related to the parent domain? Let us examine the subtle differences and similarities between the words *domain* and

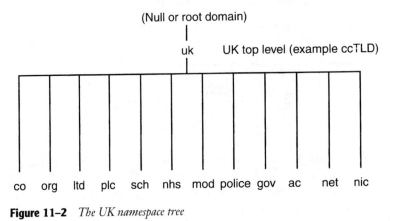

Figure 11-2   *The UK namespace tree*

zone, and in particular, the process of delegation, which forms child–parent relationships between namespace layers.

Table 11.4 *UK (ccTLD) Subdomains*

DOMAINS MANAGED BY NOMINET	DESCRIPTION
co	Companies (companies)
org	Organizations, often non-profit making; charities; clubs; societies
ltd	Limited Companies (strict definition of company)
plc	PLCs (private limited company)
sch	Schools in the UK
net	Network Providers
nhs	National Health Service
DOMAINS MANAGED BY UKERNA	
ac	Academic Institutions
gov	Government Institutions
DOMAINS MANAGED BY SPECIFIC ORGANIZATIONS	
police	Police forces in the UK
mod	The UK military
me	New in 2002 (for individuals)

Zones of Authority and Delegation

Much of the time, the word *domain* may loosely be used to mean the same as the word *zone*, but technically there is a significant difference. A zone encompasses a domain of the same name and all existent domains beneath it that have not been delegated away. Once a domain is delegated—once it has its own SOA and NS records and is managed by a different server—it forms a new zone of authority distinct from the parent zone.

The zone gvon.com is a *zone of authority*, managed by a master and slave pair of DNS servers. If Gvon decided to create a domain beneath gvon.com called uk.gvon.com, and delegate the responsibility for the subdomain uk.gvon.com to another server (meaning that the other server would have a separate Start of Authority (SOA) record and related zone database files), the subdomain uk.gvon.com is then a separate zone of authority from the parent zone.

Basically, a new zone of authority is created when the child domain (uk in this example) is managed through an SOA (and usually through a DNS server as well) separate from that of the parent zone gvon.com. The process of handing over control of a child domain is called *delegation*.

Figure 11-3 shows this important distinction. In Figure 11-3, the oval encompassing gvon represents the zone of gvon.com. Note that even though the zone is called gvon.com, we cannot include com in the oval as well, as doing so would suggest that gvon and com are part of the same zone when they are not. The com server has delegated authority to gvon's servers for the domain gvon beneath com. The domain gvon.com therefore becomes a separate zone of authority.

The domain training.gvon.com is managed by the gvon server through the same SOA record as the parent domain, namely gvon.com.

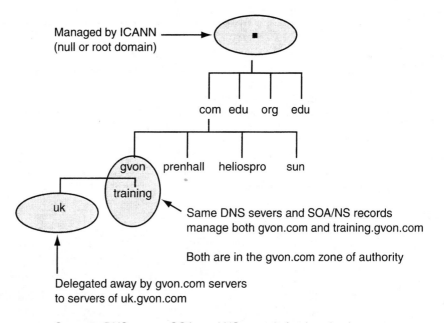

Figure 11–3 *Zones of authority*

This means that is it not a separate zone of authority, as authority for training.gvon.com has not been delegated away by the server of gvon.com.

The domain uk.gvon.com has a separate SOA, however, and so it is a separate (autonomous) zone of authority relative to that of the parent zone gvon.com.

The salient points about zones of authority are as follows:

- *All domains reside within the same parent zone unless delegated away.* For example, the domain gvon.com is in the zone gvon.com, and the domain training.gvon.com is also within the zone gvon.com.

- *All zones have a matching domain name.* The zone gvon.com has a matching domain of gvon.com, and zone uk.gvon.com matches domain uk.gvon.com.

- *Nondelegated domains do not have a matching zone name.* Domain training.gvon.com is not delegated away, so it has no matching zone name. It is, in fact, part of the gvon.com zone.

As you read through this chapter, the meaning and significance of domain and zone will be further reinforced as you see how DNS servers are configured and how DNS functions as a service.

EXAM NOTES

KEY LEARNING POINTS

- DNS domains are of two main types: generic and geographical.
- ICANN ultimately manages the gTLDs and ccTLDS.
- ICANN delegates country domains to a country-based name registry such as Nominet, who manages the uk namespace branch.
- DNS is a mapping service between names and addresses.

11.4 Types of DNS Servers

In this section, we examine the five types of DNS server, which differ among themselves in terms of their responsibilities, the domains they support, and their roles of providing domain information. The configuration information of each type of server is different, although the file syntax used by each server is the same. The five types of DNS server are:

- root—manages the top level of DNS namespace
- master—master authority for one or more zones
- slave—slave authority for one or more zones
- caching-only server—nonauthoritative
- forwarder—forwards its client requests to another DNS server

Be aware that some of these server types are not mutually exclusive. That is, a master server of one zone can also be the slave of another.

It is common to find the same DNS host supporting many zones as both master and slave server. The same server should not, however, be both the master and slave of the same zone. The factors that differentiate servers from one another are the zones they support and the type of server they are—root, master, slave, caching-only, or forwarder.

Root-Level DNS Servers

The root-level servers manage the top level of the DNS namespace and are therefore critical to the functioning of the DNS namespace. The official root-level DNS servers are managed by ICANN, which works closely with organizations such as IANA and Internic to ensure that the namespace functions smoothly.

All DNS servers need knowledge of the root-level servers (currently 13) unless you are setting up an internal DNS namespace that is private and not participating in the Internet.

To acquire the latest copy of the file that lists the root-level servers, **ftp** to ftp.rs.internic.net. Log in as a user with the name ftp (or anonymous) and provide your e-mail address as a password. You will find the named.root file in a directory called /domain.

You may automate the use of **ftp**, as shown in section 11.7, where we examine the steps to follow when setting up DNS. The named.root file lists the 13 root servers. We examine the syntax of this file in section 11.5 in greater detail; for now, just observe that the 13 root servers are named according to the syntax a.root-servers.net, b.root-servers.net, all the way to m.root-servers.net. All DNS servers have an identical copy of this file.

Nonroot Master DNS Servers and the named.root File

Following is the content of the named.root file, which was last updated in 1997, showing the current 13 original TLD servers. The contents of this file are used to prime the caches of all nonroot master DNS servers.

```
;       This file holds the information on root name servers needed to
;       Initialize cache of Internet domain name servers
;       (e.g. reference this file in the "cache  .  <file>"
;       configuration file of BIND domain name servers).
;
;       This file is made available by InterNIC registration services
;       under anonymous FTP as
;           file                /domain/named.root
;           on server           FTP.RS.INTERNIC.NET
;       -OR- under Gopher at    RS.INTERNIC.NET
;           under menu          InterNIC Registration Services (NSI)
;               submenu         InterNIC Registration Archives
;           file                named.root
;
;       last update:    Aug 22, 1997
;       related version of root zone:    1997082200
;
;
; formerly NS.INTERNIC.NET
;
.                           3600000  IN  NS   A.ROOT-SERVERS.NET.
A.ROOT-SERVERS.NET.         3600000      A    198.41.0.4
;
; formerly NS1.ISI.EDU
;
.                           3600000      NS   B.ROOT-SERVERS.NET.
B.ROOT-SERVERS.NET.         3600000      A    128.9.0.107
;
; formerly C.PSI.NET
;
.                           3600000      NS   C.ROOT-SERVERS.NET.
C.ROOT-SERVERS.NET.         3600000      A    192.33.4.12
;
; formerly TERP.UMD.EDU
;
.                           3600000      NS   D.ROOT-SERVERS.NET.
D.ROOT-SERVERS.NET.         3600000      A    128.8.10.90
;
; formerly NS.NASA.GOV
;
.                           3600000      NS   E.ROOT-SERVERS.NET.
E.ROOT-SERVERS.NET.         3600000      A    192.203.230.10
;
; formerly NS.ISC.ORG
;
.                           3600000      NS   F.ROOT-SERVERS.NET.
```

```
F.ROOT-SERVERS.NET.         3600000        A       192.5.5.241
;
; formerly NS.NIC.DDN.MIL
;
.                           3600000        NS      G.ROOT-SERVERS.NET.
G.ROOT-SERVERS.NET.         3600000        A       192.112.36.4
;
; formerly AOS.ARL.ARMY.MIL
;
.                           3600000        NS      H.ROOT-SERVERS.NET.
H.ROOT-SERVERS.NET.         3600000        A       128.63.2.53
;
; formerly NIC.NORDU.NET
;
.                           3600000        NS      I.ROOT-SERVERS.NET.
I.ROOT-SERVERS.NET.         3600000        A       192.36.148.17
;
; temporarily housed at NSI (InterNIC)
;
.                           3600000        NS      J.ROOT-SERVERS.NET.
J.ROOT-SERVERS.NET.         3600000        A       198.41.0.10
;
; housed in LINX, operated by RIPE NCC
;
.                           3600000        NS      K.ROOT-SERVERS.NET.
K.ROOT-SERVERS.NET.         3600000        A       193.0.14.129
;
; temporarily housed at ISI (IANA)
;
.                           3600000        NS      L.ROOT-SERVERS.NET.
L.ROOT-SERVERS.NET.         3600000        A       198.32.64.12
;
; housed in Japan, operated by WIDE
;
.                           3600000        NS      M.ROOT-SERVERS.NET.
M.ROOT-SERVERS.NET.         3600000        A       202.12.27.33
; End of File
```

We will examine the syntax of this file when we set up the servers. For now, it is sufficient to understand that the file contains a list of the 13 current TLD servers and that all DNS servers usually prime a DNS cache with the contents of this file.

DNS Master Servers

In earlier versions of BIND, master servers were called primary servers. We will use the term master for Solaris 8, as it uses BIND 8.1.2. For each domain there should be one master server, who holds the definitive, correct information regarding the zone and the systems within the zone.

Master servers are deemed *authoritative*—that is, correct (or at least as accurate as is possible). Essentially, they are configured to support a number of zones and are mirrored by the next category of server, called slaves. It is important to observe that if the network administrator makes a mistake in the master's zone files, the error will be mirrored on the slaves as well as cached by external DNS servers.

We shall see later that the *hostmaster* (the technical term for a DNS administrator) determines how long other DNS servers cache his or her server's records, by adjusting a time-to-live (TTL) parameter, with a time value of 12 hours as typical. From this you can see that errors can live in the caches of DNS servers for long periods of time.

To summarize:

- Masters are authoritative for the zone(s) (domains) they support or serve because they store the relevant zone data on their local disks in files.
- Masters are registered with the registry when the domain is registered and therefore must be reachable by the outside world (Internet community) in order for the domain to be seen.
- Master data is considered to be correct.
- There is usually only one master server per zone.

DNS Slave Servers

In early versions of BIND, slaves were called *secondary servers*. Each zone (domain) may have one or more DNS slave server to mirror the information stored on the master. The slave server in effect load balances with the master server, because it remains (one hopes) in synchronization with the master server for the zone(s) in question.

Slave or secondary servers are also deemed authoritative (just like the master) because they are synchronized with the master and store the information they glean from the master in local files.

Theoretically, DNS clients should be able to use either the master or the slave server for a given zone and retrieve an identical answer.

Most of the time, this works according to plan. The slave is simpler to setup than the master, primarily because it copies most of its zone information from the master.

To summarize:

- Slaves, like masters, are authoritative for the zone(s) (domains) they support because they copy a zone's data from a master through a synchronization process called *zone transfer* and write the zone data to a local disk.

- Usually, slaves are registered with the registry when the domain is registered and therefore must be reachable by the outside world (i.e., by the Internet community) for the domain to be seen.

- Slave data is considered to be correct (as correct as is possible, at any rate) because its data is identical to the master's.

- There are usually several slave servers per zone. One slave is considered the absolute minimum for the sake of avoiding a single point of failure.

We look at setting up the DNS slave in section 11.5. Next, we look at caching-only servers, which are simply a means of spreading the load and easing the pressure on masters and slaves.

DNS Caching-Only Servers

A caching-only server is different from a master and slave in that it is not authoritative for any zone but is nevertheless a fully functioning DNS server, able to answer client queries. The caching-only server is never registered with an outside authority (such as a registrar), so it is usually used to spread the load and thus relieve the master and slaves.

The caching-only server is set up to know about the 13 root-level servers and to use the 13 root servers to learn about nearly all zones. It will be seen that the caching-only server holds very little local information on disk. Everything that it learns from other authoritative servers it stores in system memory and never on disk. Precisely because it caches all the information in memory, it is said to be *nonauthoritative* and is called a caching-only server.

We will see how to set up a caching-only server in section 11.5. Setup for these servers is easier than for either master or slave, as they have very few disk-based files to configure.

To summarize:

- A caching-only server does not synchronize with a master for any zones and so is nonauthoritative.
- A caching-only server does not write what it learns to disk.
- A caching-only server is not registered with the authority through which management of the domain is delegated. That is, it is not recognized as the official server of any zones.
- A caching-only server knows about the root-level servers and so can resolve all queries by initially asking the root-level servers.
- DNS clients may use the caching-only server by adding the caching-only server's IP address to their /etc/resolv.conf file—see section 11.7.

DNS Forwarding Servers

The forwarding server is not really a different type of DNS server from the ones listed above. The forwarding server is a master, slave, or caching-only server that forwards all its questions to a specific and predetermined external DNS server. DNS servers, as we shall see shortly, ask other DNS servers questions based on the domain name they are looking up. Forwarders, on the other hand, always forward to particular, pre-defined servers and are often used for security reasons.

Think of forwarders as DNS servers whose behavior has been modified in terms of the entity to which it forwards queries. We examine a forwarder's statement in the next section.

Querying Servers: Recursion versus Iteration

We have thus far looked at the five types of DNS server. At this point, we are ready to explore how and when the servers are called. Communication in terms of queries and answers occurs between DNS clients and DNS servers as follows:

- DNS clients ask DNS servers questions (called queries).
- DNS clients should use local DNS servers (in the same network if possible) in the first instance of a query. Later in this chapter, we will see how to set up DNS clients and how they select the DNS servers they will use.

- Traffic between a DNS client and server is said to be *recursive*, because clients ask a question and wait patiently for the answer. The queried DNS server either knows the answer to the question and returns it immediately or asks one or more other DNS servers for information related to the client's questions and eventually learns the answer, at which point it returns the answer to its client. (This process usually takes only a few seconds!) DNS queries generate small UDP packets, using UDP for its low overhead and speed.

- When a DNS server asks other DNS servers questions about zones it does not support, it might need to ask more than one server and often starts with a root-level server.

- The questions that occur between peer DNS servers is said to be *iterative*, because the process is cyclic, as we see in Figure 11-4.

Figure 11-4 illustrates what happens when a Solaris 8 DNS server asks a question. Imagine a user working at a host configured to be a DNS client, who uses an application such as **ping** and issues the following command:

```
# ping www.sun.com
```

If the host we run the command on is a DNS client and correctly configured, the client host (and its resolver routines) will attempt to return to **ping** the IP address of www.sun.com, because this is the information required for a successful **ping** to occur and for IP to route the **ping** packets (ICMP in IP datagrams) to the pinged host correctly.

Because of the client's involvement in the resolving process, the DNS client is actually called a *resolver*. The Solaris routines that are used within the client's software to call the DNS servers are part of what are called *resolver libraries*.

In Figure 11-4, the user is attempting to **ping** to www.sun.com. In order to do so, it needs need the IP address of www.sun.com. The host running the **ping** calls its resolver routines to attempt to learn the IP address. Here are the steps involved in this process:

1. The resolver client first checks a file called /etc/nsswitch.conf and discovers that, for host information, it must check the /etc/inet/ hosts file and then check DNS. (In a real-world scenario, the resolver client would actually first ask the Name Server Cache Daemon [NSCD] which caches information held in the /etc/nss-witch.conf file.) For simplicity's sake, Figure 11-4 shows it checking

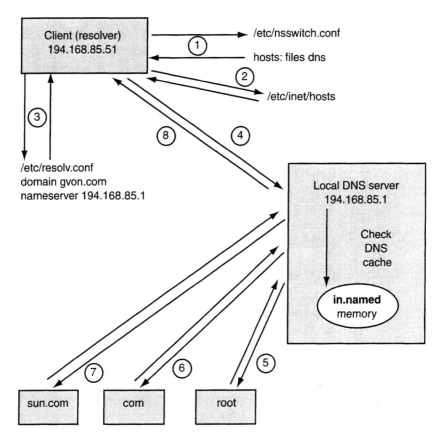

Figure 11–4 *The DNS client resolution process*

the switch file directly. Either way, it discovers it must check /etc/
inet/hosts and then check DNS.

2. Next, the resolver client asks /etc/inet/hosts (using the `gethostbyname`
   `()` Solaris function) for the IP address of www.sun.com, but the host's
   files do not have the answer.

3. It next checks DNS via the /etc/resolv.conf file (as dictated by step
   1) and the switch file's contents to identify the DNS server it is to
   use. It finds the nameserver has IP address 194.168.85.1.

4. The client resolver now sends a recursive query to the nameserver
   194.168.85.1, asking for the IP address of www.sun.com. The server
   does not support the zone sun.com, and a check of DNS servers'
   memory-based cache reveals that the cache does not contain the
   answer to the question of how to resolve it.

5. The client now waits while the server identified through the /etc/resolv.con file "walks the tree" in at attempt to resolve the name www.sun.com. Having no other choice, the DNS server sends an iterative query to one of the root DNS servers, which it chooses from its DNS memory-based cache. DNS servers prime their caches at startup (when the DNS server daemon first runs on a given host, usually after system boot) with the names and IP addresses of the root-level servers, which are held locally in a file called named.root. The root-level server IP addresses and names are called *hints*. *Iterative* simply means that the nameserver 194.168.85.1 does not expect the root server to go searching for the IP address of www.sun.com. All that is required of the root server is the IP address of www.sun.com if known; otherwise it must only provide name server (NS) records relating to the com server(s). Note that the file that contains the 13 root servers may be called whatever the DNS administrator chooses. The author has chosen to call it named.root.

6. The root server does not have the IP address of www.sun.com, but because of delegation it does know the IP addresses (A records) and NS records of the servers of com. The root server returns this information to the nameserver 194.168.85.1.

7. Next, the nameserver 194.168.85.1 sends an iterative query to the com server, whose IP address it learned in step 5. The com server does not have the IP address of www.sun.com, so instead it returns to our client server the NS information for the servers of sun.com.

8. Our nameserver is now able to send an interactive query to the server of the sun.com zone, and it gets back the IP address of www.sun.com.

9. Now, a few seconds into the process, the server is able to return to the resolver client the IP address of www.sun.com, and the client may at last attempt the **ping**. DNS, of course, provides only the IP address of www.sun.com, who may not respond to the **ping**.

To summarize the foregoing steps:

- Every server that learns new information will cache it if the learned RRs TTL permit this.
- Servers cache for performance reasons. That is, it is quicker to get information from one's own memory-based cache than it is to send out iterative queries.

- The servers' lookups were cyclic and therefore referred to as iterative.
- The client's query was recursive, so it queries server 194.168.85.1 and waits for an answer.
- The whole process usually takes less than 5 seconds!

This concludes our look at how servers are queried. In section 11.7 we examine the steps needed to set up both DNS clients and servers.

EXAM NOTES

KEY LEARNING POINTS

- There are several types of DNS server: root, master, slave, caching-only, and server in forwarding mode.
- Thirteen root-level servers manage the top level of the DNS namespace.
- Master servers hold the definitive information for a given domain.
- Slave servers of a domain(s) mirror a master's domain(s) information.
- Slaves are used for load balancing and high availability of domain information.
- A DNS server may be both master and slave for different domains.
- Clients (by default) send recursive queries to servers.
- Servers (by default) send iterative queries to other servers.
- Servers usually cache what they learn for performance reasons.

115 The Main Configuration File /etc/named.conf

All DNS servers have a main configuration file called /etc/named.conf, which lists the zones that the DNS server supports. The /etc/named.conf file in turn points to zone database files (one for each zone supported), which contain the actual host names and IP addresses. These files also contain other critical information, such as which mail server will accept mail for the zone in the form of Mail Exchanger (MX) records and DNS host name aliases in canonical name (CNAME) records.

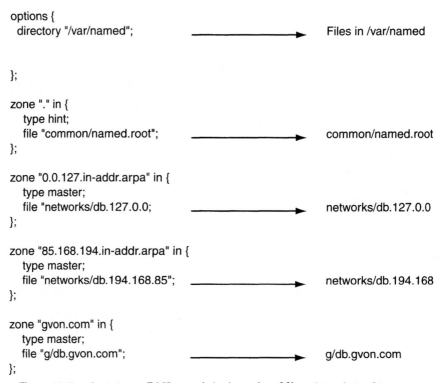

```
options {
    directory "/var/named";                    ──────────►    Files in /var/named



};

zone "." in {
    type hint;
    file "common/named.root";                  ──────────►    common/named.root
};

zone "0.0.127.in-addr.arpa" in {
    type master;
    file "networks/db.127.0.0;                 ──────────►    networks/db.127.0.0
};

zone "85.168.194.in-addr.arpa" in {
    type master;
    file "networks/db.194.168.85";             ──────────►    networks/db.194.168
};

zone "gvon.com" in {
    type master;
    file "g/db.gvon.com";                      ──────────►    g/db.gvon.com
};
```

Figure 11–5   *A minimum DNS server's /etc/named.conf file and its relationship to zone database files*

Named.conf Entries

One of the biggest challenges students encounter when learning DNS is determining which file does what and how the files relate to one another. Do not be concerned about the exact meaning of file entries at this point; we will concentrate on the content of the named.conf file in this section and devote section 11.6 to the zone database files.

Figure 11-5 should help clarify your understanding of the relationship between the /etc/named.conf file and related zone database files that are either directly stored in /var/named or in its subdirectories.

The /etc/named.conf Main Configuration File

All Solaris 8 DNS servers have one main configuration file called /etc/named.conf, which contains six main types of information (commonly called *directives*). As Table 11.1 shows, DNS servers running BIND 4 call this configuration file /etc/named.boot. We will look specifically at entries that are usable by BIND version 8.1.2 rather than by later BIND version directives, as BIND 8.1.2 is the basis for the examination.

The Directives in /etc/named.conf

Directives are essentially reserved words that are understood by **in.named** to denote the start of a particular type of entry. The configuration file consists of sections and comments. Sections end with a semicolon (;) and contain multiline directive blocks or statements enclosed in braces ({}).

Six main sections are supported in the named.conf file:

- `options`
- `server`
- `zone`
- `acl`
- `include`
- `key` (reserved for future use and so ignored by BIND 8.1.2)

Let us examine the syntax of the /etc/named.conf file and look at each type of directive, its syntax, and how to use it. These directives are referred to as *keywords* because they have a special meaning in the /etc/named.conf file.

Options

The options section of the /etc/named.conf file sets default main parameters for all zones defined in the file. Some of the options parameters may be changed for individual zones, as you will see when we explore zone definitions in this file. Only one options directive is allowed in the named.conf file, and it should occur at the head of the file.

The file contains code blocks that start and end with braces ({ }). Code blocks occur within statements, which are terminated with a semicolon (;).

The following statement is a general `option` statement that usually appears at the head of the file. The lines that begin with double forward slash characters (//) denote comments, which are ignored by the server daemon **in.named**:

```
//my default options
options      {
    directory "/var/named";
    allow-transfer { 194.168.85.2 ; };
};
//end of options statement
```

The double forward slash characters (//) in line 1 of the foregoing fragment indicate that what follows is a comment, in this case, `my default options`. Line 2 denotes the start of the `options` statement, and the open brace character ({) shows the start of the start of a block of code. In line 3,

```
directory "/var/named";
```

indicates that the zone resource files are found in the directory /var/named. We will see how to create zone resource files in a later section of this chapter. The next line,

```
allow-transfer { 194.168.85.2 ; } ;
```

is the `allow-transfer` statement, which determines which slaves may zone-transfer from this server. (Zone transferring is the act of synchronizing with a master and will be discussed shortly.) Only 194.168.85.2 may zone-transfer from this particular server.

The final closing brace (}) in line 5 closes the `options` statement, and the block ends with a comment to that effect.

Many other options are permitted in the options directive; you can find a listing of them in the Solaris manual pages. Use the following command to view the listing:

```
# man in.named
```

One option, `forwarders`, merits a closer examination, as you can create forwarding servers simply by adding extra options. Following is a modified `options` statement that serves as an example of how to use this statement to force a server to become a forwarding server.

```
//my default options
```

```
options      {
    directory "/var/named";
    forwarders  { 62.254.198.1 ; } ;
};
//end of options statement
```

If the server we forward to (address 62.254.198.1 in our example) fails to supply the answer that the forwarding server requires, it may access other DNS servers in an attempt to retrieve the information. If we use a `forward only` option, we can prevent that from happening and force the forwarding server to ask none but the server we forward to, even if the forwarded to server fails to return an answer. Here is how such a modification might look:

```
//my default options
options      {
    directory "/var/named";
    forwarders  { 62.254.198.1 ; } ;
    forward only;
};
//end of options statement
```

The foregoing example tells the DNS server to forward all zone lookups other than lookups to the zones that the server supports. Later versions of BIND (version 8.2 and later) allow for forwarding to selected zones only. As this is not a feature of Solaris 8, which ships with BIND 8.1.2, we will not cover it.

Server

Server directives are completely optional and may be omitted altogether. One use of server directives is to define a remote DNS server that you believe is *bogus* (false) and is giving out bad data. Using the `bogus` statement causes your server to ignore the bogus server and cease sending queries to it. Here is an example of how to define a server as bogus:

```
//bogus DNS server.
server 62.254.198.1  {
    bogus yes;
}
```

Line 1 of the foregoing fragment identifies a comment. Line 2 says that what follows refers to a DNS server with an IP address of 62.254.198.1. The opening brace ({) also shows that we are opening a code block. Line

3 says that the IP address in the previous line is a bogus server. (Changing the `yes` in this line to `no` rescinds the designation of this server as bogus.) The closing brace in the final line of the fragment denotes the close of the `server` statement.

Multiple server directives are allowed in the /etc/named.conf file.

Zone

Zone definitions form the bulk of the /etc/named.conf file because for each zone supported, a zone directive is required. If a server supports a thousand zones, for example, its /etc/named.conf file will contain a thousand zone directives.

Within the zone options category there are four main types of entries:

- `hint`
- `master`
- `slave`
- `stub`

Let us look at a single example of each, starting with hint entries.

ZONE ENTRY OF TYPE `hint`

This zone definition points to the local file that lists the current root-level servers. As we saw earlier in the chapter, the root servers are listed in a file called /var/named/named.root. In section 11.3, you saw how to retrieve that file from ftp.rs.internic.net.

The following sample zone entry is of type `hint` because the contents of /var/named/named.root are used to prime the DNS server's memory-based name cache (maintained by **in.named**) and provides hints about how to reach the 13 root-level servers. Please note that the file that contains the list of root-level servers is called named.root and is usually stored in /var/named.

```
//file containing root servers list
zone "." in {
        type hint;
        file "named.root";
};
```

In line 1 of the example, the line beginning with a double forward slash (//) shows that what follows is a comment, in this case, `file containing root servers list`. The next two lines say that for the root zone (denoted by .) there is hint information that should be added immediately to the cache. Line 4 says that the file named.root is in the directory called /var/named. Notice that the path is relative—it does not begin with a forward slash character. In this case, the directive called *directory* /var/named, is automatically prepended to the path. The path is seen as /var/named/named.root. The very reason for defining the directory directive in the `options` statement was to allow for the use of relative names like `named.root`.

ZONE ENTRY OF TYPE `master`

This zone definition points to a local file that contains the zone information for the supported domain. We will show two sample zone definitions of type `master`: forward zones and reverse zones.

THE FORWARD ZONE • The resource record (RR) data of a *forward zone* enables a DNS server to map a host's name (such as voyager.gvon.com) to an IP address. The DNS server will then return the IP address associated with the name when it is queried. This type of information is provided by the DNS record type called an *A record* (address record). DNS has several record types, which we examine in detail in section 11.6.

DNS can also perform the reverse of this function. That is, it can be given an IP address and asked to return the host name that matches the IP address. Reverse zone database files use a type of record called a pointer (PTR), which we will examine shortly.

Here first is an example that shows the named.conf files entry for the forward zone gvon.com.

```
zone "gvon.com" in {
        type master;
        file "g/db.gvon.com";
};
```

The fragment tells us says that for zone `gvon.com`, the server is the master and holds the authoritative zone information in a file called `/var/named/g/db.gvon.com`.

THE REVERSE ZONE • Our second example shows the named.conf files entry for the reverse zone 85.168.194.in-addr.arpa.

```
zone "85.168.194.in-addr.arpa" in {
        type master;
        file "networks/db.194.168.85";
};
```

The `master` zone in this case relates to network address 194.168.85.0. What looks peculiar (to the unfamiliar eye) is that the network 194.168.85.0 is shown as the zone `85.168.194.in-addr.arpa`. This is correct. The network address is reversed (yielding 85.168.194), and the TLD of in-addr.arpa is tagged onto the end of the reverse network address.

All DNS reverse zone information is stored under the official TLD zone called `in-addr` (for Internet address) a subdomain of arpa, which is used solely for reverse zones.

The zone database file in the example just given is called

```
/var/named/networks/db.194.168.85
```

The administrator has chosen to put zone files relating to reverse zones in a subdirectory of /var/named called networks. This is not compulsory. This zone file contains the PTR records that map IP addresses back to host names.

The choice of name for the zone file lies with the administrator, who here has chosen db.194.168.85. As long as the file exists in the directory /var/named/networks and contains the correct information for the zone 85.168.194.in-addr.arpa, things will function correctly. Because reverse zones always relate to a network address (here, 194.168.85.0) and to the IP addresses of hosts on that network, the hostmaster has decided to add it to the directory /var/named/networks. This is simply a means of organizing zone files hierarchically on the system, rather than putting them all in the /var/named directory. In section 11.7 we will explore file storage more thoroughly.

ZONE ENTRY OF TYPE `slave`

```
zone "domainbank.co.uk" in {
        type slave;
        masters { 194.168.85.105; };
        file "secondary/d/db.domainbank.co.uk.";
};
```

The foregoing fragment says that for zone domainbank.co.uk, this server is of type `slave` and must contact the master (who is defined in braces and who has an IP address of 194.168.85.105) for the zone data.

Once the server has acquired the zone data (which it will do automatically when **in.named** is started on the slave server), it must dump the zone data into an automatically created file with the name /var/named/

secondary/d/db.domainbank.co.uk. Note that the dump file will be created automatically only if the directory /var/named/secondary/d exists.

As line 4 shows, this hostmaster has decided that all slave zone data will be stored in a directory called /var/named/secondary and that within this directory, a directory called d will store the zone transfer information for domainbank.co.uk (because the domain name begins with the letter "d").

ZONE ENTRY stub

The entry type stub is unlike the previous three types (hint, master, and slave) because none of the others are related to the subject of *delegation*. The named.conf stub zone entry allows us to delegate away authority for a given zone to another DNS server, in effect creating a new zone of authority. Here is an example entry:

```
zone "support.gvon.com" in {
        type stub;
        masters { 194.168.85.2; };
        file "stubs/db.support.gvon.com";
};
```

In this zone definition, we are type stub. We are the master of the zone gvon.com and are delegating subdomain support to master server 194.168.85.2, in effect creating a new zone of authority called support.gvon.com. As we acquire information about this zone from the master to which we have now delegated authority, we will store the information in a file called /var/named/stubs/db. support.gvon.com.

The acl *Directive*

The ACL /etc/named.conf entry tightens a given DNS server's security. Here is a simple ACL definition:

```
//Gvon ACL called internal

acl "internal"  { 194.168.85/24; };
```

Having now defined the acl internal, we may use it in the global options statement that is always located at the start of the /etc/named.conf file. (Recall from Chapter 5 that we may use CIDR notation to indicate the netmask that applies to a given network address, thus we may use the notation 194.168.85/24 in our acl called `internal`. Here is the `options` statement:

```
//my default options
options
{
directory "/var/named";
allow-transfer {
internal
};
//end of options
```

Through this statement, we are allowing any DNS slave in the network 194.168.85.0 to zone transfer (synchronize) with us. As you will see shortly, you may override this statement for individual zones.

The `include` *Directive*

The final entry type in the /etc/named.conf file is `include`, which makes it possible to include the contents of a file in the /etc/named.conf file. Here as an example of its use:

```
Include       "named.conf.master";

Include       "named.conf.slave";
```

These two lines tell the server to read (insert) into the current /etc/named.conf file the contents of the two files named.conf.master and named.conf.slave. In effect, the include directive allows us to build a named.conf file from multiple files.

EXAM NOTES

KEY LEARNING POINTS

- The /etc/named.conf file is the default master configuration file and is found on all DNS servers of type BIND 8.
- BIND 4 used a default bootfile called /etc/named.boot.
- A zone of authority contains all domains that are not delegated away.
- The 8.1.2 /etc/named.conf file contains entries of type `options`, `server`, `zone`, `acl`, `include`, and `key`. Newer versions of BIND might have additional options not relevant to our study of DNS and Solaris 8.

- Zone entries define the zones for which a given DNS server acts as either master or slave. Zone entries make up the bulk of the /etc/named.conf file.

11.6   The Zone Database Files and the Resource Record (RR) Format

The /etc/named.conf file references per-zone database files, which are in a format called *resource record* (RR) format. We will refer to them in this book as *zone database files*. Some texts refer to them as *resource record files*.

The /etc/named.conf directive that specifically points to the zone database files is the zone directive, in which the `file` statement indicates the filename that stores the zone data. An example of the file directive in use is shown here as it occurs in the block of lines from the /etc/named.conf entry for the zone gvon.com:

```
zone "gvon.com" in {
        type master;
        file "g/db.gvon.com.";
};
```

The file directive points to the zone files we examine in this section, which hold the crucial zone (domain) information for a specific zone, in this case gvon.com.

At the start of the /etc/named.conf file, we defined a directory directive that pointed to the directory /var/named. Following this reasoning, all file directives that show a relative file name will have /var/named prepended to them. For example, the full pathname of g/db.gvon.com is really /var/named/g/db.gvon.com.

The zone line defines the zone in double quotes, in the above case it is "gvon.com." In the zone database file itself, we may refer to the zone by simply using the metacharacter "@" which in the zone database files is called the "current origin." That is, in the above gvon.com zone block, the current origin is "gvon.com" and "@" is a metacharacter for (is equal to) "gvon.com."

Syntax of the Resource Record (RR)

In this section, we examine the syntax of individual resource records and follow with a look at the list of resource record types used in the RRs. Be aware that most RRs occupy one line at most, with the exception of the Start of Authority record, which usually occupies several lines. The general syntax of RR records is

```
[NAME]      [TTL]    [CLASS]        RECORD-TYPE      RECORD-DATA
```

The record values are not case sensitive, but we show them in upper case so they may be differentiated from the rest of the text. Let us next examine the five fields of the RR format.

[NAME] *Field*

The name field usually contains a host or zone name, such as www.gvon.com or simply the zone itself (gvon.com). There are exceptions to this rule, as you will see when we look at pointer (PTR) records, where the name field is part of a complete IP address.

The bracket characters ([]) denote that the field is optional if it is not included in a given zone record. When this field is omitted in the real world, its value is presumed not to have changed from the previous resource record.

Here are two additional rules to remember when dealing with the name field:

- If the name field is blank, the previous record's name field is assumed to be correct for the current line. That is, in most zone files, the first field of the first RR is the current origin (@)— gvon.com in this case. So, if the lines were

  ```
  gvon.com.   IN        NS            auriga.gvon.com.
              IN        NS            centauri.gvon.com.
  ```

  the second line's first field would be gvon.com, because it is blank. A blank name field assumes the value of the last fully qualified name field used in the nearest (but previous) line.
- If the name field is not qualified, the current origin is appended. For example, if the name field were voyager and the current origin were gvon.com, the name field would be interpreted as voyager.gvon.com.

[TTL] *Field*

The TTL field determines how long, in seconds, the RRs supplied by an authoritative DNS server are cached by other nonauthoritative DNS servers. When a DNS server supplies answers in response to queries it receives, it supplies a TTL value with the RRs it returns, which determine the life of the RR record in the DNS cache of the nonauthoritative or querying server.

If the TTL field is blank in a particular RR, as defined in the zones database file, the DNS server supplies the default TTL from the zones SOA record, which is always located at the start of the given zone file.

[CLASS] *Field*

The class field always has a value of IN. There are other classes under development, but the Internet class (IN) is the main one in use today. This field is optional. If the class field is omitted, it defaults to the class IN, which is by far the most common.

[RECORD-TYPE] *and* [RECORD-DATA] *Fields*

We will examine the record-type and record-data fields together because one describes the format of the other. There are many record types, as Table 11.5 shows. We will explore each of these types later when we see them used in actual zone database files.

Table 11.5 *Common Resource Record (RR) Types*

RECORD TYPE KEYWORD	BRIEF DESCRIPTION
SOA	Start of Authority Record. Contains the name of the master server, the hostmaster mail address, slave synchronization information, plus the default TTL
A	Address record, an IP address
NS	Name server name
MX	Mail exchanger name
PTR	Pointer record name
CNAME	Canonical name used to create host aliases
HINFO	Host information (CPU+OS)
TXT	A text field, which is not often used

The Zone Database Files

All DNS servers have zone database files describing the zones they support. These are saved in RR format. The number of zone database files held by a given server depends on the number of zones the server supports or serves. Although the actual number of these files vary from one DNS server to the next, all zone database files are one of just three possible types:

- *Forward zone files*—A zone file is required for each forward zone that the DNS server hosts. We will examine a sample forward zone file for the gvon.com zone.

- *Reverse zone files*—A zone file is required for each reverse zone that the DNS server hosts, i.e., for each network that the server supports.

- *Root zone files*—A root zone file (named.root) contains the addresses and names of the 13 root-level servers. This file is identical on all Internet-facing DNS servers. You do not have to create the named.root file. Simply ftp to ftp.rs.internic.net and log in as anonymous (or as ftp). When asked for a password, give your e-mail address. Change directory (cd) to the directory /domain and **get** the file called named.root. In section 11.7, you will see how to automate the collection of this file using ftp.

A Forward Zone File Example

Here is a sample zone file for the forward zone gvon.com. For the sake of brevity, we show only a few examples of each type of record. The number of resource records in a zone file will vary; each zone file will contain one SOA and two or more NS records, but the number of A records will depend on the number of hosts in the domain whose name we wish to look up using DNS. For example, if we wish to acquire the IP addresses of 10,000 machines through DNS, we will have 10,000 A records.

```
# cat /var/named/g/db.gvon.com

;Forward zone file for gvon.com
;first the SOA record
@      IN    SOA    auriga.gvon.com.   hostmaster.gvon.com. (
                          76381     ; Serial
                          10800     ; Refresh every 3 hours
                          3600      ; Retry every hour
                          604800    ; Expire after a week
```

```
                                 43200   )  ; Default TTL 12 hours
;List of masters and slaves
                    IN            NS                auriga.gvon.com.
                    IN            NS                centauri.gvon.com.
;mail exchangers (running SMTP) for zone
                    IN            MX          5     hercules.gvon.com.
                    IN            MX          10    ophelia.gvon.com.
                    IN            MX          15    orion.uk.gvon.com.
;IP addresses of hosts
localhost  IN       A             127.0.0.1
auriga     IN       A             194.168.85.1
centauri   IN       A             194.168.85.2
hercules   IN       A             194.168.85.60
ophelia    IN       A             62.254.198.60
;machine aliases
www        IN            CNAME          voyager.gvon.com.
smtp       IN            CNAME          ophelia.gvon.com.
pop        IN            CNAME          hercules.gvon.com.
ns0        IN            CNAME          auriga.gvon.com.
ns1        IN            CNAME          centuria.gvon.com.

;delegation of zone uk.gvon.com to orion.uk.gvon.com
follows
;unqualified name field (first field)will have current
origin,   ;gvon.com appended
uk         IN            NS             orion.uk.gvon.com.
orion.uk   IN       A             62.254.198.1
;END of Zone database File
```

The following explanation of the contents of our sample forward zone file gives line numbers and also shows the file lines being referenced.

LINES 1–2

```
;Forward zone file for gvon.com
;first the SOA record
```

Lines 1 and 2 are comments, as denoted by the leading semicolons. It is a good practice to add comment lines in the zone files to make the contents of the file explicit. In this case, our comments tell us that this file is the forward zone file for the zone gvon.com.

LINES 3–8

The long Start of Authority (SOA) record starts with the at character (@) and ends with the closing parentheses character()).

```
@   IN   SOA   auriga.gvon.com.   hostmaster.gvon.com.  (
                        76381     ; Serial
                        10800     ; Refresh every 3 hours
               3600      ;  Retry every hour
               604800    ; Expire after a week
               43200  )  ; Default TTL 12 hours
```

The name field denoted by the @ character is a metacharacter and is referred to as the *current origin,* which simply means the zone to which this file relates. The zone lines from the /etc/named.conf entry that reference this zone database file determine the current origin and, thus, the value of @:

```
zone "gvon.com" in {
        type master;
        file "g/db.gvon.com.";
};
```

The in field denotes that the SOA record is of class Internet. The SOA field denotes that the RR is of type SOA. (Each zone database file has only one SOA entry, which is always at the head of the zone file.)

The record data of the SOA is far more complex than that of any other RR. The DNS server who is the Start of Authority (SOA) for the zone file and its data is auriga.gvon.com. The mail address of the hostmaster who manages the zone is hostmaster.gvon.com. You would mail the address as hostmaster@gvon.com. The opening bracket character (() at the end of line 3 means that the SOA record continues until a closing bracket character ()) is encountered. Following the opening bracket are five critical fields. The five numerical fields of every SOA record in every zone file have the same meaning, even though the actual values of the five fields vary from file to file.

Note

The values of the four lines that follow the serial field (lines 5 through 8 in our example) are given in seconds.

LINE 4 (PART OF SOA RECORD) • `76381; serial`

The serial value denotes the version number of the file. If the zone file is modified on the master server, this value should be incremented by at least one. The slave servers, when synchronizing, check this value against the serial number in their respective copies of this file. Failing to increment this number when updating the master zone file can lead to slaves having old copies of the zone data for the given zone, in this case gvon.com.

LINE 5 (PART OF SOA RECORD) • 10800; Refresh every 3 hours
This field dictates to slaves that they should revisit the master every three hours to check whether the serial number from the previous line has changed. If the file on the master has been modified, the slaves should synchronize by taking a copy of the updated file. This synchronization process is called a zone transfer and uses TCP rather than UDP for the sake of greater reliability.

LINE 6 (PART OF SOA RECORD) • 3600; Retry every hour
If a slave fails to synchronize with the master during a clocked refresh (every three hours, in our example), it does not wait until the refresh (line 5) value elapses. Rather, it retries hourly until it is successful. Once it has synchronized, it resumes its standard refresh cycle as dictated by the refresh value in line 5.

LINE 7 (PART OF SOA RECORD) • 604800; Expire after a week
If the slave fails to synchronize after trying continually, it has no choice but to give up attempting to mirror the master's data for the zone in question. After one week (604,800 seconds) in our example, the slave will cease serving the zone.

LINE 8 (PART OF SOA RECORD) • 43200); Default TTL 12 hours in seconds
The four fields in lines 4 through 8 pertain to keeping a slave in sync with the master by supplying a file version number and slave synchronization instructions, which the slave obeys. The final value of the SOA field in line 8 is the default TTL for RR lines that lack a specific TTL.

That concludes our examination of the crucial SOA RR.

LINES 10–11

We now look at RRs that are much simpler than the SOA record and that occupy a single line of the file. We start with the name server (NS) RR lines:

```
IN      NS      auriga.gvon.com.

IN      NS      centauri.gvon.com.
```

These lines denote that auriga.gvon.com. and centauri.gvon.com. are Name Servers (NS) for the gvon.com zone. Auriga, as we have seen in the SOA, is the master server. Centauri, therefore, must be a slave, as it is a name server, but not the master.

The first field (the name field) is usually left blank, in which case the current origin denoted by the at character (@) is automatically assumed. In our example, the current origin is gvon.com, so functionally, the same lines could just as easily read

```
gvon.com.    IN      NS      auriga.gvon.com.
gvon.com.    IN      NS      centauri.gvon.com.
```

LINES 13–15

```
IN          MX      5       hercules.gvon.com.
IN          MX      10      ophelia.gvon.com.
IN          MX      15      orion.uk.gvon.com.
```

Again, the first field is blank, which tells us that it assumes the value of gvon.com. The MX record identifies the hosts who act as SMTP mail relays for the gvon.com domain. The MX record-data field has an additional value, called the *preference value*. In the example, the preference values are 5, 10, and 15, representing the mail exchangers hercules, ophelia, and orion, respectively.

Note DNS simply makes SMTP mail server and preference values available, and other applications (such as super sendmail, the Internet's most popular and powerful UNIX mail server) obey the preference value.

LINES 17–21

```
localhost    IN      A       127.0.0.1
auriga       IN      A       194.168.85.1
centauri     IN      A       194.168.85.2
hercules     IN      A       194.168.85.60
ophelia      IN      A       62.254.198.60
```

The A field stands for IP address and associates an IP address with the name in the name field. Notice that the name field in our example does not end in a qualifying full stop (.). Unqualified name fields have the current origin appended when loaded into the cache. The current origin is still gvon.com, derived from the @ character of the SOA record.

LINES 23–27

```
www            IN          CNAME          voyager.gvon.com.
smtp           IN          CNAME          ophelia.gvon.com.
pop            IN          CNAME          hercules.gvon.com.
ns0            IN          CNAME          auriga.gvon.com.
ns1            IN          CNAME          centuria.gvon.com.
```

Essentially, CNAME is a DNS alias record. For example, www is an alias for voyager. If www is requested, we return the A record of voyager.gvon.com. Note also that the alias is shown in the name field. The canonical name (voyager.gvon.com) is in the record-data field.

LINES 31–32

```
uk          IN      NS         orion.uk.gvon.com.
orion.uk    IN      A          62.254.198.1
```

Here, we delegate uk.gvon.com to nameserver (NS) orion.uk.gvon.com. Notice that the first field (the name field) is unqualified, which is intentional. Remember that the current origin is gvon.com. Therefore, the DNS server qualifies these names when it adds them to its cache, which reflects its interpretation of their meaning. Functionally, they are the same as

```
uk.gvon.com.            IN      NS         orion.uk.gvon.com.
orion.uk.gvon.com.      IN      A          62.254.198.1
```

These lines show the name field qualified, which, although correct, is superfluous and can lead to errors and unnecessary work. Refer back to Figure 11-3 in section 11.3, which will help you further understand the concept of zone delegation.

We have now examined every line in the db.gvon.com zone file. Next, we examine the lines of the reverse zone file.

The Reverse Zone File

The reverse zone file we use as an example is pointed to by the following /etc/named.conf zone block, seen in section 11.4.

```
zone "85.168.194.in-addr.arpa" in {
        type master;
```

```
            file "networks/db.194.168.85";

    };
```

We now look at the file db.194.168.85, which as can be seen, has an origin of 85.168.194.in-addr.arpa. The origin, remember, is the zone defined in the zone line and enclosed in double quotes. Here is the complete reverse zone file for zone 85.168.194.in-addr.arpa.

```
# cat /var/named/networks/db.194.168.85

;the reverse zone file for network 194.168.85.0
;zone 85.168.194.in-addr.arpa.
@    IN    SOA    auriga.gvon.com. hostmaster.gvon.com. (
                          76381  ; Serial
                          10800  ; Refresh every 3 hours
                          3600   ; Retry every hour
                          604800 ; Expire after a week
                          43200 )  ; Default TTL 12 hours
     IN    NS     auriga.gvon.com.
     IN    NS     centauri.gvon.com.

1         IN         PTR         auriga.gvon.com.
2         IN         PTR         centauri.gvon.com.
50        IN         PTR         alpha.gvon.com.
51        IN         PTR         voyager.gvon.com.
;end of zone file
```

We have looked at the forward zone file in depth. The first 12 lines of the reverse zone file are identical to those of the forward zone file, apart from the comments. The current origin (@) in this file, however, is 85.168.194.in-addr.arpa. The lines that are different in the reverse zone file are:

```
1         IN         PTR         auriga.gvon.com.
2         IN         PTR         centauri.gvon.com.
50        IN         PTR         alpha.gvon.com.
51        IN         PTR         voyager.gvon.com.
;end of zone file
```

The name fields (as can be seen) have values of 1, 2, 50, and 51, respectively. Recall that if the name field is unqualified, the current origin is appended to it. The lines that are qualified are placed in the current DNS server's cache as

```
1.85.168.194.in-addr.arpa. IN PTR auriga.gvon.com.
2.85.168.194.in-addr.arpa. IN PTR centauri.gvon.com.
50.85.168.194.in-addr.arpa. IN PTR alpha.gvon.com.
51.85.168.194.in-addr.arpa. IN PTR voyager.gvon.com.
```

For example, if a DNS server (client) asks for the host name that matches IP address 194.168.85.1, the name auriga.gvon.com. is returned.

The Root Zone File

Unlike the forward and reverse zone files—which are needed for the zones the server supports—the root zone file is needed so you can prime a server's cache with information relating to the 13 root name servers that manage the top level of the namespace. We saw how this file was referenced in /etc/named.conf as a zone entry of type hint, which means that the files contain information we use to prime the server's cache (see section 11.5). Rather than include the whole file again here, we include just a few lines for brief analysis:

```
.   3600000   IN   NS     A.ROOT-SERVERS.NET.
A.ROOT-SERVERS.NET. 3600000 A 198.41.0.4
```

The first of these two lines says that for the root zone (identified by a lone dot), the class is Internet (IN) and the Name Server (NS) is called A.ROOT-SERVERS.NET.

   The second line provides the address record of this root server, which is 198.41.0.4. The rest of the file (as seen in section 11.4) simply lists the other 12 root servers in an identical fashion and syntax. This file is different from most other files referred to with the named.conf zone directive, in that it does not begin with an SOA record. This is simply because the current server is not the SOA for the information it contains. The root level servers themselves are authoritative for the information in the named.root file. All nonroot servers simply use the contents of the named.root file to prime their cache so they know how to look up the root-level servers for nonlocal domains.

EXAM NOTES

KEY LEARNING POINTS

- **Zone database files are in resource record (RR) format.**
- **The name field (first field) in a zone database file is the subject of a DNS query.**

- The `TTL` field determines how long servers cache a learned RR.
- Zone database files relate to zones of type `forward` and `reverse`.
- An unqualified `name` field has the current origin value appended in order to qualify it.
- The official root zone file (named.root) is the same on all DNS servers.

11.7   Creating a DNS Server and Client Step by Step

We have now examined examples of the files needed to create a DNS server. We now summarize this task by examining, step by step, the process of creating a DNS server and client. If you need to review any technical details along the way, please refer back to the section in which a configuration file is examined.

Creating a DNS Server

In our example, we will create a server for a single forward zone (testing.com) and network address 194.168.85.0, which has three hosts. Our server is called rigel 192.168.20.1, and its two hosts are capella and antares. The IP addresses of these servers are:

- DNS server rigel: 192.168.20.1
- DNS client capella: 192.168.20.2
- DNS client antares. 192.168.20.3

Creating the server involves the following steps:

1. Create the /etc/named.conf file and add zone definitions to /etc/named.conf for the zones your server supports, without creating the actual zone files at this point.
2. Create the directory referenced in /etc/named.conf that will contain the zone database file (called /var/named in our example).
3. Create the zone files in /var/named that contain the resource records for each supported zone.
4. Modify the /etc/nsswitch.conf file and add `dns` to the `hosts` line, which instructs your system to use DNS as a client.
5. Start the **in.named** server daemon.
6. Create an /etc/resolv.conf file if you want the system to be a DNS client as well as a DNS server. We look at creating a DNS client and the /etc/resolv.conf file later in this section.

Creating The Main /etc/named.conf File on Server rigel

The named.conf file is a simple text file created with an editor of your choice. Ensure that you add support in /etc/named.conf for

- forward zone training.com
- reverse zone 192.168.20.0
- the root zone using the named.root cache hints file
- the simple localhost DNS file

We did not previously discuss the localhost DNS file; it is simply a reverse zone except for the loopback address, which is always 127.0.0.1. Your /etc/named.conf file will look exactly like this:

```
//Main Options
options {
        directory           "/var/named";
        };
};
zone "." in {
        type hint;
        files "common/named.root";
};
zone "0.0.127.in-addr.arpa" in {
        type master;
        file "common/db.127.0.0";
};
 zone "20.168.192.in-addr.arpa" in {
        type master;
        file "networks/db.192.168.20";
}
 zone "training.com" in {
        type master;
        file "t/db.training.com";
};
```

Creating a /var/named Directory and Desired Subdirectories

The /var/named directory contains the per-zone db file. You may store the zone files in a directory of your choice, but you should ensure that they are modifiable only by authorized users like root. Set the correct Solaris permissions. Make the directory using the Solaris **mkdir** command:

```
# mkdir /var/named
```

Following is a simple shell script that will make directories for all letters of the alphabet and numerics from 0 through 9. This script needs to be stored as a file and made executable. We have chosen to call the script (command) **makedirs**. Make it executable and run it as `root`.

```
# cat   /var/named/makedirs

#!/bin/sh
NAMED=/var/named
for CHAR in a b c d e f g h i j k l m n o p q r s t u v w x
y z 0 1 2 3 4 5 6 7 8 9
do
    #make dirs under /var/named

        echo Creating $NAMED/$CHAR

            mkdir -p $NAMED/$CHAR

        echo $NAMED/$CHAR has been created
done
```

Ensure that the file is executable by setting the correct permissions. Enter the following basic **chmod** command:

```
# chmod 700 /var/named/makedirs
```

and run it by typing its name at the prompt:

```
# /var/named/makedirs
```

You will see output as the directories are recreated.

Creating Zone Files for Each Zone Supported

You need to create zone files for each zones you intend to support, as listed in the named.conf file you created in step 1. Use the following shell script to automate the collection of the all important named.root file.

```
#!/bin/sh
MAILADDRESS=hostmaster@gvon.com
NICSERVER=ftp.rs.internic.net
DNSDIR=/var/named

ftp  $NICSERVER  <<!
user ftp $MAILADDRESS
cd /domain
get named.root $DNSDIR/named.root
```

```
!
#END of SCRIPT
```

Now follows a brief explanation of the script.

LINE 1

```
#!/bin/sh
```

This line instructs the shell that runs the script to run the script (call) the Bourne shell (/bin/sh).

LINES 2–4

```
MAILADDRESS=hostmaster@gvon.com
NICSERVER=ftp.rs.internic.net
DNSDIR=/var/named
```

These three lines setup variables, which are referenced later in the script.

LINES 5–9

```
ftp  $NICSERVER  <<!
user ftp $MAILADDRESS
cd /domain
get named.root $DNSDIR/named.root
!
```

The <<! and ! characters (technically denoting the start and end of what is called a *here document*) cause the ftp command to read input (stdin) from the following lines up to the closing !, rather than to expect keyboard input.

These lines cause the system to run **ftp**, connect to ftp.rs.internic.net, log in as a user called ftp or anonymous, and provide the mail address hostmaster@gvon.com as the password. Once logged in, we **cd** to /domain and get the named.root file, and transfer it to the local directory called /var/named.

In these lines, the variables will be substituted for the actual values of the variable. Technically, the variable is said to have been *expanded*. The named.root file is now available for use and resides in the local directory called /var/named.

Now create zone files for:

- /var/named/db.127.0.0
- /var/named/db.training.com
- /var/named/db.192.168.20

Following are examples of what each file will look like.

FILE: /var/named/db.127.0.0

```
; zone file for 0.0.127.in-addr.arpa zone
@ IN  SOA  rigel.training.com. hostmaster.training.com. (
                    1  ; Serial
                    10800 ; Refresh every 3 hours
                    3600    ; Retry every hour
                    604800  ; Expire after a week
                    43200 ) ; Default of  12 hours
           IN      NS       rigel.training.com.
1              IN      PTR       localhost.
```

FILE: /var/named/db.training.com

```
;zone file for traning.com zone
@ IN  SOA  rigel.training.com. hostmaster.training.com. (
                    1  ; Serial
                    10800 ; Refresh every 3 hours
                    3600    ; Retry every hour
                    604800  ; Expire after a week
                    43200 ) ; Default of  12 hours
           IN      NS       rigel.training.com.

rigel          IN    A    192.168.20.1
capella        IN    A    192.168.20.2
antares        IN    A    192.168.20.3
```

FILE: /var/named/db.192.168.20

```
;zone file for the 20.168.192.in-addr.arpa zone
@ IN  SOA  rigel.training.com. hostmaster.training.com. (
                    1  ; Serial
                    10800 ; Refresh every 3 hours
                    3600    ; Retry every hour
                    604800  ; Expire after a week
                    43200 ) ; Default of  12 hours
           IN      NS       rigel.training.com.

1    IN    PTR    rigel.training.com.
2    IN    PTR    capella.training.com.
3    IN    PTR    antares.training.com.
```

We have now created all the zone files referred to in the /etc/named.conf file that was created in step 1.

Modifying the /etc/nsswitch.conf File

Next, edit the /etc/nsswitch.conf file and add `dns` to the `hosts` line, as follows. Edit the file using any Solaris editor:

```
hosts:  files dns
```

As a DNS client, the system will now attempt to use the DNS server(s) listed in /etc/resolv.conf. We look at creating the DNS client very soon.

Starting in.named

The DNS server daemon **in.named** will read the /etc/named.conf and zone files we have already configured. Start the daemon by entering

```
# in.named
```

Ensure that the daemon is actually running by using the **ps** command (which lists processes) as follows:

```
# ps -ef | grep in.named
```

If the daemon is not running, check the tail end of the Solaris /var/adm/ messages file for errors using the command

```
# tail /var/adm/messages
```

Startup and error messages are added to the /var/adm/messages file by in.named as it starts.

Please note that DNS servers are usually set up as clients also, so create a resolv.conf file on the server. We show the format of the /etc/ resolv.conf file in the section on creating the DNS client.

Creating a DNS Client

Creating a DNS client is simple and involves only two files:

- /etc/nsswitch.conf
- /etc/resolv.conf

Here are the steps:

1. Modify /etc/nsswitch.conf to show
   ```
   hosts:      files      dns
   ```
2. Create the /etc/resolv.conf file that enables a DNS client to locate its DNS server, 192.168.20.1, in the example that follows:

```
domain training.com
nameserver 192.168.20.1
```

In our example, we list only one DNS server in etc/resolv.conf, namely 192.168.20.1. You are allowed to add up to three DNS servers in this file, which are checked in the order in which they occur in the file.

3. Send SIGHUP to **nscd**, which forces **nscd** to reread /etc/nss-switch.conf:

```
# pkill -HUP nscd
```

4. Use **ping** to test whether DNS is working:

```
# ping rigel.training.com
rigel.training.com is alive
```

The client setup is now complete. If **ping** fails, ensure that you have performed the foregoing steps correctly. Table 11.6 summarizes the DNS configuration files and their purposes.

Table 11.6 *A Summary of DNS Configuration Files*

SOLARIS FILE NAME	PURPOSE
/etc/named.conf	Read by **in.named** (DNS server daemon); and identifies which zones are supported by the server.
/var/named	Contains zone files for each zone supported by the server.
/var/named/db.zone	One needed for each domain and zone supported. Each db.zone file is referenced by a zone definition block in the /etc/named.conf file.
/var/named/common/named.root	This file contains a list of root servers.
/etc/nsswitch.conf	This file determines which name services will be used by the host, and in which order. DNS clients must have this file.
/etc/resolv.conf	This file lists the DNS servers available to the client. DNS clients must have this file.

EXAM NOTES

KEY LEARNING POINTS

- **DNS servers are set up to support zones.**
- **DNS servers run the daemon in.named.**

- DNS clients are enabled through the /etc/nsswitch.conf file.
- DNS clients use the server(s) listed in their /etc/resolv.conf files.

11.8   DNS Debugging and Dumping the DNS Cache

This section briefly introduces you to some useful switches for debugging DNS. Equally important, it provides information on how to manipulate the memory-based DNS cache. The **in.named** DNS server daemon responds in a specific way when it receives certain signals.

Sending Signals to in.named

You can issue signals to **in.named**, causing it to behave in a number of different ways. It has signal handlers that control its behavior.

The INT Signal—Dumping the DNS Server's Cache

The INT signal causes **in.named** to dump its DNS memory cache, which provides invaluable information about how the server sees its own local zone information and the information in its cache. To dump the cache, issue the following command, which dumps the cache into a text file called named_dump, which you will find in the /var/named directory. You may then examine the text dump using a standard UNIX editor such as vi, the versatile interface.

```
# pkill -INT named
```

In the following fragment from the dump, we see some lines related to gvon.com zone:

```
$ORIGIN gvon.com
tgt       43200    IN       A        194.168.85.104    ;Cl=2
imap4     43200    IN       CNAME    hercules.gvon.co.uk.
;Cl=2
smtp      43200    IN       CNAME    hercules.gvon.co.uk.
;Cl=2
phobos    43200    IN       A        194.168.85.11     ;Cl=2
cri       43200    IN       A        194.168.85.101    ;Cl=2
news      43200    IN CNAME     ispc-news.cableinet.net.  ;Cl=2
```

```
localhost          43200    IN      A         127.0.0.1
;Cl=2
opensolve          43200    IN      A         194.168.85.102
;Cl=2
surreyserve        43200    IN      A         194.168.85.65
;Cl=2
hercules           43200    IN      A         194.168.85.60
;Cl=2
nexus2    43200    IN      A         62.254.198.254    ;Cl=2
bb        43200    IN      MX        5 hercules.gvon.co.uk.
;Cl=3
43200    IN      MX        10 ophelia.gvon.co.uk.    ;Cl=3
43200    IN      NS        auriga.gvon.co.uk.         ;Cl=3
43200    IN      NS        centauri.gvon.co.uk.       ;Cl=3
43200 IN SOA  auriga.gvon.co.uk.ostmaster.gvon.co.uk.
11155 10800 3600 604800 43200 )
```

As you can see, the dump shows the origin as gvon.com and a collection of records relating to the zone.

The HUP Signal—Reloading the Server's Configuration Files

The HUP signal causes **in.named** to reread its /etc/named.conf and related zone files. Use this signal when you update the server's files but wish to retain the current cache. The command is

```
# pkill -HUP  named
```

Lines in the log file /var/adm/messages will show you that the daemon had actually reloaded the zone data. The log files entry will look something like

```
July 17 17:15:46 auriga named[27551]: [ID 295310
daemon.notice] reloading nameserver
July 17 17:15:46 auriga named[27551]: [ID 295310
daemon.notice] Ready to answer queries.
```

The USR1 Signal—Activating Real-Time Debugging

The USR1 signal causes **in.named** to write real-time debug output into the file called /var/named/named_run. To turn on debugging to go to debug level 1:

```
# pkill -USR1 named
```

Repeat the command to go to debug level 2:

```
# pkill -USR1 named
```

Use signal USR2 to turn off debugging:

```
# pkill -USR2 named
```

The TERM and KILL Signals—Killing in.named

The TERM and KILL signals will both terminate the **in.named** daemon and hence, the DNS service. Use KILL, however, only if TERM fails to work. Here we terminate **in.named** and restart it:

```
# pkill -TERM in.named
```

and if this fails and the **ps** command shows **in.named** still running when you type:

```
# ps -ef | grep in.named
```

Use the stronger and more severe:

```
# pkill -KILL in.named
```

To restart the DNS server daemon in.named, issue the command:

```
# in.named
```

Additional Tools

Although the following topics are not covered by the Sun examination, it is nevertheless important to use them to probe the DNS namespace. The following tools allow you to do this:

- Dig
- Nslookup

EXAM NOTES

KEY LEARNING POINTS

- To dump the DNS cache, send the INT signal to the **in.named** demon.

- To reload the DNS cache, send the HUP signal to the **in.named** daemon.
- Turn on debugging by issuing the USR1 signal to **in.named**.
- Turn off debugging by issuing the USR2 signal.
- Use **nslookup** and **dig** to probe and query the namespace.

SUMMARY

In this chapter we examined DNS, a globally distributed, text-based database, which manifests as a hierarchical tree of names to which we refer as the namespace. DNS is built from BIND software, which enables the namespace to be managed by countless DNS servers spread around the globe, each one responsible for zones that have been delegated to them by higher level servers.

We examined top-level domain names (TLDs) of type gTLD and ccTLD, which are known as generic and geographic domains. We also explored the process of delegation, in which new zones of authority are born as parent zone servers give away authority over child domains to other servers.

We discovered that there are five main types of DNS servers, the most important three being root, master, and slave servers, which manage zones and zone database files. The master file /etc/named.conf enables **in.named**, the DNS server daemon, to identify which zones it supports and the location of the zone files that contain the zone information itself, usually stored in the /var/named directory.

We discussed the resource record (RR) format used in the zone database files and looked at the RR types used to categorize the zone data, such as A, NS, SOA, CNAME, and PTR.

Finally, we took a step-by-step look at how to create a DNS server and client and followed this with a discussion of debugging DNS and related tools.

TEST YOURSELF

MULTIPLE CHOICE

1. *What is the process of passing authority for a zone to another DNS server called?*
   A. dedication
   B. deliberations
   C. domination
   D. delegation
   E. deliberation

2. *Which of the following usually asks recursive questions? Choose 2.*
   A. root level servers
   B. master servers
   C. slave servers
   D. forwarding servers
   E. clients

3. *What is the default main DNS server configuration file called?*
   A. /etc/resolv.conf
   B. /etc/named.root
   C. /etc/named.cache
   D. /etc/named.conf
   E. /etc/nsswitch.conf

4. *What does the @ symbol stand for when it is found in RR zone database files?*
   A. the master server's name
   B. the current network
   C. the current origin
   D. the host's IP address
   E. the parent domain

5. *What record type should never be found in the zone file that deals with forward resolution?*
   A. NS
   B. PTR
   C. SOA
   D. A
   E. CNAME

6. *Which of the following RR types determines the master server (but never slave servers) for the zone in which it occurs?*
   A. NS
   B. PTR
   C. SOA
   D. A
   E. CNAME

7. *Which of the following RR types is only found in zone files that deal with reverse resolution?*
    A. NS
    B. PTR
    C. SOA
    D. A
    E. CNAME

8. *Stub zones are specifically a means of doing what?*
    A. defining a parent zone
    B. creating a domain name
    C. delegating a zone to another server
    D. identifying a slave server to the master
    E. dumping the DNS cache

9. *Which of these is the correct RR format?*
    A. `[name] [ttl] [class] record-type record-data`
    B. `[ttl] [class] [name] record-data record-type`
    C. `[name] [class] [ttl] record-type record-data`
    D. `[ttl] [name] [class] record-type record-data`
    E. `[name] record-data record-type [class] [ttl]`

10. *Which of the following commands dumps the DNS server cache?*
    A. `# pkill -HUP named`
    B. `# pkill -TERM named`
    C. `# pkill -INT named`
    D. `# pkill -KILL named`
    E. `# pkill -USR1 named`

FREE RESPONSE

1. *If a DNS slave server fails to synchronize with the DNS master, what is the most likely reason?*

2. *How does a DNS server prevent other DNS servers from caching RR data that we supply to them?*

REFERENCES

Albitz, Paul and Cricket Liu. *DNS and BIND.* Sebastopol, CA: O'Reilly & Associates, Inc., 1992-2000. ISBN 0-596-00158-4.

12

The Network Time Protocol (NTP)

EXAM OBJECTIVES

12.1 Solaris 8 NTP Features and Terminology

12.2 Solaris 8 NTP Configuration Files

12.3 Configuring a Solaris 8 NTP Client and Server

After completing this chapter, you will be able to meet the following Network Administration Exam objectives:

- Describe NTP features and terminology.
- Identify NTP configuration files.
- State the purpose of NTP files.
- Describe how to configure NTP.

To help you meet these objectives, this chapter covers the following topics:

- terminology related to the Network Time Protocol (universal time coordination, reference clocks, stratum time servers, and so on)
- the importance of NTP to encryption, logging, and network management software
- the NTP configuration files /etc/inet/ntp.conf, /var/ntp/ntp.drift, /etc/init.d/xntpd, and /var/adm/messages
- configuring NTP clients and servers, synchronizing clients, and using the NTP commands **ntpq** and **ntptrace**

121   Solaris 8 NTP Features and Terminology

In this section we introduce the terminology used to describe the features of the Network Time Protocol (NTP) as it is implemented on Solaris 8. We start with a brief explanation of universal time coordination (UTC), which is the internationally accepted time standard used by NTP and is based on an atomic clock.

NTP Basic Terminology

The Network Time Protocol bundled with Solaris 8 is used to synchronize the time of one Solaris client or server to that of another server or reference time source, such as a satellite receiver or radio. Accuracy is provided to within 1 ms on LANs and up to a few tenths of 1 ms on WANs relative to Universal Time Coordination (UTC) via a global positioning service (GPS) receiver. Typical NTP configurations use multiple redundant servers and several network paths in order to achieve great accuracy, availability, and reliability. NTP then is basically a distributed, network-based, clock (time) synchronization protocol.

Before entering into a full discussion of NTP, we need to familiarize ourselves with certain essential terms pertaining to this protocol. These terms include:

- *Universal Time Coordination (UTC)*—Was adopted as the official time for the world on January 1, 1972. The International Bureau of Weights and Measures plays the role of official timekeeper of world atomic time. This composite timescale is calculated using 230 atomic clocks in 65 worldwide laboratories.
- *Reference clock*—A clock that provides current time by accurately following a time standard such as UTC and acting in turn as a reference clock for other systems. Stratum-1 servers are examples of systems that act as reference clocks.
- *Strata*—Stratum time servers are organized into a hierarchy of levels, also known as strata. A stratum-1 server (the most accurate clock available) is more accurate than a stratum-2 server, which in turn is more accurate than a stratum-3 server, and so on.
- *Stratum-1 server*—A highly available, highly accurate NTP server that has its own reference clock. The stratum-2 sever is

used to synchronize the stratum-3 server, and so on. The organizations that manage the stratum servers recommend that the public use the stratum-2 to stratum-5 servers rather than the stratum-1 server, which would become overloaded from heavy public use.

- *Resolution*—The smallest increment in time that a clock offers. For example, a standard wristwatch usually has a resolution of one second, but some stopwatches have a resolution of one tenth of a second.
- *Jitter*—The difference of the differences encountered when measuring time repeatedly. It follows that the most accurate of servers (the reference clock) has the smallest amount of jitter.
- *Accuracy*—How closely a clock follows an official time reference such as UTC. Naturally, reference clocks keep greater accuracy than other clocks.
- *Wander*—All clocks suffer from frequency variations. These variations are called *wander*. Again, the most accurate reference clocks are subject to very little wander.
- *Drift file*—This file, typically the /var/ntp/ntp.drift file, contains the frequency offset of the local system's clock oscillator. The drift file causes a system's clock to be more accurate.
- *Local clock*—The clock of the Solaris 8 host. When located on a client, this local clock is kept in sync with a local Solaris 8 NTP server. When located on an NTP server, the local clock is kept in sync with a reference source, such as a stratum-2 or stratum-3 server.

A Brief Description of Solaris 8 NTP

The Solaris 8 operating system is shipped with a bundled version of NTP, which is a protocol for synchronizing a set of clocks between distributed clients and servers that communicate across networks. The UDP transport protocol provides NTP with a suitable connectionless service and avoids the overhead of the TCP protocol. UDP is well-suited to the NTP protocol, which tends to generate small packets frequently, as do most applications that use UDP.

The NTP service is implemented through the Solaris 8 **xntpd** daemon that sets and maintains a UNIX system time-of-day in agreement with Internet standard time servers. The Solaris 8 **xntpd** daemon and time-keeping service is a complete implementation of Network Time

Protocol version 3, as defined by RFC 1305. The daemon also retains compatibility with version 1 and 2 servers as defined by the earlier RFCs 1059 and 1119.

The principle upon which NTP operates is essentially that a less-disciplined clock may synchronize with a system that has a far more precise reference clock. In this context, *synchronizing* refers to the process whereby a system with a less accurate clock has its time corrected and updated by a reference clock that keeps the most accurate time available.

NTP servers typically use a multicast address to learn about and disseminate server information about the current time. NTP clients may use a broadcast, multicast, or unicast address to acquire the time from the local time server.

It should be understood that although it is important for most computers to keep accurate time, certain types of software applications malfunction completely if a system's time drifts by too much. For example, the following types of software require that the systems they run on maintain highly accurate time:

- *System auditing, accounting, and logging tools*—These types of applications use time stamps, logging the precise times when specific events occur. For example, systems that deploy Solaris 8 features such as auditing, where transactions are precisely recorded in a transaction log, need to ensure that the timestamp is accurate.

- *Encryption key technology*—Encryption algorithms can break completely if the time difference between communicating systems is too great. For example, time stamps are sometimes included in packets sent between systems (as with NIS+, for example), in which cases agreement about the current time is very important.

- *Network management*—When systems are managed using network management tools and protocols such as Sun's Solstice Enterprise manager (see Chapter 10), which uses the SNMP protocol, agreement on the current time between the components of the managed networks (clients, servers, switches, routers) is critical in terms of responding to current events correctly.

On Solaris 8, we set up one or more hosts as NTP servers, which synchronize their local clock with an external reference clock such as a stratum-2 or stratum-3 server. These local NTP servers are then used by local NTP clients, which acquire the correct time from them. In this sense, NTP is hierarchical. Let's go on to examine how this hierarchy works and how to configure the NTP servers and clients.

EXAM NOTES

KEY LEARNING POINTS

- NTP is a distributed, network-based clock (time) synchronization protocol.
- NTP uses universal time coordination (UTC), which is based on atomic measurements.
- UTC is time zone independent and global.
- A stratum-1 server has the most accurate time possible and is referred to as a reference clock.
- NTP uses UDP at the transport layer for speed and low overhead.
- Some software applications are more dependent on time accuracy than others; encryption, logging, and network management software are examples of such application types.

122 Solaris 8 NTP Configuration Files

This section briefly lists the Solaris 8 NTP configuration files and describes their purpose, but we avoid showing their content until the next section describing configuration steps. Although NTP is a standard protocol supported by many UNIX vendors, the actual filenames used by different UNIX vendors tend to vary.

The Primary NTP Configuration Files

Let us examine the three most important NTP configuration files: /etc/inet/ntp.conf, /var/ntp/ntp.drift, and /etc/init.d/xntpd. We also examine the log file that the NTP daemons write to, called /var/adm/messages.

/etc/inet/ntp.conf

This file is the main configuration file and identifies the system as either an NTP client or an NTP server. The files differ in terms of both complexity and content depending on the identity of the system on which NTP is installed. The server configuration file is more complex than the client file, which typically contains just a few lines and enables the client to reach an NTP server.

The /etc/inet/ntp.conf file is a copy of either the Solaris 8 NTP template file called /etc/inet/ntp.client (used on client systems) or /etc/inet/ntp.server (used on NTP servers). If we are setting up an NTP client, we copy the /etc/inet/ntp.client template file, naming the copy /etc/inet/ntp.conf, and modify it as necessary to suit the environment. When setting up an NTP server, we copy the /etc/inet/ntp.server template file, naming the copy /etc/inet/ntp.conf, and modify it to suit the environment.

Both NTP client and server read their configuration information from this file, as shall be seen in section 12.3.

/var/ntp/ntp.drift

The drift file allows Solaris to store the frequency error it has calculated for the system's clock, which then enables Solaris to adjust the system's clock at bootup if necessary. In essence, this file enables the host system to calculate how much its clock has drifted from the correct time and adjust accordingly. NTP creates this file automatically.

/etc/init.d/xntpd

This file is the script that starts the NTP daemon in client or server mode, depending on the content of the file /etc/inet/ntp.conf. If the file /etc/inet/ntp.conf exists, the shell script /etc/init.d/xntpd (which is linked to /etc/rc2.d/S74xntpd) starts the **xntpd** daemon with either client or server options.

/var/adm/messages

This is a standard log file to which the NTP daemon writes. It provides useful debugging information and enables NTP tracking and monitoring. We may configure NTP to write to a separate log file, although this is usually not necessary.

Verifying That Solaris 8 NTP Packages Are Installed

On Solaris 8, NTP is supplied in two Sun packages. We may verify that the packages are installed (which does not imply that NTP is configured) by searching for them with the Solaris **pkginfo** command. Rather than list the hundreds of packages that are typically installed, we run the **pkginfo** command but pipe (|) the output to the **grep** command, asking it to show only lines with the string ntp in them. We issue the command

```
# pkginfo | grep ntp
```

and here is the output from the command, which shows that two packages (SUNWntpr and SUNWntpu) are installed:

```
system       SUNWntpr      NTP, (Root)
system       SUNWntpu      NTP, (Usr)
```

EXAM NOTES

KEY LEARNING POINTS

- NTP's main configuration file on both client and server is /etc/inet/ntp.conf.
- The /var/ntp/ntp.drift file records server clock drift.
- The Solaris shell script **/etc/init.d/xntpd** starts the NTP daemon, **xntpd**.
- The NTP protocol is bundled in the Solaris 8 packages SUNWntpr and SUNWntpu.

---

123 Configuring a Solaris 8 NTP Client and Server

To demonstrate how to configure NTP clients and servers under Solaris 8, we develop an example scenario in this section. We configure the host voyager to be a Solaris NTP server, and to ensure that NTP server voyager (with address 194.168.85.51) has accurate time, we synchronize it with an external stratum-2 server, ntp2c.mcc.ac.uk. Next, we configure an NTP client (apollo, with address 194.168.85.75) and intentionally set its clock to be five minutes slow. Having set the clock to be slow, we observe the client communicating with its NTP server and, on learning the correct time, adjusting or synchronizing its clock to it. The two systems, apollo and voyager, are on the same network (refer back to Figure 6–6 in Chapter 6).

First, we must configure the local NTP server voyager, which is where we begin.

Configuring a Solaris 8 NTP Server

In this section, we set up a Solaris 8 host (voyager) to be an NTP server for our network, but we keep it in sync with an external reference (stratum) server. We could choose to set up voyager to use one of the following time sources:

- *its own local clock*—said to be *undisciplined* because it is not a stratum server and does not use any external reference server. With this configuration, the NTP daemon running on voyager will use the local time as stored on voyager, which is derived from voyager itself and is therefore hardly guaranteed to be very accurate.
- *a stratum server*—configuring voyager to send continual UDP packets to an external reference server (ntp2c.mcc.ac.uk) so that it can continuously check that its own local time has not drifted. If it has drifted, the server is configured to adjust its time until it is correct.

We choose to keep voyager in sync with a stratum server, because voyager will then maintain as accurate a time as is possible for a Solaris host.

Creating the NTP Server Main Configuration File

Our first step is to create the NTP main configuration file, /etc/inet/ntp.conf. Sun facilitates this process by providing an NTP server template file called /etc/inet/ntp.server. The template file contains most of the standard lines needed by the NTP configuration file.

Change directory to the standard Solaris 8 /etc/inet directory. Next, copy the file /etc/inet/ntp.server and rename the copy as /etc/inet/ntp.conf. Here are the two commands to execute these steps:

```
# cd /etc/inet
# cp ntp.server ntp.conf
```

Configuring the NTP Server

Next, we configure the new /etc/inet/ntp.conf file for our local NTP server, voyager. We may configure our NTP server according to one of the following methods:

- *Method 1*—Configure the NTP server to use its own internal clock.
- *Method 2*—Configure the NTP server to synchronize with an external reference clock (stratum-1 server). This is the preferred method.

METHOD 1: CONFIGURING VOYAGER TO USE ITS OWN LOCAL INTERNAL CLOCK

We start by editing the file /etc/inet/ntp.conf using a Solaris editor, such as **vi**. Locate the line that begins `server 127.127.Xtype.0` and modify it as follows. Change

```
#server 127.127.XType.0 prefer
```

to

```
server 127.127.1.0 prefer
fudge 127.127.1.0 stratum 12
driftfile /var/ntp/ntp.drift
```

The drift file is described above. The `fudge` line allows us to indicate to clients that this local server is a low-ranking stratum-12 NTP server. The reserved address `127.127` is used only by the NTP protocol, as dictated by the Internet Assigned Number Authority (IANA). See http://www.iana.org.

The third octet (`xtype`) is now 1 in our example, as we wish to use the "local," undisciplined clock. The following code fragment shows the `xtype` values. You can find this table in the Solaris 8 ntp.server template file. Observe that type 1 is the `Undisciplined Local Clock` or `LCL` type. Here is the table of clock devices as shown in the Solaris NTP server template file /etc/inet/ntp.server:

```
# This is the external clock device.  The following devices are
# recognized by xntpd 3-5.93e:
#
# XType Device      RefID  Description
# -----------------------------------------------------------------
#  1    local       LCL    Undisciplined Local Clock
#  2    trak        GPS    TRAK 8820 GPS Receiver
#  3    pst         WWV    PSTI/Traconex WWV/WWVH Receiver
#  4    wwvb        WWVB   Spectracom WWVB Receiver
#  5    true        TRUE   TrueTime GPS/GOES Receivers
#  6    irig        IRIG   IRIG Audio Decoder
#  7    chu         CHU    Scratchbuilt CHU Receiver
#  8    parse       ----   Generic Reference Clock Driver
#  9    mx4200      GPS    Magnavox MX4200 GPS Receiver
# 10    as2201      GPS    Austron 2201A GPS Receiver
# 11    arbiter     GPS    Arbiter 1088A/B GPS Receiver
# 12    tpro        IRIG   KSI/Odetics TPRO/S IRIG Interface
# 13    leitch      ATOM   Leitch CSD 5300 Master Clock
# 15    *           *      TrueTime GPS/TM-TMD Receiver
```

# 17	datum	DATM	Datum Precision Time System
# 18	acts	ACTS	NIST Automated Computer Time Service
# 19	heath	WWV	Heath WWV/WWVH Receiver
# 20	nmea	GPS	Generic NMEA GPS Receiver
# 22	atom	PPS	PPS Clock Discipline
# 23	ptb	TPTB	PTB Automated Computer Time Service
# 24	usno	USNO	USNO Modem Time Service
# 25	*	*	TrueTime generic receivers
# 26	hpgps	GPS	Hewlett Packard 58503A GPS Receiver
# 27	arc	MSFa	Arcron MSF Receiver

Our system is now ready to use its own internal clock as the time reference for NTP. We have now changed the only lines we need to in order to use voyager's local, internal clock. Next, we examine how to synchronize voyager's clock with an external time server, which is preferred because the external stratum server keeps highly accurate time.

METHOD 2: CONFIGURING VOYAGER TO USE A REFERENCE CLOCK (STRATUM-2 SERVER)

Although synchronizing a server with a reference clock generates additional network traffic, it is the preferred method because it allows the server to keep perfect time. You may find a list of stratum-1, stratum-2, and stratum-3 reference servers at the official (IANA-recommended) Web address maintained by David L. Mills, who maintains the NTP RFCs and is considered an expert in this field. Here are the URLs that list the stratum servers:

```
http://www.eecis.udel.edu/~mills/ntp/clock1.htm
http://www.eecis.udel.edu/~mills/ntp/clock2.htm
http://www.eecis.udel.edu/~mills/ntp/clock3.htm
```

Notice that the filenames referenced at the end of each URL are

- clock1.htm, which lists the stratum-1 servers
- clock2.htm, which lists the stratum-2 servers
- clock3.htm, which lists the stratum-3 servers

Having looked at the Web address

```
http://www.eecis.udel.edu/~mills/ntp/clock2.htm
```

choose an NTP server that has *open access*, which means that you are permitted to use it and that is within your geographical service area. We choose server ntp2c.mcc.ac.uk. Its Web page entry says:

```
UK ntp2c.mcc.ac.uk (130.88.200.6)
Location: University of Manchester, Manchester, England
Synchronization: NTP secondary (S2), PC/FreeBSD
Service Area: UK
Access Policy: Open Access
Contact(s): timelords@mcc.ac.uk
Note: Please use DNS for address, subject to change
```

Proceed as following to configure /etc/inet/ntp.conf to use your chosen NTP server. We have chosen ntp2c.mcc.ac.uk, which is a DNS CNAME alias (see Chapter 11) for utserv.mcc.ac.uk, the reference server's real name. We have now added the following lines to our ntp.conf file on voyager:

```
server ntp2c.mcc.ac.uk
server 127.127.1.0
fudge 127.127.1.0 stratum 12
driftfile /var/ntp/ntp.drift
```

Server ntp2c.mcc.ac.uk is the preferred server because it is an external stratum server. The other server we reference (127.127.1.0) is our local undisciplined clock and therefore our second-choice server. Server 127.127.1.0 will be used only if ntp2c.mcc.ac.uk is unavailable, because ntp2c.mcc.ac.uk has a higher-level stratum number than 127.127.1.0.

Our NTP server is now ready to reference and synchronize its clock with an external reference server called ntp2c.mcc.ac.uk. We may enter either the IP address or the DNS name in the ntp.conf file. The DNS name is recommended (so we must acquire the IP address though DNS), just in case the IP address changes without warning.

STARTING THE NTP SERVER PROCESS (XNTPD)

We are now ready to start the **xntpd** daemon by running the **xntpd** shell script. Enter the following command:

```
# /etc/init.d/xntpd start
```

To verify that the NTP daemon (**xntpd**) is actually running, we use the **ps** command with the **ef** option. The **ef** option tells **ps** to list all running system processes. We also use our trusty **grep** command to display only the lines of interest. We enter the command:

```
# ps -ef | grep xntpd
```

and here is the output, showing that the daemon is running as /usr/lib/inet/xntpd:

```
root 21872 1  1 15:13:18 ? 2:14 /usr/lib/inet/xntpd
```

If the server is not running (in which case **ps** will not display any output lines), check the syntax of your previously configured /etc/inet/ntp.conf file and the /var/adm/messages file for error messages. We check this log file because the NTP daemon (**xntpd**) will report any errors on startup to the /var/adm/messages file.

We have been successful, and the log file entry shows the following lines, which have been added by the **xntpd** daemon:

```
Apr 25 15:13:16 voyager ntpdate [21868]: [ID 558275
daemon.notice] adjust time server 130.88.200.6 offset
0.000500 sec
Apr 25 15:13:18 voyager xntpd [21872]: [ID 702911
daemon.notice] xntpd 3-5.93e Mon Sep 20 15:47:11 PDT 1999
```

The foregoing log file snippet shows that the NTP server has started and consulted 130.88.200.6, and that voyager's clock was offset by 0.000500 of a second.

Before we examine the log entries further, we configure NTP client apollo. Once both NTP client and server are configured, we set apollo's clock back by five minutes and observe the log file entries.

We may use the **ntpq** command to show us the time reference that our local timehost (voyager) is now configured to use:

```
# ntpq -n
remote          refid       st t when poll reach delay offset disp
==================================================================
127.127.1.0   127.127.1.0 12 1 23   64   377   0.00  0.000   10.01
*130.88.200.6 129.132.2.21 2 u 50   64   377   16.24 19.101  10.01
```

As you can see from the asterisk character (*), we are indeed using time server **130.88.200.6,** whose name is ntp2c.mcc.ac.uk. Observe that 127.127.1.0 (local clock) is defined as a stratum-12 server and that **130.88.200.6** is a stratum-2 server—see the st column of the **ntpq** command, which indicates the stratum level.

Configuring a Solaris 8 NTP Client

We now configure apollo as an NTP client and set its clock five minutes slow so that we can observe it synchronizing with local NTP server voyager.

Configuring the Client's ntp.conf File

Change directory to the /etc/inet directory, and copy /etc/inet/ntp.client to /etc/inet/ntp.conf on NTP client apollo:

```
# cd /etc/inet
# cp ntp.client ntp.conf
```

The default Solaris 8 client template file contains only one line, which we show using the **cat** command:

```
# cat ntp.conf
multicastclient 224.0.1.1
```

The only line of significance is the one that indicates which multicast address the ntp client should listen on, namely, 224.0.1.1, which is officially set aside by IANA for the NTP client.

Note

This multicast address is not the same one that is used by the routing daemon in.rdisc (Chapter 6, Table 6.4), although it may easily be mistaken for it. The in.rdisc routing daemon uses addresses 224.0.0.1 and 224.0.0.1. The NTP protocol, on the other hand, uses IANA-assigned (and therefore official) NTP multicast address 224.0.1.1.

If you wish, you may change the multicast address to the broadcast address of the client's network, because in this case both the NTP server (voyager) and the NTP client (apollo) are on the same logical network (194.168.85.0) and may therefore communicate using a shared broadcast address. The broadcast address for both hosts is 194.168.85.255, and the client NTP file (ntp.conf) would be changed as follows:

```
# cat ntp.conf

broadcastclient      194.168.85.255
driftfile            /var/ntp/ntp.drift
```

In addition, you may choose to specify the NTP server by name (voyager) or by a suitable host name alias, such as timehost. If you choose to use an alias, remember to define it in /etc/inet/hosts. Here is a line from the client /etc/inet/hosts showing `timehost` as an alias for voyager. Alias names simply appear in the client's hosts file on the same line as the primary name (voyager), making them aliases for voyager:

```
# cat /etc/inet/hosts | grep voyager
194.168.85.51    voyager timehost
```

The /etc/inet/ntp.conf file is as follows:

```
# cat ntp.conf

server              timehost
driftfile           /var/ntp/ntp.drift
```

We are now ready to start the **xntpd** daemon on the client.

Running the xntpd Daemon

Start the NTP client on apollo by running the shell script called /etc/inetd/xntpd:

```
# /etc/init.d/xntpd start
```

This runs a command called **ntpdate** on the client, which immediately attempts to learn the time from the NTP server and adjust the client's time accordingly.

Note   The ntpdate command runs immediately on the client to quickly set the correct time on the NTP client apollo. It should be understood that if we used xntpd immediately, the rules of the protocol require that the client time be seen to be wrong several times before the client adjusts it. Immediately running ntpdate is therefore much faster and appropriate to use for the initial synchronization of NTP client and server. Solaris also has a simple rdate command, which may be used to synchronize one host's time to that of another.

Once the timeserver has been contacted, **ntpdate** terminates and **xntpd** continues to run to maintain the time and keep it in sync with the NTP server voyager.

Client Synchronization and the Log File Entries

One way to learn how synchronization is monitored in actual practice is to set a client's clock to an incorrect time deliberately and then observe the log entries that occur. In our example, we set the time of apollo back by five minutes. First we use the Solaris **uname –n** command to check the identity of the current host and then run the **date** command to check the current time. We start from the NTP server voyager:

```
# uname -n
voyager
# date
Thu Apr 26 17:03:15 BST 2001
```

As you can see, voyager's time is 17:03:15.

Our task is now to set apollo's time five minutes behind voyager. We now access apollo. First, we check the current host's name:

```
# uname -n
apollo
```

We are indeed on apollo.

Next, check the current time by running the **date** command:

```
# date
Thu Apr 26 17:03:29 BST 2001
```

As you can see, the time is currently in sync with voyager. We need to set it back by five minutes using the **date** command:

```
# date 0426165801
Thu Apr 26 16:58:00 BST 2001
```

Client apollo's clock is now five minutes behind that of voyager.

Apollo is an NTP client that learns its time from voyager, the local NTP server. We previously observed the log entry that was created when voyager synchronized with the external reference, stratum-2 server ntp2c.mcc.ac.uk. Now, let's take a look at the log entries revealing the interaction between the NTP client and server. You can use the Solaris 8 **snoop** analyzer to see real-time network interaction between NTP client and server, but the log file entries are succinct and show the result we wish to observe. Following are the significant lines from apollo's log file, /var/adm/messages.

```
Apr 26 16:58:05 apollo ntpdate[10406]: [ID 774510
daemon.notice] step time server 194.168.85.51 offset
338.539012 sec
```

The log snippet shows NTP client apollo adjusting its time by 338.539012 seconds, which represents the five minutes by which we set its clock back.

Back on client apollo, the time is now the same as the time on local NTP server voyager and hence accurate according to external stratum server 130.88.200.6. In this indirect way, clients learn (through a go-between NTP server) the time according to a stratum server.

In addition to analyzing the logs, we may run commands to investigate the sources of time and the current state of time servers. We look next at two such commands.

Some Useful NTP Commands: ntpq and ntptrace

Solaris provides us with some useful commands to investigate which time server we are using and the path back to the original source of time. The **ntpq** command queries NTP servers—which implement the recommended NTP mode 6 control message format—about their current state. The **ntpq** command also can request changes in that state. We use it here on the client apollo, which reveals that apollo's remote time server is 194.168.85.51 (voyager) and that its time reference (refid) is 130.88.200.6:

```
# ntpq -pn
remote        refid        st t when poll reach delay offset disp
==============================================================
194.168.85.51 130.88.200.6 4 u 43 64 17 0.52 -14.863 1879.46
```

From the client or server, you also may trace back to the source of the reference time using the Solaris 8 **ntptrace** command:

```
# ntptrace

localhost: stratum 4, offset 0.000015, synch distance 0.05818
voyager: stratum 3, offset -0.000071, synch distance 0.04784
utserv.mcc.ac.uk: stratum 2, offset 0.008028, synch distance 0.02132
ntp1.ja.net: stratum 1, offset 0.012621, synch distance 0.00085, refid
'GPS'
```

What we see here is that the local host (apollo) acquires its time from voyager, which in turn acquired it from utserv.mcc.ac.uk, which in turn acquired it from ntp1.ja.net. Each server in the trace-back to the stratum-1 server reveals its stratum.

You can see the Solaris manual pages for the exact meaning of the other (less important) fields by entering the following Solaris 8 command:

```
# man ntptrace
```

This concludes our examination of Solaris 8 NTP and NTP clients and servers.

EXAM NOTES

KEY LEARNING POINTS

- NTP clients use either a predefined multicast address or the NTP host's local broadcast address, which is determined by the network it is on.
- Multicast address 224.0.1.1 is reserved by IANA for use by the NTP protocol and NTP clients and servers
- The /etc/inet/xntpd script, when run on NTP clients, first executes the **ntpdate** command to perform the initial synchronization.
- NTP clients and servers log to the /var/adm/messages file on Solaris.

SUMMARY

The purpose of NTP is to ensure that our computer systems maintain time as accurately as possible, primarily by synchronizing with other systems that keep more accurate time. Stratum servers act as reference servers, with stratum-1 servers being the most accurate, stratum-2 the next most accurate, and so on. This hierarchy provides a means by which to spread the load across multiple servers.

We saw the NTP files used to configure NTP on Solaris 8 and examined the purpose of each file. We observed that NTP clients and servers use broadcast, multicast, and unicast addressing.

Finally, we reviewed the steps that should be performed in order to set up a Solaris 8 NTP client and server and to run the essential NTP daemons, primarily **xntpd** and **ntpdate.** We also examined the commands, **ntpq** and **ntptrace.**

TEST YOURSELF

MULTIPLE CHOICE

1. *What does UTC stand for in the context of the NTP protocol?*
    A. Universal Time Consortium
    B. United Time Coordinated
    C. Universal Time Conducted
    D. Universal Time Composition
    E. Universal Time Coordinated

2. *What does the word "jitter" mean?*
    A. The difference of the differences encountered when repeatedly measuring time
    B. The drift time (in milliseconds) experienced by NTP servers
    C. The smallest increment in time that a clock offers
    D. The precise frequency fluctuation of an NTP server's clock
    E. The difference between an NTP client's clock and a server's clock at the precise moment of the NTP client starting up **xntpd** for the very first time

3. *What is the name of the NTP client template file supplied with Solaris 8?*
    A. /etc/init.d/xntpd
    B. /etc/inet/ntp.conf
    C. /etc/inet/ntp.client
    D. /etc/inet/ntp.server
    E. /etc/inet/clientd.ntp

4. *What file acts as the main configuration file on Solaris 8 NTP clients and servers?*
    A. /etc/inet/ntp.conf
    B. /etc/inet/ntpconf
    C. /etc/inet/xntpd.conf
    D. /etc/inet/server.conf
    E. /etc/inet/client.ntp.conf

5. *What daemon implements NTP on Solaris 8 servers?*
    A. **xntpd**
    B. **ntpdate**
    C. ntpd

D. **rdaemon**

E. **timed**

6. *What multicast address, officially allocated to NTP by IANA, is used by NTP?*

    A. 224.0.1.0

    B. 224.0.1.1

    C. 224.0.0.1

    D. 224.0.0.2

    E. 127.1.0.1

7. *Which special IP address is used by an NTP server that uses its own local undisciplined clock rather than an external stratum reference server?*

    A. 127.1.0.1

    B. 127.0.0.1

    C. 127.0.1.1

    D. 127.127.1.0

    E. 127.127.0.0

8. *By default, to what log file do NTP servers and clients write log messages?*

    A. /var/log/syslog

    B. /var/ntp/ntp.drift

    C. /var/adm/messages.ntp

    D. /var/adm/messages

    E. /var/tmp/messages

9. *What daemon is first run by the /etc/init.d/xntpd shell script on Solaris 8 NTP clients when the NTP client runs for the first time?*

    A. **xntpd**

    B. **ntpdate**

    C. **ntpd**

    D. **rdaemon**

    E. **timed**

10. *Which NTP file indicates to the system how far its clock has drifted and contains the frequency offset of the local system's clock oscillator?*

    A. /var/log/syslog

    B. /var/ntp/ntp.drift

    C. /var/adm/messages.ntp

D. /var/adm/messages

E. /var/tmp/messages

FREE RESPONSE

1. *Describe briefly the official international standard for time known as UTC.*

2. *What is the purpose of NTP as a network protocol, and why is NTP important to Solaris?*

REFERENCE

Mills, David L. *RFC 1305, Network Time Protocol (Version 3) Specification, Implementation.* March 1992. (Format: TXT = 307085, PDF = 442493 bytes) (Obsoletes RFC 0958, RFC 1059, RFC 1119) (Status: DRAFT STANDARD)

13

The New Internet Protocol: IPv6

EXAM OBJECTIVES

13.1 IPv6, the New Internet Protocol

13.2 The IPv6 Datagram Header

13.3 The IPv6 Address Format

13.4 The Three Types of IPv6 Addresses

13.5 Configuring an IPv6 Network Interface

After completing this chapter, you will be able to meet the following Network Administration Exam objectives:

- Describe IPv6, its importance, and its potential benefits.
- Configure an IPv6 network interface.

To help you meet these objectives, this chapter covers the following topics:

- the reasons why IPv6 came into being as a new Internet protocol
- the fields of the IPv6 datagram header
- notation conventions of the IPv6 address format and their importance
- unicast, multicast, and anycast IPv6 address formats and reserved IPv6 addresses
- steps involved in configuring an IPv6 network interface

13.1   IPv6, the New Internet Protocol

In the early days of the Internet, a 32-bit address space seemed vast—a huge resource that could never be depleted and would last for centuries. But let us remember that in 1912, an "unsinkable" ship sank all the way to the floor of the Atlantic ocean, demonstrating once again that an ostensibly perfect design can still have an Achilles heel. Whether that heel is the limited IPv4 address space, unable to scale as the Internet grew far more quickly than could possibly have been predicated back at the dawn of the Internet, or a leviathan iceberg set deep in a freezing, (but very still) black ocean, there is a serious lesson to be learned in this embryonic age of technology.

IPv6 (Next Generation) is the new version of IP, which came about primarily because of the progressive depletion of available IPv4 addresses. The introduction of CIDR in 1993 (see Chapter 5) was the initial response to the exhaustion of IPv4 address space exhaustion, followed by the introduction of the new IP, also commonly referred to as IPv6 or simply Next Generation (IPng).

Interestingly, although most IPv4 addresses are allocated, only a small proportion of the allocated IPv4 addresses are actually in use. This discrepancy reveals a fundamental flaw in the way IPv4 addresses are organized.

For example, how many companies with class A addresses—with a potential of 16 million addresses for systems—actually use all 16 million addresses? Very few, which means that literally millions of IP addresses are wasted because they are unavailable though unused. IPv6 is the solution to this dilemma, as we shall see shortly.

There are many good reasons for deploying IPv6, although the number of companies actually using IPv6 on today's company networks is fewer than had been expected originally. IPv6 was first discussed back in the early 1990s, when it became obvious that IPv4 addresses were becoming in short supply, and only now, 10 years later, is it starting to be used. Solaris 8 was Sun's first-ever version of its OS to offer both IPv4 and IPv6. Our exploration of IPv6 starts with the IPv6 datagram header, which is far simpler than its IPv4 counterpart.

EXAM NOTES

KEY LEARNING POINTS

- The IPv6 protocol (also referred to as IPgn or IP Next Generation) was introduced because of the near exhaustion of the IPv4 32-bit address space and resulting inability to scale with the growth of the Internet.
- IPv6 is also referred to as IPng or IP Next Generation.

13.2   The IPv6 Datagram Header

In Chapter 5, we examined the IPv4 header, which reveals much of the functionality of the IPv4 protocol. Here, we examine the IPv6 header, which is larger but simpler in design and has fewer fields than the IPv4 header. The fields up to, but not including, the source and destination address total 64 bits (8 bytes). The source and destination IPv6 addresses are 128 bits each (16 bytes), with the result that the total size of the IPv6 minimum header is 320 bits (40 bytes)—twice the size of the minimum IPv4 header.

From the standpoint of the Solaris 8 exam, there is no need to memorize the fields of the IPv6 header, but becoming familiar with the header fields is useful because it helps you understand the protocol. Figure 13-1 shows the fields of the header, with each numeral 4 representing 4 bits.

Fields of the IPv6 Header

Let us look briefly at each field that makes up the IPv6 header.

Version

The version field is 4 bits in size. The current version number is 6.

Traffic Class

This field, as yet undefined, consists of all zeroes and is 8 bits in size.

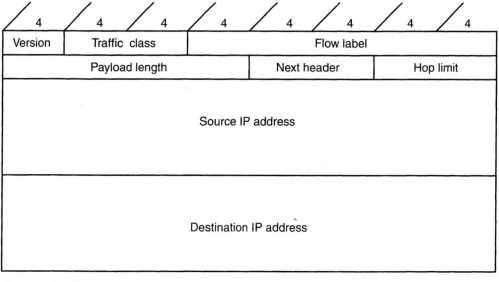

Figure 13–1   *IPv6 header*

Flow Label

Packets traveling from a source to a destination are said to be in the same *flow* and are identified by a label. Systems can be involved in several flows at once. Flows can be identified by routers and given special priority, which is a particularly useful feature for real-time applications. The flow label field is 20 bits in size.

Payload Length

Datagram payload size is measured in bytes, but this does not include the IPv6 header itself. This field is functionally the same as the total length field in the IPv4 header. The IPv6 header, however, is a fixed size, so this field records only the length of the datagram payload (data carried). The field is 16 bits wide.

Next Header

This 8-bit field is similar to the protocol field of the IPv4 header, in that it stores a number that identifies what header-plus-data is encapsulated in the IPv6 datagram. A value of 6, for example, indicates that the next header is TCP and that the IPv6 datagram is carrying a TCP segment. A value of 17 indicates that the next header is UDP and that the IPv6 datagram is carrying a UDP datagram. The next header could also be an *extension header*, which replaces the Options field of the IPv4 header. In summary then, the Next Header field shows that following the IPv6 header there will be either a transport layer header (UDP, TCP), an ICMP header, or one of many extension headers. The IPv6 header, then, might contain several extension headers, each indicating the type of header that follows it. The final extension header in the IPv6 datagram usually indicates what transport protocol the IPv6 datagram has encapsulated.

The current IPv6 specification defines six extension headers, which allow for additional control information relating to the following areas:

- routing
- fragmenting
- encrypted security payload
- authentication
- destination options
- hop-by-hop options

See the References section at the end of the chapter for documents that cover IPv6 in greater detail than we do here.

Hop Limit

This 8-bit field, like the IPv4 TTL (time-to-live) field, contains a number that is decremented by 1 each time the datagram passes through a router. When the value reaches 0, the datagram is discarded.

Source IP Address

The 128-bit source IP address is stored in this field, which represents the IPv6 address of the originator of the IPv6 datagram.

Destination IP Address

The 128-bit destination address is stored in this field. The destination address may be a unicast, multicast, or anycast address.

Comparing the IPv6 and IPv4 Headers

By comparing the structure of the IPv6 and IPv4 headers, we can see what changes have been made. Changes in the headers indicate changes in the IP protocol and so are worth reviewing at closer range. Following is a discussion of the IPv4 header fields that have been omitted from the IPv6 header.

IPv4 Options Field

In the IPv4 header, the Options field enabled a basic IPv4 20-byte header to grow to a maximum size of 60 bytes. The basic IPv6 header size, on the other hand, is fixed at 320 bits (40 bytes), precisely because the Options field has been omitted. The functionality of IPv4 options is retained in IPv6, however, through the use of IPv6 extension headers, which contain optional IPv6 information. (Refer to the "Next Header" section of this chapter for more information about extension headers.)

Checksum Field

The checksum calculation in IPv4 has been dropped as unnecessary overhead in IPv6 because TCP, UDP, ICMP, and other protocols using IPv6 perform their own checksums. So do the networks over which IP is framed, such as Ethernet and ATM.

Router Fragmentation Field

We saw in Chapter 5 that IPv4 routers fragment IPv4 datagrams if that is required by restrictions in the MTU size of network interface layers (Ethernet, for example). The IPv6 behavior, however, is somewhat different. A system sending IPv6 datagrams learns the maximum acceptable datagram size in terms of the devices through which the datagram will pass through on its journey from source to destination. For this reason, all header fields from IPv4 that are related to fragmentation—such as the Don't Fragment, Last Fragment, and Fragment Offset fields—are removed in IPv6.

A system that sends IPv6 datagrams must use a procedure called *path MTU discovery*, which allows a source (sender) to learn the MTU size of all hops along the routing path between itself and the destination. Having learned this maximum MTU size, the sending server will be able to send datagrams that all hops between source and destination can accept without fragmenting.

Finally, it is worth noting that a new *end-to-end fragmentation* is allowed in IPv6 but that it is quite unlike IPv4 fragmentation. Recall from Chapter 5 that IPv4 fragmentation is performed by network routers on the receiving end of datagrams that require fragmenting because their underlying network interface layers and MTU demand it. IPv6 end-to-end fragmentation, on the other hand, is performed by the sending host of the IPv6 datagram because a protocol such as UDP or TCP demands it. If such end-to-end fragmentation occurs, an IPv6 extension header is used to indicate this.

EXAM NOTES

KEY LEARNING POINTS

- The IPv6 header has a fixed length of 320 bits (40 bytes).
- Extension headers allow IPv6 to indicate what is encapsulated in the IPv6 datagram and provide some of the functionality of the IPv4 header Options field.
- The Source IP Address and Destination IP Address fields in the IPv6 header are 128-bit addresses.
- The IPv6 header has no checksum field.
- The IPv6 header contains no fragmentation fields because IPv6 does not fragment its datagram in the way that IPv4 did.

13.3 The IPv6 Address Format

The IPv6 address structure and architecture are described in RFC 2373 and RFC 2460. RFC 2373, titled "IP Version 6 Addressing Architecture," describes IPv6 addresses as 128-bit identifiers. Like an IPv4 address, the IPv6 address is associated with an interface rather than with a host. That is, hosts with several interfaces may have multiple IP addresses or identifiers.

We start by looking at the format of IPv6 addresses. IPv6 addresses are more involved than IPv4 addresses and do not use the notion of classes.

Text Representation of IPv6 Addresses

You might recall from Chapter 5 that IPv4 addresses use a notation referred to as dotted-decimal notation (or *dotted quad notation*). IPv6, however, uses a completely different notation, known as *colon notation*, which uses colons (:) rather than dots (.) as delimiters.

RFC 2373 describes the format as follows: "The preferred form is *x:x:x:x:x:x:x:x*, where the '*x*'s are the hexadecimal value of the eight 16-bit pieces of the address."

Before investigating IPv6 addresses further, recall the IPv4 addresses you are familiar with. Let us abbreviate a familiar IPv4 address using the new and unfamiliar colon notation. This will help you to learn the new colon notation and revisit the process of converting binary to hexadecimal while using a familiar (and much shorter) IPv4 address.

Colon Notation Example Using an IPv4 Address

We will convert IPv4 address 194.168.85.50 to colon hexadecimal notation. This will reinforce your understanding of binary, hex, and decimal and also illustrate the underlying colon notation used by the IPv6 addressing scheme. We will break down IPv4 address 194.168.85.50 into four octets and then demonstrate how to convert the IPv4 address into the split hex notation used by IPv6. Here is 194 in decimal and binary:

Decimal   194

Binary   11000010

We may also show binary 11000010 (decimal 194) in two pairs of four bits, which are usually referred to as *nibbles*. With split binary notation, we split the binary number (11000010 in our example) into two blocks of four bits (1100 0010), but we do not change the binary number. Next, we use column values of 8 4 2 1 for each of the two blocks of four bits to ascertain a decimal number between 0 and 15 for each four-bit block, which we then convert to a hexadecimal value. Such notation makes it easy to then convert the binary number to hexadecimal. Following is binary 11000010 shown in 4-bit split binary notation:

8421   8421

1100   0010

Remember that in hexadecimal, decimal values 10 through 15 are represented as follows:

Hex A = 10 decimal
Hex B = 11 decimal
Hex C = 12 decimal
Hex D = 13 decimal
Hex E = 14 decimal
Hex F = 15 decimal

We may further convert the two nibbles to hexadecimal as follows: The first binary nibble, 1100 (decimal values 8 + 4) is decimal 12 and, therefore, hexadecimal c. Similarly, the nibble 0010 (decimal value 2) is decimal 2 and also hexadecimal 2. So far, then, we may represent 194 as shown in Table 13.1. Make the same calculation for all four octets of 194.168.85.50, and you will obtain the results shown in Table 13.2.

Table 13.1 *Representing 194 in Decimal, Hex, and Binary Notation*

NUMBER BASE	BASE REPRESENTATIONS OF 194
Decimal	194
Binary	11000010
Split binary	1100 0010
Hexadecimal	C2

Table 13.2 *Decimal and Hexadecimal Representations of the Four Octets of an IPv4 Address*

DECIMAL REPRESENTATION	HEXADECIMAL REPRESENTATION
194	C2
168	A8
85	55
50	32

So, finally, we have 194.168.85.50 translating to C2:A8:55:32.

It is important that you understand this basic notation before looking at IPv6, which uses 128 bits rather than 32 bits and uses four hex values to represent each of eight groups of 16 bits.

Colon Notation Example Using IPv6 Addresses

IPv6 addresses are made up of 8 groups of 16 bits, which are represented as eight hex pairs. Whether an address is of type unicast, multicast, or anycast (the three types of IPv6 address), we can represent it in one of the following three possible formats. The format that is applicable will depend on whether it contains one or more groups of zeroes or leading zeroes at the start of any of the 8 (16-bit) address groups, or is an IPv4 address being represented in IPv6 environment by a host that supports IPv6.

There are three different formats in which to represent an IPv6 address. These three formats do not directly correspond to the three main types of IPv6 address referenced previously. Let us explore each format in turn.

LONG-FORMAT IPV6 ADDRESSES

The long format shows the IPv6 address in full. Here is an example IPv6 address:

```
1080:0000:0000:0000:0008:0800:200C:417A
```

Focus on these attributes of the long-format IPv6 address:
- There are 8 groups of 16 bits delimited by colons (:).
- Each group is 16 bits, shown as 4 nibbles (4 bits per nibble), in which each nibble is shown in hexadecimal. For example, 417A represents 16 bits, where the 4, 1, 7, and A are hex values and represent 4 bits each.
- Each IPv6 address is 8 groups of 16 bits. Multiplying 8 by 16, therefore, yields 128 bits, which is the total number of bits in the IPv6 address.
- Many groups consist of zeroes only (0000).

The IPv6 notation allows for zeroes to be compressed. Until IPv6 comes into wider use, there will be many addresses that contain zeroes. For this reason, it is important that we be able to compress groups of zeroes in IPv6 addresses. This brings us to the short format of IPv6 addresses, which is essentially the same as the long format but with zeroes compressed.

SHORT-FORMAT IPV6 ADDRESSES

RFC 2073 uses the term *compress* to describe the act of shortening IPv6 addresses by the compression of zeroes. Using this technique, we will compress the long address we used when we examined format 1. Here is the address again:

```
1080:0000:0000:0000:0008:0800:200C:417A
```

In the short form of an IPv6 address, leading (or trailing) groups of zeroes (`:0000:`) may be removed completely. Our example address now becomes

```
1080::::0008:0800:200C:417A
```

Notice that the three groups of four-zeroes that followed `1080:` have been removed and compressed. A pair of empty colons (`::`) means the same as a value of one or more groups of `:0000:` in IPv6 short-address notation.

In addition to compressing groups of zeroes, we are also allowed to remove leading zeroes in the address, leaving us with just

```
1080::::8:800:200C:417A
```

We may not remove trailing zeroes, however, unless they are a complete group, as in the example `:0000:`. Notice in our short-form example that

- `0008` was truncated to `8`, and
- `0800` was truncated to `800`.

There is one more compression technique we may apply. It is legal to reduce multiple colons to a single colon pair, so the address becomes

```
1080::8:800:200C:417A
```

Notice that

```
::::
```

was compressed to

```
::
```

Recalculating the original address from the truncated form merely involves adding zeroes according to the following rules:

We must retain at lease two colons (::) because the two colons indicate where in the address the compression of groups of zeroes has occurred.

- Add leading zeroes to groups that are not made up of 4 nibbles (16 bytes). For example, `:8:` becomes `:0800:`, and `:800:` becomes `:0800:`.
- Change the lone colon pair (`::`) to as many `:0000:` pairs as is needed to expand the IPv6 address back to 8 groups. For example, `::` becomes `::::` in our example address, and `::::` becomes `:0000:0000:0000:0000:` when the zeroes are reinserted.

We have now examined the long and short (truncated) formats of the IPv6 address. Table 13.3 contains additional examples of conversion between the two formats.

Table 13.3 *More Examples of Legally Abbreviated IPv6 Addresses*

ORIGINAL LONG FORM OF IPV6 ADDRESS	SAME IPV6 ADDRESS IN SHORT (COMPRESSED) FORMAT
FEDC:BA98:0000:0000:0000:0000:7654:3210	FEDC:BA98::7654:3210
FEDC:BA89:7654:3210:0000:0000:0000:0000	FEDC:BA89:7654:3210::
0000:0000:0000:0000:FEDC:BA98:7654:3210	::FEDC:BA98:7654:3210

The double-colon abbreviation technique may be used only once inside an address because if we reduce multiple double colons in more than one place, it would not be clear what the original address had been. To illustrate this, the following IPv6 address has groups of four zeroes at both ends of it (that is, both leading and trailing):

`0000:0000:0000:BA98:7654:0000:0000:0000`

This address may be legally truncated to

`::BA98:7654:0000:0000:0000`

or to

```
0000:0000:0000:BA98:7654::
```

but definitely not to

```
::BA98:7654::
```

This last example would be illegal because we have now applied the compression technique to both ends of the IPv6 address. This is not allowed because it would then be unclear which of the following versions is the correct expanded address:

```
0000:BA98:7654:0000:0000:0000:0000:0000
0000:0000:BA98:7654:0000:0000:0000:0000
0000:0000:0000:BA98:7654:0000:0000:0000
0000:0000:0000:0000:BA98:7654:0000:0000
0000:0000:0000:0000:0000:BA98:7654:0000
```

Be very careful, then, to use the colon abbreviation technique only once within a given IPv6 address.

We can represent IPv4 addresses in the IPv6 address space as well, which gives us a third address format.

IPV4 ADDRESS REPRESENTATION IN AN IPV6 ENVIRONMENT

For the representation of IPv4 addresses within an IPv6 environment, there is a special compression technique. Essentially, it leaves the four bytes of the IPv4 address in dotted-decimal notation, prefixing a double colon pair (::) to indicate that we are using IPv6 to represent an IPv4 address. Using this format, we transform

```
194.168.85.50
```

into

```
0:0:0:0:0:0:194.168.85.50
```

or, in short format,

```
::194.168.85.50
```

IPv6 Subnet Prefixes

We may select a leading part or portion of an IPv6 address through the use of a prefix. Prefixes are similar to (and used instead of) the netmasks used in IPv4. The notation form looks like this:

```
ipv6-address/subnet-prefix-length
```

In this format,

- `ipv6-address` is any of the three formats mentioned in the previous sections (long format, short format, or IPv4 address representation).
- `prefix-length` is a decimal value specifying how many of the leftmost contiguous bits of the address comprise the prefix. The prefix picks out the subnet (as did the netmask of IPv4 as seen in Chapter 5).

For example, here is an example of a long-format IPv6 address (128 bits):

```
12AB:0000:0000:CD30:1234:4567:98AB:CDEF
```

We may mask (select) any number of bits. Starting at the high-order end, here we select the first 60 bits, which identify the node's network or subnet. The first 60 bits are:

```
12AB:0000:0000:CD3
```

which we may show as

```
12AB:0000:0000:CD30::/60
```

It follows, then, that when writing a node address and a prefix of that node address (the nod's subnet prefix), the two can be combined as shown here—the node address as

```
12AAB:0000:0000:CD30::1234:4567:98AB:CDEF
```

and its network number as

```
12AB:0000:0000:CD30::/60
```

This notation is similar to that of the CIDR notation used with IPv4, as we discussed in Chapter 5.

KEY LEARNING POINTS

- IPv6 addresses are 128 bits in length.
- IPv6 addresses are shown as eight colon-separated groups of 16 bits (2 bytes).
- Each of the 16 bits is shown in hexadecimal notation.
- There are three types of IPv6 addresses: unicast, multicast, and anycast.
- Techniques exist for truncating IPv6 addresses and for representing IPv4 addresses in the IPv6 address space.
- We may identify an IPv6 subnet by using a subnet prefix.

13.4   The Three Types of IPv6 Addresses

In the previous section, we focused on the format of IPv6 addresses and the text representation of 128-bit addresses or identifiers. Now, we look at the types of IPv6 address. Each type has a discrete range in which it may be used (local LAN, local site, globally) and is composed of specific subcomponents. What is common to all three address types, however, is that all are made up of 128 bits.

There are three types of IPv6 addresses:

- unicast (used in both IPv4 and IPv6)
- multicast (used in both IPv4 and IPv6)
- anycast (IPv6 only)

The meaning of unicast is identical in the IPv4 and IPv6 environments and identifies a single interface. There are several types of IPv6 unicast addresses, and they are more complex than IPv4 unicast addresses.

Multicast addresses identify a group of systems; traffic to a multicast address will be delivered to a group of interfaces (and, therefore, to a group of hosts). Once again, the meaning of multicast is identical in both IPv4 and IPv6, although its scope is far greater in the IPv6 arena.

The anycast address type is new to IPv6 and combines features of both unicast and multicast. Like a multicast address, it identifies a group of systems, but IP datagrams addressed to an anycast address are delivered to only one member of the anycast group—the one considered the nearest in the group.

Note

It is worth stressing that broadcast addresses (so familiar in IPv4) are not used in IPv6. Their functionality is superseded by multicast addresses.

The Three Types of IPv6 Unicast Addresses

There are three types of unicast addresses. We start by showing the core unicast address structure, followed by a brief explanation of the various types of IPv6 unicast addresses.

The IPv6 address architecture or space is hierarchical, facilitating effective global, hierarchial routing. IPv4 addresses, as we saw in Chapter 5, used five classes, A through E. IPv6 does not uses classes at all, but rather breaks the 128-bit address space into components.

To make things more complex, the three types of unicast addresses use different internal structures, which determines what kind of usage is viable for them.

- *aggregatable global unicast*—Internet usage as an example
- *site-local unicast*—not allowed out of site by the access router but may be used within a single site
- *link-local unicast*—not allowed through routers at all

We now show the format of each of the three types of unicast addresses. It will be apparent that each of the unicast address types is structured internally because of its intended usage, namely global, site, or local usage. We start with the global unicast, which is intended for Internet consumption.

Aggregatable Global Unicast Addresses

This type of unicast address is for global use beyond a single corporation or enterprise—across the Internet, for example. The term *aggregatable* means that it is designed so that single routing table entries can identify vast numbers of networks (see RFC 2373 for more information about aggregatable routing). Figure 13-2 shows the internal structure of an aggregatable unicast address.

Let us briefly analyze each component of the address structure, starting with the prefix. The most important thing for you to keep in

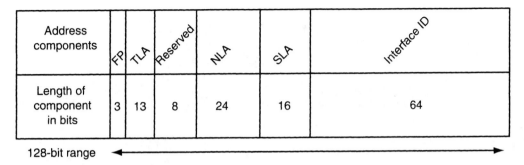

Figure 13–2 *The IPv6 aggregatable unicast address format*

mind while examining these fields (especially the TLA, NLA, and SLA) is that they allow an IPv6 address to be routed and identified globally. These fields are what differentiate aggregatable addresses from site and link-local unicast addresses.

FORMAT PREFIX (FP)

The Format Prefix field for aggregatable unicast addresses is 3 bits in length, and its value is always 001. This first component (3-bits) is combined with the four following components (the TLA, Reserved, NLA, and SLA fields, together comprising 61 bits) to make a 64-bit address. This is then combined with the Interface-ID field to form a unique 128-bit address.

TOP LEVEL AGGREGATOR (TLA)

The second component is the Top Level Aggregator (TLA) field, 13 bits in length. IANA is expected to allocate these ranges to large providers such as ARIN, APNIC, and RIPE (see Chapter 5), who in turn may allocate subranges to country-based organizations like AT&T or MCI (US) and BT (UK). Thirteen bits is currently considered enough for this purpose; if this proves not to be the case, the 8-bit Reserved field can be used.

RESERVED

The third component, 8 bits in length, is reserved as a possible extension for the TLA if needed.

NEXT LEVEL AGGREGATOR (NLA)

The Next Level Aggregator (NLA) field is 24 bits in length and will be used for the next level below the TLA range. The official RFCs avoid the words *subscriber* and *provider*, simply identifying this layer with a long-haul provider (AT&T or MCI, for example), who in turn may identify second tier providers within the 24-bit range.

SITE-LOCAL AGGREGATOR (SLA)

The Site-Local Aggregator (SLA) field, a 16-bit field, will be allocated to a link within a site. If a site changes its provider, the TLA and NLA components of an address will change, but the SLA and the interface ID will remain the same.

INTERFACE-ID

The last field, Interface-ID (64 bits in length) is based on the IEEE EUI-64 format. It will have a unique value based on the interface that connects to the link. We examine the way in which a 48-bit ethernet address makes up the basis of this field in this section.

Next, we look at the two types of local unicast addresses, namely site-local and link-local.

Site-Local Unicast Addresses

Site-Local unicast addresses are intended for use within a site but not over the Internet. Be aware that the uniqueness of site-local addresses is only guaranteed within the site and site-controlled routers, so they should never be allowed onto the Internet. Routers that support the IPv6 protocol and connect a site to the Internet will refuse to forward over the Internet any IPv6 datagrams that are addressed to (or from) a site-local unicast address. Within the site-local scheme, however, the site's internal routers will understand and be able to route IPv6 datagrams to the correct destination.

Site-local addresses always begin with binary 1111111011 or hexadecimal FEC, as shown in Figure 13-3.

We now briefly analyze each component of the address structure, starting with the prefix.

FORMAT PREFIX (FP)

The 10-bit Format Prefix (FP) field is always binary 1111111011 (hex FEC). This field identifies the address as a site-local unicast address, which may be used within a site where an organization has complete control of the subnets it uses for internal routing.

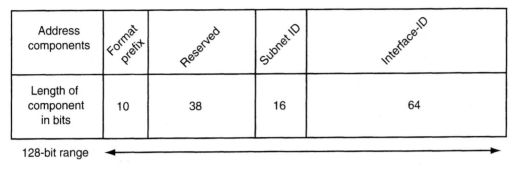

Address components	Format prefix	Reserved	Subnet ID	Interface-ID
Length of component in bits	10	38	16	64

128-bit range

Figure 13–3   *The IPv6 site-local unicast address*

SUBNET ID

This 16-bit field is used by the organization as it chooses—for example, to identify networks within an organization.

INTERFACE-ID

The last field, the 64-bit Interface-ID field, is based on IEEE EUI-64 format and will have a unique value based on the interface that connects to the link. We examine the way a 48-bit ethernet address makes up the basis of this field in this section.

Link-Local Unicast Addresses

This second type of unicast address is limited in range to a single LAN and must never be forwarded through any routers, even within a site. They are intended for use by hosts on the same link. Link-local addresses should always start with binary 1111111010 or hexadecimal FE8. They usually are autoconfigured, which means that the IPv6 link-local address is created without administrator intervention. Figure 13-4 shows the structure of link-local addresses.

We now briefly analyze each of the components of the link-local unicast address structure, starting with the prefix.

FORMAT PREFIX (FP)

The 10-bit Format Prefix (FP) field is always binary 1111111010 (hex FE8). This field identifies the address as a link-local unicast address that may be used only by systems on the same link. They function as if routers did not exist.

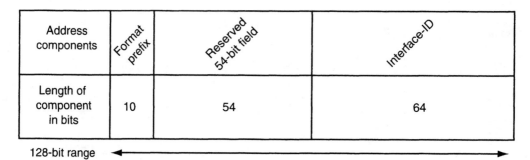

Address components	Format prefix	Reserved 54-bit field	Interface-ID
Length of component in bits	10	54	64

128-bit range

Figure 13–4   *The IPv6 link-local unicast address*

RESERVED 54-BIT FIELD

The second field has no name and is unused at present.

INTERFACE-ID

The last field, the 64-bit Interface-ID field, is based on the IEEE EUI-64 format and will have a unique value based on the interface that connects to the link. We examine the way a 48-bit ethernet address forms the basis of this field in this section.

IPv6 Special Unicast Addresses

We have thus far looked at the three main types of unicast addresses, namely aggregatable global (Internet usable unicast), site-local, and link-local addresses. You should be aware that there are some special IPv6 address types, namely

- unspecified addresses
- loopback addresses
- IPv6 addresses with embedded IPv4 addresses

UNSPECIFIED IPV6 ADDRESSES

An IPv6 address consisting totally of zeroes is called an *unspecified address* and must never be assigned to a node. It may, however, be used temporarily by a host as a source address in the field of the IPv6 header, which indicates that the host does not yet have an IPv6 address. It may be written as

```
0:0:0:0:0:0:0:0
```

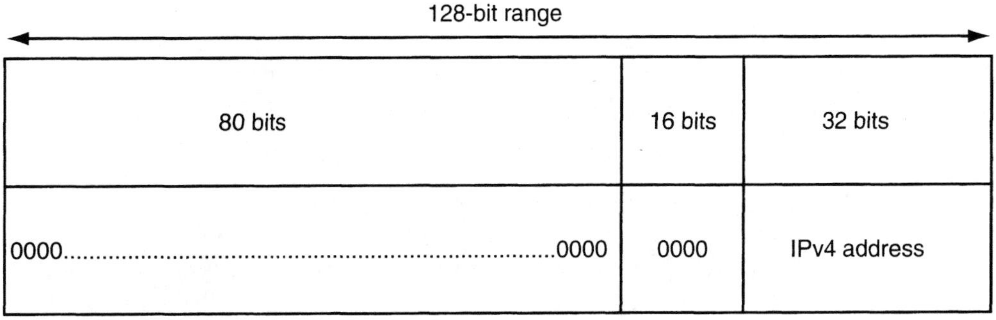

128-bit range

80 bits	16 bits	32 bits
0000..0000	0000	IPv4 address

Figure 13–5 *The IPv4-compatible IPv6 address*

or alternatively, in short form simply as two colons:

`: :`

LOOPBACK ADDRESSES

This is the familiar IPv4 loopback address of 127.0.0.1. It may be used by a host to send a packet to itself and is in effect a virtual address. It is written as

`0:0:0:0:0:0:0:1`

or alternatively, in short form as

`: :1`

IPV4 UNICAST ADDRESSES IN AN IPV6 ENVIRONMENT

There are two ways to represent IPv4 addresses in the IPv6 address space. The two formats for representing IPv4 in the IPv6 address space are

- the IPv6-compatible IPv4 address
- the IPv6-mapped IPv4 address

The IPv6 transition mechanisms include a technique for hosts and routers to tunnel IPv6 packets dynamically over an IPv4 routing infrastructure. IPv6 nodes that use this technique are assigned special unicast addresses that carry an IPv4 address in the low-order 32 bits. This type of address is termed an *IPv4-compatible IPv6 address* and has the format shown in Figure 13-5.

Let us look at some examples of IPv6 addresses in the IPv4 compatible format, using the example of IPv4 address `194.168.85.50`. Here first is the long format, which is shown as 6 times 16-bit fields (96 bits) of 4 zero (0000) groups followed by the 32-bit IPv4 address. Add 96-bits to 32 bits to get 128 bits, which is the size of the IPv6 address. Please note that the IPv4 component (the last 32-bits, or 194.168.85.50 in this case) is shown in the familiar IPv4 dotted-quad notation described in Chapter 5:

```
0000:0000:0000:0000:0000:0000:194.168.85.50
```

We saw previously that we may truncate groups of zeroes to a double-colon representation (::), so in the short format, the address becomes

```
::194.168.85.50
```

The RFCs also define a second type of IPv6 address that holds an embedded IPv4 address. This type, known as an *IPv4-mapped IPv6 address*, represents the addresses of IPv4-only nodes (those that do not support IPv6) as IPv6 addresses. It has the format shown in Figure 13-6.

Notice that in the IPv4-mapped type of address, the 16-bits just before the 32-bit embedded IPv4 address is FFFF, but that in the IPv4-compatible address, the same 16-bits had a value of 0000. By looking at these 16 bits we can differentiate between the two types of embedded IPv4 address.

Next, we look at an example of an IPv4 mapped address and the same address in truncated format. Here is the long format of IPv4 address 129.144.52.38:

```
0000:0000:0000:0000:0000:FFFF:129.144.52.38
```

If we truncate it, it becomes

```
::FFFF:129.144.52.38
```

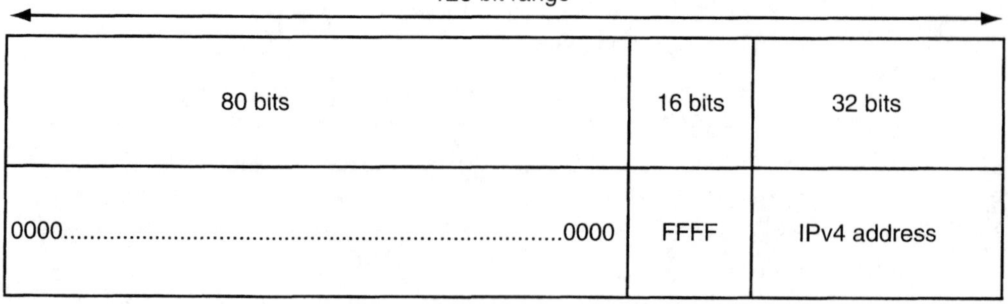

128-bit range

80 bits	16 bits	32 bits
0000..0000	FFFF	IPv4 address

Figure 13–6 *The IPv4–mapped IPv6 address*

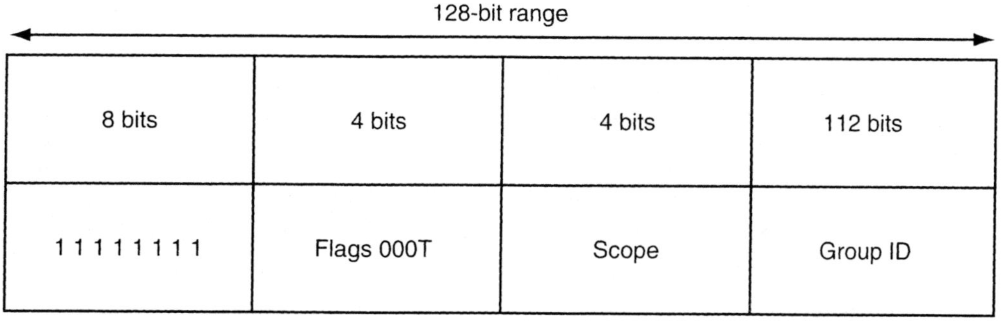

128-bit range

8 bits	4 bits	4 bits	112 bits
1 1 1 1 1 1 1 1	Flags 000T	Scope	Group ID

Figure 13–7   *The IPv6 multicast address format*

That concludes our examination of IPv6 unicast addresses. Next, we look at the second type of IPv6 addresses—the multicast address.

IPv6 Multicast Addresses

Multicast addresses completely replace broadcast addresses in IPv6 (rather than being used alongside them as in IPv4). Multicast addresses always begin with binary 11111111 or hexadecimal FF.

The IPv6 Multicast Address Format

An IPv6 multicast address identifies all members of the multicast group rather than an individual interface, as we saw in Chapter 5 when we discussed multicasting in the context of IPv4. Nodes can choose to belong to a multicast group, and in addition, multicast traffic (unlike IPv4 broadcasts) may be forwarded through routers. Figure 13-7 shows the multicast address format.

FORMAT PREFIX (FP)

The first eight bits of all multicast addresses are always set to binary 11111111 or hexadecimal FF.

FLAGS

Only the fourth bit of the Flags field is defined in the current IPv6 specification; it is referred to as the T (for transient) bit. The first three bits of the Flags field should be initialized as zeroes.

The transient bit can have a value of either 0 or 1. A value of 0 indicates a permanently assigned (well-known) multicast address, assigned by a global authority such as IANA. A value of 1 indicates a non-permanently-assigned (ephemeral) multicast address (used privately with an Intranet).

SCOPE

The values for the four bits defining the scope of a multicast address (the size of the network an address encompasses) are shown in Table 13.4. The 4-bit values are shown in hexadecimal.

Table 13.4 *Scope of Multicast Addresses*

SCOPE VALUE	DESCRIPTION
0	Reserved
1	Node local
2	Link-local
3	Unassigned
4	Unassigned
5	Site-local
6	Unassigned
7	Unassigned
8	Organization-local
9	Unassigned
A	Unassigned
B	Unassigned
C	Unassigned
D	Unassigned
E	Global
F	Reserved

GROUP ID

The last 112-bits of the multicast address define the actual multicast group ID. IANA has reserved a large number of multicast addresses for special use on the Internet. One such example includes the multicast addresses used by the Network Time Protocol that we explored in Chapter 12.

Multicast Addresses Used by the Network Time Protocol (NTP)

Let us examine a specific example of how a protocol—in this case, NTP—uses multicast addresses. NTP uses multicast addresses that are node-local (scope 1), link-local (scope 2), site-local (scope 5), organization-local (scope 8), and global (scope E). That is, the size and number of networks that will be targeted or "reached" by a given multicast address is determined by its scope. Group identifier 43 (hexadecimal) has been assigned to the NTP protocol by IANA, as can be seen in Table 13.5.

In our examples of NTP multicast addresses, the groups of zeroes have been truncated to double colons (::). Table 13.5 shows the truncated, short form of the IPv6 addresses.

Table 13.5 *NTP Multicast Addresses*

NTP MULTICAST ADDRESSES	REPRESENTS ALL NTP SERVERS ON...
FF01::43	The same node as the sender
FF02::43	The same link as the sender
FF05::43	The same site as the sender
FF08::43	The same organization as the sender
FF0E::43	The Internet

All NTP servers and clients will know these addresses, which are hard-coded into the NTP protocol. Let us examine one of these multicast addresses in further detail. Take, for example, the address in the last line of the table,

FF0E::43

which identifies all NTP servers on the Internet. An examination of its five components follows.

FF

All multicast addresses begin with FF, without exception.

0

The four bits containing the flags (see Figure 13-7) are shown as 000T. The zero represents a Flags field value of 0000 (with the T bit set to 0), because as explained previously, T = 0 identifies an official IANA-assigned multicast address.

E

In our example, a value of E means that the scope of the multicast address is global, as shown in Table 13.5.

DOUBLE COLON (::)

The double colon is the truncated form of :0000:0000:0000:0000:0000 :0000:, that is, six 16-bit groups of zeroes.

43

In our example address, the 43 (from the low-order 16-bit group) is the truncated form of :0043:. This value has been assigned to NTP by IANA and is used by all NTP multicast addresses.

Node-Local, Link-Local, and Site-Local Multicast Addresses

In addition to the NTP examples just given, three other IPv6 multicast address types (node-, link-, and site-local) are worthy of note. Multicasting will be used heavily across Solaris 8 LANs because it replaces broadcasting and supplies equivalent functionality plus additional features. The following permanent multicast group identities are therefore expected to be understood by ALL Solaris 8 systems. Specific multicast addresses are used to identify node-local, link-local, and site-local addresses. We show only the first 16-bits in the following examples:

- FF01 (node-local)
- FF02 (link-local)
- FF05 (site-local)

Remember that all multicast addresses start with FF and that the values 01, 02, and 05 represent node, link, and site, respectively. So to identify a specific multicast group ID, just use the values shown in Table 13.6. The multicast group identifier (the boldface **1** or **2** in the table) identifies a specific multicast group ID. Notice that a group ID of 1 refers to all nodes and that a group ID of 2 refers to all routers.

Note

Multicast addresses are always destination addresses, but never source addresses.

Table 13.6 *Node and Router IPv6 Multicast Addresses*

SCOPE	GROUP IDENTIFIER
1	All the IPv6 nodes' addresses
	Scope 1 (FF01::1) all nodes on this node
	Scope 2 (FF02::1) all nodes on this link
2	All the IPv6 routers' addresses
	Scope 1 (FF01::2) all routers on this node
	Scope 2 (FF02::2) all routers on this link
	Scope 5 (FF05::2) all routers on this site

IPv6 Anycast Addresses

The anycast address is new to IPv6 and was not part of the IPv4 specification. The principle of anycast is simple: Instead of sending a datagram to a specific server, one can send it to a generic address that is shared by a group of servers, perhaps offering a given service such as DNS.

Sending a datagram in this manner requires that an anycast address be assigned to more than one interface and that the interfaces be on different nodes. It is the job of routers to route the traffic addressed to the anycast address to the "nearest" node using that anycast address, according to the router's measure of distance.

Anycast addresses are syntactically indistinguishable from unicast addresses. A unicast address becomes an anycast address when it is assigned to more than one node. Very little field experience with anycast addresses has been gained to date, however.

Some restrictions have been placed on the use of anycast addressing because of the possible hazards and complications of using them. The following rules (according to RFC 2373) are in place to date:

- An anycast address must not be used as the source address of an IPv6 packet.
- An anycast address must not be assigned to an IPv6 host; it may be assigned to an IPv6 router only.

EXAM NOTES

KEY LEARNING POINTS

- IPv6 has three types of addresses: unicast, multicast, and anycast.
- There are three main text representations of IPv6 addresses. The long format leaves all zeroes in the address. In short format, groups of contiguous zeroes and leading zeroes are truncated. Finally, multiple pairs of colons may be reduced to a single pair of colons (::).
- There are three main types of unicast addresses: aggregatable global unicast, link-local unicast, and site-local unicast.
- Multicast addresses replace IPv4 broadcast addresses.
- IANA has preassigned certain multicast groups and multicast scopes to specific protocols (NTP, for example).
- A prefix functions like the familiar IPv4 netmask and may be used to identify a subnet (network) within an IPv6 address.
- Only link-local unicast addresses are autoconfigured.

13.5 Configuring an IPv6 Network Interface

Countless extensions have been added to Solaris 8 to support IPv6. Many of them are related to how we configure IPv6 interfaces and to the commands used for viewing the ethernet-to-IPv6 address mapping. Currently Solaris 8 cannot be configured for IPv6 only. Rather, Sun has implemented a dual-stack approach to IP networking, allowing a system to use IPv4 and optionally, IPv6.

One powerful feature of IPv6 is its ability to automatically (or if you prefer, automagically) configure an IPv6 address for use on the local link. In this section, we investigate the how-tos of autoconfiguration.

Earlier, we noted that Solaris 8 can autoconfigure a link-local, non-routed IP address. Let us look at an example of this. Be aware that IPv6 provides two forms of autoconfigured addresses:

- *Stateful*—Using DHCP as in IPv4; requires that an administrator already maintain and configure a DHCP server.
- *Stateless*—For link-local addresses only; requires absolutely no intervention by the network administrator and is based on the host's ethernet address, which is unique.

Autoconfiguring IPv6 Link-Local Addresses

We have already examined the three types of unicast addresses—global, site-local, and link-local. We examined their 128-bit address format and observed that all three types had a 64-bit interface ID as part of their 128-bit IPv6 addresses. A format called IEEE EUI-64 is used to build the interface ID from the 46-bit Ethernet address. We now look at the process of how a 48-bit Ethernet address makes up the basis of the 64-bit interface ID as found in all three types of unicast addresses.

Autoconfiguration, it should be understood, is a process whereby a link-local address is automatically generated using the EUI-64 format. In our example, host apollo has IPv6 enabled. First, we use the **uname** command to ensure that we are on apollo:

```
# uname -n
```

Here is the command output, showing that we are on apollo:

```
apollo
```

Next, we use the **ifconfig** command to check the interface characteristics. As we saw in Chapter 5, we may supply parameters to the **ifconfig** command. In this case, we supply the interface name (hme0) and the version of the IP protocol whose address we wish to see (inet6):

```
# ifconfig hme0 inet6
```

Here is the output from the command. Pay special attention to the boldface parts of the output, which indicate that we are looking at an IPv6 address:

```
hme0: flags=2000841<UP,RUNNING,MULTICAST,IPv6> mtu 1500
index 2 inet6 fe80::a00:20ff:fefc:8dd6/10
```

Notice the `FE80` element of the IPv6 address, and recall that the prefixes `FE8`, `FEC`, and `FF` identify the type of IPv6 address (link-local, site-local, and multicast, respectively). We see from this that

```
fe80::a00:20ff:fefc:8dd6/10
```

is indeed link-local, as it starts with `fe8`.

Solaris 8 interfaces may have both an IPv4 and an IPv6 address on the same interface. Solaris 8 interfaces support the use of multiple IP addresses on a single physical interface (virtual addresses, as you saw in Chapter 5) and the concept of both versions of IP on the same interface.

The following steps illustrate exactly how the link-local IPv6 address is generated, and why. We refer to the host we are working on (apollo) as the current host. Please note that you do not have to perform the steps we describe. In fact, the IPv6 link-local address we are examining (`fe80::a00:20ff:fefc:8dd6`) is autoconfigured. The purpose of the steps is to illustrate how the host calculates the IPv6 link-local address automatically.

Obtaining the Host's Ethernet Address

First, we must obtain the current host's ethernet address. Here is the **arp** command, which will reveal apollo's ethernet address:

```
# arp -a | grep -i apollo
```

The command's output is as follows, with the boldface representing the ethernet address:

```
hme0    apollo    255.255.255.255 SP    08:00:20:fc:8d:d6
```

Converting to Binary

Next, we convert the hexadecimal ethernet address into binary notation. We convert every 4-bit nibble to 4 binary bits. Remember that the 4-bits of the nibble have column values of 8, 4, 2, and 1 as shown here, where we convert the example nibble of 8:

```
8 4 2 1
1 0 0 0    = 8
```

Figure 13-8 shows the converted nibbles below the hexadecimal ethernet address. From the figure, we see the binary equivalent of apollo's hme0 ethernet address of `08:00:20:fc: 8d:d6`.

Inverting Bit 7 (High-Order Byte)

Next, we need to invert the seventh bit of the first octet (the universal bit), which converts the ethernet address to what IPv6 terms an Interface Identifier. Notice that the highlighted nibble in Figure 13-9, which now contains a value of `A`, contained a value of `8` in Figure 13-8. This is because the nibble's values were changed from `1000` to `1010`. That is, we have raised the seventh or universal bit from `0` to `1`. It is referred to as the seventh bit because it is the seventh bit of the leading byte (8 bits) of the address.

Inserting 0xFF and 0xFE between the CID and VID

Recall from Chapter 3 that we may split the ethernet address into CID and VID components. We need to insert `0xFF` and `0xFE` between the two, which is always the case when link-local addresses are autocalculated. That is, hex `FFFE` goes in the middle of the ethernet address. Here's the result:

```
0A00:20FF:FEFC:SDD6
```

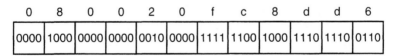

Figure 13–8   *Ethernet address in hex and binary notation*

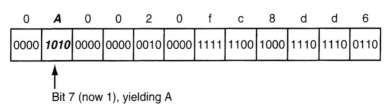

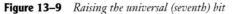

Bit 7 (now 1), yielding A

Figure 13–9   *Raising the universal (seventh) bit*

Notice that the address thus far is not 128-bits, so it is not a legal IPv6 address. We must add to it to make it a legal IPv6 address.

Adding the Prefix

Next, the prefix FE80 is added to the beginning of the address to indicate that the address is of type link-local.

Only link-local addresses are autoconfigured. Link-local addresses never pass through routers.

Thus far, we have

```
FE80:0A00:20FF:FEFC:8DD6
```

which needs to be padded out with groups of zeros to form a 128-bit address. The zeros are always added after the first 16 bits. Here is the address with the zeros inserted, shown in bold:

```
FE80:0000:0000:0000:0A00:20FF:FEFC:8DD6
```

This now forms a complete 128-bit address. The **ifconfig** command, however, showed the address as FE80::A00:20FF:FEFC:8DD6/10, which is the truncated form of the address. The /10 indicates that the address is of type link-local, the first 10 bits being FE8.

As you have seen, autoconfiguration is extremely useful and reduces administration overhead. But remember that a stateless autoconfigured link-local address is never routed and so is useful only to the host on its immediate ethernet link or network.

Configuring an IPv6 Permanent Address Manually

Next, we examine how, as administrators, we can configure an interface to use an IPv6 address. We use the **ifconfig** command (as with IPv4) to achieve this. Enable IPv6 Interfaces by creating and editing the following files:

- An /etc/hostname6.*interface* file, where *interface* represents the actual interface name—for example, /etc/hostname6.hme0.

- Add to the /etc/hostname6.hme0 file the name you wish to associate with the IPv6 interface.
- Add the new hostname to the IPv6 hosts file, /etc/inet/ipnodes. This file applies only to IPv6. Recall that the IPv4 hostnames are stored in the file /etc/inet/hosts.

As with IPv4 addresses, we can create temporary (virtual and non-virtual) and permanent IPv6 addresses that are retained across reboots. In the example you're about to see, we plumb in a virtual interface, but the same steps apply to a nonvirtual address. Following are the steps require to plumb in the interface hme0:10.

Plumbing in Interface hme0:10

Use the **ifconfig** command to plumb in the virtual interface:

```
# ifconfig hme0:10 inet6 plumb
```

We may now check whether the interface has been correctly plumbed in using the following command:

```
# ifconfig hme0:10 inet6
hme0:10: flags=2000840<RUNNING,MULTICAST,IPv6>mtu 1500
index2 inet6 ::/0
```

Notice that the interface is not up yet and so has no address, because we have not yet assigned one to it.

Bringing Up and Assigning an IPv6 Address

We have decided to assign the following address to hme0:10 with subnet-prefix 64:

```
fec0::a00:20ff:fefc:8dd6/64
```

We achieve this by issuing the following **ifconfig** command:

```
# ifconfig hme0:10 inet6 fec0::a00:20ff:fefc:8dd6/64  up
```

Next, we check whether the interface has been correctly configured using the following **ifconfig** address:

```
# ifconfig hme0:10 inet6
```

Here is the output from the **ifconfig** command, showing the most important parts in bold:

```
hme0:10: flags=2000841<UP,RUNNING,MULTICAST,IPv6> mtu 1500
index 2 inet6 fec0::a00:20ff:fefc:8dd6/64
```

Notice that the interface is up and has the correct IPv6 address. To make the address permanent across reboots, use the **echo** command to add the address to /etc/inet/ipnodes and the name to the /etc/hostname6.hme0:10:

```
# echo  "fec0::a00:20ff:fefc:8dd6  apollo-ip6" \
>>  /etc/inet/ipnodes
```

Next, enter the hostname into /etc/hostname6.hme0:10 file using the **echo** command:

```
# echo "apollo-ip6"  > /etc/hostname6.hme0:10
```

Because we have added this information to the relevant files, the interface information will be retained across a reboot.

Testing with the ping Command

We may test whether the address is enabled by pinging both the IPv6 address and the hostname. First, we ping the address using the IPv6 address:

```
# ping fec0::a00:20ff:fefc:8dd6
```

Here is the command's output, which indicates that the interface is enabled (alive):

```
fec0::a00:20ff:fefc:8dd6 is alive
```

Next, we ping the same address, but using the hostname we have mapped onto the IPv6 address in the /etc/inet/ipnodes file:

```
# ping apollo-ip6
```

Here is the command's output, which indicates that the interface is enabled (alive):

```
apollo-ip6   is alive
```

As you can see, the IPv6 interface is now fully enabled, and the existence of the entry in /etc/inet/ipnodes and etc/hostname6.hme0:10 will reestablish the interface at boot time.

EXAM NOTES

KEY LEARNING POINTS

- Solaris implements a dual-stack approach to IPv4 and IPv6.
- Solaris 8 does not support IPv6 without IPv4.
- We can test the interface with **ping** and **ifconfig**.
- The /etc/inet/ipnodes file holds IPv6 host names.

SUMMARY

This chapter explored the new version of IP, version 6, referred to as Next Generation or simply IPng. It solves the problems of a depleted address space, although it introduces greater complexity than IPv4 with more complex address architecture and address types.

IPv6 uses multiple unicast address types—global, site-local, and link-local. It uses multicasting far more extensively than IPv4 and replaces the familiar broadcast address format with multicast addresses. IPv6 has been around for several years and is now bundled with Solaris 8, but it cannot be used on Solaris in the absence of IPv4; Sun has implemented a dual-stack approach where IPv4 and IPV6 work together in harmony.

We saw how link-local addresses are autoconfigured and deploy a format called IEEE EUI-64 to form an interface ID that becomes part of its 128-bit link-local IPv6 address. Finally, we saw that the **ifconfig** command may be used to configure an IPv6 unicast address manually.

TEST YOURSELF

MULTIPLE CHOICE

1. *Which of these are valid types of IPv6 address? Choose 3.*
    A. anycast
    B. unicast
    C. broadcast
    D. multicast
    E. netmask

2. *How many bytes are in an IPv6 header without extensions?*
    A. 120
    B. 28
    C. 128
    D. 40
    E. 32

3. *Which of these are valid IPv6 addresses? Choose 3.*
    A. FEDC:BA98:0000:0000:0000:0000:7654:3210
    B. FEDC:BA98:0000:0000:7654:3210
    C. ::
    D. FE:DC:BA:98:0000:0000:0000:0000:7654:3210
    E. ::194.168.85.51

4. *Which of these are unicast addresses? Choose 3.*
    A. site-local
    B. link-local
    C. multicast
    D. aggregatable global
    E. broadcast

5. *Which one of these prefixes is the Format Prefix (FP) of the site-local unicast address?*
    A. FF
    B. FEE
    C. FEC

D. FE8

E. 001

6. *Which of these prefixes is the Format Prefix (FP) of the link-local unicast address?*

    A. FF

    B. FEE

    C. FEC

    D. FE8

    E. FF

7. *Which of these prefixes is the Format Prefix (FP) of the global aggregatable unicast address?*

    A. FEE

    B. FEC

    C. FE8

    D. FF

    E. 001

8. *Given the address FE80::**A00:20FF:FEFC:8DD6**/10, how much of the address does the /10 suffix select?*

    A. FE80

    B. FE80::A00:

    C. ::8DD6

    D. FE8

    E. **FE80::A00:20FF:FEFC:8DD6**

9. *Which file stores the IPv6 address to hostname mappings?*

    A. /etc/inet/hosts

    B. /etc/inet/hostname6.hme0

    C. /etc/inet/ipnodes

    D. /etc/nsswitch.conf

    E. /etc/net/hosts

10. *Which of these address types are autoconfigured?*

    A. site-local unicast

    B. link-local unicast

    C. aggregatable unicast

    D. multicast

E. anycast

FREE RESPONSE

1. *In what sense is the IPv4 address architecture too simplistic?*

2. *In IPv6 addresses, is there an equivalent of IPv4 classes?*

REFERENCES

Heutema, Christian. *IPv6: The New Internet Protocol.* Saddle River, NJ: Prentice Hall, 1998. ISBN 0-138-50505-5.

Hinden, R. and S. Deering. *RFC 2373: IP Version 6 Addressing Architecture.* July 1998. (Format: TXT=52526 bytes) (Obsoletes RFC1884) (Status: PROPOSED STANDARD)

Hinden, R. and S. Deering. *RFC 2460: Internet Protocol, Version 6 (IPv6) Specification.* December 1998. (Format: TXT=85490 bytes) (Obsoletes RFC1883) (Status: DRAFT STANDARD)

A

Multiple-Choice Answers

A.1   Chapter 1: Network Models and Protocols

1. Answers A, B, and E are correct. The Session, Presentation, and Application layers are all layers of the OSI/ISO 7-layer reference model.
2. Answers B, D, and E are correct. The Physical, Transport, and Internet layers are layers of the TCP/IP model.
3. Answer D is correct. Ethernet functions at the Network Interface layer of the TCP/IP model.
4. Answer B is correct. UDP is a transport protocol and functions at the Transport layer of the TCP/IP model.
5. Answer D is correct. UDP stands for User Datagram Protocol.
6. Answer C is correct. TCP stands for Transmission Control Protocol.
7. Answer D is correct. Peers are communicating entities operating at the same layer of the protocol stack.
8. Answer B is correct. ICMP is encapsulated in the IP protocol.
9. Answer E is correct. The size of the UDP header is 8 bytes.
10. Answer A is correct. The size of the IP header is always a minimum of 20 bytes.

A.2   Chapter 2: Introduction to Local Area Networks

1. Answers A, C and D are correct. Star, bus, and ring are all LAN topologies.
2. Answer B is correct. A segment is indeed a length of contiguous (continuous) cable.
3. Answers C and D are correct. Bridges deal with MAC and Ethernet addresses. An Ethernet address is an example of a MAC (Media Access Control) address.
4. Answers A and B are correct. Routers deal with IP addresses, which are also referred to as software addresses.
5. Answer C is correct. A router maps onto the Internet layer (3) of the TCP/IP model because routers deal with IP addresses and IP functions at the Internet layer.
6. Answer D is correct. A bridge maps onto the Network Interface layer (2) of the TCP/IP model because bridges deal with Ethernet/MAC addresses and Ethernet functions at the Network interface layer.
7. Answer E is correct. Repeaters map onto the Physical layer of the TCP/IP model.
8. Answer C is correct. Hubs are also referred to as multiport repeaters.
9. Answers A and E are correct. Switches and bridges filter packets based on Ethernet addresses.
10. Answer D is correct. Routers route packets based on IP addresses.

A.3   Chapter 3: The Ethernet LAN

1. Answer B is correct. The CD in CSMA/CD stands for Collision Detect.
2. Answer C is correct. A collision occurs as the result of two or more hosts attempting to transmit Ethernet frames simultaneously.
3. Answer A is correct. Token Ring is defined by IEEE standard 802.5 and is not to be confused with CSMA/CD (Ethernet), which is defined by IEEE standard 802.3.
4. Answer C is correct. IEEE is the organization that allocated the first three bytes of Ethernet address (24-bits) known as CIDs (Customer IDs) to manufacturers such as Sun Microsystems, Inc.
5. Answer B is correct. The Type field of a V2 Ethernet frame is 2 bytes in length.

6. Answer B is correct. All Ethernet addresses, whether source or destination, unicast, multicast, or broadcast, are 48-bits in length.

7. Answer B is correct. The Ethernet overhead (which does not include the Ethernet preamble or data field) is 18 bytes.

8. Answer A is correct. The CRC (checksum) field of the Ethernet frame is calculated by the sending station and checked by the station receiving the frame.

9. Answer A is correct. The Ethernet broadcast address is 48 bits worth of 1s in binary notation or ff:ff:ff:ff:ff:ff in hexadecimal notation.

10. Answer A is correct. The **ifconfig** command configures Solaris interfaces.

A.4 Chapter 4: The ARP and RARP Protocols

1. Answer E is correct. Opcode 2 identifies the ARP reply.

2. Answer C is correct. A value of 0x0806, when found in the Ethernet frame's type field, means that the frame has ARP encapsulated.

3. Answer A is correct. ARP is attempting to learn an Ethernet address when it issues an opcode 1 request.

4. Answer E is correct. RARP is attempting to learn its own IP address when it issues an opcode 3 request.

5. Answer D is the correct answer. The **in.rarpd** daemon must run on a RARP server.

6. Answer C is correct. The **arp** command's **–d** option deletes an entry from the ARP cache.

7. Answer B is correct. The U flag in the ARP cache indicates that the entry with the U flag is unresolved.

8. Answer C is correct. ARP entries are usually cached for 20 minutes.

9. Answer B is the correct answer. The ARP/RARP frame is 28 bytes in size.

10. Answer C is correct. In the RARP request (opcode 3), the target and the source host are seen as the same host.

A.5 Chapter 5: The Internet Layer and IPv4

1. Answer A is the right answer. The scope of the first octet of the Class B range of addresses runs from 128 through 191.

2. Answer B is correct. The scope of the first octet of the Class A range of addresses runs from 0 through 127.

3. Answer C is the right answer. The scope of the first octet of the Class C range of addresses runs from 192 through 223.

4. Answer E is correct. The host portion of a nonsubnetted class A address is identified by 24 bits.

5. Answer A is correct. The host portion of a nonsubnetted class C address is identified by 8 bits.

6. Answer D is the correct answer. Address 194.168.85.255 is a broadcast address because 255 includes all possible bits of the fourth octet.

7. Answer D is correct. IP datagrams are fragmented when a router attempts to send an IP datagram (or fragment) of a size greater than its interface's MTU size.

8. Answer B is the correct answer. The /etc/inet/netmasks file holds netmask values on Solaris 8.

9. Answer C is correct. Interface names of the type *interface:number* (such as hme0:88) are virtual addresses. The actual interface is *interface* (in this case hme0) and the virtual component is 88, yielding a usable (complete) interface name of hme0:88.

10. Answer D is correct. **Ifconfig** acquires and interfaces actual IP address from the Solaris /etc/inet/hosts file.

A.6   Chapter 6: Routing over TCP/IP with Solaris 8

1. Answers A, C, and D are correct. The three types of routing table entry are default, network, and host routes.

2. Answer B is correct. The **in.routed** daemon implements RIP on Solaris 8.

3. Answer C is the correct answer. RDP uses multicast addresses.

4. Answer A is correct. RIP servers (running in.routed) are started with the –s option, which causes them to advertise their routes.

5. Answer C is the right answer. To view the host's routing table, run the command **netstat –r**.

6. Answers A and D are both correct. The **in.rdisc** daemon uses Class D address 224.0.0.1 (known also as ALL_HOSTS) and also 224.0.0.2, known as ALL_ROUTERS.

7. Answer C is correct. The /etc/gateways file is used to add additional static routes.

8. Answer C is the right answer. An indirect route is one that requires a router. *Indirect* specifically means that the destination is not on the same logical network as the source; if they were on the same network, the route would be described as *direct*.

9. Answer A is correct. 10.1.1.0/24 means that a 24-bit netmask is to be applied to network 10.1.1.0. This subnet prefix notation is used when defining CIDR blocks on IPv4.
10. Answer B is the correct answer. Setting the kernel parameter *ip_forwarding* to 0 disables packet forwarding.

A.7 Chapter 7: The Transport Layer Protocols

1. Answer C is correct. The TCP segment is composed of the TCP header plus TCP data.
2. Answer C is the right answer. Both source and destination port fields in the TCP header are 16-bits, allowing for a total of 65,535 ports, which is 16^2.
3. Answer A is the correct answer. MSS stands for Maximum Segment Size.
4. Answer D is correct. During the TCP three-way handshake, the SYN bit is set in the first two segments.
5. Answer B is correct. The minimum size of a TCP header is 20 bytes.
6. Answer C is correct. The minimum size of a UDP header is 8 bytes.
7. Answer E is correct. Both source and destination port fields in the TCP header are 16 bits, allowing for a total of 65,535 ports, which is 16^2.
8. Answer D is the right answer. The UDP pseudo header, which is prepended to the UDP data for the purpose of generating a checksum, is 12 bytes long.
9. Answer A is correct. TCP's protocol number, as shown in the Solaris 8 file /etc/inet/protocols, is 6.
10. Answer C is the right answer. UDP's protocol number, as shown in the Solaris 8 file /etc/inet/protocols, is 17.

A.8 Chapter 8: The Client-Server Model

1. Answer B is the correct answer. RPC functions at the session layer of the OSI 7-layer model.
2. Answers D and E are the correct choices. Standalone servers are started either manually by an administrator or through shell scripts.
3. Answer B is the correct answer. The inetd configuration file is called /etc/inetd.conf. This file enables the **inetd** daemon to know which servers are enabled and which ones it should start when a client request arrives on an **inetd**-monitored port.

4. Answer D is correct. TI-RPC server program numbers are stored in the file /etc/rpc. Do not confuse these with port numbers. TI-RPC servers have dynamic ports, which are allocated by the **rpcbind** daemon.

5. Answer A is the correct answer. The /etc/services file associates the traditional non-RPC server with a fixed port number.

6. Answer B is correct. The **rpcbind** daemon allocates ephemeral port numbers to TI-RPC servers.

7. Answer B is correct. The **rpcinfo** command is used to check which TI-RPC servers are actually running. **Rpcinfo** causes **rpcbind** to dump its database of registered (enabled) servers.

8. Answer B is correct. XDR functions at the Presentation layer and is a standard used by TI-RPC servers to ensure that data is delivered in a uniform, standard fashion.

9. Answer D is correct. The **rpcbind** daemon always listens on port 111.

10. Answer B is correct. The *.* shown in **netstat –a** output means "any IP address.any port."

A.9   Chapter 9: Dynamic Address Allocation with DHCP

1. Answer B is correct. The BOOTP relay allows DHCP clients and servers to communicate when they are on different networks.

2. Answer C is correct. When a DHCP server is using a DHCP server, it is said to be bound. In effect, the DHCP client is using an IP address and other information supplied by the DHCP server.

3. Answers A, B, and E are correct. The three types of DHCP allocation mode are dynamic, automatic, and manual.

4. Answer E is correct. A fixed address is always allocated when the DHCP manual address mode is used by the network administrator.

5. Answer B is correct. IP addresses allocated through automatic mode are assigned for an infinite time period and are therefore not lease-based.

6. Answer A is correct. IP addresses that are allocated through dynamic mode are assigned for a finite time period and are therefore allocated on a leased basis.

7. Answer C is correct. The command **dhcpconfig** may be used to set up the DHCP server.

8. Answer B is correct. The file /var/dhcp/194_168_85_0 would hold the pool of addresses for network 194.168.85.0. The filename that holds

the pool of addresses for a network is always the same as the network (or subnet), with the dots (.) replaced by underscore characters (_).

9. Answer B is correct. Code 04 means that the IP address is unusable, which is usually the result of the address already being in use.

10. Answer C is correct. The command **dhtadm** is used to configure the /var/dhcp/dhcptab file.

A10 Chapter 10: Network Management Using SNMP

1. Answer A is correct. SNMP operates at the Application layer of the TCP/IP stack and uses UDP (for speed and low overhead), which operates at the Transport layer.

2. Answers A, B, and E are correct. The SNMP protocol does indeed have functions called **get**, **set**, and **trap**, which modify and access objects stored in the SMI.

3. Answer B is correct. The object tree used by SNMP contains Object Identifiers, which are part of the SMI.

4. Answer D is correct. ASN stands for Abstract Syntax Notation.

5. Answer C is correct. RFC1156 does not list *network* as one of the SNMP object groups. All the protocols and objects that it does list, however, function by using networks.

6. Answers C and D are both correct. ISO and CCITT are at the very top of the OID tree.

7. Answers C and D are correct. Solstice Site Manager and Solstice Enterprise Manager use SNMP.

8. Answers B, C, and D are correct. UDP has a very quick startup because it does not perform a handshake and has less overhead than TCP.

9. Answer A is correct. An OID is a sequence of integers which traverse a global tree.

10. Answers A, B, C, and D are all correct and may be used when managing networks.

A11 Chapter 11: Domain Name Service (DNS)

1. Answer D is correct. When a DNS server passes authority for a child domain to another DNS server, it is called delegation.

2. Answers D and E are correct. Clients and DNS servers in forwarding mode (forwarders) generate recursive queries or questions.

3. Answer D is correct. Version 8 of DNS/BIND (Solaris 8 is bundled with 8.1.2) uses a main configuration file called /etc/named.conf. Prior to version 8, the file was called /etc/named.boot.

4. Answer C is correct. The @ symbol is a metacharacter that represents the current origin (the current zone).

5. Answer B is correct. PTR records are found only in zone DB files, which deal with reverse resolution. The other four types of resource record listed—NS, SOA, A, and CNAME—may occur in any forward or reverse zone file.

6. Answer C is correct. Both slave and master have an NS record, but only the master has an SOA record. Even when the master's zone files are transferred to the slave, the SOA still identifies the master as the start of authority (SOA) for the zone.

7. Answer B is correct. PTR records specifically deal with the reverse zone, which handles IP address-to-host name translation. On the Internet, the reverse domain is defined beneath the in-addr.arpa. branch of the namespace tree.

8. Answer C is correct. Stub zones are a means of delegating a domain to another DNS server, thus forming a child zone.

9. Answer A is correct. Note that the `name`, `ttl`, and `class` fields are in square brackets ([]) which means they are optional. They are only optional, however, in that you may omit them from a given RR line in a zone file. If you do not specify them in a given RR, the `name` field is acquired from the last-defined RR record (in which the `name` field was fully qualified), the `ttl` is acquired from the default `ttl` field (the final field of the SOA record for the given zone), and the `class` field simply defaults to `in`, which is the Internet class.

10. Answer C is correct. The **in.named** signal handler dumps its memory-based cache when it receives the `INT` signal. The dump is called named_dump.db and will be found in the directory defined in /etc/named.conf in the directory directive, used primarily to tell **in.named** where to locate supported zone files.

A.12 Chapter 12: The Network Time Protocol (NTP)

1. Answer E is correct. UTC stands for Universal Time Coordinated, which is the reference time adopted and used by the NTP protocol.

2. Answer A is correct. Jitter refers to the difference between the differences and may be calculated when time is measured many times.

3. Answer C is correct. The NTP client template file is called /etc/inet/ntp.client.

4. Answer A is correct. The /etc/inet/ntp.conf is the main configuration file for both NTP clients and servers. It is the file's content that tells the **xntpd** daemon whether it is running on an NTP client or server and determines the daemon's behavior.

5. Answer A is correct. The **xntpd** daemon implements the NTP protocol on Solaris 8.

6. Answer B is correct. The Internet Assigned Numbers Authority (IANA) specifically allocates multicast address 224.0.1.1 to the NTP protocol.

7. Answer D is correct. Address 127.127.1.0 is used to indicate that the NTP server is using its own undisciplined internal clock.

8. Answer D is correct. The default log file is the Solaris log file called /var/adm/messages, which is written to by several Solaris daemons.

9. Answer B is correct. The **ntpdate** daemon runs on the client so that the time can be set as quickly as possible.

10. Answer B is correct. The /var/ntp/ntp.drift file contains the drift information.

A13   Chapter 13: The New Internet Protocol: IPv6

1. Answers A, B, and D are correct. Anycast, unicast, and multicast are valid IPv6 address types.

2. Answer D is correct. The IPv6 header (with extension headers) is 40 bytes in length.

3. Answers A, C, and E are correct. Answer A is a correct, 128-bit IPv6 address. Answer C is the short format for 128-bits worth of zeroes (known as the unspecified address). Answer E is a valid way to represent a compatible IPv4 address in the IPv6 environment.

4. Answers A, B, and D are correct. Site-local, link-local, and aggregatable are the three types of unicast addresses. Multicast addresses are valid in IPv6 but are not unicast. Broadcast addresses are not used in IPv6, and their functionality (as used in IPv4) has been replaced by multicasting.

5. Answer C is correct. The site-local unicast address has a format prefix (FP) of binary 1111111011, hexadecimally notated as FEC.

6. Answer D is correct. Hexadecimal FE8 is the prefix used by link-local addresses, expressed in binary as 1111111010.

7. Answer E is correct. The aggregatable unicast format prefix (FP) is 001.

8. Answer D is correct. FE8 represents the high-order 10 bits and so would be identified by a suffix of 10.

9. Answer C is correct. The /etc/inet/ipnodes file maps IPv6 addresses to host names. For IPv4 addresses, the /etc/inet/hosts file performs this function.

10. Answer B is correct. The link-local unicast address is autoconfigured.

Free Response Answers

B.1   Chapter 1: Network Models and Protocols

1. *State in your own words three advantages of modularizing the design of network protocols.*

Three possible advantages are:

- *Ease of upgrading existing protocols*—Each protocol performs a specific function and interfaces with other specific protocols determined by its position in the stack, so we can upgrade it without having to modify the protocols that communicate with it.
- *Ease in troubleshooting*—Troubleshooting is simplified because we know exactly what function each protocol performs (for example, routing in the case of IP, error detection for ICMP, and delivery in the cases of TCP and UDP).
- *Ease of introducing new protocols*—When introducing a new protocol, we need only define the exact function of the new protocol and ensure that it communicates correctly with existing protocols. For example, we could introduce a new transport protocol, and as long as it communicates correctly with IP, there would be no need to upgrade IP itself.

2. *List the similarities and differences between IP and UDP as protocols.*

Both protocols have the following characteristics in common:

- They are datagram-based.
- They are connectionless.
- They are unacknowledged.

The protocols differ in several respects, including:

- IP operates at the Internet layer of the protocol stack, while UDP functions at the Transport layer.
- UDP offers a low-overhead, fast delivery service to applications (typically between client and server processes that are usually on different hosts). On the other hand, IP offers a routing (host-to-host) service to the transport protocols, routing transport-layer data in IP datagrams from a source IP address to a destination IP address.
- UDP (with its 8-byte header) offers low overhead, whereas IPv4 has a 20-byte header and IPv6 an even larger 40-byte header.

B.2   Chapter 2: Introduction to Local Area Networks

1. *Describe briefly how a LAN specifically helps groups of users who are working on the same project and need to share files.*

Projects involving several users usually involve the sharing of files and a need to communicate ideas and plans. A LAN enables the use of file-sharing software such as Sun's NFS and SAMBA. NFS, which ships with Solaris, is the perfect tool for sharing files between Solaris servers and workstations because it is easily configured. SAMBA (see http://www.samba.org) is freeware designed to allow easy sharing of UNIX resources (files, printers, and other devices) with PCs running Microsoft Windows. PCs see the UNIX resource as a logical drive (for example, E:). The beauty of SAMBA is that is it automatically supported by Windows, which supports the protocols that SAMBA uses.

NFS can also be used to share files and printers between Solaris systems and PCs running Windows, but Sun's PC-NFS product would need to be added to the Windows environment for this arrangement to work. NFS and SAMBA do not "copy" files (as **ftp**, **rcp**, or **rdist** would) but rather allows users to literally share the "same" files transparently as if the files were on the user's own system.

2. *What could you do to increase the responsiveness of a LAN?*

One could simply spend money and buy the latest and fastest technology to modernize the LAN. Alternatively, one could use **snoop** or another utility to monitor the protocols that are evident on the LAN and remove any that are not necessary to achieve the desired functionality. For example, broadcast and multicast traffic can be reduced by using static ARP cache entries and static routing (avoiding the use of daemons like **in.routed** and **in.rdisc,** which generate broadcast and multicast traffic). Another option is to check for any Solaris daemons that need not be running at all and might be generating network load. Disable them whenever possible by modifying files like /etc/inet/inetd.conf and /etc/inet/services. Finally, one could consider segmenting—introducing switches and possibly routers in strategic locations—to reduce the number of stations in a given part of the LAN.

B.3 Chapter 3: The Ethernet LAN

1. *Which UNIX commands can you use to view a system's Ethernet address?*

The following commands may be used to view a system's Ethernet address. At the UNIX command prompt, use

```
ifconfig -a
arp -a
netstat -pn
```

At the system's Openboot prompt, use

```
banner
```

2. *Describe Ethernet's strengths and weaknesses in brief.*

Ethernet has several strengths, the most important of which are:
- Hosts may transmit when ready (no server decides when).
- There is no chance of an Ethernet server failing because no Ethernet server exists.
- It is permissible to mix Ethernet speeds and cable types. An Ethernet with mixed speeds is known as multimode Ethernet.
- One can use several different types of devices with Ethernet, such as hubs and switches.

- Configuration is easy: Simply connect host to bus via a switch or hub.
- Ethernet hosts may be connected to one another directly by using a crossover Ethernet cable.
- If an Ethernet host fails, other hosts are usually not affected.
- Ethernet is now relatively cheap to install. Hubs and switches have come down drastically in price.
- Ethernet is used by many OS platforms, including UNIX, Windows, and Macintosh, among others.
- Gigabit Ethernet is extremely fast, even by current standards.

Ethernet's weaknesses are:

- It is a bus, which means that packets are easily seen by the network analyzer or a network sniffer such as **snoop**.
- A break in the bus can cause total bus failure.
- A faulty switch or hub can also cause complete bus failure.
- Excessive collisions can result in an unusable network.
- Gigabit Ethernet is still relatively expensive.

B.4   Chapter 4: The ARP and RARP Protocols

1. *State in your own words why ARP requests are broadcast rather than unicast.*

The reason a host generates an ARP request is to glean the Ethernet address of another host. The ARP request itself, therefore, must be broadcast, as the targeted host's Ethernet address is unknown, so the unicast option is not available. Broadcast addresses are used mainly when

- the MAC address of the target is unknown, or
- we need to contact all machines at once.

Both of these conditions are true in the case of ARP. We need to acquire an unknown MAC address, so using the Ethernet broadcast address (which is always ff:ff:ff:ff:ff:ff) enables a host to contact all hosts, which will inevitably include the one whose specific MAC address is needed. That host will then return its MAC address in an ARP reply (opcode 2).

2. *Why does the ARP cache reduce network traffic and improve network performance?*

The ARP cache provides information (in the form of IP-to-MAC address mappings) that would otherwise need to be acquired by generating network requests. The contents of the cache may be added statically or are the result of network requests.

B.5   Chapter 5: The Internet Layer and IPv4

1. *Why are datagrams sometimes fragmented?*

The only reason datagrams are ever fragmented is because they are too large to traverse a given network. If an IP router attempts to transmit a datagram across a network where the datagram is larger than the outbound network interface's MTU size, the datagram is either discarded by the router (if the Don't frag bit is set) or fragmented into multiple IP datagrams (fragments), each of which is the size demanded by the MTU or smaller. Such fragmentation wastes time in the processes of fragmenting and reassembling and can be problematic. For example, if a single fragment is lost, the entire datagram needs to be retransmitted, not just the lost fragment.

In IPv6, MTU path discovery prevents the need to fragment by calculating a maximum MTU path for the entire IP datagram's journey and ensuring that the sender sends only IP datagrams of that size or smaller.

2. *If an IP datagram is fragmented, when are the fragments reassembled?*

The fragmented datagram is always reassembled at the destination host. There are several reasons for this:

- It cannot be guaranteed that all fragments will go through the same router, so they cannot easily be assembled en route.
- It is possible to force all packets through the same routers using loose or strict-source routing, but with IPv4 this is rarely done in practice.
- If datagrams were reassembled en route, we would need to wait until all fragments had arrived before we could completely reassemble the fragmented datagram(s). This would introduce delays into the routing process.
- En route reassembly would require buffering, which can be demanding in busy networks in terms of CPU and memory usage.
- If reassembly did occur en route, it would not be possible to ensure that fragmentation would not have to occur again at a

router closer to the destination. Multiple reassemblies would introduce further delays into the routing process.

Chapter 6: Routing over TCP/IP with Solaris 8

1. *Why is routing so fundamentally important in networking terms?*

Routing is fundamentally important because most network applications and protocols rely on the routing service offered by IP to ensure that their data is successfully routed to the appropriate destination host. Most Solaris network traffic is user- and application-related and the result of client-server services functioning across networks between hosts. Web, mail, dns, ftp, news, irc, and other applications all result in data being encapsulated in TCP or UDP for delivery, then being encapsulated by IP for routing, and eventually running over some kind of LAN or WAN for bit-for-bit transfer. Without effective routing, applications and Application-layer protocols such as POP, DNS, HTTP, or FTP are completely unable to function. Routing is performed by IP, rendering it a critical protocol—the bytebarge of the Internet.

2. *Describe the advantages and disadvantages of dynamic routing as opposed to static routing.*

The advantages of dynamic routing are:
- New routes are learned dynamically without network administrator intervention.
- Responses to learned changes in a network—such as routers becoming available or unavailable—are quick and automatic.
- Once dynamic routing has been configured, very little maintenance is required.

The disadvantages of dynamic routing are:
- It increases network traffic because of broadcast and multicast router advertisements.
- Clients might need to solicit a router (as in the case of **in.rdisc** clients), which introduces yet more network traffic.
- Dynamic routing poses some security risk because it heightens the chance of bogus routes (possibly introduced by a hacker) being learned.

B.7 Chapter 7: The Transport Layer Protocols

1. *Why might an application developer choose to use UDP, if TCP is so reliable?*

   UDP is often more attractive because it has extremely low overhead. In addition, because UDP is stateless, it has a rapid startup and does not require an initial handshake at the Transport layer. Using UDP therefore involves a tradeoff between reliability versus speed and low overhead. Applications that send small, discrete messages (such as a routing table update or a DNS query, both of which use small packets) can afford to use UDP, as the occasional data loss is not critical.

   As a concrete example of a UDP application that can afford to lose the occasional packet, a RIP router (running **in.routed**) would have to fail to send at least five update messages before neighboring routers would drop it from their routing tables.

2. *Describe what happens when TCP segments arrive out of order in IP fragments that have likewise arrived out of order. Describe the process from the point at which the IP fragments arrive at the destination machine.*

   IP fragments are reassembled at the destination address as soon as all fragments of a given datagram have arrived. The order in which fragments arrive is not important, If any fragment of a given IP datagram is lost, the entire IP datagram is discarded. Presuming that all fragments arrive, the IP datagram is reassembled. Given that each TCP segment is put into a single datagram at the source end and that the fragmented datagram is reassembled by IP at the destination end, it follows that fragmented segments are never passed up to TCP. Put another way, only whole segments are passed up to TCP, whether or not they were routed in one or more IP fragments.

   The IP fragmentation process is transparent to TCP. If whole datagrams arrive at the destination end or are ready to be transported to TCP in the wrong order, however, they will be passed up to TCP in the wrong order. In such a scenario, it is up to TCP to reorder the segments. To summarize:

   - IP reassembles IP fragments before passing them to TCP, but sends whole IP datagrams up to TCP in order of readiness (which might not be the order in which they were sent).

- TCP reorders segments before it passes the data in them to an application, so the application sees a stream of data in the same order in which it left the peer application. The two applications are usually client and server.

B.8 Chapter 8: The Client-Server Model

1. *Describe the senses in which a port can be said to be ephemeral.*

A TCP/UDP port is said to be ephemeral (short-lived) when it is assigned to an application for a short period of time and is not a fixed number of the type allocated to servers—for example, 23 (telnet) or 21 (ftp). Typically, these short-lived, non-fixed port numbers are allocated to clients rather than to servers.

2. *Use the analogy of a receptionist to describe the way* **rpcbind** *works.*

When they first run (typically at system boot), TI-RPC servers register with the **rpcbind** server. The **rpcbind** server allocates them a port number to use, which might be different each time the server registers. In this context, such a port is said to be dynamic.

When a TI-RPC client needs to contact a specific TI-RPC server, it contacts the **rpcbind** server (always on fixed port 111), which informs the client of the dynamic port number that has been allocated to the server. The client may then contact the server on that port number. **Rpcbind** is a receptionist in the sense that clients get a number from it so that they may contact a service, in the way that a receptionist may guide a visitor to the appropriate room in a building.

B.9 Chapter 9: Dynamic Address Allocation with DHCP

1. *What types of network environments are not suitable for DHCP?*

DHCP would not suit an environment where the hosts have fixed addresses and are never moved around the network. Neither should DHCP be used in environments where security is critical, as it introduces a degree of automation that would be undesirable. Environments where nomadic hosts (such as laptops) are not used may not benefit from using DHCP either. DHCP would also not be suitable for a server environment, because servers need a fixed address in order for clients to locate them. Finally, if a host's name and address are known to a name service such as DNS or NIS+, the information needs to remain unchanged or at least not changed frequently. This is because a change of host name or IP address would require that the name service also be reconfigured and restarted.

2. *How does DHCP differ from BOOTP? Why is it considered an enhancement?*

DHCP is an enhancement of BOOTP in that DHCP is not only able to allocate an IP address to a requesting host (as does BOOTP) but also can allocate an address on a leased basis. That is, the IP address is leased for a period of time and the lease is continually renegotiated by the client without network administrator intervention. It is the leasing component of DHCP that introduces complexity to the protocol. DHCP has the ability to behave like BOOTP and simply allocate the IP address on a permanent basis if this is desirable.

B.10   Chapter 10: Network Management Using SNMP

1. *Why does SNMP use UDP?*

SNMP needs to be able to communicate quickly and without delay, especially when network conditions are poor and bandwidth is sparse. So although UDP is not as reliable as TCP, UDP has the advantage of being fast and avoids any kind of handshake, in this way enhancing the likelihood that at least some of its datagrams will cross the network safely. SNMP needs to get only some of its packets through to be successful, so UDP is a better choice than the slower-starting, high-overhead TCP.

2. *What does the SNMP OID allow you to do, compared with what a Web address allows you do in DNS? Is there a similarity?*

The SNMP OID allows you to locate an object within the distributed SNMP database, which could contain many millions of objects of countless types and groups. For example, the OID address

```
iso.org.dod.internet.private.enterprise.sun.sunMib.sunSystem.hostid
```

maps onto the Sun system hostid. Object groups, such as those in the list that follows, may be accessed through the SNMP OID tree:

*   system

- interfaces
- address translation
- IP
- ICMP
- TCP
- UDP
- EGP

DNS addresses (such as www.sun.com) allow you to locate an object with the distributed DNS database, which contains millions of domains and object types, the most important being:

- SOA
- NS
- A
- PTR
- MX
- CNAME
- TXT
- HINFO

In the sense that they both allow a text string to index into a database tree to retrieve information, they are similar.

B.11 Chapter 11: Domain Name Service (DNS)

1. *If a DNS slave server fails to synchronize with the DNS master, what is the most likely reason?*

When a master server zone file is updated, the serial number in the zone file's SOA record must be updated, because it is this number that is checked by the slave to discover whether a zone update has occurred. Here is an example of an SOA record, which always occurs at the start of the zone file:

```
@ IN SOA auriga.gvon.com. hostmaster.gvon.com. (
                        76381     ; Serial
                        10800     ; Refresh every 3 hours
                        3600      ;  Retry every hour
                        604800    ; Expire after a week
                        43200  )  ; Default TTL 12 hours
```

The serial field (in bold for easy reference) has a value of 76,381. The slave will return every 10,800 seconds as instructed by the refresh value in the zone file. Versions 8 and 9 of BIND support the notify feature of DNS, whereby the master server can notify the slave immediately of changes to the master zone files. In either case, when the slave checks for an update, it is only the serial number of the zone file, not its content, that is checked. The most common reason for the slave not to synchronize is that the network administrator has forgotten to update the serial number in the zone file.

2. *How does a DNS server prevent another DNS servers from caching RR data that we supply to them?*

The syntax of the resource record (RR) is as follows:

```
[NAME]      [TTL]    [CLASS]      RECORD-TYPE      RECORD-DATA
```

For example:

```
jaguar        IN    A    194.168.85.100
```

In this case, the host jaguar has an IP address (an A record value) of `194.168.85.100`. We may prevent DNS servers that ask for jaguar's *A* record from caching it by simply adding a time-to-live (ttl) value of `0` to the ttl field. By this means we can determine that other servers will not cache the jaguar record at all:

```
jaguar        0     IN    A    194.168.85.100
```

Jaguar's ttl now has a value of `0` and will not be cached by other DNS servers because we are supplying a ttl of `0` with the record to any DNS server that requests it.

B.12 Chapter 12: The Network Time Protocol (NTP)

1. *Describe briefly the official international standard for time known as UTC.*

Universal Time Coordinated (UTC) is based on atomic measurements. UTC has replaced Greenwich Mean Time (GMT) as the international standard for time. In this context, "universal" means that the time is standardized globally and independently of time zones. "Coordinated" means that several institutions contribute their estimate of the current time, and UTC is built by combining these estimates.

UT1 is the time scale based on the observation of the Earth's rotation. It is now derived from *Very Long Baseline Interferometry* (VLBI). The various irregular fluctuations progressively detected in the rotation rate of the Earth lead in 1972 to the replacement of UT1 as the reference time scale. The scientific community, however, desired to maintain the difference between UT1 and UTC as smaller than 0.9 seconds to ensure agreement between the physical and astronomical time scales.

Since adoption of this system in 1972, it has been necessary to add 21 seconds to UTC time. This is due to the initial choice of the value of the second (1/86,400 mean solar day of the year 1900) and to the general slowing down of the Earth's rotation.

2. *What is the purpose of NTP as a network protocol, and why is NTP important to Solaris?*

The purpose of NTP is to synchronize clocks within a global network using UTC as the reference scale. In terms of Solaris, some applications must have as accurate a time as possible. Applications such as those using cryptography (SKIP, NIS+, secure NFS), those using network management protocols such as SNMP, and auditing and accounting systems may break or be rendered unreliable if the system time of the Solaris host upon which the software is running is not accurate.

B.13   Chapter 13: The New Internet Protocol: IPv6

1. *In what sense is the IPv4 address architecture too simplistic?*

IPv4 has been proven too simplistic in not having sufficient granularity in terms of the way address blocks are allocated. This leads to vast wastage because address blocks are allocated but not used in full. For example, if a class B is allocated to a company that then uses only 14,000 addresses, the other potential 50,000 addresses remain unused yet unavailable to others. Class A addresses contain a potential 16 million addresses, but the organizations using them are (at most) using about 10 percent of their allocated class A addresses.

2. *In IPv6 addresses, is there an equivalent of IPv4 classes?*

Yes, but the term "class" is no longer used, and in addition, IPv6 has far greater granularity in terms of an address architecture. The format prefix (FP) field determines the "type" of IPv6 address being examined. With IPv4, the leading bits in an address determined its class. The leading high-order bits of IPv4's classes were fixed as follows:

- 0   A
- 10   B
- 110   C
- 1110   D
- 11110   E

IPv6 addresses have the FP field, which also determines the type of address, for instance:

An FP of 001 identifies a global aggregatable unicast. This type of unicast address will be used on the Internet. The Format Prefix is 3 bits.

- An FP of FEC identifies a site-local unicast. This type of unicast may be used with a company intranet but will not be used on the global Internet. The Format Prefix is 10 bits.

- An FP of FE8 identifies a link-local unicast. This type of unicast is used only with a host's immediate LAN and is never allowed to pass through a router. It is also the only IPv6 address that uses stateless autoconfiguration. The Format Prefix is 10 bits.

The internal use of the 128 bits is different in IPv6 for each of these address types. This is also true of IPv4, although IPv4 addresses are far simpler and much shorter than IPv6 addresses. As can be seen, the length of the FP is different for the various types of IPv6 address. So, in summary, the nearest approximations to classes in IPv6 are format prefixes.

C

Examination Objectives

T he objectives listed in this appendix define the scope of material covered by Exam 310-043, Sun Certified Network Administrator for the Solaris 8 Operating Environment. You can also view these objectives at http://suned. sun.com/US/certification/solaris/solaris_exam_objec-tives.html #netadmin.

Table C.1 *Examination Objectives*

OBJECTIVE SECTION	OBJECTIVE	COVERED IN CHAPTER
Network model	Identify the purpose of each layer in the TCP/IP 5-layer model.	1
	Describe the functionality of the following network protocols: TCP, UDP, IP, and ICMP.	
	Describe the relationships between the following network protocols: TCP, UDP, IP, and ICMP.	
	Describe peer-to-peer communication.	
Local Area Network	Identify the LAN components: repeater, hub, bridge, switch, router, and gateway.	2
	Identify the network topologies.	
Ethernet interface	State the purpose of the Ethernet address.	3
	Identify the commands to getting and setting driver configuration.	

Table C.1 *Examination Objectives*

OBJECTIVE SECTION	OBJECTIVE	COVERED IN CHAPTER
ARP and RARP	Explain the process of address resolution using ARP and RARP.	4
	Identify the commands to manage the ARP cache.	
	Identify the configuration files and scripts used to configure a network interface.	
Internet layer	Describe IP address, broadcast address, netmask, datagram, and IP fragmentation.	5
	Describe classless inter domain routing (CIDR).	
	Identify the file used to set netmasks.	
	Identify the features and benefits of the Variable length subnet masks (VLSM).	
	Configure a network interface.	
Routing	Identify the Solaris 8 daemons that implement routing protocols.	6
	Identify the files used to configure routing.	
	Identify the purposes of the files used to configure routing.	
	Specify the purpose of the files used to configure routing.	
	Administer the routing table.	
Transport layer	Identify the features of the Transmission Control Protocol (TCP) and the User Datagram Protocol (UDP).	7
	Define the terms connection-oriented, connectionless, stateful, and stateless.	
	Describe the relationships among port numbers, network services, and the **inetd** daemon.	
Client-server model	Explain the terms client, server, and service.	8
	Administer Internet services and RPC services.	
	Collect information about services configured on hosts.	

Table C.1 *Examination Objectives*

Objective Section	Objective	Covered in Chapter
DHCP	State the benefits of the Dynamic Host Configuration Protocol (DHCP).	9
	Identify DHCP configuration files.	
	State the purposes of the DHCP configuration files.	
	Administer DHCP clients and servers.	
Network management tools	Identify tools that use the Simple Network Management Protocol (SNMP).	10
	Describe the Simple Network Management Protocol (SNMP).	
Domain Name Service (DNS)	Identify the purpose of DNS.	11
	Describe address resolution and reverse address resolution.	
	Identify the correct Resource Record syntax.	
	Explain the steps needed to configure DNS.	
	Identify the configuration files for DNS.	
	State the purposes of the DNS configuration files.	
Network Time Protocol (NTP)	Describe NTP features and terminology.	12
	Identify NTP configuration files.	
	State the purposes of the NTP files.	
	Describe how to configure NTP.	
Troubleshooting	Identify common network problems.	All chapters
	Diagnose network problems.	
	Resolve network problems.	
IPv6	Describe IPv6, its importance, and its potential benefits.	13
	Configure an IPv6 network interface.	

INDEX

4-bit header length, in TCP headers, 201

32-bit acknowledgment number, in TCP headers, 200–201

A

Acknowledgment number field, in TCP headers, 200–201

acl directive, in /etc/named.conf file, 341–342

active open, 207, 245

addresses. *See* IP addresses

address-to-name translation, **netstat -rn** command and, 189

AF_INET6 sockets, 239

aggregatable global unicast addresses, 402–404

all-subnets-directed broadcast address, 118

AND operations, truth tables and, 112

anti-spoofing rules, 146–147

anycast addresses, IPv6, 413–414

Application layer (layer 5), in TCP/IP 5-layer model, 6–7

args field, in inetd.conf, 239, 242

ARP (Address Resolution Protocol), 19, 71–97

    address mapping with, 72–73

    format of, 73–74

    opcodes (operational codes), 74–81

        opcode 1, 75–79

        opcode 2, 79–81

arpadd file, 95, 96

ARP cache, 89

    adding a static ARP cache entry with **arp -s** and **-f**, 93–95

    checking a single cache entry, 90–91

    deleting an ARP cache entry with **arp -d**, 92–93

    viewing the entire ARP cache with **arp -a**, 91–92

arp command, 89–97, 416

    -a option, 90, 91–92

    -d option, 90, 92–93

    -f option, 90, 94, 95

    options, 90–95

    -s option, 90, 94

ASN.1 (Abstract Syntax Notation One), 305–306

attenuation, 31

automatic allocation of permanent IP addresses, 267

B

backbones, 27, 30

binary logic, truth tables and, 112

BIND (Berkeley Internet Name Domain), 312, 313–316

    Solaris 8 version of, 313–314

boot file, 314

BOOTP relay, 263–264

bridges, 32–33

broadcast addresses, 47, 114–118

    special-case, 116–118

bus LANs, 27

C

caching-only servers, DNS, 328–329

cat command, 176–178, 255

ccTLDs (country code top-level domains), 318, 319

Checksum field

    IPv6 header, 392

in TCP headers, 202–204
UDP header, 218–219
chmod command, 356
CID (Company Identifier), 45
CIDR (classless inter domain routing),
134–136
Class A networks and addresses, 105–
106
Class B networks and addresses, 106–
107
Class C networks and addresses, 107–
108
Class D multicast identifiers and multicast groups, 109–110
class field, in resource records (RRs),
344
classless inter domain routing (CIDR),
134–136
clients, 230
DHCP, 262–263, 268
DNS, 359–360
TI-RPC, 234–235
client/server applications
ONC+ applications, 231–234
overview of, 230
collapsed backbone technologies, 27
collision domain, 32
collision rates, 56
collision window, 56
colon notation, 394–399
concentrators, 34–35
contention bus, 27
control bits, in TCP headers, 201–202
convergency, 167
corresponding bits, 113
countdown to infinity process, 166
country code top-level domains
(ccTLDs), 319
CRC (cyclic redundancy check) field,
53, 54
CSMA/CD (Carrier Sense Multiple
Access with Collision Detect), 55–57

D

daemons, 230. *See also* specific daemons
data field of the Ethernet frame, 54
datagrams. *See also* Headers; UDP
(User Datagram Protocol)
fragmentation of, 9, 12, 131–134
date command, 381
default routers, 167
default routes, 160–161, 172
adding, through the /etc/
defaultrouter file, 173–175
delimiter, domain name, 316
delivery service (transport service), 7,
8, 12–13
demultiplexing, 198
destination field
of Ethernet frame, 53
UDP header, 218
destination IP address field, 130
IPv6, 391
in the TCP pseudo header, 202–203
DHCP (Dynamic Host Configuration
Protocol), 18, 261–298
administering clients and servers,
286–293
server installation using **dhcpconfig**, 286–288
/var/dhcp/dhcp_network file, 288–
291
/var/dhcp/dhcptab file, 291–292
advantages of using, 264–265
binding, 264
clients, 262–263
allocating a specific address to, 268
binding between DHCP server
and, 264
configuration files, 269–285
/etc/default/dhcpagent file, 284–
285
/etc/default/dhcp file, 283–284
/etc/dhcp/inittab file, 270–274
/etc/dhcp.interface file, 283

/var/dhcp/dhcp_network file, 275–
277
/var/dhcp/dhcptab file, 277–282
disadvantages of using, 265–266
in.dhcpd server daemon, 293–295
IP address allocation with, 266–268
terms used by, 262–264
dhcpagent file, 284–285
dhcpconfig command, 275
server installation using, 286–288
dhcpinfo command, 274
DHCP-leased IP address, 264, 266
dhcp_network file, 275–277, 288–291
DHCP servers, 263
administering, 286–293
server installation using **dhcpconfig**, 286–288
/var/dhcp/dhcp_network file, 288–
291
/var/dhcp/dhcptab file, 291–292
binding between DHCP client and,
264
dhcptab file, 277–282
macro characteristics, 279–280
symbol characteristics, 278–279
dhtadm command, managing the /var/
dhcp/dhcptab file with, 291–292
digital voltmeter, 301
directives, in /etc/named.conf, 335–342
direct routing, 175
distance-vector algorithm, 163–164
DNS (Domain Name Service), 311–366
BIND (Berkeley Internet Domain
Name) and, 312, 313–316
cache, dumping, 361–363
clients, creating, 359–360
debugging, 361–363
namespace, 314, 316–323
purpose of, 312
Solaris 8 version of, 313–314
Solaris name services and, 314–316
zones of authority and delegation,
321–323
DNS servers, 323-333

caching-only servers, 328–329
forwarding servers, 329
main configuration file (/etc/
named.conf), 333–343
master servers, 327
nonroot master, 324–326
querying, 329–332
root-level, 324
slave servers, 327–328
step-by-step process of creating,
354–361
UDP and, 221–222
dntadm command, 286
dormant domains, 318
dotted quad notation, 103, 394
drift file, 369
dynamic allocation of IP addresses, 267
dynamic routing, 161

E

echo command, 180, 420
EEPROM parameter, Ethernet
addresses and, 47–49
egrep command, 253
enabling technologies, 234
encapsulation
TCP, 196–197
UDP, 216–217
endpoint-type field, in inetd.conf, 241
end-to-end fragmentation, 393
/etc/default/dhcpagent file, 284–285
/etc/default/dhcp file, 283–284
/etc/defaultrouter file, 173–175
/etc/dhcp/inittab file, 270–274
FIELD option type, 274
INTERNAL option type, 274
option categories, 270
SITE option type, 273
STANDARD option type, 271–273
VENDOR option type, 273–274
/etc/dhcp.interface file, 283
/etc/gateways file, 176–178
/etc/inet/inetd.conf file, 237–242

defining TI-RPC clients and servers in, 240–242
defining traditional socket-based servers in, 238–240
/etc/inet/ntp.conf file, 371–372, 374–375, 379–380
/etc/inet/services file, 237, 238, 243–244
   port allocation to traditional servers via, 243–244
/etc/init.d/xntpd file, 372
/etc/named.boot file, 314
/etc/named.conf file, 333–343
   creating, 354–355
   directives (keywords) in, 335–342
     acl directive, 341–342
     directory directive, 339
     include directive, 342
     options section, 335–337
     server directives, 337–338
     zone definitions, 338–341
     zone directive, 343
/etc/nsswitch.conf file, 330, 354, 359–360
/etc/resolv.conf file, 331, 358–360
/etc/rpc file, 255–257
Ethernet Access Method (CSMA/CD), 55–58
Ethernet addresses, 45–50
   global versus local port, 47–49
   scope of, 46–47
Ethernet controllers, Sun, 65–66
Ethernet LANs, 41–69
   addresses in, 45–50
   CSMA/CD (Ethernet Access Method), 55–58
   frame overhead fields, 52
   IEEE Ethernet identifiers, 42–45
   specification, 42
   V2 frame, 50–55
Ethernet V2 frame, 50–55
ethers table, 85
extension header, 391

eXternal Data Representation (XDR), 232–233

F

Fast Ethernet cards, 65
FDDI (Fiber Distributed Data Interface), 29
FIN flag, 202
firewalls, 24
flags field
   in inetd.conf, 239, 241
   IPv4 header, 129
   for multicast addresses, 409–410
   netstat command, 189
flow label field, IPv6 header, 390
Format Prefix (FP) field
   for aggregatable unicast addresses, 403
   for link-local unicast addresses, 405
   for multicast addresses, 409
   for site-local unicast addresses, 404
forwarding servers, DNS, 329
forward zone files, 339, 346–351
FQDNs (fully qualified domain names), 317
fragmentation of datagrams, 131–134
fragment offset field, IPv4 header, 129–130
frame overhead fields, 52
ftp service, 240, 252

G

gateways, 34
generic top-level domains (gTLDs), 318–319
get command, getting parameter settings with, 63–64
get function, 303, 304
grep command, 174, 181, 244, 249, 314, 373, 377
gTLDs (generic top-level domains), 318–319

H

handshake, three-way, 205–208
hash character (#), disabling a particular
    service with, 239–240
head command, 255
header(s)
    IPv4, 127–131
    IPv6, 389
    TCP, 197–204
        4-bit header length, 201
        32-bit acknowledgment number,
            200–201
        32-bit sequence number, 199–200
        Checksum field, 202–204
        control bits, 201–202
        Options field, 204
        Padding field, 204
        pseudo header, 202–204
        source and destination port num-
            bers, 197–199
        TCP data field, 204
        Urgent pointer flag (URG), 204
        Window field, 202
    UDP, 217–219
header checksum field, 130
header length field, 129
    in TCP headers, 201
hint, zone entry of type, 338–339
hints, 332
hold-down state, 167
hop count (metric count), 163
    IPv6 header, 391
    limit of RIP, 165–166
host groups
    building MAC addresses for multi-
        cast groups and, 169–171
    permanent, 169
hostmaster, 327
host number, 103
host-specific routes, 160, 171
HTTP (HyperText Transfer Protocol),
    18
httpd daemon, 236

hubs (multiport repeaters), 31–32
HUP signal, 362

I

IANA (Internet Assigned Number
    Authority), 320, 324
    IP multicast addresses reserved by,
        169–170
ICANN (Internet Corporation for
    Assigned Names and Numbers),
    317, 319, 324
ICMP (Internet Control Message Pro-
    tocol), 15–16, 19
    variables for, 63
identification field, IPv4 header, 129
IEEE Ethernet identifiers, 42–45
ifconfig command, 49, 58, 136–137,
    139–141, 180, 181, 284, 415, 418–
    421
IMAP4 (Internet Message Access Pro-
    tocol), 18
include directive, in /etc/named.conf
    file, 342
in.dhcpd server daemon, 293–295
indirect routing, 175
inetd.conf file, 237–242
    defining TI-RPC clients and servers
        in, 241–242
    defining traditional socket-based
        servers in, 238–240
inetd daemon, 235
    rpcbind daemon compared to, 257–
        258
    starting services through, 237–242
in.ftpd daemon, 240
in.named daemon, 314, 335, 359–360
    sending signals to, 361–363
in.rdisc daemon, 162, 167–168, 170,
    171, 181, 182
in.routed daemon, 162–163, 169, 171,
    177, 181, 182, 190
    options
        -q option, 163

-s option, 163
trace and debug options, 190–191
Interface-ID field
for aggregatable unicast addresses, 404
for link-local unicast addresses, 406
for site-local unicast addresses, 405
interfaces, Solaris 8, 140–149
Internet Assigned Number Authority (IANA), 320, 324
Internet Layer (layer 3), in TCP/IP 5-layer model, 9–10
Interpacket Gap (IPG), 56
INT signal, 361–362
IP (Internet protocol), 9. See also IPv4; IPv6
interface to the Transport layer, 223–224
variables for, 59–60
IP addresses, 102–111, 312
allocating a specific address to a DHCP client, 268
automatic allocation of, 267
broadcast address, 114–116
Class A networks and addresses, 105–106
Class B networks and addresses, 106–107
Class C networks and addresses, 107–108
Class D multicast identifiers and multicast groups, 109–110
classes of IPv4 address, 102–111
computing the network number using the netmask rule, 113–114
DHCP allocation of, 265, 266–268
dynamic allocation of, 267
IPv6
anycast addresses, 401, 413–414
destination IP address field, 391
format of, 393–401
multicast addresses, 401, 409–413
source IP address field, 391
subnet prefixes, 400–401

text representation of addresses, 394–399
types of, 401–414
unicast addresses, 401, 402–409
manual allocation of, 267–268
network number and host number, 103, 113–114
special broadcast address types, 117
subnetting, 119–127
virtual, 64
ip_addrs_per_if variable, 64, 65
IPC (interprocess communication), 233
ip_def_ttl variable, 64
ip_forwarding parameter, 63, 64, 158, 181
IPG (Interpacket Gap), 56
IP routing. See Routing
IP spoofing, 146–147
IPv4 (Internet Protocol version 4), 14–15
addresses. See IP addresses
fragmentation of datagrams, 131–134
headers, 127–131
netmasks (subnet masks), 111–114
netmasks file, 136–137
IPv6 (Internet Protocol version 6), 387–424
configuring a network interface, 414–421
autoconfiguring IPv6 link-local addresses, 415–418
configuring an IPv6 permanent address manually, 419–421
datagram header, 389–393
comparing the IPv6 and IPv4 headers, 392–393
IP addresses
anycast addresses, 401, 413–414
destination IP address field, 391
format of, 393–401
multicast addresses, 401, 409–413
source IP address field, 391
subnet prefixes, 400–401

text representation of addresses, 394–399

types of, 401–414

unicast addresses, 401, 402–409

IPX/SPX, 36

ISO/OSI 7-layer reference model, 3–4

J

jitter, 369

K

KILL signal, 363

L

labels, domain name, 316, 317

LANs (Local Area Networks), 23–69

  advantages and disadvantages of, 24–26

  components of, 30–35

    backbones, 30

    bridges, 32–33

    concentrators, 34–35

    gateways, 34

    hubs (multiport repeaters), 31–32

    repeaters, 31

    routers, 34

    segments, 31

    switches (multiport bridges), 33–34

  definition of, 24

  Ethernet. *See* Ethernet LANs

  topologies of, 26–30

    bus LANs, 26, 27

    ring LANs, 26, 29

    star LANs, 26, 27–28

latency port to port, 32

layered network models, 2–5

leased IP addresses, 264, 266

LeaseNeg parameter, 280–282

LeaseTim symbol, 280

length field

  IPv4 header, 129

  UDP header, 218

limited broadcast address, 118

link-level frame, 156–157

link-local unicast addresses, 405–406

  autoconfiguring, 415–418

local clock, 369

loopback addresses, 407

loopback interfaces, 140–141

M

MAC (media access control) addresses, 45

  for multicast groups, 169–171

macros, /var/dhcp/dhcptab file, 279–280

manual allocation of IP addresses, 267–268

master, zone entry of type, 339–340

master servers, DNS, 327

maximum frame length, in Ethernet LANs, 52

maximum segment size negotiation, TCP, 208–213

metric count (hop count), 163

MIBs (Management Information Bases), 305–306

minimum frame length, in Ethernet LANs, 52

mkdir command, 355–356

mountd daemon, 235–236, 247, 255

  fields for, 255

MSS (Maximum Segment Size), 208–213

MTUs (Maximum Transmission Units), 10–11

  fragmentation of datagrams and, 131–134

multicast addresses, 168, 170

  Ethernet, 46–47

  IPv4, 109–110

  IPv6, 409–412

NTP (Network Time Protocol) and, 370, 379
multicast groups, building MAC addresses for, 169–171
multihomed hosts. *See* Router hosts
multiport bridges (switches), 33–34
multiport repeaters (hubs), 31–32

N

named.conf file, 333–343
    creating, 354–359
    directives (keywords) in, 335–342
        acl directive, 341–342
        directory directive, 339
        include directive, 342
        options section, 335–337
        server directives, 337–338
        zone definitions, 338–341
        zone directive, 343
named.root file, 324–326
Name field, /var/dhcp/dhcptab file, 278
name field, in resource records (RRs), 344
name services, Solaris, 314–316
namespace, DNS, 314, 316–323
ndd command,
    setting protocol driver parameters with, 58–65
        getting parameter settings, 63–64
        protocol variables, 59–63
        setting parameter settings, 64–65
NetBEUI, 36
NetBIOS, 36
net-directed broadcast address, 118
netmasks (subnet masks), 111–114
    subnetting and, 120–123
netmasks file, 136–137
netstat -a command, 248–250
    -P udp option, 248
netstat command, 56, 190, 248–252
    getting routing information with, 186–187
    server monitoring with, 248–252

viewing the routing table with, 187–189
netstat -r command, 181, 188
netstat -rn command, 189
Netware, 36
Network File System (NFS), 233
Network Information Service (NIS/NIS+), 233–234
Network Interface layer (layer 2), in TCP/IP 5-layer model, 10–11
network interfaces. *See also* Virtual interfaces
    configuring, 139–151
network management, 299–310
    ISO definition of, 300
    tools for, 301
network models, layered, 2–5
    benefits of using, 5
network monitor, 301
network number, 103
    computing, with the netmask rule, 113–114
network protocols, 2, 11–16. *See also* specific protocols
Network Solutions Incorporated (NSI), 317
network-specific routes, 160, 171–172
Network Time Protocol (NTP). *See* NTP
next header field, IPv6 header, 390–391
next-hop routers, 72–73
Next Level Aggregator (NLA) field, 403–404
NFS (Network File System), 233
nibbles, 394
NIS/NIS+ (Network Information Service), 233–234
Nominet UK, 320
non-router hosts, 156–157
NOT operations
    broadcast addresses and, 114–115
    truth tables and, 112
NSI (Network Solutions Incorporated), 317

nsswitch.conf file, 330, 354, 359–360
NTP (Network Time Protocol), 367–386
  basic terminology, 368–369
  brief description of, 369–371
  configuration files, 371–373
  configuring a client, 379–383
  configuring a server, 373–378
  multicast addresses used by, 411–412
  verifying that NTP packages are installed, 372–373
ntp.conf file, 371–372, 374, 377–380
ntpdate command, 380
ntp.drift file, 372
ntpq command, 382
ntptrace command, 382–383

O

Object Identifier (OID), 304–305
ONC+ (open network computing) applications, 230, 231–234
  XDR (eXternal Data Representation), 232–233
opcodes (operational codes)
  opcode 1, 75–79
  opcode 2, 79–81
Open Systems Interconnection (OSI) family of protocols, 3, 35
Options field
  IPv4 header, 130–131, 392
  IPv6 header, 392
  in TCP headers, 204
OR operations
  broadcast addresses and, 114–116
  truth tables and, 112
oscilloscope, 301
OSI (Open Systems Interconnection) family of protocols, 3, 35
OSI/ISO 7-layer reference model, 3–4
OSPF (Open Shortest Path First) protocol, 138

P

Padding field, in TCP headers, 204
parked domains, 318
passive open, 207, 245
path MTU discovery, 392–393
payload length field, IPv6 header, 390
peer-to-peer communication, 16–17
Physical layer (layer 1), in TCP/IP 5-layer model, 11
ping command, 330, 332, 420–421
pkginfo command, 373
pkill command, 191, 256
pntadm command, 275, 286, 288–291
  managing the /var/dhcp/ dhcp_network file with, 288–291
POP3 (Post Office Protocol), 18
port field, rpcbind daemon, 254
portmapper. See **Rpcbind** daemon
port numbers, source and destination, in TCP headers, 197–199
positive acknowledgment with retransmission, 213–215
prefixes, Ethernet address, 45
program field, rpcbind daemon, 254
PROM (programmable read-only memory), Ethernet addresses and, 47
protocol analyzer, 301
protocol field
  in the TCP pseudo header, 203
  IPv4 header, 130
protocol stack, 2
protocol variables, 59–63
proto field
  in inetd.conf, 239
  rpcbind daemon, 254
pseudo-Ethernet addresses, 170
pseudo header, TCP, 202–204
pseudo-MAC addresses, 170
PSH control bit, 201

Q

querying servers, 329–333

R

RARP (Reverse ARP), 72–89
  format of, 73–74
  opcodes 3 and 4, 83–87
  server, configuring, 87–88
RDNs (relative domain names), 317
RDP (Router Discovery Protocol),
    167–171
reboot command, 180
record-data field, in resource records
    (RRs), 345
record-type field, in resource records
    (RRs), 345
reference clock, 368
repeaters, 31
resolv.conf file, 331, 359–361
resolver, 330
resolver libraries, 330
resource records (RRs), 343–354
  syntax of, 344–345
reverse zone files, 339–340, 346, 351–
    353ring LANs, 29
RIP (Routing Information Protocol),
    13, 162–167
  overview of the general features of,
    163
  routing process of, 163–165
  stability properties of, 165–167
root-level DNS servers, 324
root zone files, 346, 353
round-trip delay, 32
route command
  adding and deleting routes using the,
    182–185
  continuously monitoring routing
    information with, 185–186
route get command, 186
route monitor command, 185–186
router(s), 34

configuration files and their func-
    tions, 171–178
  adding default routes through the /
      etc/defaultrouter file, 173–175
  direct and indirect routing, 175
  working with the /etc/gateways
      file, 176–178
configuring a Solaris 8 system as a,
    179–181
Router Fragmentation field, IPv6
    header, 392–393
router hosts (multihomed hosts), 156
  behavior of, 157–158
routing (over TCP/IP with Solaris 8),
    155–194
  direct, 175
  dynamic, 161
  example of, 158–160
  getting routing information and dis-
    playing on standard output, 186–
    187
  indirect, 175
  protocols and daemons, 160–171
routing decisions, 9, 158
routing tables, 9, 135
  administering, with the **route** and
    netstat commands, 182–189
  congestion of, 134–135
  router host behavior and, 157
  types of routes in, 160–161
  viewing, with **netstat**, 187–189
rpcbind daemon (portmapper), 237,
    242, 243, 252
  inetd compared to, 257
  output fields for, 253–254
  port allocation to TI-RPC servers
    via, 245–246
rpcinfo command, server monitoring
    with, 252–255
rpcinfo -p command, 253–255
rpc_prog/vers field, in inetd.conf, 241
rpc/proto field, in inetd.conf, 241
RPC servers. *See also* TI-RPC servers
  program numbers of, 246–247

RRs (resource records), 343–354
    syntax of, 344–345
ruserd service, 242

S

security, subnetting and, 120
segments, 31
    TCP (Transmission Control Protocol), 196–197
sendmail daemon, 235
Sequence field, in TCP headers, 199
server_pathname field, in inetd.conf, 239, 241
servers, 230. *See also* Client/server applications
    configuring, 234–247
    DNS. *See* DNS servers
    monitoring services and, 247–258
        /etc/rpc file, 255–257
        netstat command, 248–252
        rpcinfo command, 252–255
    starting, 235–242
        multiple standalone servers, 236
        single standalone servers, 235–236
        starting services through **inetd**, 237–238
    TI-RPC, 234–235
    types of, 234
service field, rpcbind daemon, 254
service name field, in inetd.conf, 238
services, 230
set function, 303–304
shell scripts, 95
Site-Local Aggregator (SLA) field, 404
site-local unicast addresses, 404
slave, zone entry of type, 340–341
slave servers, DNS, 327–328
sliding window protocol, TCP, 215
SLIP (Serial Line IP), 19
Slow Ethernet cards, 66
SMI (Structure of Management Information), 304–305

SMTP (Simple Mail Transfer Protocol), 18
SNMP (Simple Network Management Protocol), 18, 302–307
SNMP-based management tools, 306–307
snoop command, 54, 77, 208, 209
    DNS packets captured using, 222
socket-based servers, defining, in /etc/inet/inetd.conf, 238–240
sockets, 233
socket_type field, in inetd.conf, 238
Solaris 8 interfaces, 140–149
Solstice Enterprise Manager, 307
Solstice Site Manager, 306
source Ethernet address, 53
source IP address field, 130
    in the TCP pseudo header, 203
    IPv6 header, 391
Source port field, UDP header, 218
SPF (Stealthy Packet Filter) firewall, 175
split horizon of RIP, 166
split horizon with poisonous reverse of RIP, 166
standard interfaces, 140
star LANs, 27–28
static routing, 172
store-and-forward feature, 33
stratum time servers, 368–369
strings command, 314
stub, zone entry of type, 341
subdomains, 320
subnet-directed broadcast address, 118
subnet masks (netmasks), 111–114, 120–123
subnet prefixes, IPv6, 400
subnets, 119–120
subnetting, 119–127
    creating multiple logical networks from a single network address, 119
    delegated subnet administration, 120
    mechanics of, 120–123
    on a non-byte boundary, 123–126
    security and, 120

traffic and protocol isolation, 119–120

Sun Ethernet controllers, 65–66

Sun Management Center, 307

switches (multiport bridges), 33–34

symbols, /var/dhcp/dhcptab file, 278–279

SYN flag, 202

syslog service, 249

T

TCP (Transmission Control Protocol), 6–11, 12–13, 17–19
  encapsulation, 196–197
  features of, 205–215
    connection establishment and release, 205–213
    maximum segment size negotiation, 208–213
    positive acknowledgment with retransmission, 213–215
    sliding window protocol, 215
    three-way handshake, 205–208
  headers, 197–204
    4-bit header length, 201
    32-bit acknowledgment number, 200–201
    32-bit sequence number, 199–200
    Checksum field, 202–204
    control bits, 201–202
    Options field, 204
    Padding field, 204
    pseudo header, 202–204
    source and destination port numbers, 197–199
    TCP data field, 204
    Urgent pointer flag (URG), 204
    Window field, 202
  UDP compared to, 223
  variables for, 61–62

TCP data field, 204

TCP/IP 5-layer model, 4–5
  layers of, 6–11

Application layer (layer 5), 6–7
Internet Layer (layer 3), 9–10
Network Interface layer (layer 2), 10–11
Physical layer (layer 1), 11
Transport layer (layer 4), 8–9
TCP/IP protocols, by name and function, 17–20
TCP Length field, in the TCP pseudo header, 203
tcp_mss_def variable, 63
telnet
  clients, 8
  command, 208–212
  service, 251
TERM signal, 363
three-way handshake, TCP, 205–208
TI-RPC clients and servers, 234–235
  defining, in /etc/inet/inetd.conf, 241–242
  port allocation to, via **rpcbind**, 245–246
  program numbers of, 246–247
TLDs (top level domains), 317–321
TLI (Transport Layer Interface), 233
Token Ring, 29
Top Level Aggregator (TLA) field, 403
top level domains (TLDs), 317–321
touch command, 283
traffic class field, IPv6 header, 389
Transport layer (layer 4), 8
  IP interface to, 223–224
  in TCP/IP 5-layer model, 7
Transport Layer Interface (TLI), 233
Transport layer protocols, 12–14. *See also* TCP; UDP
transport service (delivery service), 7, 8, 13
trap function, 303
triggered updates, 166
truth tables, 112
  broadcast addresses and, 115–116
TTL (time-to-live) field, 327
  IPv4 header, 130
  in resource records (RRs), 345

Type field
    Ethernet, 53
    /var/dhcp/dhcptab file, 278
type of service (TOS) field, IPv4 header,
    129

U

UDP (User Datagram Protocol), 8–9,
    13–14, 19
    encapsulation, 216–217
    features of, 219–222
    header, 217–219
    as stateless protocol, 220
    TCP compared to, 223
    variables for, 60–61
udp_do_checksum parameter, 218–
    219
UDP Length field, 218
UKERNA, 320
uname command, 90, 187, 250
uname -n command, 174, 381
unicast addresses
    IPv4, in an IPv6 environment, 407–
        409
    IPv6, 402
        aggregatable global, 402–404
        link-local unicast addresses, 405–
            406, 415–418
        site-local unicast addresses, 404–
            405
        special unicast addresses, 406–409
unicast Ethernet address, 46
UNIX, 230
URG flag, 201, 204
user (UID) field, in inetd.conf, 239, 241
USR1 signal, 362–363
UTC (Universal Time Coordination),
    368

V

Value field, /var/dhcp/dhcptab file, 278
/var/adm/messages file, 372

/var/dhcp/dhcp_network file, 275–277,
    288–291
/var/dhcp/dhcptab file, 277–282
    macro characteristics, 279–280
    symbol characteristics, 278–279
variable length subnet masks (VLSM),
    137–138
/var/named directory, creating, 355–
    356
/var/ntp/ntp.drift file, 372
vers field, rpcbind daemon, 254
version field
    IPv4 header, 129
    IPv6 header, 389
VID (Vendor Identifier), 45
virtual interfaces, 140, 145–148
    permanent, 150–151
    temporary, 144
        plumbing in, 149–150
virtual IP addresses, 64
VLSM (variable length subnet masks),
    137–138

W

Web addresses, 312
Window field, in TCP headers, 202
WUFTP, 240

X

XDR (eXternal Data Representation),
    232–233
xntpd daemon, 369–370, 372, 380

Z

Zero field, in the TCP pseudo header,
    203
zone database files, 343, 346–353
    creating, 356–358
zones of authority and delegation,
    321–323
zone transfer, 336, 341, 342

Rick P. Bushnell was born and grew up in London. After graduating from Oxford University and teacher training college, he served as a schoolteacher in the British school system, specializing in computer science, mathematics, and English literature. Around 1980, Rick switched professions and became a UNIX administrator, in which he continued for eight years before joining Sun Technical Support in 1988 as a UNIX networking support and security consultant. Later, he joined the Sun Educational Services (SES) U.K. team as a senior lecturer.

As a Sun Microsystems support consultant, Rick supported Solaris networking and security, primarily sendmail, DNS, TCP/IP, and firewall security. As a lecturer through Sun University, he has taught hundreds of Solaris TCP/IP and security courses to both Sun employees and Sun customers worldwide. In addition, Rick has written training courses for Sun Microsystems and Hewlett Packard, covering subjects as diverse as *Configuring Sendmail and DNS on Solaris 8* for Sun and *Running an ApacheSSL Web Server on HP-UX* for Hewlett Packard.

In 1998, Rick set up an ISP called Gvon.Com Ltd. (http://gvon.com), which he continues to manage. He also offers UNIX networking and Internet security consulting services to leading companies, including Sun, Hewlett Packard, BT, NTL, the British Army, U.K. Police, and other enterprises both local and abroad. Rick led the Sun certification team that developed the *Network Administrator for the Solaris 8 Operating Environment* exam in October 2000. This year, Rick is leading the Sun certification team members who are writing the Solaris 9 exam in May 2002.

He is married with three children and lives in Surrey, England.